■ A F T E R T H E L A W

A book series edited by John Brigham and Christine B. Harrington

Explorations in Law and Society

■ *AFTER THE LAW*
A book series edited by John Brigham and Christine B. Harrington

Also published in the series:

Explorations in Law and Society

TOWARD A CONSTITUTIVE THEORY OF LAW

■ ALAN HUNT

■ ROUTLEDGE NEW YORK ■ LONDON

Published in 1993 by

Routledge
29 West 35th Street
New York, NY 10001

Published in Great Britain by

Routledge
11 New Fetter Lane
London EC4P 4EE

Library of Congress Cataloging-in-Publication Data

Hunt, Alan.
    Explorations in law and society : towards a constitutive theory of law / Alan Hunt.
        p.   cm. — (After the law)
    Includes bibliographical references and index.
    ISBN 0-415-90695-4 (HB) — ISBN 0-415-90696-2 (PB)
        1. Sociological jurisprudence.   2. Critical legal studies.   3. Law and socialism.   II. Series.
    K370.H85   1993
    340'.115—dc20   92-42291
                                                                          CIP

British Library Cataloguing-in-Publication Data also available

To Ros

CONTENTS

CONTENTS

ACKNOWLEDGMENTS

I would like to thank the respective publishers and journal editors for permission to reprint the following:

"Law, State and Class Struggle", 20 *Marxism Today* 178–187 (1976) [Chapter 2]. "Perspectives in the Sociology of Law" in Pat Carlen (ed) *The Sociology of Law,* Sociological Review Monographs, University of Keele, Keele, 1976 [Chapter 3]. "Dichotomy and Contradiction in the Sociology of Law" 8 (1) *British Journal of Law and Society* 47–77 (1981) [Chapter 4]. "The Poliitcs of Law and Justice" in Diana Adlam *et al* (eds.) *Politics and Power IV: Law, Politics and Justice,* Routledge & Kegan Paul, London, 1981 [Chapter 5]. "The Ideology of Law: Advances and Problems in Recent Applications of the Concept of Ideology to the Analysis of Law" 19:1 *Law and Society Review* 101–126 (1985) [Chapter 6]. "The Theory of Critical Legal Studies" 6:1 *Oxford Journal of Legal Studies* 1–45 (1986) [Chapter 7]. "On Legal Relations and Economic Relations: A Critique of G.A. Cohen" in R.N. Moles (ed.) *Law and Economics* Franz Steiner Verlag, Stuttgart, 1988 [Chapter 8]. "The Critique of Law: What Is 'Critical' About Critical Legal Studies?" in Peter Fitzpatrick and Alan Hunt (eds.) *Critical Legal Studies,* Basil Blackwell, Oxford, 1987. [Chapter 9]. "Rights and Social Movements: Counter-Hegemonic Strategies" 17:3 *Journal of Law & Society* 309–28 (1990) [Chapter 10]. "Marxism, Law, Legal Theory and Jurisprudence" in Peter Fitzpatrick (ed.) *Dangerous Supplements: Resistance and Renewal in Jurisprudence* Pluto Press, London, 1991 [Chapter 11]. "Foucault's Expulsion of Law: Towards a Retrieval" 17:1 *Law & Social Inquiry* (1992) [Chapter 12].

CHAPTER I

EXPLORATIONS IN LAW AND SOCIETY

THE JOURNEY BEGINS

In introducing these explorations in law and society that this book undertakes it is important not to succumb to what might be called the retrospective fallacy. This is the fallacy that creates the illusion that both the path traveled and the destination arrived at were carefully planned and were fully self-conscious. It is not necessary to go to the other extreme and suggest that everything was an accident, devoid of intent or without reason. Perhaps a more serviceable analogy is to suggest that from the vantage point of a break taken for refreshment, reflection can produce insight into the presence of some themes that have served as landmarks. These landmarks may sometimes have dropped out of sight during the course of the journey, but keep reappearing with the result that they must have played some role in determining the general direction of the journey. To press this metaphor of the journey a little further, it is important to note that while landmarks appear to exist as fixed points of reference, the truth (one that anyone who has got themselves lost in the wilderness knows) is that landmarks have a remarkable habit of changing their appearance as the standpoint from which they are observed changes. Indeed it is often the case that they change their appearance to such an extent that one is often not sure that one has the same feature in view.

The best a participant can hope to do is to give the reader some sense of those features that the author has chosen to conceive as landmarks or persistent themes. To embark on such a retrospective creates the ever-present danger of the self-indulgence of autobiography. I hope to succeed is keeping in mind that the reader is very properly not interested in the personal crises and moments of elation that an author has encountered along the way.[1] The most I can promise is to attempt to avoid such self-indulgence.

The chapters that follow adhere strictly to the chronology of their production. The obvious temptation to regroup these essays to give a stronger thematic unity has been resisted. For to do so would have been to fall victim to the "retrospective fallacy." Similarly the essays are carried in their original form. The only editorial intervention has been to ensure a consistency in the citation of reference and the form of footnotes and to standardize spelling conventions; in addition a number of purely technical typographical errors were corrected. The desire to engage in extensive rewriting, to attempt with hindsight to express better or more clearly a position now held, has been severely resisted. If the organizing metaphor of the journey has any merit it must lie in the claim not to have tampered with the itinerary. No false leads or embarrassing stumblings have been removed. Whatever deficiencies this strategy may expose it is at least consistent with the aspiration to share with the reader a voyage that is still very much in progress. There is no claim that any firm conclusions have been reached or that anything that might signify an end has come into sight. What is offered is an ongoing engagement with some themes that continue to attract my attention and some suggestions about how to engage with those themes.

MAPPING THE TERRAIN

Before starting out on this journey it is perhaps wise to offer some description of the terrain through which I intend to travel. This description makes no claim to the comprehensiveness to which travel guides usually aspire; rather it seeks to keep in view that I am offering a construction of the terrain. Indeed it is through recognizing the constructed character of the intellectual scenario it is possible to recognize some topographical features while, intentionally or otherwise, ignoring others; at the same time it is important to recognize that one necessarily adopts some perspective that enlarges some features while down-grading others.

The terrain that this book traverses is most distinctly marked by the fact that it refuses to locate itself within a single privileged intellectual framework. While the designation "law and society" is often employed this needs to be understood in a way that seeks to refuse the temptation to be a part of a project that seeks to carve out a reserved subdisciplinary niche. In the first place this stems from the strongly held view that the issues and problems raised by an engagement with the role of law in contemporary societies are simply far too important to be left to the practitioners of a subdisciplinary "sociology of law." Neither can there be or should there be a neat impermeable boundary between sociological and jurisprudential approaches. One reason for a continuing enthusiasm about the prospects of the project of critical legal studies is that it has offered the prospect of a bridge between social theoretical and jurisprudential approaches.

The most difficult feature of the terrain to be mapped is its primary feature, namely, law. Certainly the terrain should not be imagined as one dominated by Mount Law. The image of Law as a towering, hierarchical pinnacle whose imposing summit rises into the clouds is not a self-evident truth; but this is not to imply that this view is merely some ideological mirage. The persistence of this image is itself a major form in which the place of law is socially constituted. Neither should we envisage a terrain as some high and soggy plateau in which law is everywhere so dispersed in its social reality that it becomes indistinguishable from any other feature of the terrain.

I seek to sustain a studied and serious ambivalence to law. There are many ways of articulating this idea, but one will serve for the rest; I seek to hang onto the idea that law is an important constituent of the conditions of social practices, but neither does it determine those practices. Hence there is an important sense in which law is unimportant, always in need of having its pretensions to self-importance punctured. The attraction of the thematic of constitutive theory is I suggest not that it offers itself as some about-to-be-unveiled "new theory" that provides approaches to the general field of inquiry. Rather its significance is that it serves as a way out of the uncomfortable dichotomy between the importance and the unimportance of law. It serves to focus attention on the way in which law is implicated in social practices, as an always potentially present dimension of social relations, while at the same time reminding us that law is itself the product of the play and struggle of social relations.

SOME ORGANIZING THEMES

This book is organized around an argument that seeks to elucidate the way in which engagement with the phenomenon of law can be shown to have significance for wider issues in social theory. There are two distinct aspects to such a claim. In the first place I confess a sympathy to the view that a focus on some specific element or feature of social life necessarily involves an engagement with all aspects of the social. Such a view embraces a resistance to the powerful trend that has marked the history of the social sciences, namely, the tendency to a successive differentiation of the field into ever more subsociologies (sociology of . . .). Thus while much that follows can legitimately be classified as an intervention in the subdiscipline, the sociology of law, it always strives to maintain an openness toward a wider conception of the social, even while it retains a healthy skepticism about such holistic ambitions. While taxonomic classifications are necessary for the librarian, this text should be read as an ongoing attempt to resist the narrowing acceptance of subdisciplinary status for the "sociology of law." I strive to maintain a claim that the focus on law provides a fruitful way of sustaining an engagement with the most general and pervasive questions in social theory.

The claim that to study law is to study society encounters two objections. In the first place this claim sits rather uncomfortably with the currently influential view that announces "the death of society" (Laclau 1983); but I am happy to take a less catastrophic view of this line of thought and to accept it as a valuable rebuttal of the equation of "society" and "nation-state" and, more generally, as a reminder that "society" involves no necessary unity or system-like integration. A second problem with the claim that to study law is to study society is that it seems to imply a commitment to a philosophy of internal relations that espouses the view that each and every type of social relation is a microcosm of the prevailing forms of sociality (Ollman 1971). While this view has some attractions its claims are too ambitious; I prefer to treat it as a more modest injunction to keep in mind the presence of the general within the particular. As I will argue a defensible commitment to the project of the sociology of law requires attention to the extent to which legal relations are implicated in the general tendencies and trends in contemporary society.

The contention is that questions generated by engaging with the phenomena of law have a central relevance to some of the most persistent general concerns of contemporary social theory. However, I insist at the outset that my argument is *not* a version of the claim that there is some single general question around which sociology is organized; for example, I want to repudiate the idea that some grand theme, such as the "problem of order" can be elaborated to provide some semblance of unity to the diversity of the social. I unreservedly accept Anthony Giddens rejection of the myth of the "problem of order" (Giddens 1972).

THE DIVERSITY OF TRADITIONS

The most palpable way in which I seek to impede the slide toward a narrowing subdisciplinary status for the sociology of law is to sustain a focus on the interaction of a range of diverse intellectual traditions. This book seeks to sustain an ongoing interrogation as to the potential contribution of such diverse intellectual traditions. This general claim is developed by sustaining an on-going interrogation of the following major lines of thought: the sociology of law that skirmishes with jurisprudence,[2] the critical legal studies movement that builds bridges toward the sociology of law, while Marxist theory is called on to engage with the classical sociological tradition, and also with contemporary social theory, particularly as represented by Foucault. This movement between alternative and competing traditions is present in the attempts to understand the intellectual location of the critical legal studies movement and within the ongoing controversies surrounding the politics of law and rights. It should be stressed that the project of these investigations self-consciously avoids any attempt either to assign priority to any one of these traditions or to propose some reconciliation between them. Instead this work advances the claim that each of these traditions, if taken on its own, always requires the supplement of the others to avoid slipping into the seductive self-limitations of congealed disciplinary boundaries. The on-going dance of law needs to sustain the mutual interrogation of social theory, in its classical, Marxian, and poststructuralist manifestations along with the more narrowly constructed descriptive traditions of the sociology of law, and, at the same time, to maintain an openness toward the controversies within the field of jurisprudence.

THE IMPORTANCE OF LAW FOR SOCIAL THEORY

That law has some distinctive significance for social theory is a thesis that belies the general marginality of the sociology of law. At an early stage I was struck by the fact that although the "founding fathers" of social theory all had much to say about law, it was significant that the sociology of law had not subsequently associated any significant place within the sociological imagination. Perhaps surprisingly it has found a home, albeit somewhat insecure and often marginalized, within the Law Schools. To defend my thesis about the importance of law for social theory I have to do more than point to the accumulated tradition of sociology of law as a subdisciplinary specialization.

In *The Sociological Movement in Law* (1978) I advanced two claims. The first was to demonstrate the rich and fertile resources that were already in existence to facilitate sociotheoretical enquiry into law; this stress on the existing intellectual resources was particularly significant during a period that was largely bereft of theoretically informed writing on law when the early sociology of law was predominantly descriptive, inspired by the quest to see "law in action" as contrasted to "law in books." My second objective was to explore a paradox. In the writings of the founding fathers there existed a rich legacy of sociotheoretical work on law. These features of their work had been largely ignored during the revival in the late 1950s and early 1960s of attention to the work of Durkheim and Weber. The paradox that I addressed was that despite the demonstrable importance of the treatment of law in Durkheim, Weber, and Marx little or no interest was shown in these issues in the sociological discussion and debates of the 1960s and 1970s.

For both Durkheim and Weber law figured as a significant constituent of modernity. For Durkheim law became the new embodiment of the "conscience collective" in an era of interdependence and reciprocity within an advanced division of labor displacing the traditional role of religion and providing a vehicle for a new civic ethic. While for Weber the transformation in the forms of rational domination that marked the shift to modernity was epitomized by the rise of formal legal rationality intimately associated with the rise of bureaucratic administration. Weber did not regard the rise of formal rational law as a simple evolutionary progression, but rather was evidence of his ambivalence toward modernity, captured in the telling phrase "the iron cage." The movement toward formal legal rationality brought with it a tension between the formalism and proceduralism of legal rationality and the ever more strongly pressed demands for substantive justice, first by the worker's movement and subsequently by an expanding range of social movements.

There has indeed been a continuing strand of engagement with the legacy, in particular, of Weber and to, a lesser extent, of Durkheim (Trubek 1972a, b, 1986; Cotterrell 1983; Pearce 1989). It was unrealistic to argue that a return to the classics could provide the necessary theoretical underpinning for a nonempiricist sociology of law. Even when the project of the engagement with classical theory had also interrogated the legacy of Marx, as sociologists of law did with considerable enthusiasm in the late 1970s and early 1980s, this was to prove no panacea.[3] This encounter with the "founding fathers" was productive, but it carried with it something that came dangerously close to the view that the sociology of law could be reestablished on a sound footing by identifying a set of central questions and associated general theses inherited from the classical tradition.[4]

What does need to be recognized is that the engagement with Marx left an indelible imprint on the trajectory of contemporary work. From Marx comes the recognition that law always remains proximate to the state and that one dimension of our enquiries always has to engage with the connection between law and power. While we have come to avoid positing any instrumental link between law, state and power, and debate, the relative significance of power in its central locations and its localized manifestations, the root of these preoccupations manifests the imprint of Marx. Perhaps the most persistent legacy of these concerns has been the recognition that law is an arena of struggle. This theme manifests itself throughout the chapters that follows, but leaves its most distinctive impact in those chapters that explicitly address general questions of the "politics of law" (Chapters 5 and 10).

In addition to these general themes the imprint of an engagement with Marx is present in this work in other themes. Its early chapters were written within a generalized commitment to a Marxism that took two related but distinguishable emphases. In the first place Marxism provided the organizing paradigm of a preoccupation with the reproduction of social domination. How is it that capitalist social relations that relegate the great majority of people, whether in the metropolitan heartlands or in the innumerable peripheries of the third world, to a life of systematic inequality and disadvantage are sustained through social mechanisms that have come to place decreasing reliance on direct mechanisms of coercion? In brief, the problematic is that captured by the Gramscian figure of hegemony, the processes whereby acquiescence to subordination is secured. This thematic is explored through the presumption that law exhibits a distinctive interaction between the imposition of relations of domination and its normative legitimation. Hence the key role played by the decisive concept of ideology. In the earlier stage the concern was to provide an explication of ideological processes that were not to be reduced simply to notions of deception, false consciousness, or mystification. The further working and reworking of the notion of ideology undergo a significant transformation the result of which is a more refined conception of "legal ideology" explored in Chapter 6. The key feature of this conception focuses on the active character of ideological processes; no longer is ideology conceived as being produced in the specialized texts of the appellate courts and from this point of production disseminated into the wider society. Rather legal ideology is conceived as a complex of distinct discourses operating at increasing distances from doctrinal discourses. Attention becomes focused on the significance of rights discourses, particularly in the significant part played by rights-claims throughout the history of modern political struggles. These considerations come to provide a key link between the theoretical discussion and the concern with the politics of law in the chapters engaging the "politics of rights" (Chapters 5 and 10).

There is one final respect in which Marxism provides the starting point for the present enquiries. Marxism is approached as systematic social theory. A distinctive feature of the intellectual explosion that was Western Marxism was a preoccupation with what now perhaps appears as an unsustainable attempt at the elaboration of a formal conceptual model each of whose concepts is subject to rigorous clarification. This style of theoretical work was most closely associated with the significance I attach to the writings of Althusser. This does not imply any particular attachment to the results of Althusser's work, but rather to the contribution that it made to the possibility of sustained theoretical "work." This feature is most clearly visible in my continuing preoccupation with the primary concept "relation." The general question that is pursued is: How is law present within social relations?

The concern to develop a "relational theory" has two major motivations. Relationalism provides an attractive alternative to methodological individualism. Relationalism involves the ontological claim that social being exists within social relations. Ryan captures the implications of adopting a relational perspective.

> Relationality imposes on theory the necessity of acknowledging that it is a practice in history, the tracking down and working out of relations, rather than the proper naming of the world. (Ryan 1982:34)

A relational approach also provides an attractive alternative to the implicit institutionalism that so marks legal theory because of the self-evident presence of the institutional apparatus of the courts. It is for this reason that most jurisprudence adopts a markedly internal view of the law as something that lives and has its being in law offices and courtrooms. Insofar as it is present outside the courts, law is conceived as a brooding normativity that provides a major element of the normative integument of social life. Relational theory does not seek to refuse the significance of institutionalization, but rather it treats this as a particular case of social relations in which clusters and patterns of social relations are condensed into the purposefully organized features that characterize institutions. It is important to stress that institutions are not the only form in which social relations become condensed; there also exist social structures that can perhaps be best understood as noninstitutionalized condensation of social relations; "the market" and "the family" are structures in that they are relatively stable patterns of social relations that may undergo institutionalization, for example, through the formation of stock exchanges or the legal institution of marriage.

The relational strategy is employed to facilitate the exploration of the connection between "legal relations" and other forms of social relations. The significance of the engagement with the work of G.A. Cohen, while grounded in interpretive issues of Marxist theory, is of wider import. Cohen's reconstruction of the classical conceptualization of historical materialism relies heavily on being able to establish that it is possible to establish that Marx's key concept "relations of production" does not involve positing any legal content to the property relations that are a major constituent of the relations of production. My discussion of legal and property relations in Chapter 8 suggests that Cohen fails. Aside from the interesting issues involved in the exegesis of the conceptual apparatus of Marxism, my concerns are wider. A relational theory holds that lived social relations be conceived as "clusters" or sets of relations that may, for analytical purposes, be broken down into unique combinations of a range of different types of relations. For example, any specific relation can be resolved into economic, political, gender, and other relations. The question that a relational theory of law posits is how "legal relations" enter into the construction of lived relations.

THE TENSION WITHIN LEGAL PLURALISM

These relational concepts make it possible to propose a solution to the tension at the heart of the notion of legal pluralism. The tension resides in the fact that while it is possible to identify distinct forms of legal ordering that coexist, there is a strongly centralizing force that gives reality to the common-sense unity of the legal order, captured by such signifiers as "the Law" and "the legal system." Legal pluralism embraces a view that insists on the coexistence of different forms of legal regulation that exist both over time (i.e., between different historical periods) and also over social space (i.e., between different types of social relations). Persistence over time is illustrated by historical traces, such as the persistence of customary rights of indigenous peoples that struggle to secure recognition from settler legal orders.[5] Coexistent legal ordering is illustrated in the distinctive forms in business relations in which formalized commercial law coexists in tension with mechanisms of arbitration. While a plurality of legal orders exists, it is always subject to a strong centralizing pressure, but is never entirely subdued or brought neatly under the dominance of state-law.

A solution to the tension inherent in legal pluralism may be illustrated in a severely simplified form by assuming the existence of only two forms of juridical order: (1) "social legislation" that corresponds to the welfare state form and that operates through the construction of the legal status of "welfare recipient" or "client," and (2) "political rights" involving the legal subject constructed as "citizen." We can distinguish two distinct corresponding legal forms, "social rights" and "political rights."[6] Through this simplified typology we can recast and throw new light on contemporary debates of which I will give two illustrations.

Recent liberal political philosophy has been preoccupied with the priority to be accorded to equality and liberty.[7] In the light of my distinction between legal forms the liberty–equality distinction should not be understood as two abstract and opposed values, but rather as an organizing principle of two distinct legal forms in which "liberty" corresponds to "political rights" and "equality" to "social rights." The implications of this approach are that we are confronted not so much with a choice between alternative values, but with determining the proper scope or range of the different legal forms in a scenario in which each has a necessary and proper place. The political implications of this approach need to be made clear. It offers a means of avoiding a false polarity between the individual and the social (or collective) that has dogged the engagement between liberalism and socialism. Nor is it necessary to represent this clash in terms of a priority to be accorded to liberty or equality. It is not that socialism gives higher priority to the social while liberalism errs on the side of the individual. Rather the engagement is better seen as being about the proper scope and limits of two appropriate and desirable forms of social ordering. This way of posing the relationship between liberty and equality also serves to avoid another commonly polarized issue, namely, that between pro- and anti-rights stances (Chapter 10).

My second illustration of the potentiality of the distinction between two different forms of law concerns the "fate of the individual." The implications of this distinction lead to a particularly fruitful way of conceptualizing the modern sociological common-sense that "the individual" or subject is socially constituted. It suggests that individuals are socially constructed by means of a number of distinguishable processes. We need, for example, to distinguish between a "classical individualism," that is the liberal problematic of the rights-bearing legal subject in respect to whom the preoccupation becomes the attempt to delineate between legitimate and illegitimate use of state-imposed constraints over individual conduct as epitomized in Ronald Dworkin's idea of rights as "trumps against the state" (Dworkin 1978). There is another and quite distinct form of individualism associated with the welfare state than can fruitfully be explored by means of the concept of "individuation."[8] This concept has the merit of addressing what I refer to as the antimonies of the welfare state in that it captures the tension between, on the one hand, the Foucauldian sense of "surveillance" ("the gaze"), the disciplinary strategies through which people are labeled, numbered, recorded on the ever-expanding computerized databases; and, on the other hand, "individuation" that speaks of a necessary form for generating the knowledges necessary for the identification of the unique needs of individuals; for example, disability classifications generate knowledge necessary for the distribution of medical and economic resources. In its strongest sense "individuation" is the positive face of atomized individualism that *prefigures* the possibility of a society that attaches importance to needs.

The approach advocated posits the coexistence of not only different legal forms, but also that other forms of social ordering compete. That competition is not only about outcomes that may be registered in the changing content of legal rules or in legislative changes, but also in more general political changes. The form of this competition and struggle between different modes of regulation can be understood as discursive struggles. I elaborate a conceptual framework for the analysis in proposing a general model of regulation (Chapter 13). The focus on discursive struggles makes it possible to understand an important feature of the connection between law and hegemony. It is that state law seems to exhibit a widely generalized capacity to pursue projects directed toward the subordination of other legal forms to eliminate difference and construct a unified conception of the legal order, to produce the ascendancy of "the Law." This project of unification plays an important role in the process of state formation; for example, in medieval England the expansion of the "King's peace" and of the jurisdiction of the Royal courts exemplify this process whereby the dominance of a new project of unification is secured over the localized and particularistic regimes of feudal and ecclesiastical law. This centralizing process manifests itself not only institutionally but also normatively through projects of legal closure that pursue aims of consistency and universality and thereby seek to subordinate other normative traditions. But this centralizing hegemonic process is always incomplete, although it is generally ideologically dominant; the variety of legal forms refuse to take their orderly and subordinate place or to accept their own extinction. Instead they hold out the possibility that things might be different in that they not only keep alive alternative traditions but also prefigure alternative constellations of social ordering.[9] An application to the contemporary arena of rights struggles is developed in Chapters 5 and 10.

LAW BETWEEN MODERNITY AND POSTMODERNITY

The engagement with the relation between law, politics, and modernity provides a route along which to explore some of the important questions of our time, to achieve what the young Marx called "the self-clarification of the struggles and aspirations of the age" (1843). I offer no easy access to such a clarification because I unearth and spend much time worrying with a significantly paradoxical feature of our late modern situation. The simplest form of this paradox is that at one and the same time law seems to be both more important and more marginal. For a long time I struggled with the need to make a choice between these alternatives or to decide which claim, for the importance of law or for its marginal role, was correct. Now I am clearer that no such choice is necessary, but this is not to say that it is not necessary to intervene on one side or the other of this alternative. Sometimes it is necessary to deflate the ambition of unrestrained "legal imperialism," the view that law is a solution to some, if not all, of our most pressing problems. Against the dream of much contemporary jurisprudence that presents law as offering the best means of resolving social conflict and, in particular, of restraining an ever-expanding state power, it is important to deflate law's self-aggrandisement (Hunt 1992a). Against those, on the other hand, who view law as little more than a passive reflection of more fundamental processes or as an ideological cloak of social power, it is necessary to insist not only on the distinctive effectivity of law, but also to draw attention to its real potentiality as a component of any serious strategy for social transformation. Necessary though such engagements are they are reactive in character. What is needed is a more sustained engagement with the guts of the paradox itself.

In a variety of different expressions contemporary social theory points to the thesis that the law continues to occupy an increasingly central and organizing place, whether for good or ill, in advanced capitalist democracies. This general thesis comes in many guises and exhibits many divergences. For the moment these differences can be set aside. For such diverse figures as Weber, Poulantzas, Habermas, and Luhmann are to be found distinct, but related, versions of a thesis that state law has been an increasingly central feature of modernity. Whether expressed as the advance of legal rationality (Weber), the centrality of the "juridico-political instance" (Poulantzas 1978), the process of 'juridification' (Habermas 1987: 356–373), or as the 'positivization' of a self-referential legal system (Luhmann 1985), these are all variants of what I will call the 'centrality of law' thesis. Another very popular version of this general thesis is that of 'legalization' that makes the general point that legal regulation penetrates more pervasively into social life.

Behind this apparent consensus that there is some important sense in which law occupies a more central place in late modernity there lurks the seeds of yet another paradox. This concerns the link that is envisaged between the state and law. The positions diverge over how the juridico-political relationship is to be conceived. It is the complex forms of both separation and integration of political and legal institutions that give the distinctive stamp to the variations in the form of the modern constitutional-representative state in which the legal and the political fields mutually constitute but never fully encompass the other. Another way of putting the same point is to use the concept of "closure" to draw attention to the interdependence in tension between the two systems that both engage in "projects" that purport to determine the proper limits and boundaries of the other.[10] In brief, the political and the legal constitute a unity but are unable to secure their own autonomy without reference to the legitimations provided by the other.

For present purposes I am content to assert this thesis rather than to defend or substantiate it. I will, however, hope to add some persuasive weight by focusing attention on an extension or elaboration that builds on the basic thesis. I will sketch this theoretical elaboration schematically in order to focus attention on the important debates and controversies to which it is intended to contribute.

In its simplest form my position can be read as an attempt to achieve some rapprochement between those two sometimes intemperate adversaries, Foucault and Habermas. From Foucault I want to take two of his most fertile ideas concerning power; first is his emphasis on the dispersion of power (as against the classical doctrines of centralized sovereignty); second is his emphasis on the positive or constitutive (rather than negative) conception of power (see Chapter 12). From Habermas I want to borrow the focus on the historical stages of the formation of the juridical component of the modern state, whose main form is the "social welfare state." I do not follow his typology in detail;

for present purposes we can use a simplified version in order to focus on what I will call the "formative bourgeois state" that gave rise to a legal form that constituted the property-owning legal subject as the bearer of rights, through a number of stages of the democratization process through which the legal-subject-as-citizen is arrived at and whose significance is that rights no longer remain exclusively tied to property relations. The culmination of this process is the emergence of the "welfare state" that is characterized by the emergence of distinct forms of "social rights."

There was a tendency in the late 1980s, reflecting on the impact of the Thatcher–Reagan decade, to pronounce the welfare state as dead. It is not simply that this judgment was wrong although the announcement of its death was certainly "exaggerated." In the 1990s the welfare state is by no means out of the wood. Its most cherished exemplar, Swedish social democracy, is at its lowest ebb for many decades. The exploration of legal autonomy in Germany, particularly in the work of Luhmann and Teubner, can be understood as a response to the weakening of the specifically corporatist form of the welfare state that had been constructed in the postwar period between the state, labor, and capital.

The welfare state remains a central political question, but it is a matter of neither celebration nor condemnation. Rather our focus should be on the antimonies of the welfare state: we need to grasp that the welfare state is, on the one hand, a set of major victories prefiguring important elements of a transformative project. At the same time, the welfare state is a bureaucratic, unresponsive, and paternalistic nightmare that renders significant sections of the people disempowered, demoralized, and passive.

My interest in Habermas on the stages of formation of the juridico-political system departs from his own account; it does so in a way that I suspect he would approve. Habermas presents a series of sequential stages in the lineage of the bourgeois state. I propose to amend this account by borrowing from Derrida the idea of the "trace" to suggest that the stages are not simply replacements but, in the simplest sense of the idea, retain "traces" of earlier stages, and also to suggest the idea that each stage is itself suffused with "traces" of "the other," that is it exists in tension with that which it is not.

This reworking of the centrality of law thesis does not make the general paradox that surrounds the thesis disappear. What it does is to overcome the sense in which the centralization of law thesis is opened up to and becomes sensitive to the other modality that draws our attention to the relative powerlessness of law. The bureaucratic and administrative face of modernity is one from which law is never absent but in which law forms a protective and enhancing patina. I use the figure of patina to refer to the process whereby a surface encrustation forms, through processes that may be both an intentional artifice or merely through the process of exposure to an atmosphere suffused with law and legal discourses. The patina of law over bureaucratic administration serves to project an invention of a legitimatory tradition.[11] This line of thought provides a rather preliminary attempt to make contact with what is likely to be an increasingly important and fruitful line of inquiry into law as a significant cultural form, as legal culture. This prospect is hinted at in a number of places (Chapters 9 and 10), but most explicitly in Chapter 6 where all that is missing is the label "legal culture."

A significant feature of law as culture is that it disrupts the taken-for-granted sense in which the preceding discussion has posed the question of the "importance" of law. Much of the discussion in the variety of work concerned with law's developmental tendencies assumes a somewhat naive positivism in which it is presumed that the impact of law can potentially be measured, usually by some undisclosed standard of causal measurement. Once this narrow conception of causality is challenged then it has the radical effect of transcending the paradox about whether law is important or marginal. In place of this one-dimensional model we can now engage with the diverse senses in which the significance of law has to be understood.

TOWARD CONSTITUTIVE THEORY

The focus on the multiple dimensions of the effectivity of law does not necessarily lead to the need to espouse a set of noncommensurate modes of analysis. The problem is to avoid a stand-off between more traditional impact studies associated with sociolegal studies on the one hand and more recent discursive readings of law as semiotic systems associated with the linguistic shift that has made its distinctive mark on the law and society movement as it has upon so many other social sciences.

The claim that is made for the regulation approach, developed in Chapters 12 and 13, is that it has the capacity to facilitate an integrated form of inquiry that can encompass an unapologetically realist approach that takes as its organizing theme a relational perspective. The distinctive feature of the relational perspective is that it seeks out the legal component of social relations that makes it possible to break out of the narrow institutional focus of both the traditions of jurisprudence and of the sociology. Once this impediment to a fully social theory of law is broken through then it generates a new way of posing the traditional jurisprudential question: what is distinctive about law? The pursuit of this question is opened up through the contention that some aspect of legal relations may be constitutive of whatever variety of social relationship is being discussed. This formulation seeks to make clear that it makes no claim that all social relations exhibit a constitutive legal dimension. Rather it suggests that it is significant to search out the legal dimension of social relations for it is in discovering the far-flung ramifications of legal ordering that we can approach answers to questions about the historical place of law in the trajectory from premodernity to modernity and beyond.

CHAPTER 2

LAW, STATE, AND CLASS STRUGGLE

INTRODUCTION

This chapter sets out to examine the way in which law operates to maintain class domination. The argument that is developed shows that law should not simply be regarded as part of the coercive armoury of the state; but also must be understood as making a major contribution to what will be called "ideological domination." Ideological domination consists of those processes that produce and reaffirm the existing social order and thereby legitimize class domination. The processes involved in creating and reproducing ideological domination play a major part in ensuring the continuation of capitalist social relations.

There has been relatively little attention paid by Marxists to law. This absence of discussion has resulted in a tendency for the more obvious repressive characteristics to be stressed; and as a consequence the more pervasive contribution of law to the maintenance of capitalist society has not been sufficiently explored. The analysis of law in this wider context is of considerable political importance. Marxists are increasingly being forced to come to grips with the fact that modern capitalism has exhibited very considerable "staying power." In the period since the Second World War capitalism in Western Europe has shown what may be best described as relative stability; that is to suggest that despite the occurrence of very deep economic, social and political crises the capitalist social order in the major Western European states has survived substantially intact. This chapter examines the extent and the manner in which legal systems contribute to the perpetuation of capitalist systems.

STATE AND LAW

In class societies the economic and social dominance of an exploiting class does not sustain itself automatically. The exploiting class always strives to turn itself into a ruling class by means of an institutional structure, the state, which operates to sustain and to reproduce that position. While the state is a product of class antagonism it takes on the appearance of being an entity which stands above society and which embodies the interests of the community as a whole. This apparently *universal* quality is especially significant with reference to legal systems:

> Right, law, etc. are merely the symptom, the expression of *other* relations upon which State power rests. . . . These actual relations are in no way created by the State power; on the contrary they are the power creating it. The individuals who rule in these conditions, besides having to constitute their power in the form of the *State*, have to give their will, which is determined by these definite conditions, a universal expression as the will of the State, as law. (Marx/Engels 1968:366)

The distinctive feature then of legal systems of class societies is the fact that they embody the material interests of the ruling class in a universal form, and thus present law as the embodiment of the interests of the community as a whole:

> In a modern state, law must not only correspond to the general economic condition and be its expression, but must also be an *internally coherent* expression which does not owing to inner contradictions, reduce itself to nought. And in order to achieve this, the faithful reflection of economic conditions suffers increasingly. All the more so the more rarely it happens that a code of law is the blunt, unmitigated, unadulterated expression of the domination of a class—this in itself would offend the 'conception of right'. (Engels 1890:504)

This striving for "internal coherence," in which law comes to be seen as the embodiment of universal notions of "justice" and "right," needs to be explored. At the hands of bourgeois legal and political theorists it has been used to provide an ideological dogma, important in bourgeois political and legal theory, of the doctrine of the "separation of powers." The essence of this view is that the character of the democratic state is defined as one in which there exists a separation between the major components of the state. Specifically it is argued that not only is there, but also that there ought to be, a separation between the legislature, which makes the laws, and the judiciary, which apply those laws.

The doctrine of the separation of powers has played, and continues to play a central part in bourgeois theory of the law and the state.

There has been a tendency for Marxists in seeking to expose the ideological character of this doctrine to react against it by asserting the identity of the state and law. Thus the legal system has been presented simply as the direct and totally subservient agent of the state. Such a position is too simple, but more importantly it obscures the real class character of the legal system as a mechanism whereby the existing form of class domination is perpetuated and reproduced.

We need to start by asking, how does it come about that a separation appears to exist between law and state? Engels provides a useful starting point:

> But once the state has become an independent power vis-a-vis society, it produces forthwith a further ideology. It is indeed among professional politicians, theorists of public law and jurists of private law that the connection with economic facts gets lost for fair (sic). Since in each particular case the economic facts must assume the form of juristic motives in order to receive legal sanction; and since, in so doing, consideration of course has to be given to the whole legal system already in operation, the juristic form is, in consequence, made everything and the economic content nothing. (Engels 1958:396–397)

If these ideological functions are to be fulfilled they cannot operate exclusively as ideological forces, they must find some expression in the actual practice embodied within the legal system. As a consequence the legal system operates in a manner which cannot be explained exclusively by reference to the dictates of the state as a whole.

The doctrine of the separation of powers appeals to the independence of the judiciary. Yet this independence is clearly very restricted. Judicial appointments are made by the highest representatives of the political apparatus of the state.[1]

But what does need to be stressed is that even the relative degree of autonomy sets up stresses and contradictions within the state as a whole. Decisions by courts do not always please the holders of state power. The protracted struggle between the courts and Nixon throughout the "Watergate affair" is perhaps the most important recent example of such a tension in operation, in which the conflict between court and state contributed in no small measure to the downfall of Nixon.

But the tension between courts and state may also have advantages for the holders of state power. The institutional complexity of the English legal system allowed the government to brush the cobwebs off the Official solicitor whose intervention facilitated the release of the

"Pentonville 5" in 1972 when faced with the prospect of a General Strike. Frequently it serves as a convenient smoke-screen behind which to hide; Roy Jenkins, as Home Secretary, consistently used the excuse of separation between government and courts to refuse to intervene and secure the release of the Shrewsbury pickets.

This discussion points toward the general conclusion that the relationship between the state and the legal system must always be a matter for concrete examination. While the general dependence of the law on the state as a whole is an important proposition within Marxist theory, this must not be treated as if it suggested a complete identity between law and state.

DOMINATION AND HEGEMONY

Domination is a universal feature of class society. It consists in the subjection of one or more classes to another class (or grouping of classes) in such a way that exploitative relations are perpetuated. But the form that domination takes varies with the form of the exploitative class relations; thus the domination of slave by slaveholder differs from the employer's domination of the factory worker. Domination must be viewed not as a single act but as a process that reproduces the conditions for exploitative social relations.

Domination can only be based for very short periods of time on direct physical coercion. Even the most barbarous and coercive systems do not rely exclusively upon coercive violence. Direct coercion will often play a major part in the establishment of a new system of class power, but, however much it continues to depend on physical repression, it will strive to promote other means of consolidating its domination.

An extremely fruitful approach to the discussion of domination is provided by the early leader of the Italian Communist Party, Antonio Gramsci, who made use of the concept of "hegemony." He used it to identify the processes that create

> the 'spontaneous' consent given by the great mass of the population to the general direction imposed on social life by the dominant fundamental group (i.e. the ruling class). (Gramsci 1971:12)

The vital characteristic of "hegemony" is that it is an active process; it is concerned not merely with the *fact* of consent, but focuses on the creation and the mobilization of that consent. One major facet of the class struggle that takes place within capitalist societies is the continual struggle for influence over the ideas, perceptions, and values of members of the different classes. The maintenance of capitalism would be impossible unless the capitalist class was able to decisively influence the ideas, attitudes and consciousness of the working class.

It is important to stress that the ideological struggle is not simply concerned with the conflict between general theories of society. It is concerned with every aspect of the way in which people think about, react to, and interpret their position in class society.

COERCIVE AND IDEOLOGICAL DOMINATION

In examining the part that is played by law in the class struggle it is useful to distinguish between two different aspects. Law plays an important role in sustaining the domination of the ruling class because it operates both as a form of *coercive domination* and of *ideological domination*. It will also be necessary to stress that they are not simple alternatives. I hope to show the way in which these two elements are closely bound together and as such contribute to the special effectiveness of law as a mechanism of social order.

Let us first consider the coercive character of law. The legal system is able to call upon the organized power of the state. This repression operates both through specific institutions, which range from the courts themselves to the prison system, probation service, etc. In addition it also operates more generally through the police system that operates with wide-ranging powers, sanctioned by law, but able to act with a very considerable degree of autonomy.

Legal coercion operates at a number of different levels. Of greatest importance is the application of coercion to protect the *general conditions* of the capitalist order. First and foremost coercion is applied to protect and reinforce the property relations of capitalist society. There exists an increasingly complex body of "offences against property" that are concerned with the defense of private property. First they are important in demarcating the "lawful" from the "unlawful"; they differentiate between the unlawful appropriation of property, the acts of the "criminals," and the lawful forms of appropriation that are the hallmark of the capitalist system. Just how close is the dividing line between lawful and unlawful appropriation has been clearly revealed by recent bribery and corruption cases. But second, it is not only the offender that is coerced, but all members of society because the coercion of the offender reinforces the values, attitudes, and behavior associated with the existence of private property. It is for this reason that it was stressed above that the coercive and ideological functions of law are closely related.

While the criminal law protects the property interests of the capitalist class it operates more generally to protect the "private property" of all members of society. Indeed it is important to recognise that the vast majority of "property offences" are committed, not against the property of the capitalist class, but rather against the property of noncapitalists. Property offences are usually directed against the privately owned consumption goods of working people.

Another way in which legal coercion is applied to defend the *general* conditions of capitalist society is with respect to "offences against the person." Again this area of the criminal law does not merely act against offences against members of the capitalist class. The significance of this type of legal coercion is that some level of general social order is a necessary precondition for the maintenance of its specifically capitalist content.

One of the most important manifestations of legal coercion is the application of law for the direct protection of the state itself. The state has at its disposal a veritable armory of measures that are ready to be invoked to defend the existing political order. These range from a number of traditional offences such as treason, treachery, and sedition (which have been invoked fairly infrequently in the recent past), through such legislation as the *Official Secrets Act* of 1911 and 1920 and the *Incitement to Disaffection Act* 1934, to the wide ranging emergency powers that the ruling class has gradually accumulated. The *Emergency Powers Acts* of 1920 and 1964 give very extensive powers to the civil and military authorities to intervene in the class struggle. These powers have been used on no less than eight occasions since the War; on four of these occasions by the Heath government against dockers, power supply workers, and the miners; Labour Governments have not shrunk from invoking them.

In the recent past Northern Ireland has been a fertile source of emergency regulations. The *Northern Ireland (Emergency Provisions) Act* 1973 and the *Prevention of Terrorism (Emergency Powers) Act* 1974 have aided the British government's struggle against the Irish people and their scope has been extended to the mainland.[2]

The ruling class also has at its disposal a wide range of legal devices that can be used against offences against public order. These range through riot, affray, unlawful assembly and breach of the peace. Of particular importance is the *Public Order Act* 1936, supposedly introduced to curb the Fascists, but used systematically against the Left. It is interesting to observe the skill of the police and courts in making use of "appropriate" legal mechanisms. A good example has been the recent resuscitation of the *Conspiracy and Protection of Property Act 1875.*

In protecting the existing political order the law does not only have at its disposal the wide ranging powers contained in the legislation discussed above. The general principles of criminal law offer not only ample scope, but also special advantage. It is often in the interest of the ruling class to seek to depoliticize the class struggle. One of the means that is frequently invoked is to charge the "political offender" with ordinary crimes. This can be achieved by using a charge that is incidental to the main social or political issue involved; the most favored police strategy being to invoke charges involving or implying violence. A very good example of this technique is to be seen in the trial of the Shrewsbury pickets. The use of such charges allows the political issues to be ignored while branding the defendants as "common criminals," a tactic favored by Roy Jenkins and Frank Chapple in their attacks on the Shrewsbury pickets.

A related prosecution strategy is to use blanket charges; much in favor in the recent past has been the use of conspiracy charges. These are not only significant in that they allow the prosecution to evade some of the restrictions with regard to evidence and procedure that normally apply. But in addition, through the orchestration by the mass media, to create impressions of the existence of an unspecified "threat to law and order."

The legal order has at its disposal this powerful armoury of techniques of legal coercion that enable it to directly intervene in the class struggle to defend the interests of the existing order. This direct intervention in the class struggle stands out most sharply in the case of industrial and trade union laws.[3] The history of trade union law, from the *Combination Act* 1800 to the *Industrial Relations Act* 1971, is testimony to the attempt to provide a legal framework favorable to the interests of capital as opposed to those of labor. Yet it is also testimony to the extent of the resistance that over the period as a whole has not only forced tactical retreats, but has also witnessed significant advances in the legal positions of trade unions. I will return later to take up this question of law as an arena of class struggle.

What stands out in sharp relief is the extent to which the ruling class utilizes a legal framework for sustaining and buttressing their class interests. But a certain degree of care is needed in drawing conclusions from this common ground. The argument is frequently advanced that in periods of crisis the capitalist class resort to an increasingly repressive strategy and embark on major attacks on civil liberties. This type of analysis is very clearly presented in John Hostettler's article *Trends to Authoritarian Rule in Britain* (*Marxism Today*, Dec 1973). This line of argument is sometimes presented in such a way that it obscures important contradictory dimensions, which if correctly considered throw much light on the specific role of law within capitalist society.

The lurch to legal authoritarianism is checked by an equally strong need on the part of the ruling class to maintain the legitimacy of their class rule. This contradiction is not an interaction between two equal forces that smoothly balance each other out; hence there are periods in which there are major shifts toward authoritarianism, but equally there are periods of movement toward more liberal and less coercive forms. The particular result at any point in time is a complex result of the level of class struggle itself.

There is a more general, and possibly more fundamental, political point that underlies this discussion that needs to be more fully discussed. Lenin was correct when he argued that

> bourgeois states are most varied in form, but their essence is the same; all these states, whatever their form in the final analysis are inevitably the dictatorship of the bourgeoisie. (CW 25:413).

Yet there has been a tendency (which is present in Lenin as well as in others) to regard bourgeois democracy as simply a sham or fraud designed to conceal the class character of the rule of the bourgeoisie. Capitalism has been in existence long enough to demonstrate that its most persistent, stable and "successful" form has proved to be the *bourgeois democratic* political form. Thus for the bourgeoisie whatever pressures manifest themselves toward the "authoritarian solution" there is at the same time a profound concern to sustain the legitimacy of the capitalist order.

This analysis does not lead to the conclusion that the resort by the ruling class to fascism or to military coup is impossible. The tragic example of Chile is too urgent to allow such a naive conclusion. But this analysis does insist that the resort to fascism is not the automatic response of a capitalist class in crisis. We should have no illusions about the fact that the capitalist class has been prepared, in the final analysis, to abandon bourgeois democracy. But we should be equally insistent that the interests of the bourgeoisie have been best served where they have been able to sustain their class rule within the bourgeois democratic form and that the ruling class itself has an interest in the preservation of bourgeois democracy.

The legal order plays a central role within bourgeois democracy.

Thus while the coercive role of the legal order has been emphasized in the first half of this article it is now necessary to draw attention to and to examine the contribution made by the legal system to sustaining the legitimacy of the bourgeois democratic order. In other words it is necessary to discuss law as a method of ideological domination.

LAW AS IDEOLOGICAL DOMINATION

Repressive and ideological domination are in no sense alternatives. On the contrary they are interdependent; they interact and reinforce each other. While the coercion of the criminal law is directed against those it punishes, its ideological effects are directed much wider. For example, the jailing of the Shrewsbury pickets was legal violence against the accused which was concerned with more than "deterring" others; it was an ideological offence against the strategy of the "flying picket" developed by the miners and applied so effectively by building workers.

Ideological domination describes those activities and processes whereby the assent to the existing social order is produced and mobilized. The notion of assent embraces both the idea of legitimacy as active assent and also acceptance as the passive form. The means by which assent is produced are ideological in that it involves the production and dissemination of ideas that affect social practice through the determination of the social consciousness of individuals, groups, and classes. This process is one of domination in that it involves two elements; first, a differential ability of groups and classes in society to produce, communicate, and disseminate ideas, and second, these ideas, directly or indirectly, have consequences for the maintenance of the existing social order.

Law is ideological in that it conveys or transmits a complex set of attitudes, values, and theories about aspects of society. Its ideological content forms part of the dominant ideology because these attitudes, values, etc. are ones that reinforce and legitimize the existing social order.

The most pervasive ideological effect of law is to be found in the fact that legal rules and their application give effect to existing social relations. The rules of law affirm the social and economic relations that exist within capitalist society. Thus the law of property is not only based on the inequality of property ownership but it reinforces it by allowing and facilitating the owners of property to make use of that property as capital. The complex of legal rules relating to mortgages, trusts, leases, etc. not only allows but also enables property to be used as capital. The law relating to contracts and commercial activity gives effect to the mechanisms of the market.

Similarly labor law facilitates the capitalist form of the relationship between labor and capital; it gives effect to the economic fact of the dependence of the majority on the sale of their labor power. It embodies the economic power of capital over labor by granting to the employer rights regarding not only the control of labor but also over the hiring and firing of labor.

Rules of law impinge on almost every form of social relations. For example, family law, despite the reforms of the past decades, incorporates the fact of the dominant role of the husband over the wife, of the parents over the children. Likewise the law of landlord and tenant underlines the power of landlords over tenants in regard to the supply of housing. It is important to stress that the legal rules do not *create* the social relations that make up capitalist society. But by stating them as principles and by enforcing them the law operates not only to reinforce these relations but also to legitimize them in their existing form. This function is further advanced by the role of law in conferring authority upon officials such as the police, magistrates, etc.

The rules of law not only define social relations but confer rights and powers on certain categories of individuals. Thus, for example, landlord and tenant law not only incorporates the economic fact of the monopolization of housing by private interests, but it also legitimizes that economic power by granting rights to landlords to extract rent, to impose conditions, and to evict tenants. The legal system not only reinforces existing social and economic relations, but in addition it confers authority on dominant social interests.

One important aspect that should not be overlooked is the extent to which law operates to regulate the mutual interests of the bourgeoisie. It provides a mechanism for the resolution of disputes and conflicts that arise *between* capitalist interests:

> The administration of . . . civil justice is concerned almost exclusively with conflicts over property and hence affects almost exclusively the possessing classes. (Marx 1958:II,34)

Company law, for example, is concerned in the main with the respective interests of shareholders and directors. Much commercial law is likewise concerned with the interests of merchants, middlemen, and dealers.

The law regulating the interests of the propertied classes is detailed and complex, but it has a significant common core. The operation of capitalistic functions is facilitated where the law provides a degree of certainty and predictability. What bourgeois legal theory fails to recognize is that it is only that element of law that regulates the mutual interests of the bourgeoisie, and not the whole of law in a capitalist society that exhibits this quest for certainty.

It is necessary to consider more closely the nature of the correspondence between legal rules and the social relations to which they relate. Legal rules do not simply "reflect" social relations. The rules of law have an added ideological dimension. To explain this it is important to recall that a central feature of capitalist society is that its essential features are obscured or concealed by the very nature of the operation of the capitalist economy. Marx insisted on the need to distinguish between how things appear (the "appearance" or "phenomenal form") and how they really are ("real substratum" or "essence").

The "real" relations that exist find themselves expressed in legal rules in a distorted or truncated form because the law gives effect to only the appearance ("phenomenal form") of social relations. This theoretical point could be taken further by applying the argument developed by Marx in the famous section on "the fetishism of commodities" in *Capital* Vol. I in which he shows how our comprehension of commodities embodies not the real social relations of production which create them, but simply as things; and as a result what are relations between people come to be seen as relations between things.

So legal rules appear abstracted from social relations, and are therefore a "fetishistic" expression of social relations. Legal rules are further divorced from the social relations to which they refer because they (like the state itself) appear separated, independent of society; they seem to have an independent origin and life of their own. Thus as ideological forms of social relations legal rules are doubly removed from the real world.

Legal rules express the appearance of social relations:

> This phenomenal form, which makes the actual relations invisible . . . forms the basis of all the juridical notions of both labourer and capitalist, of all the mystifications of the capitalist mode of production, of all its illusions as to liberty. (Marx 1961:I,540)

Marx showed how our initial perception of the capitalist economy focuses on the process of circulation and exchange, and thus ignores the production process itself. It is significant to note that legal rules follow this pattern and reduce social relations to a system of exchanges. The key legal concept of bourgeois law is that of *contract*. All the most important relations within capitalist society are moulded into the form of contractual relations.

By treating social relations as "contracts" bourgeois law strips them of their most important characteristics. Perhaps the most important example is in the labor relationship between employers and workers. At law the labor relation is a contract between individual employer and individual employee; they are therefore presumed to bargain over the terms of the contract. This individualizing of the contract of employment by focusing on it as an individual exchange excludes the social character of the relation between capital and labor. It is incapable of embracing the increasingly collective determination of labor relations through negotiations between trade unions and employers' federations. English law has reduced itself to great confusion in attempting to preserve the "individual contract" while taking some note of the real "collective contract."

It is not only economic relations that are reduced to contractual form. A wide range of other social relations is similarly treated. Thus, for example, the social institution of marriage is enshrined in law as a contract within which the "parties" have obligations that derive from the contract, and the "breach" of which can result in the contract being terminated, i.e., in divorce. Yet by expressing the marriage relationship in contractual form the law inadvertently exposes something of the real economic basis on which the bourgeois marriage is based, founded on the economic dependence of women.

The principles of contract have been so pervasive that they have been developed into a contractual ideology which continues to have wider ranging influences. Contractual ideology leans heavily on the notions of freedom and equality. But the "freedom" and "equality" to which it refers is purely *formal;* that is individuals are regarded as free if there is no legal bar to them entering into a contract, and are therefore deemed to be equal. It is a notion of equality brilliantly captured by Anatole France:

> The law in its majestic impartiality forbids rich and poor alike to sleep under bridges, to beg in the streets and steal bread. (1927:91)

These formal notions of freedom and equality are characteristic of bourgeois legal and political theory. They do violence to social reality because they are incapable of grasping the real inequality and lack of freedom that results from the dependence of all workers on the sale of their labor.

This discussion has focused on the way in which the rules of law, far from being pure or independent creations, are but a distorted expression of the existing social relations which are thereby reinforced and legitimised. This ideological character of legal rules is extended by two further considerations.

One of the difficulties in penetrating the ideological form of bourgeois law stems from the fact that it operates by abstracting the cases that come before the courts from their social and class context. They are thereby reduced to the status of being purely *technical* issues, apparently divorced from any political or ideological overtones. If, for example, a householder inquires why it is that tax relief is granted on mortgage payments but not on rent, the law replies that it is not a question of relief on mortgage or rent, but on interest repayments. By focusing on a technical distinction the law thereby obscures the social and economic reality.

Second, the law further depoliticizes social issues through the universal form of many legal rules. The fact that rules of criminal law protect the person and property of *all* members of society not only hides the fundamental class differences, but it also treats the capital of the employer and the personal belongings of the worker as if they were the same. The ideological significance is that it induces the view that all classes in society have a common interest in the protection of private property. Thereby the legal system is aided in fulfilling the ideological function of asserting the unity of interests of all classes. The ideology of the "rule of law" operates to assert and reinforce, and even seeks to celebrate, a social unity and cohesion in the face of the manifest class differentiation of capitalist society.

There is one further facet of the ideological character of law. It is directly ideological in the sense that the legal system propagates a range of views about the nature of the social and political system. This general ideological character of law is contained in what I will call "bourgeois legal ideology."

Bourgeois legal ideology is the fundamental component of the justification of the bourgeois democratic state; many of its elements directly enter into the consciousness of wide sections of the population. The central element of this ideology is the doctrine of "the rule of law." Its classic expression is to be found in Dicey:

> When we speak of the 'rule of law' as a characteristic of our country we mean, not only that with us no man is above the law, but (what is a different thing) that here every man, whatever be his rank or condition, is subject to the ordinary law of the realm. . . . With us every official, from the Prime

Minister down to a constable . . . is under the same responsibility for every act done without legal justification as any other
citizen. (1967:193)

The fundamental tenet is that both the ruled and the rulers are
equally subject to a common system of law. The "law" itself is thus
viewed as something separate from the interests of classes. As such it
plays a central role in the legitimation of the bourgeois democratic
political order.

One particularly interesting feature of bourgeois legal ideology in
the context of English law is the way in which it holds itself out as the
protector of the individual against the incursions of the state. This
antithesis between individual and state has a lengthy history in bourgeois legal thought. Its roots were in the historical alliance between the
common law judges and the bourgeois interests against the absolutism
of the Stuarts. It became more fully elaborated during the nineteenth
century as the legal reflex of laissez-faire ideology. And in the twentieth
century it has been used as the basis of antistate attitudes that characterize one element of the conservative reaction to the growth of the
Welfare State.

In addition to explicit constitutional principles bourgeois legal ideology consists of a range of important background or implicit assumptions. The intention is only to roughly sketch some of these assumptions, but at the same time to argue that the more the "law and order"
debate moves into the center of the political stage the more important
it becomes to develop a systematic critique of bourgeois legal ideology.

Almost all discussion about law is based on the assumption that the
existence of law is an inevitable or natural feature of social life. Hence
law becomes identified with "civilization"; the absence of law is seen
as synonymous with the absence of civilization. The classic expression
of this assumption is the equation of the absence of law with anarchy;
in its classical form in the political philosophy of Hobbes the absence
of law implies a condition of "the war of all against all." The whole
of society is presumed to have an interest in the existence of law, and
is therefore closely connected with the "universalism" of law discussed
above.

A closely associated assumption insists on the inherent rationality
of law. The existence of rules of social life brought together or codified
as law is presented as socially desirable in that it makes social life more
certain and predictable. Social life is viewed as if it were a game or a
sport in which it is essential that all the "players" adhere to the same
rules; without this common set of rules social life would revert to

anarchy. Such an attitude places stress on the desirability of rules *as such*, and hence leaves unquestioned the content of those rules and any questions concerning the social and economic interests that are embodied in the rules.

Flowing directly from the insistence on the naturalness and rationality of law is the insistence that adherence to law is natural, and as a corollary, that nonadherence to law is unnatural or deviant. The very existence of a state is treated as a sufficient condition to make obedience to law obligatory for all citizens. The assumption is made that the offender who violates the law is a deviant whose deviation stems from some pathological condition. While the nature of the pathology appealed to has varied, from the genetic inferiority of the "lower orders" to deficiencies in "socialization," the same assumption of the naturalness of obedience to law persists. It is interesting to note that in the recent past this essentially conservative tradition has come under increasing attack from criminologists, and that radical theories of crime are being developed which draw upon Marxism (Taylor, Walton, and Young 1972).

These interrelated attitudes and assumptions about law are not usually expressed in a coherent form; they are a cluster of ideas, but they add up to an assertion of the "sanctity of law" that forms the heart of the pervasive and powerful "law and order" ideology. This ideology finds expression not only in the moralizing editorials of the *Times*, but also forms an important part of widespread and diffuse social attitudes. The essential substance of these views is that they appeal to the sanctity of law, elevated above social life itself, and thereby ignore the class content of law and its role in legitimising the existing forms of class domination.

There is one final aspect of the ideological character of law that needs to be mentioned. The most formal and systematic expression of legal ideology is provided by jurisprudence or legal theory. The history of jurisprudence consists in successive attempts to provide a justification for obedience to law. The central concern has been to provide a socially persuasive account of the legitimacy of the existing legal order, and through that of the social order itself. However, a very interesting development has occurred within jurisprudence which is worth noting. Increasingly a number of liberal academics have been afflicted with growing self-doubt and disillusionment with the whole edifice of law, and are increasingly aware of a very real decline in the legitimacy of the existing legal order (Rostow 1970; Wolff 1971).

The operation of law is, therefore, not confined to simply giving effect to the direct and immediate interests of the ruling class. It must be understood as having an ideological function of an extensive character. Within capitalist society the legal system not only provides substantial ideological underpinnings to the existing capitalist organization of society. It also provides a consistent and coherent legitimation of a multitude of key institutions and principles that are central to the smooth operation of a system of capitalist social relations.

It is this ability to integrate two critical functions, on the one hand to give practical effect to the interests of the dominant class, and, at the same time, to provide a justification or legitimation for these interests in terms of some higher and apparently universal interest of all classes that demonstrates the real power and influence of law in capitalist society.

LAW AND CLASS STRUGGLE

Our attention has been focused on the part that law plays in the process of reproducing capitalist social order. Yet law is not simply an instrument which can be wielded at will by an omnipotent ruling class. Precisely because it is an active element in the class struggle, it is at the same time affected by and involved in the class struggle. The law and the legal system form part of the context within which the class struggle takes place, and it is itself an arena in which that struggle occurs. To recognize that class struggle occurs *within* the legal system is not to suggest that the legal system is some neutral territory over which the class struggle wrestles for control. As a major component of the state law is necessarily part of the process through which the ruling class seeks to preserve its domination.

To argue that class struggle occurs within law is only the first step in examining the way in which class struggle makes itself evident within law. It has been argued above that law plays a central part in bourgeois democratic society, not only in theory but also in practice. The form taken by the class struggle has its boundaries broadly defined by the existing law. Thus, for example, trade union activity in Britain is pursued by forms of struggle that are recognized as being lawful. Some of the most important stages in the history of British trade unionism have been periods when struggle has occurred around attempts by the ruling class to narrow or restrict this lawful sphere of operations. The struggle against the Industrial Relations Act was a classic example of this type of struggle.

While law plays this important part of defining the parameters of class struggle, it also needs to be recognized that it does not necessarily stay confined within this framework. Indeed a change in this boundary or its breach will normally mark a critical phase in the class struggle. For example, a very important stage of the struggle against the Industrial Relations Act occurred in the months after is had been put on the statute book. The right-wing inside the Labour Movement argued that despite the objection they had to the Act it was now "law" and had to be accepted. The critical phase was the decisions made in the individual unions and within the TUC (Croydon and Blackpool Congresses 1971) as to whether they would "register" under the Act, and thus come within "the law," or whether to remain unregistered and to conduct trade union activity without the forms of protection that had been established since the beginning of the century.

Not only does law play an important part in defining the parameters of the class struggle, but many important stages in the class struggle take place around demands for legislative reforms. Marx himself gave considerable attention to one very important example of such struggles, the early Factory Acts (in particular the *Factories Regulation Act* of 1833). His chapter in *Capital,* Volume I, on "The Working-Day" is a classic study of the interrelation and interaction of class forces in a struggle for legislative control of working hours.

> The creation of a normal working-day is, therefore, the product of a protracted civil war, more or less dissembled, between the capitalist class and the working-class. (1961:I, 231–302)

Elsewhere he summarized the significance of the victory underlying the Act in the following terms:

> it was the first time that in broad daylight the political economy of the middle class succumbed to the political economy of the working class. (1958: I, 383)

His analysis makes clear that the Factory Acts were not simply the direct result of class struggle between the capitalist and working classes. Two particular features of the analysis are worth drawing attention to. The first concerns the relationship between the state and the capitalist class. The advent of machinery and industrial production in the textile industry gives rise to a veritable orgy of exploitation in which the working-day is extended to such lengths that a real threat is posed to the survival of the work force. At this stage the state represents the collective interests of capital, as distinct from the interests of individual capitalists.

Second, he stresses the divisions between the various sections of the capitalist class. Not only is there the division between the landed and industrial capitalists, which led the Tories as representatives of landed capital, to support factory legislation. But more important are the divisions between the more advanced sections of industrial capital and the smaller, more traditional employers. The passage of the factory acts represented a victory not only for the working class, but also for the more advanced sections of capital, who triumphed over their less efficient rivals. The overall analysis therefore brings out with great sharpness the way in which the development of the productive forces, in association with the more or less conscious struggle of various classes, finds its expression in legislation.

In his discussion of factory legislation Marx showed clearly how each legislative victory was only partial; while each was a major practical and ideological victory, the employers, with the direct complicity of the magistrates and judges, impeded the effective enforcement of the provisions of the statutes.

CONCLUSION

In this chapter I have stressed the importance of law in capitalist society, and as a consequence argued that it is a question that requires a more thorough analysis by Marxists. While this chapter does not complete that task, it has sought to raise a number of questions, and to stress a number of areas for discussion. Some of these have been of a general nature that revolve around an assertion of law as an important agency in the maintenance of capitalist social relations. In particular I have argued the need to understand the significance of law as a system of ideological-coercive domination. It is through this emphasis on this combined process, rather than as two distinct or separate processes, that we can achieve a better understanding of the specific functioning of law within capitalist society, and is also of assistance in achieving a fuller theoretical treatment of the capitalist state.

The legal system within the bourgeois democratic state operates in such a way as to legitimize the class rule of the bourgeoisie. This legitimation involves not only the recognition and reinforcement of the social and economic relations of capitalism. It also encompasses the reification of law (through which law appears to be a power above and outside society) in which the social and political relations of capitalist society are presented as natural and universal. Law then operates to provide ideological reinforcement to those processes that make the reality of class and class power less visible.

The really difficult question is posed by the fact that bourgeois democratic society is not entirely a facade and a fraud. If it were its veils and deceits would have been stripped away long ago. Its strength and persistence result from the fact that in varying degrees it has successfully combined the continued social, political and economic dominance of the capitalist class with, at the same time, a significant level of involvement of the exploited classes sufficient to ensure a relatively high level of acceptance of, and even commitment to, the existing order.

Within the bourgeois democratic state law provides, alongside those aspects that reinforce the domination of the ruling class, an important set of rights, protections, and powers that in varying degrees incorporate certain class interests of the nonruling classes. The most obvious examples of these are such things as the right to vote, to form trade unions, to take strike action, etc.

It is important to recognize that most of these have been secured as the result of class struggle. But these facts should not lead us to view them simply as concessions wrung from the capitalist. Once granted they become woven into the fabric of bourgeois democracy. It should also be noted that we need to recognize that the range of legal rights that may be used to the advantage of the working class extends beyond the range of the more obvious "political" rights mentioned. The law confers rights and protections on all classes as "citizens" in bourgeois democracy. It is of course important to stress the inequality of their application and the inequality of access to legal redress. Yet this does not negate their political and ideological importance. Their very existence plays a significant part in securing the acceptance of, and allegiance to, the existing capitalist social order.

CHAPTER 3

PERSPECTIVES IN THE SOCIOLOGY OF LAW

THE THEORETICAL ROOTS OF THE SOCIOLOGY OF LAW

The focus of any area of academic enquiry may be identified by the way in which the "importance" of the social phenomenon under examination is presented. To understand the distinctive character of sociology of law it is essential to recognize that the location of this importance has been expressed in a number of different ways. The significance of these alternative positions is that each constitutes a different statement of the "importance" of law. This may be expressed in a slightly different way by contending that each statement of the importance of law contains a designation of a problematic. A problematic is contained in every statement of a frame of reference or a theoretical proposition; it is more than the statement of a problem or a question in that the selection of a particular focus excludes or relegates other foci and thereby presents a potential solution within itself.

The sociological movement in law takes as its starting point the law–society relationship. The problematic is extremely underdeveloped; it provides little explicit direction to study within the field. Within this orientation may be detected a number of other problematics that are concerned with providing a skeletal formulation of the nature of the law–society relationship. It will be through an examination of these alternative problematics that we can arrive at a characterization of the major trends within the sociological movement. Further, their elucidation will facilitate a statement as to the present state of development of the field currently designated as "sociology of law." The present concern is with the general tradition that underlies the sociological movement in law. For this reason the "critical" or "radical" development within the sociology of law and in deviancy theory is not considered in any detail. These developments are of sufficient importance to require independent treatment.

It is necessary to stress that the alternative problematics to be discussed are pure types. They are "pure types" not in the sense that they are not found in the real world (insofar as the realm of the theoretical basis of the sociological movement in law can be regarded as part of the real world), but in the sense that they rarely appear complete and uncontaminated. More frequently they appear in combination with other elements and in this form constitute the specific or distinctive characteristics of the particular contributors to the sociological movement.

The Sociological Jurisprudential Problematic

The first problematic may be designated as the "sociological jurisprudential problematic." It is expressed with particular clarity in Julius Stone's definition of sociological jurisprudence.

> Sociological jurisprudence, and any study which seeks to bring social science knowledge to serve legal problems, address themselves to the influence of social, economic, psychological and other non-legal factors on the process in the concrete content of legal propositions. (Stone, 1966:5)

The definition asserts the existence of law as a discrete element in social reality. As the final phrase indicates, the central reality of law is posited as its normative content, the substantive rules of law and the changes to which they are subject. The law thus conceived is subject to external forces (social, economic, etc.) that act on it and whose action results in internal changes. The model of the law–society relationship that this sociological jurisprudential perspective constitutes may be simply presented in the diagrammatic form:

What is significant about this model is that it enshrines a simple assumption of the centrality of law. For the jurist, as for the practitioner, the law *is,* and is therefore self-evidently important. Such an analysis makes clear and provides an explanation for the general contention that sociological jurisprudence, despite its efforts and protestations, did not succeed in making any significant break from the jurisprudential tradition.

What the sociological jurisprudential model provided was the assertion that law does not exist—and cannot, therefore, be studied—in a vacuum. Law is seen as being subject to the influence of external forces,

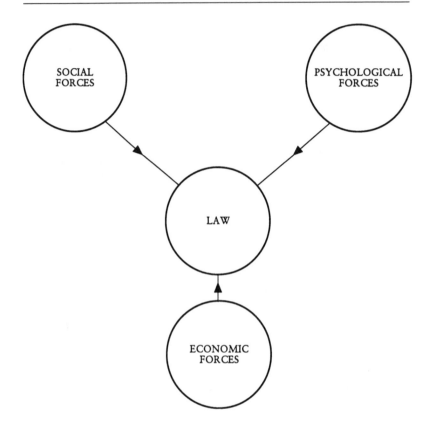

but at the same time the central focus remains the action of social forces on law, insofar as it is determinant of the internal dynamic of the legal order itself. Such a perspective gives rise to an eclecticism in the methods of study; insofar as the factors impinging on the legal system are regarded as independent variables, then these factors can be viewed in isolation. This perspective manifests itself in the predominant tendency to see the field of "law and society," or sociolegal studies as being multidisciplinary activities in which the social scientists subserve the interests of the jurist who is, if not the leader of the team, its link-pin.

A variant of this sociological jurisprudential problematic not only focuses upon the social factors that impinge on law but also includes within its implicit statement of the problematic a concern with the "social consequences of law." In other words the law remains very much the center of enquiry, subject to social forces that act on it, but is itself viewed as reacting back on the social system. This variation may be represented as follows:

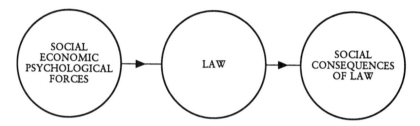

This model retains the implicit assumption not only of the centrality of law, but also persists in encouraging the same eclecticism of method. This variant manifests itself in its purest form in the behavioralistic tendencies in American Realism, and has been largely followed by the modern behavioralists.

The simple form of the sociological jurisprudential model is one that is common to both Poundian and Realist jurisprudence. Pound's version of this position is more developed insofar as it tackles the question of the form in which social forces act on law, namely in the form of claims pressed on the system that embody "interests." The Realists, insofar as they are to be differentiated from Pound, tended to a greater eclecticism in that social pressures on law were not treated as being subsumed under a general form, but remained a multiplicity of forces acting on law. The sociological jurisprudential problematic is the one that motivates many studies that are usually treated as part of the sociology of law. This is especially true of Timasheff (1939), but also provide the general pattern in the area of "emergence studies" and "impact studies."

The Law as Social Control Problematic

The second major problematic developed within the sociological movement in law is one that may be identified as the "law as a means of social control" problematic. The major change of emphasis involved is that the "importance" of law is not derived from something intrinsic to law itself, but rather stems from its classification as part of a wider frame of reference. Law then is not significant in and of itself, but as but one of the forms of social control. The situation of the discussion of law thereupon proceeds on the basis of a consideration of its relationship, first, to the social control process as a whole and second, to the other forms of social control.

The "law as social control" perspective is significant in that it has provided a central focus for both wings, the sociological and the juristic, of the sociological movement. It is one that contains the potentiality of breaking from the hallmark of jurisprudential tradition in that it avoids the assertion of the centrality of law. However, it should be stressed that this potential has not been generally realized in the application that has been made of the perspective. Thus within Poundian jurisprudence, although the social control perspective provided a major definitional role, it remained subordinate to the sociological jurisprudential problematic. Conversely, in Durkheim's sociology the social control perspective is dominant, expressed in terms of his overriding concern with solidarity in which law is treated as a form of its exemplification. The social control perspective has also played a significant role in American sociology of law, being conceived as a means of breaking with the jurisprudential tradition.

The "law as social control" perspective has undoubtedly been a unifying theme within the sociological movement, but because of its somewhat self-evident character there has been insufficient attention given to the implications that flow from its adoption. It is therefore necessary to devote some attention to these consequences for the sociology of law.

Underlying the discussion of social control is a pervasive concern with a question that has been fundamental in sociology, social philosophy, and jurisprudence, namely, the problem of order. How is it that the complexity of the actions of individuals and groups allows us to perceive "society" as an entity, as an "organic community"? The social control perspective has provided a particular way of posing the problem of order. The existence of society gives rise to certain social forces that act on society in the form of mechanisms of social control, which are social facts in the Durkheimian sense, in that they impose themselves on the members of society. Social control operates, in a sense, despite the individuals who constitute society. It is a product of society itself, never willed or wished or planned by its members but as a necessary consequence of the existence of society itself, whose preservation is a consequence of these social forces spontaneously generated.

This position manifests elements of a reified conception of society. Society is perceived as an autonomous social reality, independent of those who form it, giving rise to social forces that act on, control, and determine the conduct of its constituents. Society, through the mechanisms of social control, is perceived as "acting on" and "controlling" its members. Insofar as the sociology of law has utilized the social control perspective it necessarily becomes involved, and indeed needs to involve itself more consciously in what is one of the major debates in sociological theory, which although taking many forms revolves around the counterposing of an image of man as the product of social forces or as the creator of social reality, or as the dichotomy between determinism and voluntarism (Dawe 1970; Atkinson 1971).

An alternative perspective, pronounced in currently influential trends in sociological theory, finds its starting point in a view of the individual as an active agent in the creation of social reality (Dawe 1970). This alternative perspective tends toward subjectivism; the problem on which it founders is: with what or from what do individuals make their social reality? Where the individual consciousness of "social reality" is deemed to be the reality itself then pure subjectivism is the consequence. It is suggested that the sociological strategy that overcomes these apparently dichotomous alternatives, and that has a major potential within the sociology of law is that contained in Marx's proposition:

> Men make their own history, but they do not make it just as they please; they do not make it under circumstances directly encountered, given and transmitted from the past. (Marx, 1958:I,247).

Such a perspective provides an integrated dual focus, which makes it possible to avoid both reification and subjectivism. It insists on a conception of man as an active agent, within which the relationship between his activity and his consciousness provides the central dynamic of social action. Yet this action and consciousness exist under historically given circumstances; and only on the basis of these circumstances can the study of activity and consciousness proceed. For the sociology of law an insistence on historical specificity is a much needed corrective to the universalistic or overgeneralized conception of "law," which the sociological movement has generally utilized.

Apart from the general issues of sociological strategy there is a more immediate respect in which the adoption of the "law as social control" view has determined certain characteristics of the sociological movement in law. Since the process of social control is seen as a necessary consequence of social life itself it is located in primary social activities and, in particular, as a product of the normative process. Hence the process of social control is seen mainly in terms of the socialization process operating through the internalization of values. The means of social control that receive attention are the value-embodying processes variously identified as customs, mores, folkways, and morality.

If primacy is attached to the informal, noninstitutionalized mechanisms of social control then a certain model of the social control process is developed. This model may be schematically depicted as: social activity and interaction give rise to social values that, expressed as expectations of others, constitute norms. Adherence to normative expectations is induced by a range of socially available sanctions that are associated with the existence of the norms themselves. These sanctions are applied as a response to norm violation in the course of primary social activity within the primary social units of "group," "family," and "kinship." The constraint of society over its members is thus the constraint that flows naturally from the primary constituents of social life itself. The constraint that is exercised through the informal mechanisms of social control is seen as being essentially a process of self-regulation endemic in the postulation of social life itself.

Now if law is regarded as one of the forms of social control there is implied a view that they form a continuum ranged along a scale from informal means to the more institutionalized forms, of which law is regarded as the most specialized form. For example, the definition of law as the most specialized form of social control is explicit in Pound (1942). To treat law as one of the forms of social control carries with it the implication that it partakes of the characteristics of the other forms. The association has tended to enhance a view of law that stresses the normative character of law and lays stress on the relationship between societal values and the value content of legal propositions. Hence an apparently self-evident truth is invested in the identification of the rules of law as embodying the most widely diffused social values.

Further, the general non-institutionalised character of the forms of social control with which law is compared tends to result in an assumption that law shares with these other agencies a reliance on enforcement through widely diffused social consensus. The most extreme variant of this is Durkheim's identification of law as the direct embodiment of the "conscience collective." Such an emphasis accounts for general tendency to ignore the coercive character of law.

It is, however, important to stress that a plea for greater attention to the coercive character of law should not be read as implying a reductionist position. It is a platitude that law does not operate as an exclusively coercive mechanism. That legal systems depend on their being invested with legitimacy is also a commonplace. The problem-raising inference that is frequently drawn is that value consensus is the root of legitimacy. What is neglected is the relationship between coercion and legitimacy. One of the significant merits of Max Weber's sociology of law, with its emphasis on the relationship between law and domination, is precisely that it permits the exploration, without ignoring the normative character of law, of the coercive characteristics of legal systems. Weber's own predominant concern, however, with rational legal domination and his tendency to regard coercive forms of domination as being residual categories detracts from a rounded treatment of law as a form of domination. It is, however, suggested that such a stance makes possible the bringing together of Weber's general insights with an analysis of coercive domination that will draw on Marxist sociology. Such an approach presents the possibility of drawing upon the best of the academic tradition within the sociology of law but in such a way that avoids the deficiencies that have been identified and that are exemplified in the "law as social control" problematic.

THE PROBLEM OF THEORY IN THE SOCIOLOGY OF LAW

One of the major characteristics of modern sociology of law is the very pronounced orientation toward empirical studies. The origins of this strongly empirical bias result both from characteristics of the sociological movement in law as a whole, and from particular features of American sociology of law. This tendency is even more pronounced in the sociology of law that has emerged in Britain since the late 1960s. It has been stressed that the criticisms that have been leveled are not against empirical studies as such but the methodological empiricism on which they are founded.

Dissatisfaction with the dominant empiricist tendency has been growing both in the United States and in Britain. In a variety of different forms this response has come from such differing positions as those of Selznick, Black, and Currie; they have all consciously asserted the need for a greater attention being devoted to theory as a necessary precondition for the advance of sociology of law. In Britain this position has been strongly championed by Colin Campbell.

> If characterised by inter-disciplinary research, with little attention given to general sociological theory, and motivated by reformist ideas and a missionary zeal to educate lawyers and law students—sociology of law is likely to contribute little of lasting value. (Campbell 1972:8)

The fundamental polarization within the field is presented as that between theoretical and empiricist approaches; the latter Campbell describes as being characterised by "a lack of any explicit theoretical framework" (Campbell 1972:5). He is of course correct that empiricist work is marked by the absence of an explicit theoretical framework; but what must be insisted on is that empiricist sociology of law does contain a consistent *implicit* theoretical position. The implicit theory of the empiricists is the same as that which informs the work of those whose theoretical concerns are more explicit, namely a social control theory founded on the assumption of widespread value consensus. The central issue is not that of "theory" versus "empiricism," although it is important to recognize that the absence of overt concern with theoretical sociology is a symptom of the malaise within the field. The major question that needs to be posed to those concerned with the sociology of law is not simply the call for "theory," but rather to raise the question: *what* theory?

The call to debate "what theory" is a contention that the posing of the issues confronting the sociology of law in this way will serve to focus attention not only on the general question of the role of theory, but will also highlight the major questions that the currently competing theoretical positions will need to embrace if our understanding is to be advanced. An ongoing debate between contending theoretical positions could assist in clarifying the problems that lie at the heart of the sociology of law.

The advocacy of a theoretical debate is not, however, a call for the abandonment of empirical work. What is significant about the majority of empirical work undertaken at present is that its importance is defined by reference to topics that are of practical significance within the pragmatic reformist tradition of the sociological movement. The initiation of a theoretical debate within the sociology of law will itself provide an impulse toward empirical studies but it is hoped these will be ones whose importance will come to be defined by reference to substantive theoretical problems within the field.

If theory is other than a retreat into abstraction an understanding of its function is imperative. Theory determines the presentation of the problematic that is both the starting point for all inquiry and the determinant of the range or scope of that investigation. It is the articulation of the problematic in terms of its conceptual framework and the posited relationships between its primary concepts. Concepts and their interrelationship express what is perceived as being important or relevant. When theory appears arid or abstracted it is because the substantive issues to which it relates are either not articulated, or are not felt to impinge significantly on features that are regarded as being relevant by the user of the theory.

What is needed is a more "open" theoretical debate, that is, one which makes, a conscious effort to make explicit the general issues that are implicated in the adoption of a particular theoretical position. The "general issues" that are implicated in all theory are the social, political, and ideological questions that it throws into relief. An "open" theory is one that strives to make explicit the ideological and political implications and significance of the perspective adopted. "Closed" theory, on the other hand, which characterizes much contemporary sociological theorizing, tends to hide behind the commitment to value-neutrality, and which in seeking scientific purity renders itself opaque.

If the debate about theory is to be made as concrete as possible it is desirable to provide some account of the context in which the debate about law takes place; this attempt to situate law is a necessary precondition of a theoretical debate. The resurgence of a potentially different set of questions concerning law has been the characteristic of the sociological movement. The stress upon "potential" must be insisted on. Although a new set of questions about law has been thrown up since the end of the nineteenth century the fact that the thrust of these questions has not always been apparent is evidence of the grip of the jurisprudential problematic on the sociological movement. These new "questions about law" have therefore remained immanent within the sociological movement rather than being the active forces that have shaped it.

Bourgeois jurisprudence and sociology have for well over a century been situated in the context of capitalist societies that have undergone unprecedented development, both in the economic and the social fields. Particularly in the period since the Second World War this development of the major capitalist societies has been at an ever expanding rate and has taken place in the context of relative stability. This relative stability has not only been economic but political. Throughout much of the postwar period a climate of inevitability and self-satisfaction has been pronounced. This has expressed itself ideologically in the currency that has been accorded to such positions as "the end of ideology," "the managerial revolution," the "technocratic revolution," "postindustrial society," the "property-owning democracy," and many other keynote slogans, both academic and political.

Yet the stability has always been relative. Despite the apparent material abundance, capitalist society has persistently underachieved with respect to its major ideological goals. The expression of this underachievement has been the failure to realize the general ideals of "freedom" and "equality"; in the political arena there has been the failure of "the property-owning democracy" and the "Great Society." The self-evident perpetuation of inequality and social injustice has not always disturbed the political calm, but it has never been far below the surface. And it has taken place in the context of an ever more self-conscious international confrontation, waged both militarily and ideologically, between contending social systems.

If in the context of this sketch of relatively stable capitalism we turn our attention to law the same persistent failure to realize major legal ideals is evident. The social ideals of freedom and equality find their reflex in the ideal of justice; while the ideal remains buoyant there is persistent underachievement in its operation. The manifestation of this failure has taken varied forms. At the general level there has been a failure to achieve the ideal of equality both in the access to and in the application of law. The consequence has been a generalized crisis of the legal order. This crisis has been compounded by the extent to which the traditional distinction between the public and private realms of law has been blurred as a consequence of the increasing ramifications of state activity. The form of state intervention is increasingly legislative and as a consequence social, economic, and political conflict comes to involve conflict with respect to both the content and the application of law. Legislation more frequently exhibits, to adopt Gusfield's distinction (1966), a symbolic as opposed to an instrumental social function. Thus law becomes directly implicated in the dynamic of social change. As a consequence the perception of law as external to social conflict and integrative in its function becomes undermined. The legal system moves always closer to the vortex of social conflict.

As a further extension to this line of thought it may be tentatively suggested that this process receives further momentum from another consideration. Where the existing social order comes under increasing tensions, especially where these manifest themselves in a declining legitimacy, then because the legal system is generally enveloped in a higher level of legitimacy than other components of the social order, it is invoked more frequently in order to maintain that social order. Thus it comes to play a more direct and explicit role in the maintenance of the existing social order. The development of statutory incomes policy in Britain lends support to such an analysis.

The protracted and simmering nature of the crisis of the legal order in capitalist societies has induced a reevaluation of the ideals themselves. At the same time reformist attitudes that point toward particular operational failures within the legal system have had to take their place alongside a more general critique. It is in this context that the urgent need for a fresh examination of the theory that informs our perception of the legal system is situated. This urgency has found expression in the upsurge of sharply polemical interventions from avowedly "critical" or "radical" positions (Currie 1971; Cloke 1971; Lefcourt 1971; Quinney 1972, 1973).

Despite the general nature of the social and legal crisis through which capitalist societies are passing and the growth of more radical critiques, it is still very much the case that "the system" remains. It may be more tarnished, but it is the fact of life. It is in this sense that the emphasis has been laid on the stability and persistence of the capitalist social order and the associated legal systems. Implicit is a suggestion that the legal system plays a significant, and possibly an increasingly important, role in the maintenance of this precarious stability. It is within this context that it is possible to situate a new problematic as a potential focus for both theoretical and substantive inquiry within the sociology of law. This new problematic may be designated as law as a mode of reproduction of the social order.

It must be stressed that what is intended is not a full elaboration of a new "theory of law." The present concern is much less ambitious. Attention will be devoted only to an exploration of the potentialities and implications of such an alternative perspective.

LAW AS A MODE OF REPRODUCTION OF THE SOCIAL ORDER

If this alternative problematic is to fulfil a role that goes beyond simply serving as a polemical slogan it is necessary, first, to explore the major concepts from which it is constituted, namely "reproduction" and "social order." Second, it is necessary to examine the consequences that flow from its adoption. In approaching this latter task it will be necessary to specify the types of problems that it brings into focus and to examine the means by which they may be pursued.

The focus on "reproduction," or more accurately on "social reproduction," serves to emphasize that it is not sufficient to treat society as something that "is," that like inert matter persists in a relatively stable form over long periods of time. Society persists only insofar as the sets of activities, relations, and institutions that constitute its totality are reproduced. To highlight social reproduction provides a framework which is dynamic and adequately embodies both the features of persistence and change in social processes.

The reproduction perspective has a considerable potential in its application to the study of law. A major defect of legal theory has been the tendency to reify law, to treat it as a thing which has an independent or autonomous existence within social systems. To specify the general function of law as the reproduction of social order is also to suggest that "law" itself is reproduced. Conceived in this manner it is not merely an institution or a system of rules, but is itself a social process that is predicated on the functioning of other social processes. At the most obvious level its reproduction consists of processes such as the recruitment and training of legal personnel, the creation and enactment of rules of law. But its reproduction is also constituted in the reproduction of social relations that form its subject matter and on which it acts. Thus to adopt a reproduction perspective is to insist on law as both determined and determining within a wider set of social processes. It is thus possible to designate the sociology of law as an integral part of the concerns of sociology and not merely as a special form of jurisprudence.

The concept of "social order" serves to complement the reproduction perspective. It consists in an assertion that social order is constituted of sets of social relations, practices, and social institutions that are not merely autonomous social processes but rather have certain structural characteristics within which these practices and relationships take place. It points to the persistence of society both as structure and system. This persistence derives from the fact that the relations, practices, and institutions are continually reproduced, and that they recur as definite and determinant structures. It is the fact that social activity is reproductive of a social order that makes it possible to give meaning and substance to the very concept of society itself.

To pose the central problematic as being the reproduction of the social order naturally leads to a strategy that puts to the fore the question: what part, if any, does a particular social practice, relationship or institution play in the reproduction of the social order? What types of social practices, relationships, and institutions play decisive or determinant roles in the reproduction of the social totality? Such a problematic is firmly grounded in an insistence on historical specificity; it is not society in general that is reproduced but particular societies or social formations that are reproduced.

The reproduction of social order has so far been treated simply as a general process operating diffusely in society; it has merely been suggested that some practices and institutions participate more actively in it than others. But the social practices and institutions involved in this process each has a particular form of effectiveness within the process. Thus while, for example, the education system and the armed forces may both be regarded as significant contributory institutions, the respective forms of their activities and the social consequences that stem from them differ greatly. Law likewise has a role within the overall process that it is now necessary to specify more closely. This role may be expressed in terms of a specific problematic for the sociology of law, namely, law as a means of domination.

The reaction against the value-consensus/normative integration model within which the sociological movement in law has been confined finds its vehicle for the transition from a critique of that tradition to the possibility of substantive development within the new problematic of law as a means of domination. Such a perspective immediately renders crucial the highlighting of the coercive or directly repressive characteristics of law. That there is the need to justify such a presentation of law as a coercive expression of politically organized state power is a measure of the long intellectual ascendancy of bourgeois legal ideology.

What the domination perspective facilitates is the avoidance of a sterile and mechanical reversal of the previous academic and ideological tradition. As a reaction, a climate or a mood, such a stage is to be expected; but a "law as repression" characterization, while accounting for a major part of the reality that has been omitted or repressed within the prevailing model, does not account for that part of the social reality of law that has been extrapolated and raised to exclusive significance, namely, the widespread normative consensus and associated legitimacy accorded to law in modern society.

The domination perspective, while founded on a critique of the consensus model, makes possible the development of a position that takes up the apparently contradictory coercive and consensus characteristics of law, but not as two incompatible and mutually exclusive positions. The concept of domination provides the means of resolving the apparent dichotomy. Domination is not synonymous with repression or coercion; neither does it deny that legal systems are accorded a generalized social acceptance and legitimacy. These elements find their integration in a distinction between two forms of domination, "repressive domination" and "ideological domination." In introducing this classification of the general process of domination it is instructive to note that this distinction bears a close resemblance to that made by Gramsci between "hegemony" and "direct domination" (Gramsci 1971:12). His usage is not followed because it is founded upon a distinction between the concepts "civil society" and "political society." Within this distinction he tends to reserve the role of law, "juridical government," simply as a function of the state and therefore not pertaining directly to hegemonic control. The distinction drawn above is preferred because while insisting upon a view of law as the exercise of coercive state power it also draws attention to the function of law in the wider context than that of direct domination. However, it is suggested that Gramsci's concept "hegemony" offers fruitful potential for the theoretical construction of sociology of law and it will therefore be necessary to return to it.

The concept of repressive or coercive domination reinstates into the center of the sociology of law the law–state relation that has been largely ignored by the sociological movement. As such law is seen as part of the apparatus of the state that functions within class society primarily as a means of protecting and advancing the interests of the ruling class or classes. This much has been repeated often. What is significant in the present period is that instead of being pushed scornfully aside as political declamation or propaganda it is beginning to receive more serious attention.

Simply to identify a distinction between repressive and ideological domination, and to point to an almost total failure of the sociological movement to grapple with the repressive role of legal systems is a simple, yet nevertheless important step. However, there follows in its wake a host of major problems, which, while they cannot be treated exhaustively, must at least be identified.

First, it is important to stress that because a distinction is drawn between two forms of domination it does not follow that these forms are in any sense antithetical or alternative. To follow such a line of thought leads us back toward a counterposing of consent and coercion, found, for example, in Timasheff's counterposing of "power" and "ethics" (1939), and in Weber's unelaborated distinction between "legitimate" and nonlegitimated forms of domination (1966). On the contrary the interdependence of the forms must be insisted on; they interact and reinforce each other. Thus while it is essential that they be distinguished in order for analysis to be carried forward, this separation is made only in order that in their recombination the full complexity of the processes of domination may be explored.

The discussion of repressive domination is hampered by the paucity or weakness of most treatments. Two equally unacceptable positions must be rejected. The first of these amounts to a "conspiracy theory" that posits a malevolent ruling class whose components are integrated to such an extent that the coercive apparatus and its personnel directly and immediately subserve the interests of the dominant economic class. Such a position is too simplistic to constitute a foundation for a systematic analysis of the coercive role of legal systems (Lefcourt 1971; Cloke 1971; Pritt 1971). Equally unacceptable is what may be designated as the "connection theory" that demonstrates the social, cultural, and political linkages between, for example, the judiciary and the holders of high political offices, and therefrom deduces that the former voluntarily and naturally subserve the interests and designs of the latter (Miliband 1969; Mills 1959).

From a formal jurisprudential position all law is coercive in the sense of being backed by the threat of the application of the legitimate force of politically organized society. The concern with the repressive role of law is more restricted, being limited to the actual application of force within the legal system and which is therefore concentrated in particular areas or phases of the legal process, but is not restricted by whether or not the use of the force is legitimate. Thus the major locations of the repressive role of modern legal systems are located in the policing and punitive agencies and in the judicial application of punitive sanctions and, finally, in the judicial endorsement of the coercive conduct of the policing and punitive agencies.

The first stage in the analysis of repressive domination is to insist that an overview must be preserved that keeps in focus its relationship to the legal system as a whole in its relationship to the state. Valuable as they may appear to be, studies of police practice, judicial behavior of magistrates, or the functioning of the prison system that are not situated in the context of their relationship to the law–state complex are necessarily limited. They are limited (whether their tone be reformatory, "muckraking," or even revolutionary) either to a contrast between fact and ideal or to the descriptive level.

One of the major barriers to a general view of repressive domination is the extent to which it is obscured by the ideological forms developed by political and juristic theory and also by the relative invisibility of the decision-making process within the law–state complex. On the surface what is visible is the periodic coercive conduct by some agency within the legal system; but behind this lies the more extensive and pervasive levels that cut more deeply into the whole social and political process. This difficulty is compounded by the extreme political and ideological sensitivity of the field where even the most basic factual questions are bitterly contested. Thus, for example, with respect to any apparently accessible topic such as police violence, the discussion consists either of general countermanding assertions or simply avoids grappling with the problem (Skolnick 1966).

It is suggested that a potentially fruitful approach is through a functional analysis of repressive domination. This may be based on the hypothesis that repressive domination consists of the application of coercive means, "legal violence" by and through the agencies of the law–state complex in order to maintain and protect the existing social order. The idea of the protection of the social order should not be read in a too static way; it should be taken to include a major adaptive element in which change is a necessary ingredient in its maintenance.

This leads on to the suggestion that a functional analysis of repressive domination can take place around a proposition of a lower level of generality. It may be stated as follows: that in the pure form of the bourgeois democratic state the primary role in the maintenance of the social order is fulfilled by the process of ideological domination and that repressive domination plays a secondary and reinforcing role. Repressive domination operates to reinforce, but not to constitute the hegemonic control on which the preservation of the social order is founded. It must hurriedly be insisted that the pure form is rarely, if ever, found in practice; historical evidence tends to point to the existence of a general tension between the maintenance of the pure form and a resort to more directly coercive forms.

The nature of the relationship between repressive and ideological domination can be indicated by suggesting that repressive domination fulfills the function of amplifying the power structure within the social order that constitutes a necessary condition for the maintenance of ideological domination. This amplification function can be detected operating at different levels.

First, repressive domination is constituted by the visibility of the "power potential" of the state, that is of the forces that can be brought into operation at the behest of state power. This visibility of power is as important as the actual utilization of that power, although its application serves not merely specific repression against a particular form of behavior, but itself serves to render that power visible. Hence it can be regarded as having both a direct and indirect dimension.

Second, the application of repressive domination serves to protect and also to affirm various features of the social order. Thus, for example, the factual distribution of power is protected against attacks on or denials of that power. Thus with specific reference to the judicial process the contempt powers of the courts have a special significance. But also protected are the general social relations on which the social order is based. Of central importance among these are the property relations that are not merely protected but are, at the same time, reasserted by the application of criminal property law. Hence the interdependence of the repressive and ideological function is apparent.

Third, an important part is played by the universalism of substantive criminal law. Of special importance is the law relating to offences against the person whose universalism manifests itself in the apparent protection or at least retribution, offered to all citizens. The protection to some of the most visible areas of law of common or universal social interests has, as will be suggested, an important ideological dimension. The provision of certain universal minimum levels of social protection plays an important role in delineating legitimate and illegitimate forms of coercion, and in providing the mechanism for the legitimation of "legal violence" itself.

In carrying out these functions the legal institutions and the substantive law can be viewed through the analogy of an armory. In modern systems it is generally a very well stocked armory of techniques, means, and procedures. To pursue the "armory" analogy suggests that a major focus of enquiry should be the decision-making process that underlies the actual application of the power potential of the legal system. Variations are detectable in the forms of conduct against which the power potential is directed; similarly the intensity of the application of legal power varies considerably as do the methods and techniques applied.

This discussion of repressive domination serves to suggest a framework within which its analysis can be developed. To advance hypotheses gives a directional quality to the discussion that goes beyond the mere assertion of its importance. The direction suggested has the merit of focusing attention on the coercive role of law in a context which relates it to a wider perspective for the analysis of legal systems within social structures.

Particular importance is attached to the concept of "ideological domination." It serves to provide the sociology of law with a perspective which avoids the anithetical posing of coercion and consent. Ideological domination, though involving consent, retains its paramount characteristic as a form of domination. The special significance of its adoption is that it suggests a very specific focus of attention on, not the fact of consensus, but rather the processes whereby consensus is produced. Coercive and ideological domination are not alternatives. Thus we hold, not as repudiated, but as requiring critical examination the apparently self-evident proposition of the inverse proportionality between coercion and consent as the basis of legal order which has been encountered, in a variety of different forms of expression in Pound (1942), Timasheff (1939), Durkheim (1964), and Parsons (1959).

The concept of "ideological domination" is taken to signify those activities and processes whereby the assent of members of society is produced and mobilized. The notion of "assent" embraces both the idea of legitimacy as active assent and that of acceptance as the passive form. The means by which assent is produced are ideological in that the process involves the production and dissemination of ideas that affect social practice through the determination of the social consciousness of individuals and groups. This process is dominating in that it involves two elements, first, a differential ability of groups and classes in society to produce and communicate ideas and, second, that these ideas, directly or indirectly, have consequences with respect to the maintenance of an existing form of social order. Ideological domination is a process that operates at different levels in society, and has both institutional and noninstitutional expression. Thus, for example, language in its specific temporal forms functions at the most diffuse level, while the education system operates as an institutionalised system of ideological domination. Law, therefore, is only one of the means of ideological domination, but it is a particularly powerful form.

The ideological domination function of law operates at a number of different levels and, without a systematic analysis, some of its major features can be indicated. The normative content of law provides authoritative definitions of social relations. In providing authoritative definitions of social relations legal norms do more than passively reflect the existing reality of these relations as lived and practised in society. Following Marx's usage we can regard legal norms as "fetishes"; that is they are a modified or transmuted expression of social relations, but they are not simply falsifications thereof. Thus, in an often distorted or inverted form, the content of the legal norm is a representation of the existing social relation.

Legal norms contain concepts that impart an authority-conferring function. Of particular importance are the "rights–duties" range of legal concepts. These concepts have the role of moulding and inducing acceptance of the power differentials that are encapsulated within them; in defining the enforceable parameters of social relations they have a special significance because they are self-referring concepts. This makes the authority-conferring function of legal rules very extensive and potentially powerful. They frequently operate in such a way as to encourage a perception of legal regulation as a technical question, and thus obscure the social content of the relation that is subject to regulation.

The self-referring authority-conferring role of legal norms and propositions is dependent on the wider legitimacy of the legal order itself. The legitimacy accorded to the legal system can be a powerful and active social force. It is in this respect that the ideological function of law is most apparent. The legitimacy of law figures in an important, but somewhat distorted context, in Max Weber (1966). The distortion that he introduced resides in his designation of "rational legal authority" as the major form of legitimate domination. This distortion stems not only from his neglect of coercive forms of domination, but also from the specific form of his treatment of rational legal domination.

He tends to assume rather than to explore the basis of its legitimacy. The needs of entrepreneurial classes for predictable law are transposed to the whole society.

The significance of the legitimacy of law lies in the associated process of the reification of law; it is "the law" that becomes perceived as intrinsically deserving of obedience. At the same time the legitimacy of law is also closely connected to the most general level of legal concepts which constitute the major elements of the prevailing legal ideology; in particular the content of the legal ideals of "justice" and "legality" plays an important part. The adherence to the reified conception of law is associated with the goal-performance of the system in realizing these ideals. But it is also the case that these ideals may themselves be reified in so far as perceptions of "justice" and "legality" may be abstracted from either the substantive content of law or from goal-performance. Thus the forms of legitimacy of the legal order may become a circular interaction between "legality" and "the law" as was very much the case in Weber's treatment of the problem.

The ideological significance of the legitimacy of the legal order as a whole resides in the fact that law represents the most general level of the assertion of the unity and integration of the social system. This is of special importance within modern capitalist society because of the relative decline in religion and nationalism as the symbolic embodiment of social unity, and within bourgeois democratic society because of the limited reliance on charismatic political figures (Poulantzas 1973). The function of ideological domination within class society is implicated in the universalism of bourgeois law. The concept of citizenship, formal equality of participation in the public affairs of society, is transposed in the field of law through the "rule of law" and associated concepts. Thus the assertion of the legitimacy of law is a celebration of social unity facilitated by the formal universalism of its symbolic content.

The universalism of law at a lower level plays a major part in the process of ideological domination. The universalism of the majority of legal concepts plays a major part in providing an underpinning for the social unity proclaimed in law. This feature can best be illustrated by utilizing some examples. The universalism of the legal category "contract" reduces all transactions subsumed under it to the same level, and therefore negates differential social and economic significance; a petty consumer contract is as much a "contract" as a government order for a new aircraft-carrier. By protecting and enforcing contract *in general* the law asserts an applicability, and therefore a relevance for all in protection of contractual interests.

Another major example is to be found in the use of the concept "ownership," particularly with reference to its application in criminal law. The law protects the property of every individual irrespective of the economic and social function of that property; thus it protects both the ownership of private consumption goods and capital goods. As Kahn-Freund observes:

> the property concept can ultimately serve the political function of creating the illusion that factual situations are identical because they happen to be reflected in the same legal institution. (Kahn-Freund 1949:xxxvi)

Thus again the universalism of the normative content functions ideologically to produce perceptions of social integration.

It should be stressed that although placed within the context of a changed problematic some of the features of law as a means of domination are consistent with many of the functional analyses of law discussed earlier in the work. There are, for example, some close parallels with Llewellyn's specification of the functions of law (Llewellyn and Hoebel 1941), and even with Durkheim's reinforcement view of law (Durkheim 1973). However, the distinctive features of the perspective developed here stand out more clearly when related to the concept of "hegemony."

Gramsci defined hegemony as referring to

> the 'spontaneous' consent given by the great mass of the population to the general direction imposed on social life by the dominant fundamental group [ruling class]. (Gramsci 1971:12, my addition)

The context in which he used the concept was in attempting to understand the characteristics not only of particular political systems, but also the processes whereby major shifts in political power occur. His general view was that a necessary condition was that a "leading group" or political party must exercise hegemony not only over that class or classes that constitute its base but also over other classes either by way of ideological cooptation or neutralization. Gramsci tended to see "hegemony" as a feature of civil rather than of state society. Such a position imports a too mechanical a divide, particularly with respect to the increasingly diffuse role of the modern state. It is suggested that use may be made of Althusser's concept "ideological state apparatuses," which are not necessarily themselves part of the state but which function to maintain the power of a particular state form. Such a concept provides a potentially valuable tool in bringing within the framework of a single analysis both the state and nonstate features of legal systems. A vital characteristic of "hegemony" is that it is an active process. Hegemony designates not merely the fact of consent but the process of creation and mobilisation of that consent. Further, hegemony is active in that social classes contend in the exercise of hegemonic control.

It is now possible to suggest the relevance of this concept to the elaboration of a conceptual framework for the sociology of law. Its application facilitates a socially active view of legal institutions and norms, not simply in the narrow "law-in-action" sense, but in the sense of presenting the reproduction of social order as a dynamic social process. It sees neither consent nor dissent as "natural," rather they are the result of the activities that constitute the hegemonic struggle in society, and in which law participates.

Further it facilitates the incorporation of a view developed within the sociology of deviance, which has criticized as naive the traditional jurisprudential and sociological views of normative consensus and obedience to law. The social perception and therefore consciousness of law relating to its authority and legitimacy will often be contradictory because although hegemony necessitates the dominance of particular forms of consciousness, this is always a relative rather than an absolute dominance. Not merely is the consciousness of law a product of the struggle for hegemony, but so also is the content of law. The relative strengths of different social forces both materially and ideologically are represented in the changing content of law, its emergence, and its relation to the process of social change.

The position developed here does not purport to constitute a sociological theory of law. At best it provides some of the major elements for the conceptual framework for such a theory. In advancing this suggested theoretical framework an attempt has been made to indicate the direction of enquiry and the type of questions involved in its further development.

CHAPTER 4

DICHOTOMY AND CONTRADICTION IN THE SOCIOLOGY OF LAW

INTRODUCTION

This chapter sets out to review developments over the last decade that have had an impact on the sociology of law.[1] In particular I focus on two lines of development. First the reemergence of theoretical explorations in the sociology of law after the barren years stretching into the 1970s during which time the sociology of law was almost exclusively characterized by empirical investigation of "the legal process." I will concentrate my attention on the work of Unger, Black, and Trubek who will represent the awakening of theoretical consciousness within the sociology of law. The second major development to which attention will be given is the emergence of an extensive and varied body of work from a Marxist perspective directed toward advancing a theorization of law. The most recent stage of development involves the tentative beginnings of a meaningful debate between very different theoretical traditions, in particular Marxist and non-Marxist, directed toward the project of the theorization of law.

It is important to stress at the outset that my intention is not to engage in a bibliographical exercise of simply cataloguing recent developments. Rather it is my intention to make use of this overview to identify current problems confronting the sociological examination of law. In particular I will advance one general thesis that it is best to introduce at the outset. The thesis is that there exists a fundamental unity between the concerns of contemporary Marxist and non-Marxist theories of law that manifests itself in the extent to which both traditions are impaled on a dichotomy that inhibits their further advance. This dichotomy finds a variety of expressions within differing theoretical and conceptual traditions. Its varieties will be discussed later but its general form is the dichotomy between *coercion* and *consent*.

In contending that there exists a manifest unity between the otherwise opposing theoretical traditions I do not hold to a convergence theory. On the contrary I want to argue that the different positions enshrine radically different attempts to grapple with the theoretical and practical implications of the general dichotomy that they embody. Thus the issue under discussion is not a theoretical convergence but is a parallelism in which alternative or divergent theories grapple with a common set of problems, albeit these problems being differentially identified and conceptualized within the specific theoretical trajectories. Additionally I want to draw attention to the political and practical implications of the positions advanced. But I would wish to comment that the possibility exists, and is to some limited extent being realized, of a fruitful exchange and debate between Marxist and non-Marxist perspectives in the sociology of law. This possibility exists because of developments within both traditions that have allowed them both to go beyond the ritual encounter between Marxist instrumentalism and normative integration positions.[2]

The themes introduced above will be explored through a consciously selective discussion of some of the more important texts; it is therefore necessary to reiterate that this essay does not engage in an extensive bibliographical survey of recent developments. The range of substantive work, both theoretical and empirical, that falls under the very general label of "non-Marxist" is very diverse. The discussion will focus on the work of Roberto Unger, Donald Black, and David Trubek. The selection of these authors must be taken to imply an assertion of the importance of their work not only in itself but more specifically because it highlights the parallelism referred to above. With regard to work within the Marxist tradition I am anxious to emphasize the recent development of a number of divergent theoretical and political tendencies; but again I consciously eschew a comprehensive bibliographical survey.

TRAJECTORIES IN THE SOCIOLOGY OF LAW

This chapter has the objective of assessing the current condition of the sociology of law. Attention will be focused primarily on the trends in the theoretical resources and developments deployed. This focus on "theory" is not intended to minimize the importance of empirical studies but rather to argue against the common misapplication of the distinction between empirical and theoretical studies that posits them as two distinct and separate fields. On the contrary there is a basic continuity in that all empirical studies are "theoretical" irrespective of the intentions of their authors in that they necessarily deploy, whether consciously or not, concepts, classifications, hypotheses, etc., that have their origins in the arena of theory, and have necessary and unavoidable consequence when they are deployed within any specific piece of empirical enquiry. The most significant criticism that can be leveled against empirical studies is that they are, all too often, inadvert to the theory that they deploy and consequently are unable to take account of its problems and limitations.

There is another justification that may be claimed for focusing on *theoretical* work within the sociology of law in that it reveals much more directly the major changes of emphasis and the associated implications and problems that are brought into play.

There is a further reason for concentrating on theoretical developments. It was a characteristic criticism during the early 1970s that one of the major weaknesses of the dominant tradition of American sociology of law was the weakness of its theoretical development (Currie 1971). It is therefore of considerable significance that there has more recently been a revival of serious theoretical contributions; this development marks both a response to criticism from radical commentators but more significantly to a growing sense of dissatisfaction within the dominant tradition. This was in turn sparked off by a deeply felt "crisis" that enveloped law and legal institutions from the end of the 1960s, which the untroubled perspective of normative integration theories of law was incapable of grappling with.[3] As Unger argues,

> the crisis of social order becomes a conscious subject of human concern whenever consensus breaks down or loses its ability to command allegiance. (Unger 1976:14)

It has become a commonplace for writers of widely divergent theoretical and political positions to deploy the contention that there exists a "crisis" in contemporary society or more specifically that there exists a "crisis of law and order." While writers, otherwise widely opposed, agree that there is a "crisis" they differ significantly in the nature of the crisis posited. We need at this stage only to enter the caution that the existence and nature of this invoked crisis should not be accepted uncritically but must be examined at two levels. First, as to whether an identifiable "real" crisis does in fact exist and second as to the role that the posited crisis plays in the different theoretical positions.[4]

The character of the period in which the reemergence of a wide-ranging theoretical debate has occurred is one in which law has become increasingly politicized. There exists a tendency within bourgeois democratic systems for law to become more centrally and directly implicated in governmental and political processes.[5] This process poses very sharply the inherent limitations of any analysis founded on an uncritical acceptance of the doctrine of the separation of powers or of legalism in general. Where law is impelled by the logic of events to play an even more central role the hallowed ideological tenets of such positions become undermined. One major feature of the greatest importance is that the question of the relationship between law and the state has become a central concern in non-Marxist sociology of law. This is apparent, for example, in Donald Black's more recent text in sharp contrast with its absence from his earlier writing which in other respects provide a significant continuity.[6]

His concern about the return to anarchy that he posits and the decrease in law is not premised on any diminution of the role and scope of the state; quite the contrary it is the very growth of the interventionist state that creates the conditions for this new anarchy.

The concern with the law–state relation is even more directly apparent in Unger's *Law and Modern Society*. At the very center of his concern is the tension between bureaucratic law and legal order. It is also apparent in his emphasis on the disintegration of the rule of law: "in seeking to discipline and to justify the exercise of power, men are condemned to pursue an objective they are forbidden to reach" (Unger 1976:18). Conflated with his religious anxiety about modern society with its "consensus without authority" and "stability without belief" is a central focus on the impact and implications of the welfare or interventionist state, or to pass to the terminology of a different tradition, with the phenomenon of statism.

A similar set of concerns is found in the work of Tay and Kamenka in which their concern is focused around the rise of "bureaucratic–administrative" regulation, which poses a challenge to individualistic or *Gesellschaft* law. They are not so much concerned with its impact on modern capitalist societies but rather problematize the extent to which modern socialism in advancing a critique of individualism has not inescapably committed itself to bureaucratic–administrative regulation with some admixture of *Gemeinschaft* attributes with its appeal to spontaneous community regulation (Kamenka and Tay 1975). Extending beyond the concerns of Kamenka and Tay it should be noted that one central feature of contemporary socialist and Marxist debates about law resolves around the problem of the place of law in socialist society. The two most important poles of recent debates have, on the one hand, been those that have revived the work of Pashukanis, with his insistence on the withering away of law and the development of a nonlegal social order (Beirne and Sharlet 1980). On the other hand E. P. Thompson in his commitment to the rule of law is committing himself to a perspective in which socialist legality completes the mission of bourgeois legality by overcoming the formalism of its concepts of individual rights and justice (Thompson 1975).

The extreme form of the concern with the law–state relation is to be found in Hayek's jurisprudence, which is explicitly directed to the project of delegitimizing the whole positivist (and in Hayek's strange identification of positivism and socialism) socialist tradition by refusing the title "law" to state legislation, which is presented as the major contributor to the undermining of the rule of law and of the Great Society in general (Hayek 1973–1979).

Yet this concern is not the property of liberal sociologists of law or conservative economists; it has its ramifications in recent Marxist writings. The question of the law–state relation figures strongly in Poulantzas' characterization of new stage of "state authoritarianism" that he explicitly sought to distinguish from a simple instrumentalist theory of a reversion of liberal democracy toward fascism (Poulantzas 1978). A similar set of concerns is also present in the much more politically and theoretically heterogeneous writings of those concerned with the question of corporatism.[7]

THE GENERAL DICHOTOMY: COERCION AND CONSENT

The most significant trend within contemporary theoretical studies is the parallelism exhibited between different and competing theoretical orientations. These apparently divergent theoretical positions make use of a conceptualization of "law" that is developed around a shared dualism. The general form of this dualism is that between "coercion" and "consent"; but it should be noted that this conceptualization takes a variety of verbal forms. To take an example in which the dualism is very explicit and is posed in its most simple form we may look briefly at Timasheff, one of the earlier pioneers of theoretical sociology of law. In developing his definition of law as "ethico-imperative co-ordination" we note the particular terminological form within which he develops his dualistic conception of law, which rests on two variables "ethics" (consent) and "power" (coercion). Law for Timasheff is essentially "ethics + power," which "may be thought of as two circles which cross one another. Their overlapping section is law" (Timasheff 1939:248). In the development of law his crudely evolutionist treatment of "the triumph of law," the upward march of civilization, is marked by law with a larger ethical content and conversely lesser reliance on power. Law then is conceived as a simple paradigm lying between the polarities of ethics and power and its advance and progress is marked by an increase in its ethical basis and a decline in its reliance on power.

This evolutionary dualism, presented with estimable sharpness in Timasheff, is but a clearer statement of a much wider and pervasive dualism that characterizes and marks the history of both sociological and jurisprudential debates. Its presence is to be found in such diverse locations as Durkheim's distinction between repressive and restitutive law on the one hand and, on the other, in the trajectory of the controversy over the role of sanctions that is the keystone of the debates surrounding jurisprudential positivism.

Nor, it must be stressed, is dichotomy and dualism restricted to theories of law. The whole history of sociology is characterized by the successive engagement between rival dichotomous conceptions. I have enjoyed, and repeat for others who have not come across it, Philip Corrigan's observation that of all the different ways in which social theory has attempted to depict the social world, they all come like the animals to the Ark, two-by-two (Corrigan 1975:211). It is not the object of this chapter to engage in an excursion into the sociology of sociology, but one last general comment on the wider location of dichotomous conceptions of law may be in order. The consent/coercion dualism with reference to law has a particular direct relationship with that unproductive and schematic divide in the sociology of the late 1960s and early 1970s between conflict and consensus models in sociology. The two terms stand as direct embodiments of the apparent polarity of concerns of that largely negative and unproductive phase; and to some degree elements of that opposition necessarily live on despite the timely death of that wider confrontation. Its echoes will recur in the subsequent discussion. The baldly stated negative assessment of conflict sociology must not detract from its positive historical contribution of disrupting the dominant complacency engendered by the long reign of structural functionalism. Conflict theory played a particular important role in the development of radical criminology and radical sociology. In fostering these trends its positive contribution was to create the conditions for the emergence of more adequate and sophisticated debates of the present period. It is to be welcomed that some of the prime movers of radical criminology and sociology such as Chambliss, Quinney, Taylor, Walton, and Young have come a long way to correct the excesses of the conflict theory period.

The persistence in the theorization of law of the coercion–consent dichotomy leads one to ask: what is the harm? Why should its persistence be seen as a stumbling block over which divergent theoretical positions continue to stumble? The specific negative consequences of particular manifestations will be examined in the more detailed discussion that follows.

The general deficiency inherent in dichotomous conceptions of law is that they have, as a necessary effect, a tendency to result in an unstable analysis that lurches between the polarities set up. They produce an "either-or" effect in which each theorization is reduced unavoidably to emphasizing "either" the element of consent "or" the element of coercion. The commitment is made, and in the views to be examined, it is found in every one of them, to conceptualizing law as not being reducible to either one of the two elements and consequently to searching for a theorization that stands on the *combination* of the elements as a reality not reducible to either element. Yet in all cases the analysis that emerges fails to escape from a view in which law is presented as constituted of particular proportions of consent and coercion along a unilinear dimension between the two polarities. In its most simple form individual theorist (A, B, or C) can be differentiated as proposing a location of law within a linear paradigm

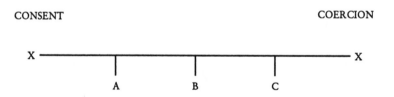

The result is that the elements themselves remain discrete and, despite the commitment thereto, are not seen in the combinatory effect.

This deficiency is but a specific manifestation of the ubiquitous dilemma of social philosophy that resolves around the oppositions of freedom–unfree, consciousness–being, determinism–voluntarism, etc. The dichotomy between consent and coercion is but a specific embodiment of these wider oppositions. In particular it has its root in the individualistic problematic that underlies the theorization of law, namely, that of the basis of individual adherence to law. Coercion and consent are but the most general form of the variety of solutions that philosophy, jurisprudence, and sociology have provided at one time or another. While it is neither the claim nor the intention of this essay to offer a general solution that supersedes the deficiencies inherent in dichotomous conceptions of law, it is my purpose to show the way in which that problem must be seen as deriving from some of the most important and perennial intellectual problems.

There is a further level of difficulty that stems from the linear consent–coercion model of law. Its impact is greatest on the non-Marxist or liberal positions to be discussed, but it is not absent from Marxist texts. It arises from the inherent tendency of liberal theory to place a positive valuation on consent; in simple terms for law to be based on consent or for consent to constitute the preponderant element is "good." It is most frequently associated with a metatheoretical or ideological evolutionary view of a historical process toward consent and freedom and away from unfreedom and coercion. The effects of such evolutionary positions often have these most serious effects where they remain implicit. They are frequently expressed in terms of some variant of "social contract" theory that is premised on the positive evaluation and thus evaluation of positive or active consent as a condition of human freedom.

The general dichotomy has been introduced and some of its wider implications considered. The next two sections of the chapter examine its role in two broadly drawn and contrasting theoretical traditions through the discussion of the work of some of their more important contemporary exponents.

CONTEMPORARY SOCIOLOGY OF LAW: OLD PROBLEMS AND NEW VARIANTS

There have been some significant theoretical developments in the sociology of law in the last few years. During the formative period of the sociology of law in the United States in the 1950s and early 1960s there existed a widespread consensus as to the nature of the project of the sociology of law. This consensus was formed around the interweaving of two apparently different traditions. Most pronounced and visible was the continuing dominance of the perspectives of American Realism organized around the problematic of examining the operational failures of the legal process to meet legal ideals operating with the presumption of the perfectability of the legal process to meet these ideals. Indeed it is important to place due emphasis on the continuing impact of the Realist perspective. This is nowhere more apparent than in Trubek's proposed "new realism" (Trubek 1977). Harnessing yet again the realist aphorism of the contrast between "law in books" and "law in action," that is, between the ideal and reality, he seeks to harness this as an articulated methodology for checking reality against the ideal. Yet the original Realist unproblematic presumption was of the perfectability of law; they presumed some operational deficiency revealed through empirical study followed by scientifically informed reform, "social engineering," could be overcome such that "the gap" between reality and ideal could be narrowed or closed. The manner in which the relation between legal ideals and legal reality has been theorized, particularly by Trubek and Unger, is more sophisticated than the version offered by the early Realists. Yet nevertheless both the theoretical terms and their practical points of reference remain central to modern sociology, and, as I shall argue in a later section, are not by any means distant from the concerns of contemporary Marxist writers.

Our discussion of contemporary liberal legal theory should properly start with Roberto Unger since he has rapidly come to exercise a powerful influence within recent legal theory. His earlier and most generalized excursion into social theory in *Knowledge and Politics* is itself impressive if only for the breadth of its concerns and for its sweeping claims to provide an alternative to the classical tradition of social theory, which is taken as embracing almost every major form of social theory developed over the last three centuries. It is important to note that Unger himself locates the problems of legal theory as "the immediate subject of my interest" (Unger 1975:3). It is, however, in *Law in Modern Society* that he addressed problems of legal theory. In this text, despite the continued presence of an overarching concern with the development of "total criticism" he nevertheless takes his stand more firmly within the terrain of positions that are part of the partial criticism that in *Knowledge and Politics* he had argued were irremediably scarred by the antinomies inherent in liberal theory.[8] He now proposes to resolve the predicament of social and legal theory through an attempted integration of the two major contemporary competing paradigms, the instrumentalist or conflict perspective and the consensus perspective. Yet despite his commitment to a synthesis that overcomes the systematic deficiencies of both, his method of combination is inherently additive and nonsynthetic; his general hypothesis is "that some social settings might best be understood in light of the doctrine of consensus and others from the perspective of the theory of instrumentalism" (Unger 1975:127).

He proceeds to posit the existence of two types of law that embody the general characteristics of the two alternative theoretical perspectives. "Interactional law" is allied to consensus theory and "bureaucratic law" to instrumental theory. The strength of Unger's analysis, although I shall argue it is severely limited, resides in the break he effects with the normative integration theories of contemporary sociology of law within which law operates as a general and pervasive mechanism of societal integration through the linked processes of social control and socialization buttressed by the legitimizing properties of law. He effects this breach with normative integration theories through his emphasis on the conflict or tension between the two different "modes of order" that coexist within the contemporary legal order.

It should, however, be noted that this position is not particularly original. It is firmly and powerfully present in Weber's classic discussion of the tension between formal and substantive justice. It is only the more crude appropriations of Weber that emphasized a simpler and therefore more evolutionary thesis of the triumph of formal rationality in the legal order of capitalist society. But even though Weber's analysis rests on the problematic tension between formal and substantive rationality he nevertheless places unqualified priority on formal rationality, which he saw as the only alternative when confronted with the rising demand for substantive justice articulated in its most powerful form by the labour and socialist movement. Just so does Unger throw in his lot with legal rationality/formalism. He identifies three functionally significant components of legal systems—formal, procedural, and substantive; but of these three it is formalism that lies at the core of the development of modern Western rule of law. His emphasis is such that formalism in his analysis wholly subordinates the other components. The result is that he presents, as did Weber before him as does Hayek today, the demand for substantive justice as the source of the dangerous erosion of formalism. As I will argue more generally, despite his apparent commitment to liberal political values he is led inexorably toward conservatism and pessimism, which even his sociological version of Christian theology cannot disguise.

We find then in Unger a specific variant of the general dichotomy that lies at the heart of the tension inherent in the liberal doctrine of the rule of law. It is expressed as the tension between "collective values" and "bureaucratic welfare tyranny." Despite his apparent commitment to achieve synthesis he evades the challenges and thereby reinforces the fundamental conservatism of his position by the evasive observation that it is beyond the remit of his present enquiry (Unger 1976:129). However the general outline of the synthesis that he desires is clearly indicated. Yet his "solution" cannot be treated as one that marks a development in social theory that overcomes or supersedes the dualism.

Rather his transcendental theology posits an immanent process of social transformation, the resultant of which abolishes both the theoretical problem and the dichotomy within law. He relies on the assertion of an immanent essentialism reconciling "individual freedom" and "community cohesion." "The more perfect this reconciliation becomes, the more does the society's emergent interactional law reveal the requirements of human nature and social existence" (Unger 1976:264). Far from advancing a theoretical synthesis we return to the old "search for this latent or living law," which seeks to "discover a universal given order in social life" (Unger 1976:242). This quest for an immanent or spontaneous normative order in large measure marks a return to an older and more conservative tradition epitomized in general by Durkheim's search for the "ideological community" and more particularly within the sociology of law by Ehrlich's espousal of "living law" (Ehrlich 1962). Yet the temptation should be avoided to immediately apply a conservative label to Unger's position. His claim, most explicit in *Knowledge and Politics,* to discern evidence of the realization of his synthesis in the contemporary developments within the "Welfare-corporate state" and within actual socialist societies should caution us against too hurried political labeling. It is sufficient to note that Unger's attempt to resolve the general dichotomy in the social and legal order takes the form of a synthesis whose starting point is an essentially metaphysical concept of "community."

The pursuance of community is grounded in a general pessimism about the trajectory of modern legal development. Talcott Parsons late and perceptive review of *Law in Modern Society* provides a very striking illustration of the contrast between two generations of sociological theorists. Parsons notes important areas of agreement and convergence between his own position and that advanced by Unger. I am disposed to place considerable weight on what Parsons identifies as his fundamental disagreement, which leads him to brand Unger's theoretical position as unacceptable. "Perhaps the main reason I am critical of Unger is that I do not share his—perhaps fashionable—pessimism about the drastic erosion of the rule of law" (Parsons 1977:148).

Parsons has been the embodiment of the most systematized commitment to a positive evaluation of the modern trajectory of the capitalist democracies. Unger can be read as representative of the more recent self-doubt and anxiety, which find its reverberations at all levels of political and social theory and which cut across traditional political and theoretical boundaries. The pessimism to which Parsons refers finds its expression within both neoconservative jurisprudence and contemporary Marxist debates about law (Hayek 1973–79; Jenkins 1980).

Donald Black presents an apparently sharp contrast to Unger's social philosophical theorization. I confess at the outset to a deep-seated dislike for the rigid positivism and formalism that characterizes his most general theoretical intervention *The Behavior of Law* (Black 1976). Such a response is sufficient to discourage me from engaging in a general review of his work. Yet despite the profound difference in methodology and theoretical orientation between Black and Unger I will seek to demonstrate that there are two important continuities. Black presents his own specific formulation of the general dichotomy and, second, his position is marked by a pervasive pessimism about the role of law in modern capitalist democracies in spite of his apparent commitment to universalistic sociology purged of all concern with current policy objectives (Black 1972).

Black has noted the continuing impact of the legal realist tradition; he rejects its prostitution of scientific method to the pursuit of policy objectives subsumed under the dichotomy between "law in books" and "law in action." But in seeking to impose a strict divide between "pure sociology of law" and "applied sociology of law" and thereby to break with the tradition imposed by legal realism, he actually bears witness to its influence by adopting its underlying positivism and behaviorism (1972:1087). His injunction that "law consists in observable acts, not in rules" (1972:1091) replicated Oliver Wendell Holmes aphoristic characterization of law as "the prophecies of what the courts will do in fact, and nothing more pretentious, are what I mean by the law" (Holmes 1897:461). The step that Black effects is to transform the pragmatic positivism of the early realists into a formalistic behaviorist variant.

To locate the presence of the general dichotomy it is necessary to trace briefly Black's methodology. His starting point, as the title of his book indicates, is to treat law as a behavioral phenomenon, purged of all value judgments and ideals. Law "behaves" or varies in relation to other observable social phenomena or "dimensions." He posits two dimensions to the variation of law; the first is quantitiative, reducible to "more law/less law." The second dimension is provided by "the style of law," which in turn corresponds to styles of social control. The styles of law are merely listed, no indication is given of where the classification is derived from, but it may be noted in passing that like many other typologies that have been advanced within the sociology of law, they have a scarcely concealed evolutionary implication in the transition from the "penal" style (i.e., primitive), through "compensa-tory" and "therapeutic" to (the more advanced) "conciliatory" style (Black 1976:4). "Style of law" as the second dimension in the variation of law plays little part in the subsequent elaboration. The variations in styles of law are introduced in an arbitrary manner and are not systematically integrated within the body of the theory. The difficulty in quantifying "style" and the ever present danger that the identifica-tion of "style" may carry evaluative connotations probably explain the limited attention it receives.

The book thereafter is predominantly concerned with advancing quantitatively expressed hypotheses concerning the behavior of law. In the main they are couched in terms of variations of "more" or "less" law. He nowhere indicates how this quantification of law is to be undertaken. It is assumed without specification of any method of mea-surement that quantitative variations are self-evidently identifiable. Thus, to take just one example, in dealing with the relationship between law and stratification he advances the hypothesis that "law varies directly with stratification," i.e., the more stratification a society has, the more law it has (Black 1976:13). The startling evidence for this hypothesis is to repeat the well-trodden anthropological data about the limited role and extent of law in "simple" society. This taken with the assumption that in some self-evident sense "modern" society has more law. The spurious scientificity of his appeal to quantification does not, however, appear to permit any exploration of the relation between law and the variety of forms and degrees of stratification in "modern" society. Stripped of their scientism his hypotheses are sociological commonplaces distorted to fit universalistic pretensions. Black's pur-portedly sophisticated theoretical enterprise is nothing more and noth-ing less than systematic common sense; and no systematization of common sense can turn it into good sense.

Yet behind the appeal to the quantification of legal phenomena we find lurking the general dichotomy between coercion and consent. The general couplets that run through his hypotheses of less/more law, undifferentiated/differentiated society, and simple/modern society are completed by noting their congruence with the dichotomy between consensual and coercive characteristics of law. This emerges most explicitly in his rejection of the Durkheimian equation between simple/undifferentiated society and repressive law (Black 1976:37).

It is further manifest in his predilection for curvilinear hypotheses; for example, in positing the quantitative growth of law with social differentiation he posits a subsequent diminution of law "as social life evolves beyond interdependence to symbiosis . . . law declines"

(1976:40). The complex symbiotic differentiation of modern society manifests itself not only, according to Black, in a decrease in law but a growing emphasis on "conciliatory," in contrast to "penal," styles of law.

The variety of curvilinear hypotheses that is advanced provided evidence not only of the presence of the coercion/consent dichotomy but also of the deep social and political pessimism that underlies his apparently neutral and apolotical stance. His evolutionary perspective posits first an increase in the quantity of law and then its decrease; it is this decrease that he decrees as the "return to anarchy" (1976:132). Black's predilection for quantitative behavioralism commits him, since it constrains him to see the variance of law in terms of increases and decreases, to a cyclical vision of legal and social development. Such a cyclical element is as Eder argues the reintroduction of an archaic philosophy of history (Eder 1977). Far from the value-freedom whose shrine he prays before, Black's sociology of law is transparently ideological. It is but an ideological anxiety that besets liberal intellectuals and paves the way for neoconservatism. "Encounters replace the social structures of the past, and people increasingly have closeness without permanence, depth without commitment" (Black 1976:135). The breakdown of community and the advance of social equality combine to produce conditions in which law tends to decrease; the result is the situational society in which there is no place for the rule of law and the values of liberal legalism. It is remarkable how, despite the sharp theoretical differences between them, the conclusions arrived at by both Black and Unger replicate the deep pessimism of the liberal intelligentsia in the United States.

David Trubek's project of developing a "new realism," referred to at the beginning of this section, marks the clearest and most explicit continuity that has stamped American sociology of law with much of the intellectual imprint of the pre-War realism. It needs to be stressed that his "new realism" marks a significant attempt to go beyond the unproblematic treatment of "the gap between legal ideals and legal reality." His position is further significant in that it is marked by an explicit commitment to engage in a meaningful dialogue with the more recently emerging Marxist trend within American sociology of law. It is for this reason that my attention will be primarily focused on his lengthy review article of Isaac Balbus' *Dialectics of Legal Repression.* I will not at this stage be concerned to comment on his critique of Balbus but rather to concentrate on the second half of his essay in which he advances his "new realism" (Trubek 1977). With respect of Trubek's earlier writing I only want to draw attention to the extent that he more than any other contemporary writer in the field of the sociology is concerned with the theoretical lineage of the field; this concern manifests itself in the extent to which he goes beyond the conventional deferential bow to the legacy of Max Weber (Trubek 1972a, b). He has sought to reexamine the Weberian legacy and this concern has its reverberations in the more recent essay.

The element that is "new" in Trubek's realism is the way in which he problematizes "the gap" between legal ideals and reality by abandoning the assumption of the perfectability of law; "the gap" is presented as itself being a necessary consequence of the structural characteristics of liberal democracy. "The gap between the ideals of law and its performance is a central and pervasive feature of legal existence" (Trubek 1977:544). Yet it is significant that, despite the abandonment of the simple-minded social engineering of the early Realists, its effects remain contagious such that despite the apparently greater sophistication of his "mediative perspective" his concern is still with "the cure" for the realist dichotomy, in that "law represents an effort to mediate fundamental conflicts" (1977:542) but one that is doomed to remain imperfect.

Within this reworking of the problematic of legal realism and of mainstream sociology of law we find lurking the general dichotomy. Law in books/law in action is the manifestation of the opposition between ideal/reality; the central content of this opposition within liberal democracy is seen as that between the ideal of social equality and the persistence of structures of hierarchy and dominance. The polarity between equality and hierarchy is, of course, but another form of the opposition between consent and coercion.

There are two significant features to be found in the development of Trubek's attempt to overcome the simple opposition of ideal and reality, consent and coercion. The first concerns the methodology he proposes; it is this that ties him closest to the realist tradition but to which he gives a significantly idealistic inflection. This arises because he insists on giving methodological priority to ideals as the starting point against which legal reality is to be examined. "Such a system *must begin* with ideals basic to our society . . . I propose that we examine law in terms of its contribution to these values" (1977:546). And again, "A legal order is not an end in itself. The system must be justified by its contribution to more fundamental social ideals" (1977:547). It should be noted that a very similar idealism is present in Unger's work and constitutes an important continuity, which is made explicit by Trubek's frequent citation of Unger. For Unger "the deepest root of all historical change is manifest or latent conflict between the view of the ideal and the experience of actuality" (Unger 1976:157). Two negative consequences follow from such idealist positions. The first is that in giving priority to ideals, the ideals themselves are regarded as unproblematic, they form the taken for granted and uncontested presumption of society as a purposive and organic enterprise of Hegelian character bent on the realization of ideals that march through the pages of history. No space is left for a critical examination of, for example, the ideological role of the ideal of equality in capitalist democracies. The second consequence of the idealist methodology is that it necessarily involves the positing of a conception of a universal human nature, which is realized in the historical process. This is most explicit in Unger and is not disputed by Trubek. "The universal is human nature . . . the particulars are the forms of social life and the individual personalities by which that humanity is represented" (Unger 1976:261).

Trubek seeks to combine this methodology with theoretical elements appropriated from the Marxist tradition, or more particularly from the historical analysis of law developed by E. P. Thompson in *Whigs and Hunters* and his colleagues in parallel work (Thompson 1975; Hay et al. 1977). Thompson's emphasis upon the complex and contradictory character of law clearly, from his explicit acknowledgments, made a considerable impact upon Trubek.

> We reach, then, not a simple conclusion (law = class power) but a complex and contradictory one. On the one hand it is true that law did mediate class relations to the advantage of the rulers. . . . On the other hand, the law mediated these relations through legal forms, which imposed, again and again, inhibitions upon the actions of the rulers. (Thompson 1975:242)

Thompson makes a more specific contribution to Trubek's position because it was *Whigs and Hunters* that "first suggested to me the perspective outlined in this essay" (Trubek 1977:543), which he identifies as "the mediative perspective" which asserts that "a significant feature of legal life in liberal capitalist societies is the simultaneous assertion and negation of basic ideals of equality, individuality, and community. The legal order neither guarantees these ideals, nor does it simply deny them: it does both" (1977:544). Trubek does not adopt the specifically Marxist connotations of "mediation" that, for reasons he does not explain, he sees as closely related to the theory of alienation. Rather he proposes to adopt "the ordinary English language sense" which he identifies as "a communicative intervention aimed at reconciling or compromising conflicting ideas or interests" (1977:543).

What Trubek has failed to notice that there is in "the ordinary English language sense" a second meaning to the word, and it is this one, which both Marx and Thompson employ, of mediation as the process of the forming a link or connection between different objects or processes.

This is not a semantic disputation; important consequences follow from the initial identification of the concept. My reservation about Trubek's mediation = conciliation is threefold: first, that it imports a consensual character to the process of mediation; second, that it implies ends and objectives of human agencies as constitutive of the process; and third, that it carries unavoidably functionalist implications. What Trubek misses about the alternative definition of mediation, and which is developed in Marxist literature, is that all social activity involves processes in which "things" (whether they be artifacts, language, institutions, etc.) mediate between people and the social and natural environment in which they live *and* which have differential effects in transforming the nature of that relation. Applying this directly to problems of the sociology of law, one of the most important questions that Marx asked (but it should be noted did not provide a direct answer) was: "the really difficult point to be discussed is how the relations of production as legal relations take part in the uneven development (of material production)" (Marx 1969:109). Marx here poses the role of law as a process of "mediation" of legal relations as the form in which relations of production are operative and which have definite effects and consequences. It is this set of central issues that Marx and Thompson pose without importing the "solution" that is introduced by Trubek's identification of mediation as conciliation.

The above exploration of the concept "mediation" is not intended to teach lessons to Trubek about "ordinary English language" or to claim a privileged interpretation of Marx, but it does serve to emphasize two points. First, the joining of a meaningful exchange between Marxists and non-Marxists involves certain problems that make it unwise to attempt simply borrowing or lifting from one theoretical tradition into another. It should be emphasized that this caution should be seen as applying not only to the adoption of elements of Marxism but likewise applies to the incorporation within Marxism from other traditions. An interesting example of the latter problem can be seen in the problems that arise when Marxists seek to make use of the Weberian concepts of legitimacy and domination; the difficulty arises from the way in which Weber's concepts are produced and thus linked to the analysis of the interpersonal relation between rulers and ruled, which is not directly compatible with the theoretical framework of class analysis. To avoid misunderstanding let me stress that I do not seek to place any barrier in the way of cross-fertilization between disparate theoretical traditions but rather to enter a caution against the simple borrowing or transplanting of individual concepts.

The manner in which Trubek employs the concept of mediation as the equivalent of conciliation has one further interesting consequence. His general position does, as I have argued, provide evidence of the presence of the general dichotomy between coercion and consent as the underlying mode of theorization of his sociology of law. Beyond this general presence Trubek gives a particular inflection through his equation of mediation and conciliation which emphasizes the proximity of Trubek's position to the sociology of law of the 1950s and 1960s, with its central assumption of the normative integration or consensual character and function of law.

One significant point of differentiation between Trubek on the one hand and Unger and Black on the other is that there is no note or sign of the pessimism regarding the trajectory of law in contemporary capitalist democracies that has been pointed to in the case of both Unger and Black. Rather Trubek exhibits a much closer lineage with the liberal confidence in the effectivity of law. He holds out a continuing and renewed faith in the role of law in the contemporary period.

THE GENERAL DICHOTOMY AND MARXISM

The most significant trend within contemporary theoretical discussions of law is the general parallelism between Marxist and non-Marxist orientations. The major manifestation of this congruence is the extent to which both positions operate with the shared dichotomy between "coercion" and "consent." The general dualism of the concept "law" within the history of jurisprudential and sociological thought has been discussed earlier, but the presence of this same dualism within Marxist approaches requires more comment.

The more Marxism has succeeded in overcoming its greatest general weakness, namely its tendency toward an instrumental reduction of law to the state and the state in its turn to organized violence, the more it has, paradoxically, manifested the dualism coercion/consent that characterizes "bourgeois" legal thought.[9] Those Marxists who still cling to a simple faith in the necessary abyss between Marxism (= "science") and non-Marxist thought (= "bourgeois ideology") may see in this shift within Marxist studies of law evidence of revisionism, of the ever-present vice of contamination with bourgeois sociology. The import I draw is very different: it is that the fundamental difficulty and problem confronting all legal theory lies in the exploration and resolution of the dualism of coercion and consent.

The coercion–consent dualism finds its most general expression in Marxist theory through the very widespread recent influence of Gramscian theory. The somewhat belated "discovery" of Gramsci, in particular by British and American Marxists, has focused primarily on the issues posed by the concept of hegemony, through which Gramsci struggled to come to an understanding of the social processes through which particular forms of class relations are sustained and reproduced in such a way that relations of exploitation and domination persist without general or frequent recourse to state coercion. Thus law cannot adequately be understood as a dependent instrument of state coercion but must be understood in its educative and moral dimension securing the conditions of class relations. Central to Gramscian thought is a reworking of the theory of ideology such that there is no invocation of an instrumentalist view of ideology as a mechanism of deception, "brainwashing," or mystification.

Within such a perspective the central focus has been on the noncoercive face of law seen as contributing to the securing and reproducing of "the 'spontaneous' consent given by the great masses of the population to the general direction imposed on social life by the dominant fundamental group" (Gramsci 1971:12). Yet there coexists in Gramsci an emphasis on the repressive role of law and state. Perry Anderson, in seeking to defend the Leninist continuity in Gramsci and to salvage a "revolutionary" Gramsci from the hands of modern revisionism, documents a continuing recognition in Gramsci of the repressive dimension of law and state (Anderson 1976–1977:5). But this presence only demonstrates the significance and problematic character of coercion and consent since Gramsci nowhere attempts to grapple with the implications of holding both the "traditional" thesis on the role of coercion and his own primary focus on hegemony as "permanently organized consent" (Anderson 1976–1977:80). The solution offered by Anderson, whilst exhibiting both Leninist and Trotskyist respectability, merely asserts the primacy of coercion over consent. The controversy within Marxism epitomized by Anderson's discussion of Gramsci has advanced little beyond the rival assertion of the primacy of coercion or consent.

Despite this perhaps pessimistic overview of the impact of Gramsci it should be stressed that in a more general sense the espousal of a

Gramscian perspective has had profoundly positive results. Gramsci has been the main vehicle that has facilitated the emergence of Marxist analyses of law precisely because it no longer requires an invocation of the primacy of coercion in state and class relations. In this sense the very existence of Marxist analyses of law owes much to the wider dissemination of Gramsci's writings.

The important place attributed to Gramsci in the genesis of Marxist approaches to law needs one important qualification. It is Gramsci's general concerns and problems that have been influential and have both encouraged and facilitated the examination of law. Yet there is an element within his writings that presents something of a barrier to the development of a systematic Marxist theory of law. It is well known that he relies heavily on the distinction between "state" and "civil society"; it enables him to direct attention to the hegemonic processes operative in civil society. Yet precisely this distinction creates an initial obstruction in the theorization of law since its location within the state–civil society distinction is problematic. The immediate and self-evident proximity of law and state suggests that law should be located within the state and yet it is precisely the concern with hegemonic processes that are most suggestive for the theorization of law and yet are obstructed by the state–civil society distinction itself.

It should perhaps be stressed that this problem of the initial location of law is not only present in Gramsci. Exactly the same problem presents itself in Althusser's work. His key paper "Ideology and the Ideological State Apparatuses" introduces the distinction between the ideological and the repressive state apparatuses (ISA and RSA) (Althusser 1971). He engages in no substantive discussion of law, it is simply "placed" as part of the RSA. The result of both Gramsci's and Althusser's conceptualization of the relation between the state and the remainder of the social totality, in so far as it has consequences for the theorization of law, is to introduce an undesirable bifurcation in our approach to law. On the one hand it is approached as an apparatus of the state, but on the other, it is studied precisely because of the extent to which law is implicated in every facet of social life.

The practical consequence of this bifurcation or rupture within the conceptual framework within which law is located is the presence of two rather different bodies of theory; the first focuses on the regulation of the social relations of production (in particular property and contract relations) and the second on the role of law in the preservation of class domination (in particular embodied in criminal and constitutional law). The two differential emphases it should be noted, correspond to the general dualism between consent and coercion, and at the same time to the commonplace legal distinction between private and public law.[10]

The general theoretical problem that presents itself in the development of Marxist theory of law is the manner in which the common sense reality of the opposition between "consent" and "coercion" is to be theorized in such a way as to produce a unitary theory. It is this difficulty on which work written under the influence of Gramsci has suffered in its failure to integrate its conceptual framework.

This theoretical flaw is present in what is the most sustained attempt to develop and apply a Gramscian analysis of law that has so far been published: I refer to the important text by Stuart Hall and his collaborators, *Policing the Crisis* (Hall et al. 1978).

Policing the Crisis takes as its central concern precisely the period in contemporary political history which it is argued marks a shift from "a consensual to a more coercive management of the class struggle by the capitalist state" (1978:218). The text documents in great detail the political and ideological conditions under which the "shift" from consensual to coercive management is prepared and orchestrated. What is omitted, despite two extensive theoretical discussions, is an analysis of the part played by law and legal apparatuses in the shift toward coercion and political authoritarianism. In keeping with the explicitly Gramscian approach, stress is laid on the manner in which the autonomization of law in bourgeois democracies contributes to the creation and reproduction of consent. Yet in the transition to authoritarianism, law reappears dressed in different clothing of coercive legislation and punitive judges as the bearer of an unavoidably instrumentalist relationship to the capitalist class and capitalist state (and this despite the conscious attempts of the authors to root out all traces of instrumentalism in their Marxism). The new coercive face of law is for the time being enshrined by the protection of its universal above-the-struggle legitimacy which is the legacy of its consensual role. It should be noted in passing, although not made explicit in the text, that this facility of law to act as the bearer of repression is limited temporally: repressive law cannot hide behind the consensual mask indefinitely. The imagery that reoccurs in much Marxist and radical writing on law is of "the iron fist in the velvet glove."[11] The fundamental weakness of this imagery is that it necessarily rests on a theorization that ascribes axiomatic priority to the repressive character of law. Yet it is precisely this necessary primacy that the authors seek to avoid. Their attempt to overcome this apparent contradiction in their theorization deserves some comment.

They seek to provide a theoretical unification by introducing a single fundamental process identified as domination that is articulated as having two faces, the repressive and the consensual/hegemonic forms of domination. I should make clear that my criticism of *Policing the Crisis* carries major elements of self-criticism. I have attempted to resolve a growing awareness of the problem posed by the coercion–consent dichotomy by advancing a distinction between "repressive domination" and "ideological domination" (Chapter 3). The proposed synthesis, in its basic formulation very similar to that found in *Policing the Crisis*, lay in the extent to which both are forms of a single general process, namely, domination.

In these formulations I was at pains to insist that the distinction between ideological and repressive domination was an analytical distinction made in order that in their re-combination the full complexity of the processes of domination may be explored. In very similar terms *Policing the Crisis* proposes the theoretical unification by means of power as the central concept taking two distinct forms, coercion/domination and consent/direction.

It now seems to me that positions of this type are semantic solutions which contribute little to the difficulties posed by the persistence of the general dichotomy between coercion and consent. The necessary effect of the presence of the dichotomy is that law comes to be seen as being constituted of two different characteristics and in its existence to oscillate like a pendulum between them. Paul Hirst makes the interesting observation that there are two distinct schools of Marxist analysis of law; one trend focuses on law as a mechanism through which the regulation of property relations is achieved and the other gives priority to the role of law in the maintenance of class rule, that is whereby the subordinate classes are repressed. These two variants identified by Hirst embody at the most general level the dualism between coercion and consent (Hirst 1969).

Hence it follows that although considerable attention has been focused on Gramscian trends in the theorization of law, the same problems and difficulties manifest themselves in other trends within Marxist theory of law. It is not intended to embark on a comprehensive survey of the different trends that can be identified, but rather to focus attention on two other influential tendencies: Pashukanis' theory of the "legal form" and Edward Thompson's historical antistructuralist analysis.

At first sight it appears most strange that early legal debates and controversies in the young Soviet Republic should have attracted so much attention in the 1970s. The writings of Evgeny Pashukanis have received special attention and new translations have become available.[12] Their contemporary relevance manifests the general tendency within recent Marxist theory to construct its theory in such a manner as to avoid the accusations of simple economic and/or class reductions so frequently directed against Marxism by its critiques. More specifically in relationship to the theory of law is that Pashukanis set out deliberately to advance a theoretical alternative to the prevailing orthodoxy of instrumentalism in which law is presented as an instrument to be wielded in the self-conscious pursuit of the interests of a dominant economic class. It is further not without significance that Pashukanis' attempt to found his theorization of law on a sophisticated understanding and application of the methodology elaborated by Marx in the opening chapters of *Capital* coincides with the tendency of contemporary Marxism to reimmerse itself in detailed reading of and exegetical controversies around Marx's major theoretical texts. The reverberations and adaptions of Pashukanis in recent Marxist debates are exemplified in Balbus, Picciotto, and Hirst (Balbus 1977; Picciotto 1979; Hirst 1979).

Pashukanis sought to go beyond the mere attribution of a class content to substantive law. In place of such limited analyses he proposed to derive the irreducibly bourgeois character of the legal from the indissoluble internal connection between the commodity exchange relationship and the legal form characterized by exchange relations between formally equal legal subjects. It is not my intention to examine the problems associated with Pashukanis' derivation of the legal form from commodity relations, but rather to examine its relation to the dualism of coercion and consent.[13]

Pashukanis directed his critique explicitly against two trends in Marxist and sociological thought: the one places primary emphasis on the ideological dimension of law and the other on the instrumental or coercive dimension. Although he did not express it in the terminology used here it is clear that Pashukanis' object of attack is both wings of coercion–consent dualism. For him no mere combination of the contradictory elements of coercion and consent adequately provide a basis for the theorization of bourgeois law. To what extent did Pashukanis succeed in providing a theory that overcame the limitations of the dichotomous conceptions of law? With due recognition for the wider heuristic significance of Pashukanis' analysis of the legal form it can only be concluded that not only did he fail, but that albeit in amended form he reproduces the same dualism. Indeed there is some evidence that he was himself aware of the problematic implications of his early commodity form analysis; the basis for this contention is to be found in subsequent modification and self-criticisms. Care should be taken about how much reliance should be placed on these works because it is difficult to determine the extent to which these were self-criticisms or accommodations to Stalinist pressure.[14]

Pashukanis reproduces the dualistic analysis of law in the radical separation between private law and state law, particularly criminal law, on which he insists. In combating legal positivism he insists on the primacy of private law as an organic social form that has its origin in the juridic relation of separation and exchange between legal subjects within commodity relations. Thus all law is necessarily private law in that it is the embodiment of the relations of commodity exchange. This organic conception of law bears marked similarities to Eugen Ehrlich's sociological conception of the origin of law in spontaneous customary norms, although he does not, of course, lapse into the latter's metaphysical conception of essence of law residing in the social or popular will of a people.

In sharp contrast he retains a theory of the state as a coercive apparatus, "bourgeois society supports its class state by its system of criminal law and thereby holds the exploited class in obedience. . . . The criminal jurisdiction of the bourgeois state is organized class terror" (Beirne and Sharlet 1980:115). Thus he introduces a sharp polarity between two modes of law, the criminal law as a means of securing class domination and the civil law as the mechanism governing the exchange relations between atomized legal subjects.

He was not entirely unaware of the conflict between his express theoretical objective and his reproduction of that which he sought to replace. To provide a bridge that overcame the dualism between private law and state law he introduces what is undoubtedly the weakest feature of his general theory. He subsumes his attempt to theorize state and criminal law into a theory of punishment.[15] His focus on punishment allows him to erect a correspondence between the "equivalence" inherent in the commodity exchange, enshrined in the labor theory of value, and the "equivalence" established in punishment through the absolute divisibility of both imprisonment and monetary fines that characterize punitive sanctions in bourgeois societies.[16] The weakness of his treatment lies precisely in the fact that the identity he seeks to establish lies in nothing more than the verbal equation achieved by the dual usage of equivalence and the assertion that the verbal correspondence evidences a real correspondence.

The identification of Pashukanis' failure to overcome the dualism between private law and state law, between coercion and consent, should not detract from the importance of his analysis of the legal form of exchange relations and its consequential role in modern legal systems. His failure is testimony to the intractable nature of the problem posed.

The other major trend within Marxist studies of law is epitomized by the interventions of Edward Thompson. It should be noted that there are important parallels between Thompson's work and the earlier discussion of Gramscian theory of law. Thompson's work has a dual significance. It insists, first, on the essential contribution of historical analysis as a primary characteristic of Marxist methodology, and with it seeks to deny the possibility of general theoretical solutions that are divorced from concrete historical analysis. I will, however, argue that the very prominent critique of structuralist Marxism, in which Thompson requires Louis Althusser to stand in the dock on behalf of widely divergent positions, involves a theoretical position that no more satisfactorily resolves the problems that have formed the focus for this essay than the position that he seeks, through the most vivid polemic, to demolish. The second dimension of Thompson's intervention raises more directly than any of the positions that have been discussed throughout this essay the explicitly political implications of the theorization of law. It is a mark of the contemporaneous character of Thompson's historical work that whatever the historical period he studies, it is always linked to what he sees as currently important political questions. The politics of legal theory is highlighted in the current controversy over the "rule of law."

Thompson's impact on the field of Marxist legal theory is a result of the shift of his own concerns from the nineteenth to the eighteenth century. In *Whigs and Hunters* and in the parallel volume *Albion's Fatal Tree,* the focus is on the manner in which law and legal developments are implicated into the construction and constitution of the modern English society. The most general form of his conclusion is developed most fully by his collaborator Douglas Hay: law assumes preeminence in the course of the eighteenth century in so far as it became the most pervasive expression of the legitimizing ideology, replacing the role of religion in the preceding epoch and in constituting the new form of hegemony of the modern bourgeoisie.[17] Thompson's individual study of "the Black Act" of 1723 starts quite deliberately with a period that marks the darkest, most repressive period in the history of English criminal law, expressed in the dramatic rise in the number of capital offences added to the statute books. Yet it is this repressive law, manifest in the Black Act, that Thompson chooses to employ against those he accuses of reducing law to a direct expression of class rule. The contemporary political implication should not be missed: as the 1980s opened with conservatism in the ascendant and with the banner of "law and order" at the head of their advance, the temptation to see law as a direct expression of "their" interests had to be resisted.[18]

The reality of law reveals a deep paradox. "It is true that the law did mediate existent class relations to the advantage of the rulers. . . . On the other hand, the law mediated these class relations through legal forms, which imposed again and again, inhibitions upon the actions of the rulers" (Thompson 1975:264). It is the task of historiography and of theory to explore and expound this paradox and to draw out its implications for current political practice. My objective in discussing Thompson is to examine two aspects of his writing: first to examine the theoretical treatment of the paradox of law and, second, to consider the politics of law that he advances.

The question that must be addressed to Thompson's theoretical position is the extent to which he succeeds in breathing substance into the paradoxical historical reality of law. The investigation of the paradox may on the other hand reduce itself to yet another version of the ubiquitous dichotomy that has been traced in this essay through such an array of disparate authors.

Thompson's onslaught against "schematic Marxism" revolves around their application of the base—superstructure metaphor. If law is pigeonholed as part of the superstructure it can only be a dependent entity adjusting itself to the requirements of the economic infrastructure. On the contrary he insists that far from being separated off within a dependent superstructure "law is deeply imbricated within the very basis of productive relations, which would have been inoperable without this law" (1975:261). Yet in *Whigs and Hunters* Thompson offers no alternative to the discredited reductionism of base—superstructure.

These theoretical issues are taken up again in the iconoclastic text of *The Poverty of Theory*. Here he announces a more ambitious project: to restore Marxism to its original inspiration as historical materialism by saving it from the distortion introduced by Marx's obsessive concern with the critique of bourgeois political economy. The sins of Althusser can be traced to this vice in the old man. But in belaboring Althusser with every argument that can be pressed into service Thompson, to avoid the risk of contamination, also dispenses with the need for close examination of the concepts he deploys. One senses that he experiences some discomfort at realizing that much of Althusser's project amounts to an attempt to provide some conceptual and theoretical clothes on the frame of Marx and Engels' tentative formulations of "relative autonomy," for Thompson has long insisted on "relative autonomy" to rebut economistic interpretations, "a helpful talisman against reductionism" (Thomson 1978:289). To establish his distance Thompson in his overtly theoretical text finds the means of differentiation in the terms "human experience" as the "necessary middle term between social being and social consciousness. . . . It is by means of experience that the mode of production exerts a determining pressure upon other activities" (1978:290). Human experience does service as "the missing link" whose mission it is to overcome the aridity of Althusser's determinism. Yet the extraordinary feature of Thompson's solution, which without a trace of even false modesty, he likens to Mendel's genetic solution to Darwin's unspecified process of transmutation of species, is that having unveiled it before his expectant audience it undergoes no examination and no elaboration.

The actual role fulfilled by Thompson's "human experience" is twofold. At the most general it necessitates the reaffirmation of historiography as the primary root to social knowledge and understanding; it is historical study rather than theoretical discourse that generates new knowledge. It is important to emphasize the contradictory dimension of this celebration of historical study. The positive dimension is to be found in the very encouraging trend in recent sociology of law to engage in detailed historical studies of the development and effectivity of law for which Thompson's own study, *Whigs and Hunters,* will long remain a major beacon and measure of achievement. But on the other hand Thompson's procedure is far less acceptable in so far as he advances historical study as a proof of his solution of the great intellectual problem of social causation. In theoretical terms it is no solution and is certainly far less thought out than that offered by Althusser or for that matter by his ally Raymond Williams (Williams 1977:83–89) or by G. A. Cohen (Cohen 1978) or even by that advanced within the Althusserian tradition by Erik Olin Wright (Wright 1978). In the absence of any theoretical solution what remains is Thompson's vivid imagery of the contradictory reality of law.

> I found that law did not keep politely to a "level" but was at *every* bloody level; it was imbricated within the mode of production and productive relations themselves (as property rights, definitions of agrarian practice) and it was simultaneously present in the philosophy of Locke; it intruded brusquely within alien categories, reappearing bewigged and gowned in the guise of ideology; it danced a cotillion with religion, moralizing over the theatre of Tyburn; it was an arm of politics

and politics was one of its arms; it was an academic discipline, subjected to the rigour of its own autonomous logic; it contributed to the definition of the self-identity both of rulers and ruled; above all, it afforded an arena for class struggle, within which alternative notions of law were fought out. (Thompson 1975:288)

Behind this dazzling inventory lies our old friend the dichotomy between coercion and consent. We must at the end of a long journey relish and value the historical insights of his work, but adjudge him to have committed a grave theoretical misrepresentation in that he fails to resolve the paradox of law but breathes fresh life into the dichotomous conception of law.

I have argued that the different trends in recent discussions about law exhibit a range of responses concerning the contemporary politics of law. One of the major elements that accounts for the impact of Thompson's recent writings is the explicitly political implications which he draws out and has subsequently elaborated. The concluding chapter of *Whigs and Hunters* seeks to derive contemporary lessons concerning the rule of law. His argument is mounted against "orthodox Marxism," which he accuses, in the main I believe with justification, of adopting the position that "the rule of law is only another mask for the rule of class. The revolutionary can have no interest in law, unless as a phenomenon of ruling-class power and hypocrisy; it should simply be his aim to overthrow it" (Thompson 1975:259). The critique of the Left's response to law is made more explicit in subsequent writings and is applied to current controversies within the politics of law: the defence of the jury as a profoundly democratic institution, opposition to jury vetting, state trials and state secrets and police powers (Thompson 1979a, 1979b:1980). These contemporary interventionist essays raise two separable but related sets of questions. The first concerns the orientation of radicals and socialists to the role of law in modern capitalist democracies and the second concerns the role of law and legality in socialist societies.

I have argued that modern sociology of law exhibits, more or less directly, concerns with the politics of law. It is not surprising that those writing in the context of the Marxist tradition are more explicit and directly concerned with the political implications of their positions. The position of liberal and non-Marxist writers reveals a marked pessimism concerning the trajectory of law in contemporary society. This concern is mirrored in Thompson's writings but is given a very distinctive and much more optimistic inflection.

Thompson broadly accepts that current of recent discussion that points toward the emergence of more authoritarian forms of state power within the capitalist democracies. His dispute with "orthodox Marxism" is that he accuses it of sitting back and complacently interpreting these trends as conformation of the necessarily repressive character of the bourgeois state. This position further results in a cynical lack of concern with the politics of law encouraging a denunciatory response to the erosion of civil liberties; its emphasis is to greet such developments as the shedding of the consensual mask of capitalist law and state to reveal, ever more starkly, its repressive essence.

The root of the disagreement with orthodox Marxism lies in radically different conceptions of the lineage and historical role of class societies. Orthodox Marxism presents each phase of class society (slavery, feudalism, capitalism) as replacing one form of class domination by another; each system of class dominance exhibits state forms that are overturned by the succeeding class to be replaced by a form appropriate to its class interests. The capitalist state and capitalist law is the form appropriate to the maintenance of its class domination. Hence the task of socialist action is to remove capitalist law and state and to replace it with socialist law and state. There is no continuity between the different orders and any defense of elements within capitalism, except for purely tactical reasons, can only breed illusions and obscure the necessity of the ultimate goal of smashing the bourgeois state. The result, "the ambivalence *within the 'Left'* towards civil liberties is the most alarming evidence of all that the libertarian nerve has become dulled" (Thompson 1979a:10). Thompson's scenario is radically different: the achievement of class power by the bourgeoisie, and the advent of the rule of law which was one of its major achievements, as an aspect of "revolutionary inheritance" (Thompson 1979b:8). The kernel of the radical and democratic content of civil liberties and the rule of law remains even though it is also at risk in the current stage from the hand of the bourgeoisie and their state and political institutions. The bourgeois epoch heralded an advance in the long haul toward freedom; bourgeois freedom has always been limited in its development by social and economic inequality on the one hand and the narrow integument of the formalism that marks bourgeois legalism. The more the limited gains of the bourgeois inheritance are threatened the more is it politically essential for socialism, as the inheritor of the radical democratic transition. His writings are peppered with reference to the "free-born Englishman"; a major part of Thompson's socialist humanism rests on his insistence that this radical democratic legacy persists and in it resides "the peculiarities of the English," and that it can be reignited in the name of a political perspective that is at one and the same democratic, humanist, and socialist (Thompson 1965).

Within Thompson's general perspective the politics of law takes on its specific significance. His position is encapsulated in two formulations that take on something of the quality of slogans: "law matters" and "the rule of law seems to me to be an unqualified human good" (1975:266). The first slogan points toward the need for socialists to intervene in the politics of law: to defend the jury, to protect civil liberties, to advance affirmative legislation, etc. The more controversial and important position that he advances concerns "the rule of law." The controversial character of his position derives from its rejection of the almost instinctive response to the Left to regard the rule of law as a prime example of an ideological fiction, to be denounced and exposed along with the separation of powers and judicial neutrality as the most transparent guises of bourgeois constitutionalism. What Thompson defends in the name of the rule of law is not entirely clear or consistent. Certainly he tends to conflate the rule of law and civil liberty; thereby he hangs the defence of the former on the more self-evident defense of the latter. But he also emphasizes the importance of the rule of law as constituting a mechanism of restraint on rulers. He adds a further dimension by proposing a conception of the rule of law as constituting a framework within which the class struggle can be fought out. The implications of Thompson's thesis in defense of the rule of law have not received systematic attention but the need is revealed as soon as the importance of its implications becomes clear; the great importance of his intervention lies precisely in the fact that it is now placed firmly on the contemporary political and intellectual agenda of the Left.

The second dimension of Thompson's excursions into the politics of law, and most directly through his treatment of the rule of law, is the question of the relationship between law and socialism. Thompson's position is a manifestation of his response to "actual socialism" and his anti-Stalinism takes the form of a declaration of faith in the inseparable connection between legality and democracy and the centrality of socialist legality and socialist democracy in a future socialist society. Thompson refuses the apparently libertarian perspective offered, for example, by Pashukanis of identifying the emergence of an explicitly nonlegal social order as the basis for founding advanced participatory democracy. These issues play a limited role in Thompson's argument yet their presence adds a wider perspective. My intention in drawing attention to them is to stress that the debate about the trajectory of law has for socialists this added dimension, in which law constitutes a "problem" raising difficult issues concerning the nature of the socialist project. It is in this context that his perspective on the politics of law is on the one hand activist stressing law as an arena of struggle, and indeed has led him to direct involvement therein; but on the other hand there is an absence concerning the theorization of the rule of legality under socialism. Thus, despite his insistence that his perspective is not restricted to a defensive struggle to retain bourgeois legality and civil liberties, the strategic direction remains cloudy and ill-defined. This problem of identifying a strategic direction for the politics of law poses an important challenge to those who stand by Thompson's insistence on the contemporary significance of legal politics but have reservations concerning his failure to explore more fully the different dimensions of "the rule of law" and its wider implications for socialist strategy.

CONCLUSION

The examination of the major trends within recent sociological theories of law has revealed the enduring presence within the different theoretical perspectives of a dichotomous conception of law organized around the polar opposition between coercion and consent. It has been argued that at one level to conceptualize law in terms of the dimensions of coercion and consent succeeds in embracing important characteristics of law. Yet none of the positions examined succeed in advancing a coherent presentation of a mode of combination of the apparently opposed characteristics of law so as to produce a unitary conception not reducible to a choice between opposites or a fluctuation between them. On the contrary, each of the positions examined is forced to make a choice, conscious or otherwise, between the polarities. Liberal theorists have understandably opted for attaching primacy to the consensual dimension or potential of law. For very different reasons recent Marxist theories, in reaction to positions that had previously held sway within Marxism, have also been anxious to give emphasis to the consensual face of law.

Thus by different roots and within the logic of their respective theoretical frameworks both trends exhibit major elements of continuity. One important consequence of this marked parallelism between liberal and Marxist theories of law is that it creates the conditions that make possible a meaningful and potentially fruitful dialogue. The greater the recognition that can be achieved of the proximity of their theoretical concerns the greater will be the motivation toward the engagement in this dialogue. The emergence and clarification of theoretical problems are not unconnected with the more explicit concern with and attention to the politics of law. Sociology of law is emerging from a period in which its primary concerns were limited to the internal examination of the "legal process" within a largely taken-for-granted social engineering set of assumptions, while the realist tradition has been shown to have continuing effects that reinforce and bolster this narrow conception of the role of sociological study of law. The persistence in widely different positions of some conception of a crisis of law or legal order has given rise, despite the lack of clarity or agreement as to the nature of "the crisis," to a more conscious concern with the wider problem of the part played by law within the social order and thus with the politics of law.

CHAPTER 5

THE POLITICS
OF LAW
AND JUSTICE

INTRODUCTION

Law and justice are important. The need to state such a truism is a mark of the extent to which the left in Britain has over a long period of time failed to recognize that law and justice have a significant political dimension. But I would argue further that political questions revolving around law are becoming increasingly important and, indeed, central to the political problems of the present.

The left *does* have a politics of law; the real problem is that it is deficient in a number of major respects. It is, first, rudimentary, for law is given little priority either in the theory or the practices of the left. Second, these responses, whether theorized or part of a less articulated set of attitudes, are significant impediments to the development of a politics of law. Third, responses that the left invokes in different circumstances are frequently incompatible and even contradictory; it is little wonder that it is confused, and even less surprising that the positions it takes up meet with very limited popular support. It will therefore be necessary to examine in some detail the varieties of left positions with respect to law and justice and to explore and criticize their implications. The arena of law and justice, studded as it is with highly significant values and symbols, has been handed over without effective resistance to the right, thus allowing them to make effective and powerful interventions with wide-ranging political consequences.

This paper argues that law must be regarded as an *arena of struggle,* a field in which different class and political positions engage, with consequences that are not deducible from any general theory of law. It thus rejects any instrumentalist theory of law, which presents law as being available to any particular class or dominant group as an instrument or means of effecting their will or furthering their interests.

This does not imply that law is neutral, equally available to all political or social forces. The social and political "limits" to intervention in law are a pressing political concern, and they are determined in each historical period as the outcome of struggle, whether that struggle is waged consciously or not.

The designation of law as an arena of struggle implies the rejection of a general politics of law, for such an approach would require law to be a unitary phenomenon. On the contrary, a politics of law requires specific political evaluation of possibilities and tactics with respect to each and every instance of legal regulation. However, consistency and coherence with reference to particular instances of legal struggle are necessary; I argue that one of the weaknesses of prevailing positions on the left is that they frequently lack both internal consistency and coherence in respect of related areas of legal struggle.

Once the weaknesses in the positions taken up on the left have been identified, my final section will be concerned to set out, first, a general framework within which a progressive politics of law and justice can be advanced and, second, to discuss a number of the more pressing contemporary issues of the politics of law. In this latter task I advance a number of positions that conflict with what have traditionally come to be regarded as socialist or progressive positions.

The objective of this chapter is not to engage in discussion of specific areas of legal and social policy. It is clear from the foregoing that such an exercise cannot be undertaken through derivation from general theoretical considerations. While consideration of individual areas of legal intervention requires detailed empirical investigation, these run the risk of lapsing into a narrow empiricism if conducted outside the context of wider theoretical and political considerations. For this reason this chapter focuses attention on some of these more important and often neglected considerations.

THE IMPORTANCE OF LAW

Law is important and socialists must take it seriously.[1] Let me briefly examine some areas in which this importance for socialist politics is manifested.

Law is important in that it exhibits a symbolic or ideological dimension. Law mobilizes important ideological symbols. The process of the legalization and legitimation gives both direct advantage and encouragement to some social forces and the corresponding delegitimation of criminalization hampers, penalizes, or discourages other social forces. For example, an understanding of the recent history of abortion law reform can be facilitated by an understanding of the symbolic dimensions of the "victories" and "defeats" recorded in the various stages of legislative process. An important question is whether the symbolic dimensions of law are direct effects of the legislative process itself or require a more complex analysis in which, for example, the symbolic content of law is significant with respect to the extent to which it facilitates the mobilization of political action and sentiment.[2]

Law displays and invokes an array of ideologically significant terms. The language of law, both technical and popular, is studded with appeals to "rights," "duties," "equality," "justice," and so forth. Indeed much of the history of political thought, in both its academic and popular forms, abounds with appeal to legal concepts and ideas (Skillen 1977). It is important to recognize that the very terms of political argument and debate are unavoidably "legalistic." For example, there has been considerable discussion of the problems inherent in invoking "rights" with its consequential invocation of the atomized "legal subject." Yet no amount of critical commentary removes the appeal to "rights" from the language of politics and therefore from the terms within which politics are fought out.[3]

The importance of law is further underlined by discussions pointing toward its growing centrality. From different theoretical and political perspectives it has been contended that one of the significant characteristics of contemporary capitalist democracies is that law is increasingly becoming a primary mechanism of social control or social order. There are at least three versions of the "centrality of law" thesis. Recent Marxist discussions, initiated by Althusser's discussion of "ideological state apparatuses," suggest that law is increasingly becoming a primary form of social regulation. There has been increasing attention to the significance of the "juridification" of social relations, the twofold process whereby wider areas of social life become subject to legal regulation and control and social relations themselves come to be treated and regarded in legalistic terms.

From a diametrically opposed perspective neoconservatism has identified, albeit in different terms, the same trend. Indeed conservative theorists have quite consciously set out to attack the modern extension of legal regulation, by emphasizing "the limits of law" (Hayek 1973–1979). The third version of the "centrality of law" thesis is to be found in the much wider middle ground focusing variously on the welfare state, social justice, and corporatism. It is clear that almost the full spectrum of political and theoretical discussion agrees that law has become more important or central in contemporary capitalist democracies as an expanding mechanism for the regulation of social life.

Law is important also for the part that it plays in the formation of popular consciousness. Anyone who has spent any time on the doorstep canvassing must recognize that it is no invention of the opinion polls or the popular tabloids that people in very large numbers persistently refer to "crime" as an area of concern, fear, or anxiety. The prevalence of and the attention given to "street crime," that is visible offences against person and property, play an important part in the way people form and express their attitudes toward the condition of contemporary social life and the quality of life. The specific focus of attention shifts, often with a considerable volatility, heightened by and through the mass media. One very obvious form of this process is the identification of an enemy/villain to be scapegoated (e.g., black muggers, trade union pickets, football hooligans, the Yorkshire Ripper).[4] There are equally powerful yet less personalized and less studied forms of social anxiety embodied in reaction to street vandalism, car thefts, and housebreaking, etc.

The political importance of popular responses to "law" and its correlative "crime" lies in the two interconnected dimensions referred to above, at the immediate level the specific anxiety/fear involved in the particular problem and the deeper social anxiety about changes in the wider pattern of social life that often underlies it. For example, concern surrounding youth vandalism and football hooliganism also expresses disquiet at the transformation of intergenerational relations, the decline in the cohesion of family life and parental control, and, beyond the problem of generations, a more profound concern with declining levels of "social responsibility" and "community." It is necessary to insist on the reality of the specific and to avoid dismissing popular reaction as a manifestation of false consciousness or of a traditional ideology. The general failure of the left to say anything about the immediate level of the "crime phenomenon" itself is a manifestation of political weakness and failure of political response.

The popular response to crime tends to be politically articulated toward the right. Yet it is necessary to insist on the contradictory nature of popular responses, for this points toward a general political basis for a progressive response to problems of crime. In *Policing the Crisis* the "social anxiety" surrounding mugging is presented as embodying a "traditional consensus" that is a *cross-class consensus,* composed of a number of interwoven commonsense notions, such as "respectability," "work," "social discipline," "respect for authority," and, perhaps most powerful of all, the sense of "Englishness" (Hall et al. 1978). I do not want to take issue with the detailed constituents of this imagery, but it is less than clear that all of these elements are traditionalist. Interwoven is another notion that, while present in their analysis is never fully discussed, that of "social responsibility"; it appeals to ideas about how people should behave, about care and concern for others. Now as social historians have so often observed, progressive sentiments and response often deploy images of a preexisting ideal state or golden age. Indeed a persistent theme in the appeal to social responsibility is a view that in "the good old days" people were more responsible, caring, etc. Yet that appeal bears a positive morality about how things should be and in its more optimistic phases of how things could be. It is the progressive thrust and potential of concepts of social responsibility that set out the basis for a progressive politics of law, and to which, therefore, I will return.

THE LEFT AND THE POLITICS OF LAW

The responses of the left fail to take law seriously and are a major barrier to effective intervention in legal politics. The positions taken up are pervasive and their crippling effect has to be recognized before a progressive politics of law and justice can be developed. It is therefore necessary to consider the varieties of left positions or responses. While I am critical of the range of positions customarily associated with the left, it is also necessary to register the presence of some long-standing and serious progressive traditions in the politics of civil liberties or, perhaps more accurately, the politics of political liberties.[5] I shall however argue that this important strand of progressive politics is not without problems.

The fundamental problem with left responses is that they manifest themselves as deductions or derivations from general theories of law and the state. This both causes and reinforces a reluctance to come to grips with more concrete issues in the broad field of the politics of law.[6] Where concrete issues are discussed there is a pronounced tendency for this to be done in a manner that is in fact the simple application of the general theory that points to the class-discriminatory character of law in general. The result is a complacency of circularity, in which the general theory is celebrated and the concrete, presented as its proof.

My objection to the derivation of legal politics from general theory requires some comment because it appears to conflict with what is frequently claimed as a strength and virtue by the Marxist left, that it is precisely the existence of the general theory, Marxism, that makes it possible to avoid the pitfalls of pragmatism, reformism, and opportunism. The problem is not general theory as such, but the nature of the presumed direct connection between the theoretical concepts (e.g., "capitalism") and the concrete (e.g., law in Britain in the 1980s), in which the concrete is treated as an expression or embodiment of the theoretical category. Such a position constantly veers toward idealism and is a barrier to the detailed analysis of the concrete or empirical reality.[7]

The general theory most commonly deployed by the left is in its simplest form the "class-state, class-law" thesis. It has its intellectual and political roots in Marxist theory of the state, particularly in the version that has had such widespread impact through Lenin's *State and Revolution* in which the state is a mechanism of class rule. This theory of the state unproblematically links law to the state as one of its major instruments or agencies. Law is but an expression of the needs and will of a dominant class. However much it may be argued that such a theoretical position does not grasp the fullness or complexity of Marxist theory, it is powerful and extensive in its influence; and it has considerable textual support. For example, *The Communist Manifesto* proclaims: "Your [bourgeois] law is merely the will of your class, erected into legislation—a will whose content is defined by the material conditions of the existence of your class" (Marx 1958:I,49). The "class-state, class-law" thesis provides the general framework within which the left develops its politics of law. It expresses itself in several variants that are either loosely combined or differentially accentuated.

The first variant is a conspiracy theory in which the emphasis is on the capacity of law to mask or hide its specifically class character. Law is thus frequently presented as the emanation of a state endowed with extensive foresight and long-term planning objectives; there is a strong tendency to see the state itself as the embodiment of political will and intention. A recent example of this tendency has been the emphasis on the campaign against the Criminal Justice (Scotland) Bill, which suggests a conscious strategy of the "ruling class" to use this legislation as a dry run for an attempt to impose increased police powers on the rest of the United Kingdom.[8]

An important pressure toward conspiratorial views of law arises from versions of ideology theory that emphasize the legitimizing function of the legal ideology through which legal provisions are expressed. Legitimation tends to be seen as a conscious state policy facilitated by the formalism through which law invokes "equality," "fairness," and other legal symbols. Its classic expression is Anatole France's ironic declamation on French law "which forbids both rich and poor from sleeping under the bridges of the Seine." It is an easy but nevertheless dangerous slippage to move directly from functional analysis of law to assumptions about the political intentions of classes and legislatures. It is not that law is neutral, above classes or politics, but that there are risks of oversimplification in reading off or deducing class and political intentions either about law in general or about specific legislation.

The second variant of the class law thesis insists, both with respect to the content of law and to its administration, that law is class discriminatory. This critique operates by exposing the gap between the universalistic claims of law and its discriminatory reality. It leads to two very different versions of legal politics. One is essentially negative, in the form of the expose of legal inequality. It is a counsel against holding any illusions about the possibility of law realizing the ideals of equality and fairness, for class discrimination is seen as the inevitable and unavoidable face of law in a class divided society. The alternative political orientation is one which emphasizes the necessity and possibility of legal reform. The class discriminatory character of the institutions and practice is highlighted in order to demand a strategy of reform aimed at the gap between legal ideals and legal reality. This position is well exemplified by the movement to extend legal services; it starts by emphasizing inequality of access and it demands administrative and financial arrangements designed to widen and simplify access to legal services. This orientation has been the organizing theme of the "law centres movement" to make legal services available to the communities disenfranchised by the existing distribution and operation of the legal profession. This position is not necessarily wedded to a simplistic piecemeal or accumulative reform strategy. Its more radical thrust stresses the contradiction between the ideological commitment of bourgeois democracy to ideals of equality and the fundamental inequality in capitalist society. By working on this tension, through demands that seek to realize ideologically legitimate goals, it seeks to bring about a heightened political consciousness of the inherent limitation of capitalism and bourgeois democracy, and to create some of the conditions for a more substantive social equality.

It is important to stress that the "class state–class law" position does not give rise to a single political expression. Yet it tends toward a rejectionism in which the possibility of a progressive politics of law is so circumscribed by its class nature that little significance is attached to struggle in the legal field. The gap between rejectionism and legal reformism tends to be viewed in the light of the dichotomy between "reform" and "revolution," although it is important to note that wider support from the left is given to specific reform campaigns whenever these are seen as having politicizing or radical potential.

The "class state–class law" position also finds other manifestations.

One which relies on the most explicitly "revolutionary" inspiration counterposes "bourgeois justice" to "proletarian justice." In some versions it is little more than an apology for the legal practice of "actual socialism"; but even in its nonapologist interpretation it dismisses the ideals of bourgeois law, which are doomed to remain "pure ideology" and which must be replaced with other goals and organizational principles. Individual rights and liberties are irredeemably bourgeois in character and are counterposed by appeal to goals of class and social justice to be realized by proletarian institutions and practices. The goal of class justice is seen as requiring an escape from the formalism of bourgeois law through informal and popular institutions pursuing goals of substantive justice untrammelled by too much concern with proceduralism.

One of the most common manifestations of the generalized "class law" thesis attributes the genesis of crime and antisocial behavior more generally to the very nature of capitalist society itself. The etiology of crime is traced to the antisocial, dehumanizing character of capitalist social relations, and the conclusion is drawn that it is not the individual law-breakers but capitalism itself or "society" that is "responsible" for or "causes" crime. "Don't blame the individual, blame society" becomes the general slogan of the left or, as expressed in one placard seen on a demonstration, "Fight Crime, Smash Capitalism." It is a perspective in which the advent of socialism is seen as leading to the long-term eradication of crime.[9]

This line of thought has disastrous consequences for the left's political response to crime. The slogan "blame society, not the criminal" persistently deflects the left's response to crime-related problems toward long-term social reform programs directed toward the removal of the social conditions that are seen as giving rise to crime; in so doing the left tends to have little to offer by way of immediate or short-term response to crime phenomena themselves. When this is associated with an anticorrectional attitude, discussed below, it gives rise to the popular picture that the left has nothing to say about the response to the law-breaker. In the light of the importance attached above to popular responses to the most readily visible forms of "street crime," this is a serious absence. It is especially noticeable in relation to youth offences, whether it be football hooliganism or street vandalism: the left emphasizes youth employment and the lack of youth facilities, yet has very little to say about what should be done either to minimize the incidence of offences or with regard to the appropriate response towards the offenders themselves.

The reluctance to blame the offender has origins in a long-standing distrust of the assumption of free-will and moral responsibility that underpin classical criminology, and is reinforced by a libertarian hostility to the demand for social order. It is taken for granted that the demand for "law and order" is *inherently* reactionary. The immediate and unavoidable consequence is that the whole political space of debate concerning social and moral order is ceded without a struggle to the right. For a period, in the late 1960s and early 1970s, radical deviancy theory provided a veritable celebration of disorder in which the denial of value consensus, coupled with a moral relativism, collapsed not only the distinction between normalcy and deviancy, but that between social and antisocial conduct. Deviancy was celebrated as a form of primitive rebellion against the existing social order; Taylor, Walton, and Young produced that "any acts of deviance must be taken to be acts of resistance (however inarticulately expressed or formulated)" (Taylor et al. 1973:252). This period found a political rapport with the political commitment to "the underdog" as the bearer of revolutionary potential articulated by Marcuse and Fanon. For radical deviancy theory it was prisoners, prostitutes, and gypsies that elicited moral solidarity. These heady days of radicalism waned for even in the earlier period the realization existed that the property that was the site of the struggle for possession was invariably the property of the worker, just as it was the worker's personal safety that was violated by crimes of violence. Yet the hostility to "order" has been retained and is shared by much of the left. The content of this agreement lies in the association of "order" and the "status quo"; yet what is adopted in the equation is not a necessary connection but one which is the result of the highly successful assertion of this identity in conservative theory and rhetoric.

The tendency of the left to "blame society, not the individual" is reinforced by a pervasive hostility to "correctionalism," since law in general is viewed as repressive so necessarily are punishment and other agencies of social control (e.g., social workers, schools, psychiatrists, etc.) all geared to relocating offenders/deviants within capitalist social relations. This approach is of course reinforced by the evident lack of "success," when judged against reformatory criteria, of the conventional range of punitive sanctions. This hostility is particularly directed toward the prison system where the general patterns of high recidivism are buttressed by a critique of the disciplinary processes employed.

The reservation or hostility toward prisons and correctionalism more generally leads the left to share with sections of liberal opinion a general call for the reduction of the prison population, opposition to imprisonment for young offenders and first offenders that has been the dominant legislative trend for over a decade. Yet the left exhibits a greater skepticism than mainstream liberal thought with regard to "alternatives to prisons," for example, parole, halfway houses, community service, etc., which are viewed as exhibiting continuity with traditional correctionalist concerns.[10] This hostility to both "old" and "new" correctionalism leads the left to a profound silence, an absence of policy, an embarrassed shuffle, or a diversionary attack on the evils of capitalist society when pressed by the question "but what should we do with offenders?"

However, anticorrectionalism does not provide the whole of the penal policy of the left. There are a number of fields in which the left has no such hesitancies about the need to punish firmly and demonstrably. The left has persistently called for the imposition of punitive sanctions on fascists and racists.[11] Is this response in contradiction with the generalized anticorrectionalism or does it have a distinguishable rationale? I would suggest that it is a mixture of two elements. First, an incoherent reliance on simple political criteria, thus expressing gut hostility to racism and fascism but running the risk of legitimizing the adoption of a "political penology" directed against the left. Second, and more coherently, it insists on the presence of an individual responsibility for "political" action. It sees fascist or racist action as conscious and deliberate, thus both requiring and justifying punitive response while insisting that "nonpolitical" acts cannot be regarded as attracting the same level of "responsibility." What is significant about this rationale is that it is an application of principles of "classical criminology" premised on the insistence on the moral responsibility of individuals for their own conduct. To point to this connection with classical liberal thought is not intended to argue against holding fascists "responsible" for their conduct, but to point to the need to reexamine the general premises on which the left's responses are based.

The left also departs from anticorrectionalism with respect to "the crimes of the powerful," for which it demands the application of the full rigor of the law. Here the focus on the crimes of the powerful serves to illustrate the class discriminatory character of the law; the content of the law biased such that important areas of antisocial conduct, oppressive or exploitative action are not criminalized. In recent years a pervasive symbol has been the hounding of supplementary benefit recipients in contrast to the judicial and political encouragement of tax evasion. Pointing the finger at the crimes of the powerful has contradictory implications. On the one hand it is a potent symbol of class inequality, and it invokes a positive criterion for law enforcement based on the *degree of social harm* occasioned. For example, the financial value of the crimes of the powerful far outstrip the relative triviality of the crime of the poor (Pearce 1976). Yet crimes of the powerful frequently are "crime without victims" in that the losses are suffered by the state, financial institutions, or are widely dispersed in the "social costs" incurred. In contrast, working-class crime is often more immediate, being inflicted on individual members of the community. "Social cost" does not provide an unproblematic criterion of moral responsibility; we may wish to maintain that to rob an old age pensioner *is* worse than to defraud a multinational corporation. But does it provide a basis for a coherent penal philosophy? The focus on ruling class crime can serve as a mechanism of deflection; to point to the widespread nature of tax evasion is not in itself a response to the political question of what attitude should be taken up toward violations of social security regulations. Does pointing the finger at tax evasion exonerate petty social security fiddles? Can we legitimately fail to censure working-class crime while the universal criminality of capitalism and imperialism is still rampant?[12]

The "class-state–class-law" position has had harmful and pervasive consequences for socialist politics of law; some of the variants give rise to less flawed political conclusions, but even these entail either a general political passivity or an incapacity to confront problems of law, crime, and order.

THE POLITICS OF CIVIL LIBERTIES

The left has a second perspective on the politics of law that is organized around "the defence of civil liberties." What is noticeable, and in some respects surprising, is the limited extent to which the demand for defense of civil liberties has been discussed, let alone theorized, by the left. The liberal political and philosophical tradition has had a virtual monopoly over both the terms and the content of the debate.

The left has recently been forcefully invited to give its attention to the arena of justice and its relation to civil liberties. This challenge has been laid down with customary publicist flair by Edward Thompson. His concern is that "the ambivalence *within the "Left"* towards civil liberties is the most alarming evidence that the libertarian nerve has become dulled" (1980:165). I share his concern about "ambivalence" on the left. But he is profoundly in error to place the responsibility at the door of Althusser and structuralist Marxism. The "ambivalence" of the left is of much older lineage; responsibility lies in the extent to which the left has operated, as I have argued, by appeal to both the "class-state–class-law" position and the espousal of civil liberties. The underdeveloped state of the left analysis of civil liberties has often tended to give an apparently greater political weight to "class law" analysis resulting in either a rejection of civil liberties (as Thompson complains) or, as I want to suggest, an equally problematic tactical adoption of civil libertarian positions.

Thompson, however, has done more than direct attention to the question of civil liberties. He has also provided a theoretical and historical account that, if accepted, provides a powerful political case for giving a major place in socialist strategy to the struggle to protect and advance civil liberties. The seeds of his theory of civil liberties are found throughout his major historical writings, in particular in *The Making of the English Working Class* and *Whigs and Hunters*. He argues that these liberties were born in the struggle against absolutism; they were pioneered by independent, radical, and republican activists and thinkers. This tradition was not simply the creature of a struggle by the bourgeois against the old order, although many aspects were taken up and articulated in the creation of the modern bourgeois state. But they remained most active and potent in a radical tradition that retained a political and intellectual independence. Although often repressed and sometimes quiescent, they persisted and were revitalized by the developing working class and formed an important inspiration for Chartism and later for trade unionism. The signpost of the historical independence of the civil libertarian tradition is expressed most graphically in Thompson's imagery of the "free-born Englishmen." An important "proof" of the irreducibility of civil liberties to bourgeois ideology lies in his defence of the jury as the classical embodiment of an independent banner of liberty: "The jury system is not a product of "bourgeois democracy" (to which it owes nothing) but a stubbornly maintained democratic *practice*" (Thompson 1980:169).[13]

Thompson's appeal is thus to an independent radical political tradition that is currently at greatest risk not only because of state sponsored attempts to extinguish it but, perhaps most importantly, because the left is in danger of abandoning it. His position is by no means idiosyncratic. Tony Benn has also advanced a very similar position: "Our liberties have been won by political and industrial campaigns . . . democratic development has not been achieved by courtesy of the judges" (Benn 1979:3). Even more evocative of Thompson is Benn's argument that the reassertion of civil libertarian demands in the present "will strike a chord in the collective memory of our own people" (1979:13).

The civil liberties perspective advanced by Thompson has wider repercussions for political strategy. It separates him decisively from that element of the socialist tradition that sees capitalism as the last of a succession of forms of class society that it is the historical role of the socialist revolution to replace. Rather Thompson's scenario is one that emphasizes greater elements of continuity between the bourgeois and the socialist revolution; in the course of the bourgeois revolution (but not reducible to it) the people embarked on a struggle for liberty and democracy which it is the socialist project to *complete,* to rescue from the limitations imposed within capitalist social relations. Civil liberties are, therefore, not a political gloss to socialism, even less a tactical expedient: rather they are a central and constitutive element of socialism itself.

Thompson's is the *strongest* and most thoroughgoing espousal of civil liberties on the socialist left. But he should not be thought to be alone; however, a number of other socialist positions are *weaker* versions of the commitment to civil liberties. There are two important variants. The first is often difficult to fully separate from Thompson's. It stresses, in the words of Tony Benn, "liberties won by political and industrial campaigns" but it sees these as victories won by the working class *against* the bourgeoisie which during the struggles of the nineteenth century were forced to concede civil liberties that were inimical to its class interests. The bourgeoisie is thus presented as having a predisposition to antidemocratic and anti-civil libertarian positions. It follows that the need to struggle for civil liberties can be summed up as the need to "defend hard-won rights" that are always at risk of being snatched back.

This position has some rather ambiguous implications. Like Thompson it stresses the historical connection between the working class and the struggle for civil liberties, but it tends to ignore or underplay the role of other classes and social forces. More seriously, it produces a very strange and ultimately unsatisfactory account of the relationship between capitalism and bourgeois democracy in which the political forms most characteristic of advanced capitalism are presented as the product of struggle by the working class and as having been conceded grudgingly by the capitalist class even though they have subsequently succeeded in turning these structures and practices to their own advantage in securing the conditions for their class rule. At its worst this weak civil liberties position comes down to a *tactical* defense of civil liberties both to expose the antidemocratic nature of the capitalist state and also because the preservation of civil liberties provides the "most favourable conditions" for prosecuting the general struggle against capitalism. Such a political line is tactical because it requires no commitment to the principles or practices defended; thus making it all the easier to dispense with them later once the immediate objective of overthrowing capitalism has been achieved.

The second version of this position has a markedly more positive thrust and places much less emphasis on the defensive character of civil liberties politics. The struggle for civil liberties is presented as a *continuing* struggle for the creation of new liberties and rights, extending beyond the scope of "formal political liberties" into fields that allow the struggle for rights of substance in the organization of production and distribution. The most distinctive demands of this type are exhibited in calls for "the right to work" and in the "industrial democracy" movement. Such demands are also very much a part of the commitment of the left to ideas of "distributive justice" to be discussed below.

The civil liberties politics of the left may also be informed by another tradition. The Leninist theory of monopoly capitalism insists that one of the significant features of this final stage of capitalism is that it marks the abandonment of bourgeois democracy. "The political superstructure of this new economy, of monopoly capitalism (imperialism is monopoly capitalism) is the change *from* democracy *to* political reaction" (Lenin 1960–70 23 C.W. 43). This theory of the trajectory of contemporary capitalism is widely diffused beyond those who would either accept or recognize its Leninist origin. It allows two rather divergent lines of political practice. One accepts the inevitability of the antidemocratic direction of modern capitalism and sees each new onslaught on civil liberties as confirmation of an "iron law" of increasing authoritarianism; in its most extreme form this position sees the direction of modern capitalism as the drift toward fascism. The second version has undergone considerable development in recent years and is embedded in the "authoritarian statism" theory advanced by both Poulantzas and Stuart Hall (Poulantzas 1978; Hall et al. 1978). Without discussing this theory fully it is necessary to note its implications for the politics of civil liberties: it finds expression in a commitment to "the democratic road to socialism" that emphasizes the importance of strategies that seek to achieve a defense of formal civil liberties alongside a transformative commitment to the development of popular democratic practices with an emphasis on new forms of direct or participatory democracy.

The multiplicity of forms of the politics of civil liberties to be found on the contemporary left reveals the general lack of sustained attention to developing a coherent and comprehensive political strategy. Often these different positions are found in various combinations or even more frequently different versions are invoked at separate stages in political argument. There is an inevitable sense of confusion that is the direct result of the failure on the part of the left to examine systematically the basis of its positions on questions of civil liberty. Beyond the inherent problems of such confusions is the more important consequence: the position on civil liberties is seen, both by the left itself and more importantly by the audience it addresses, to lack conviction and consistency and thus providing some confirmation to the criticism leveled by both liberals and conservatives that the left has an inadequate and unacceptable position on problems of civil liberties.

THE PROBLEM OF RIGHTS

The language of rights provides an organizing framework in and through which political struggles are fought out. All political issues involve, usually quite directly, appeals to rights; whether it be the "right to work" or "the right to a fair profit," "a woman's right to choose" or "the right to life," politics and political demands invoke appeals to rights or to the analogous language of "freedom." So persistent is this appeal to rights that it makes little or no sense to dismiss this reality, as some on the left seek to do, by arguing that "rights" are merely ideological masks disguising naked interests. Equally unhelpful is the tendency to counterpose collective to individual rights, the former being seen as politically progressive, the latter "bourgeois." What is problematic about individual rights is not that they may be secured by or on behalf of particular persons by resort to legal institutions. Indeed collective rights are no rights at all unless they can be secured by particular persons. All too often the espousal of collective rights, e.g., in defense of denial of rights in actual socialist states, is an actual denial of rights *as such*. While there is scope for arguing about the political priority of competing rights, socialism is at risk of lapsing into authoritarianism if it constructively denies the importance of rights.[14]

The left, however, exhibits a pervading ambivalence toward rights. On the one hand it frequently organizes its campaigns and demands around the politics of rights; Tony Benn even appeals to "the idea of inherent rights implanted by the very fact of human existence" (Benn 1979:1). But on the other hand it exhibits systematic doubt and in many cases hostility toward rights that are seen as inherently bourgeois categories riddled with individualism and subjectivism. Before considering the way in which the left deploys "rights" in political argument, I want first to consider the question of the theoretical hostility to rights as such since this has important theoretical and political ramifications, not least in providing some measure of justification to the critique from the right that socialists are not and cannot be committed to rights and their defense.

The theoretical objection to the discourse of rights has its roots in the extent to which rights are necessarily conceived as being given or assigned to "legal subjects," individuals as citizens, who exercise their proprietorial rights in relations with other legal subjects. The Soviet jurist Pashukanis insists that the very concept of the legal subject as possessor of rights is a direct consequence of the existence of commodity relations and provides the form for the resolution of conflicts between the parties to commodity relations. Even if Pashukanis is not followed in equating rights with the very existence of capitalist relations, objections to the language of rights remain. First, the consent of rights abstract from the socioeconomic relations within which people live and act, and in lifting them outside this reality it cloaks them with property in a right that they may exercise, through the institutions and procedures of law, against other individuals. Thus "rights" are seen as inherently *abstract*. Second, rights invoke the "legal subject," the atomized individual as citizen: thus rights are seen, not only as abstract, but as individualized.[15] Finally, rights either explicitly or implicitly refer to some view about the basic or fundamental character of people that provides grounds for giving priority to certain classes of claims as constituting rights; in other words the concept of rights is seen as invoking some ontological view of the character of the species, where different ontological views clash they express themselves by giving priority to different rights.[16] The general objection then is that the idea of rights involves some reference to the essence or universal nature of people.

For some or all of the above reasons, the left has exhibited a certain caution or reluctance in making use of the appeal to rights. Now the general power and persistence of the politics of rights has resulted in political activists not being too concerned about the philosophical problems of the slogans they use. But these intellectual concerns are not without importance precisely because the left, especially in its Marxist expressions, has generally been concerned with its theoretical rigour and consistency.

I will explore one theoretical attempt to purge "rights" of its abstract, individualized, and ontological features by considering Paul Hirst's essay "Law, Socialism and Rights" (Hirst 1980). He recognizes the political importance of rights and seeks to avoid the simple equation of rights within the bourgeois form of law (this is especially important to his argument that it is essential to reject notions of the withering away of law under socialism). Having considered the objections to the concept of rights, he proposes an alternative conception which is purged of these deficiencies. His alternative requires rights to be conceived as "specific capacities sanctioned by laws . . . they serve certain socially determined policy objectives and interests . . . they have no inherent unity or a single point of reference," and he suggests that "the composition of legislation must be discussed on grounds that go beyond existing rules of law," thus seeking to go beyond a narrowly positivist view of law to include, for example, reference to extra-legal considerations of the policy objectives embedded in statutes (Hirst 1980:104).[17]

The general formulation proposed by Paul Hirst is a view that insists that rights have no autonomous existence, they are created by legislation or law-making activity. Without entering too fully into the controversies of jurisprudence, it must be recognized that this position is open to major objection. Hirst's definition of rights as the creation of legislation requires us to accept that it is the legislature that determines what rights to create or to remove. Consider the following examples: (1) the government, in the wake of hostility to street demonstrations, proposes legislation banning all demonstrations and this is passed by the legislature; (2) a future parliament passes legislation, which in pursuit of a more egalitarian education removes the right of parents to exercise any choice in the school their children will attend. Forget whether we approve or disapprove of either piece of legislation, can we say that the extinction of the "right" in question will prevent political action in favor of "the right to demonstrate" or "parents right to choice." To insist, as Hirst does, that the only rights that can be said to exist are those present in current legislation is to view rights as being in the gift of the current political majority in the legislature. Yet the political reality is that rights are not coterminous with the content of legislation. The "right to demonstrate" or "the right to choice" will in an important sense be more active and powerful in the act of their repeal; it is a hostage to authoritarianism to insist that the legislative act can by itself extinguish the right in question. This should be particularly problematic for Hirst given his insistence, with which I concur, on the necessity of rights of opposition, criticism, etc., in socialist societies. The extinction of such rights through the practices of legal institutions in socialist states does not extinguish these "rights"; rather it makes more essential, as he himself argues, that the necessary institutions able to defend these rights and to restrict their violation be created within a socialist state with democratic aspirations.[18]

Hirst's attempt to tighten the definition of rights and to avoid the pitfalls of ontology and abstractness fail because of the inherent statism of the positivist position which he adopts. His conclusion largely negates the purpose of his own discussion, to take rights seriously in the context of a stress on the concreteness of law as an "instance of regulation" with respect to which definite struggles for and against particular policy objectives occur; in stressing the concreteness of legal regulation he ends by reducing law to the technical content of legal rules and procedures.

In developing a theory of rights it is necessary to make use of a concept of rights which explicitly spans both their legal form, as specifically created powers and capacities assigned to legal agents, and their character as expressions of particular social policy objectives. Thus we can distinguish between "legal rights" and "sociopolitical rights," but while insisting that this distinction embodies a continuity rather than a stark legal/nonlegal boundary. Thus "legal rights" designate not only the capacities created but also the policy objectives embodied in legislative form. This allows us, with reference to any particular area of law, to identify along a continuum legal capacities which are capable of giving full or satisfactory effect to social policy objectives. Using Hirst's own example of the Abortion Act 1967, we may study the degree to which the legal capacity conferred on women to seek an abortion is limited by the particular organization and procedures of medical services and of the legal statuses of doctors, charities, etc., and the relationship to an analysis of the policy objectives embodied in the 1967 Act. This type of analysis makes it possible to analyze areas of legislation where the capacities created are ineffective in securing policy objectives (e.g., race relations legislation, equal pay legislation etc.), but where the creation of the "right" is significant in lifting the policy objective to a higher level by virtue of its incorporation in legislation. Here we may note the significance of the role played in the politics of legislation by the symbolic dimension and of the role of secured social policy rights in effecting political mobilization for continuing struggles for implementation (Gusfield 1963; Carson 1974).

Outside the sphere of actual legal regulation "social rights" express social policy objectives and differentiate rights from mere claims, in that the appeal to rights facilitates the articulation of coherent grounds for the policy objective in terms of related sociopolitical conceptions. The existence of social rights is therefore not dependent on the content of legal provision; they are advanced as claims on the legal system and/ or on other agencies of decision.

The use of notions of legal and social rights can embrace both the specific consequence of designated legal capacities and at the same time can include the sociopolitical dimension. It allows theoretically important distinctions to be made while at the same time facilitating the expression of popular conceptions of rights. The left can and must abandon its ambivalence toward rights; they are a field of engagement between alternative social policies and political objectives, and are at the same time important sources of mobilization and for securing political advances (and defeats of course!).

THE POLITICS OF JUSTICE

The rhetoric of justice plays an important part in political struggles. Contending political forces articulate and justify their actions through appeals to justice and this in turn contributes to their capacity for political mobilization. The contemporary left exhibits an ambivalence toward justice, which needs to be explored. The right exhibits no such inhibitions or self-doubts and it has tended to secure a *de facto* monopoly of the banner of justice that has further reinforced the equivocal response of the left. I advocate a strategy that seeks to wrest from the right political slogans with important mobilizing capacity by breathing new substance and life into them, and integrating their present application with the political goals of socialism.

The hesitancy of the left toward justice has a number of dimensions. The first has its roots in the opposition of Marxism to any theory founded on the primacy of a moral doctrine, whether it be justice or any other ideological category.[19]

This tradition has had lasting reverberations in producing not an absence of political references to justice, but their use only at the most general and rhetorical level. The most characteristic form of this invocation of "justice" is as a condemnation of capitalist society as "unjust" and the sketching out of the possibility of the essential justice of future socialist society. The experience of "actual socialism" has in most sections of the left diminished the unproblematic juxtapositioning of the contrast between capitalism and socialism as that between injustice and justice. Rather the general thrust of argumentation tends frequently to seek other forms of expressing the opposition between capitalism and socialism. This caution is further reinforced by the long historical association of "justice" with liberal individualist theories to such an extent that the term has often become synonymous with this variant in liberal political and legal philosophy.

Before considering left interventions in discussion on justice and their political ramifications, some comments are necessary on the contemporary crisis of liberal theories of justice. At its center lies an increasing disillusionment with a narrow identification of justice with "procedural justice" or "legal justice." Procedural justice identifies the arena of justice as *internal* to legal systems and revolves around the primacy attached to the principle of "treating like cases alike," and its consequent individualization in the atomized environment of the legal action before a court. The heightened awareness of social inequality in all its diverse forms attacks the doctrine of "treating all alike" at its philosophical and political achilles heel.

In light of these debates, the recent adoption of the "justice model" (von Hirsch 1976) by several progressive trends is of considerable interest. It reflects a widespread dissatisfaction with existing, reformist and rehabilitary approaches to punishment. In calling, as a consciously progressive demand, for the readoption of the classical view that the only basis for punishment is that the offender's act "deserves" to be punished it is recognized that the reality of inequality poses a considerable difficulty. This difficulty concerns whether it can ever be just to punish the disadvantaged in an injust society. The force of this concern has tended to push the left toward an abstentionist position where it has been very close to opposition to punishment itself. I argue that the left must recognize the necessity of punishment in liberal democracies marked by substantial injustice, precisely in order to make possible political and legal challenges to the specific forms of injustice that characterize capitalist society. The specific objects for legal regulation are, of course, subject to detailed political argument and debate. But a socialist approach must deploy the demand for justice and, in the process, transform the content of justice itself.

Aside from the general left ambivalence concerning justice, there have been present over a long period of time associated ideas that, in a variety of combinations and emphases, demarcate a distinctive social-democratic theory of justice. A central organizing role is played by the objective of "equality," which is seen, not in opposition to liberty, but as a prior condition (Rawls 1971). This emphasis on equality is central to social-democratic conceptions of justice and it is substantially congruent with more radical versions of the liberal theory of justice, such as that presented by Ronald Dworkin (Dworkin 1978). The focus of equality avoids a direct commitment to a leveling egalitarianism; egalitarian objectives identified as the realization of social justice are seen as the cumulative result of the provision of equality of opportunity. These ideas are very closely linked to an insistence on the central role of the welfare state as operating in such a manner as to improve individual life chances freed of the vagaries inherent in the operation of the market economy. This conception of the role of the welfare state goes well beyond the much more restricted notion inherent in the tradition from the Poor Laws through to Beveridge where the objective is that of minimum provision. Concern with equality of opportunity focuses attention on such arenas as educational and health provision as positive arenas of compensatory activity. This thrust has, in the more recent period, been reinforced by the rise of wider fields of compensatory legislation, in particular concerning sex and race equality, and even more explicitly with the growth of positive discriminatory legislation (a trend that has been more important in the United States than in Britain).

There has also been a strong strand of utilitarian thought within the social democratic tradition of justice. The objective of the maximization of human wellbeing, when the majority are in major respects disadvantaged, gives rise to a concern with the aggregation of social benefit, that is with the sum total of benefits or advantages provided to the disadvantaged majority. Maximization through aggregation reveals the inherent tension within utilitarian thought and politics between individualism and collectivism. Social democratic views of justice exhibit a range of positions within this tension; in some instances justice is conceived as the provision of universal individual rights and benefits; in others it is more collectivist, arguing for the interests of the majority, and placing a lower priority on individual rights. The question of justice should sharpen our awareness of the problems generated by majoritarian democracy; it is this problematic area that has given rise to the assault on "elective despotism" from the right, but the problems posed in the relationship between majorities and minorities are central problems for all varieties of democratic roads to socialism.

A more radical strand to socialist politics of justice has been the demand for a "popular justice," which would dispense with the exercise of justice from above by the state or by professionalised judiciary. Popular justice is concerned with direct participation in the processes of social control with a minimum degree of procedural formalism. There has been an interest in the forms of popular participation developed, for example, in China and Cuba, and in the examination of the applicability of participatory politics of justice in prerevolutionary conditions, for example, developments in Portugal after 1974 (Santos 1979). The central concern has been with the potentialities of prefigurative legal politics, that is, with strategies designed to create some of the elements of the structures and practices of a socialist system of justice within the framework of capitalist society. Thompson's defence of the participatory character of the jury trial is in this sense prefigurative since it implies a goal of an extended popular participation in legal processes; so also are calls for a strengthening and democratisation in lay participation in the magistrates courts in Britain (Pearson 1980).

However, some problems concerning popular justice as prefigurative politics should be considered. The first is that, as de Sousa Santos' discussion of Portugal shows, such developments are possible only because of the generalized crisis of the legal system, or more widely, what he calls "the global situation of dual powerlessness" (Santos 1979:158). In stable capitalist democracies the degree of existing forms of popular participation is very limited (e.g., jury, lay magistrates, lay participation in tribunals, etc.) although these elements can, and indeed should, be defended. A more difficult task is posed in interventions in professionalised legal structures. The extent to which there is a general hostility to such structures and the opportunities they present, articulated most systematically by Bankowski and Mungham, has inhibited serious discussion of transformative possibilities (Bankowski and Mungham 1976). Attention has been focused, particularly through the law centers movement, on the provision of more effective legal services and representation *within* existing institutions. The general political conclusion must be that there are very limited opportunities for parallel popular justice, but that political attention needs to be focused on transforming and democratizing strategies.[21]

One final comment on the topic of popular justice concerns the question of "delegalization"; it is assumed in much of the literature that the complexity of law, in both its procedural and substantive form, is an inherent barrier to popular participation. There has therefore been a general assumption at work that posits the necessity of simplification and the introduction of broader criteria in the process of adjudication that dismantle the barriers between legal, moral, and political wrongs. The more important question is whether the abandonment of distinctions between legal, moral, and political is in principle desirable. Such an objective runs the risk of the reduction of all forms of social control to political control. The practices of "actual socialism" provide evidence of the dangerous consequences of that reduction. Retention of a distinctive form of legal regulation clearly separated from other regulatory processes is necessary if formal sanctions are to be applied since a degree of certainty, predictability, etc. seems to be an essential condition of civil liberty. Expansion of the arena of popular participatory social control should be clearly separated from processes of legal control, for example, through the express exclusion of most, if not all, the range of sanctions associated with legal systems. The range of fields of social control subject to legal regulation should be restricted, but this should be distinguished from a more general "delegalization" of the whole field of social control.

It is in the context of the discussion of the trends within both liberal and socialist traditions that the position adopted by E. P. Thompson in his discussion of the rule of law is all the more startling. At a time when the liberal theory of justice has become aware of the limitation of legal (or procedural) justice and there has been a widespread shift to concern to the problems of social justice, we find Thompson expressing commitment to the rule of law. It has not been sufficiently widely recognized that his is a surprisingly narrow view of the rule of law that equates it with adherence to procedural justice. These comments are made not to deny Thompson's conclusion but to point to the rather limited frame of reference that his intervention has stamped on the debate amongst socialists. This is reinforced by one important feature of the civil liberties response that focuses its concern primarily on what are perhaps most accurately identified as "political liberties." The positive feature of this in relation to the politics of justice is that it provides a potentially powerful intervention with respect to the relations between state and individual. It is a powerful alternative both to the statist tendencies of social democracy discussed above, but also against the prevailing judicial ideology, forcefully expressed by Hailsham, who poses the judiciary as the protective barrier between the leviathan of the modern state and the hapless individual, thus reproducing the same passivity as the statism that it opposes.

It seems clear that legal or procedural justice is not enough. The real problem is to achieve an integration of the wider socialist concern with social justice with the maintenance of legal justice. Justice is necessarily concerned with how particular persons are treated; this is equally true for questions of social justice since it is always concrete individuals or organizations (and never classes as such) that are involved. The challenge for the socialist politics of justice is to realize an integration of two rather separate and divorced traditions; this integration cannot proceed on the basis of simple conflation because at its root lies the importance of overcoming the contradiction between individualism and collectivism.

CONCLUSION

This chapter has examined a range of issues that are fundamental to the development of a socialist politics of law and justice. It has not been intended to arrive at specific policy suggestions on individual topics. Rather a major object has been to argue for these issues to make their proper place in the priorities of socialist politics. It has therefore been essential to examine those elements in current socialist responses that inhibit or prevent that development. It has also been a conscious intention to bring together a number of strands discussed in more specialist and academic forums and to make the issues more accessible to a wider audience. The central focus of the argument, the focus on "the politics of law," has been directed to advocating an interventionist strategy. Such a strategy rejects both the view that law is a technical field above and beyond politics and also the view that a general critique of capitalism is a sufficient basis for arriving at socialist analysis and socialist politics of law. In particular it has been important to examine in some detail the political problems inherent in what has been called the "class state–class law" position. The argument is that the prevalence of the unexamined political consequences constitutes a major inhibition to the development of a meaningful socialist intervention in this field. No such inhibition has affected the political right who have been successful over a long period of time, in achieving a virtual monopoly of the politics of law and justice. Even the considerable growth in recent years of socialist and radical work in criminology and the theory of law has, in the main, failed to realize a viable political position.

The reasons for this failure are complex and result from the interweaving of a wide range of positions which it is hoped to have gone some way towards identifying. The substance of this critique of left positions is threefold. The left has been widely influenced by an abstentionist position that has led it not to give political priority to significant areas of legal development that have played an important part in determining the character of the regulative framework of modern capitalist democracies.

Second, the left has often resorted to an oppositionism with fundamentally negative political results. A very important exemplification of this opposition is to be seen in the reaction of the left to the Royal Commission on Criminal Procedure. The left has been entirely correct in identifying the fundamental weakness of the Commission's proposals in its failure to address itself adequately to the question of "safeguards" against the abuse of police powers and its preparedness to rely on internal police organizational and disciplinary procedures. Yet the left has engaged in this purely negative or oppositional response that has its root in a very simple and obvious failure. None of the active left commentators, whether it be the Labour Party or the specialist bodies such as the NCCL or Legal Action Group (LAG), sees it as any part of their concern or responsibility to improve the effectiveness of policing. This failure ensures that their opponents are able to effectively marginalize the validity of the criticisms made. This attitude toward policing is a classic example of the abstentionism of the left; the effectiveness of policing is seen as someone else's problem, the left contents itself with problems of abuse of police powers, civil liberties, etc. Such a position is strategically incorrect and also tactically inept because, not only does it marginalize the important criticisms made, but it also leaves uncontested the view promulgated by the right and by the police themselves that an extension of police powers of arrest, search, detention, etc. are central to improving the effectiveness of policing. The result is that opposition to the extension of police powers is widely interpreted as opposition to effective policing.

The third general criticism of the left's positions is that they generally *deflect* from the immediate political issues posed in the politics of law towards a general critique of capitalism and assume that the development towards or the advent of socialism would resolve the problem. Popular concerns or anxieties are thus largely ignored and real social problems are identified as indexes of the evils of capitalism and not as a field for current action.

The really difficult problem for socialists is developing a political response which both addresses the immediate and pressing issues on the political agenda whilst at the same time making the connection with its contribution to kindling and mobilizing a perspective that things could be other than they are, that other forms of social organization and relations are both desirable and possible. There is no simple prescriptive solution, but one essential condition is largely absent, namely an awareness of this as a fundamental problem of socialist politics. Of themselves, neither immediate policies nor sustaining a vision of socialism are solutions to the questions posed.

The requirements of an interventionist politics of law require certain changes for the left which are likely to appear at first sight unpalatable: this unpalatability arises from the impossibility of an abstentionist or oppositionist position. Some of the more important examples have been touched upon. For example, a left politics concerned with issues of policing, sentencing and administration of punishment is an unavoidable necessity. The brief discussion of the justice model indicates that, although not without problems, it offers one framework within which socialist consideration of some of these issues can be developed, however much this may offend deeply embedded assumptions of hostility to punishment itself.

I have suggested that the notion of social responsibility provides a criterion for the evaluation of legal policies which can assist in identifying both political objectives and in specifying progressive legal principles. But it also provides a basis for political mobilization for specific objectives. It does carry the explicit recognition that it involves the struggle for social responsibility within capitalist social relations, not as an objective that is to be postponed to the future socialist society. It can be used not only to assess existing legal regulation, but also to determine alternative fields of legal regulation.

The principle of social responsibility provides also a potentially coherent basis for intervention in the politics of policing. It provides a basis not only for assessment of existing policing practices but also for mobilizing forms of popular and community participation in the broad field of social control and regulation. It may be that an alternative extra-institutional popular justice or direct community self-policing is not a political possibility within institutionally stable capitalist democracies. Yet it provides a basis for the development and mobilization around the content and direction of policing. In so doing it provides the basis for a perspective of transformation of both practices and institutions consistent with the requirements of pre-figurative politics.

Finally it has been a central strand of the argument that the extension of a socialist politics of law requires an entirely different and more rigorous approach to the question of rights and justices. We must contest the dismissal of those questions, which has been the main feature of the existing discussions. The widespread popular caution towards the left with respect to the content and form of its commitment to rights and to justice is not just a product of hostile anti-progressive propaganda. We must insist on the necessity of a politics of rights and justice which advances from the basis of existing bourgeois legality. This approach is certainly hostile to abolitionist attitudes on the left and argues that positions which express concern with 'transcending' bourgeois legality are not in fact political, or for that matter theoretical, solutions. Individual and collective rights and justice cannot be counterposed, nor should socialism elevate collectivism at the expense of individual rights. Rather what is needed is a struggle to transform the content of rights and the terms in which interests are identified and given priority.

We require an *extension* of existing rights in the course of which the content of rights and their priority is transformed. This does not imply that all individuals will accept and approve this transformation and indeed the very need for law and legal regulation lies precisely in the capacity to secure enforcement. This transformation is never one of a change from a capitalist to a socialist content for such a manner of assessing the content of particular rights or forms of justice has no meaning: there is no inherent political litmus test of socialist or capitalist content of rights or justice.

There will be a protracted struggle to secure political and legal legitimacy through concrete forms of legal regulation during the transition from and extension of bourgeois legality. Such a struggle is a necessary constituent of a socialist politics of law and justice consistent with an overriding political commitment to a democratic road to socialism.

CHAPTER 6

THE IDEOLOGY
OF LAW

INTRODUCTION

The application of the concept "ideology" to the analysis of law has been one of the distinctive features of the strand of critical legal studies that draws upon the Marxist tradition. My objectives in this chapter are

1. to situate the "ideological analysis of law" within contemporary Marxism,
2. to locate its relevance to the current concerns of the sociology of law and of critical legal studies,[1]
3. to explore the substantive contribution of work written under the imprint of "the ideological analysis of law" and to identify its major variants,
4. to show that theoretical and methodological clarification of both the components and scope of the ideological analysis of law is needed, and
5. to outline some elements of a theory of ideological analysis.

There is an extensive literature that refers variously to "the ideology of law," the "ideological dimension of law," or "legal ideology." Behind the apparent homogeneity of this writing lie diverse conceptions of ideology and even greater diversity in the way these conceptions are used. Its effects are regularly taken for granted when they should be treated as problematic, and its heuristic potential for the analysis of law is often thwarted by the vagueness and imprecision that one encounters in probing apparently sophisticated conceptualizations. "Ideology," like "dialectics," is all too often invoked as an evasion rather than a solution. If the concept of ideology is poorly used by many of those who write in the Marxist tradition, it is hardly used at all by those who approach the study of law from other perspectives. In the major texts on the sociology of law, both old and new, the concept "ideology" is noticeable by its absence. While no single concept provides a magic key to the mysteries of law, the idea of ideology is important in understanding legal life. There is no concept within the sociology of law that plays the role that is given to ideology within the Marxist tradition. Thus, the ideological analysis of law is not only significant in its own right, but it provides an instructive point of differentiation between Marxist analyses of law and mainstream sociology of law.

Perhaps the closest alternatives to "ideology" within mainstream sociology of law are the concepts "symbolic,"[2] as used by Gusfield (1963) and later by Carson (1974), and "legitimation," as used within the Weberian tradition (Weber 1966). Neither of these alternatives has, however, either the breadth or the specificity provided by the concept "ideology." If we aspire, as I do, to break what Trubek has aptly characterized as "the stifling debate between instrumental Marxism and liberal legalism" (Trubek 1977:553), we must explore the potential utility of the Marxist concept "ideology," not to show the superiority of one tradition over another but to advance the explanatory power of social theory in its application to the analysis of law.

MARXISM AND IDEOLOGY

We must, at the outset, recognize that a "correct definition of ideology cannot be discovered from a search of Marx's texts. Marx used the concept in a variety of ways. Sometimes ideology refers to all ideas, sometimes it refers only to those ideas that are deemed unscientific ("false consciousness"), and sometimes it refers to those ideas that serve the interests of dominant classes, "class beliefs" (cf. Williams 1977:66). Not only is the concept open in its texture, but it is also multidimensional. Nevertheless, there are a number of uses of the concept that must be eliminated because they make a definitional assumption about the relationship between "ideology" and "class."

My objective is to use the concept to explore the connection between ideas, attitudes, and beliefs, on the one hand, and economic and political interests, on the other. We can thus ignore ideology as "Ideology," which refers only to a systematic and totalized world view (*Weltanschauung*). Consistent world views may exist, but they must be treated as special or exceptional cases. Second, the idea that ideology necessarily entails some sort of "false consciousness" should also be discarded because it removes the empirically important issue of the association between ideas and interests. For similar reasons we should reject the view that ideology necessarily has a class designation or derivation. For example, the idea that "nationalism" is necessarily traceable to the interests of the "petty bourgeoisie" is empirically problematic and should be replaced by an approach that sees such connections as raising empirical rather than conceptual issues.

While the concept of ideology has often been misused in the ways described above, there have been important advances toward a theory of ideology in recent Marxist writing. The next step is to identify these advances and to relate them to the analysis of law as ideology.[3]

The concept of "ideology" has played a key role for Marxist theorists who make up the "Western Marxist" tradition that has sought to liberate Marxism from the ossification of orthodox "Marxism–Leninism." Central to this project has been the need to reformulate Marxist theory in a way that avoids the related deficiencies of "economism" and "reductionism." If social institutions and ideas are not a simple reflex of economic or class interests and yet are linked to such interests, a sophisticated concept of ideology is needed to explore such linkages in a thorough, empirically grounded manner.

It is thus no accident that the more recent development of a Marxist theory of law, a subject that had previously received little attention, should follow close on the heels of developments in Marxist theories of ideology. Law is interesting and important because it is both close to yet distinct from the state and is, at the same time, the bearer of important ideological values. Albrow characterizes the development within Marxist theory as a movement "from a Gramscian interest in politics to an Althusserian interest in ideology and finding in law a bridge between the two" (Albrow 1981:127).

The main thrust of the renewed concern with ideology has been directed towards elaborating a conception of ideology that plays more than the epiphenomenal or marginal role attributed to it within Marxism–Leninism. This goal reflects a political agenda that sees the need to grapple with the persistence of capitalism, while, at the same time, elaborating non-insurrectionary political strategies for socialist transformation within the advanced capitalist democracies. Theorists have realized that to do this ideology needs to be understood in its role of preserving and reproducing capitalist social and economic relations. While much of the debate has often taken an abstract and theoretical form, these real and pressing political concerns are very much present.

As an example of the recent developments in the theory of ideology, consider the use made of the concept of "relative autonomy." The term "relative autonomy" refers to the partial independence of different social elements, such as the legal, political, and ideological, both from each other and, more importantly, from the general interests of a dominant class. This concept serves the interests of the new Marxism because it acknowledges the fundamental importance of the economic base (albeit "in the last instance") while allowing the ideological realm to be treated as an arena of struggle that is not simply the reflex of economic class conflict. This places a heavy theoretical and political burden on the fragile shoulders of the concept, and despite the attractiveness of the idea of "relative autonomy" difficult theoretical problems remain. The primary problem is to achieve what Althusser (1969) described as the necessity of holding on to "both ends of the chain" at the same time; that is, to encompass both the relative autonomy of ideology (or law or state) and the determination of ideology (or law or state), in the last instance by economic relations. There are those within the Marxist tradition who argue that the concept "relative autonomy" cannot overcome such theoretical hurdles and that "there is no middle way (Cutler et al. 1977:I,172).

Nevertheless, some real and important advances have been made during the course of the debate on ideology. These achievements can best be illustrated if we look separately at three major issues that Marxist scholars have explored with the aid of the concept of ideology.

Ideology and Human Subjectivity

A major but insufficiently recognized thrust of the Althusserian tradition was to develop a theory that could at once accommodate the traditional socioeconomic concerns of Marxism and a concern for human subjectivity. While this results in some of the most difficult and opaque discussion in Marxist theory, one element is especially important for the analysis of law. The human being according to the Althusserian tradition has three "instances": as a biological being, as a "subject," and as a participant in social relations. For Althusser the "subject" is created by and through a range of different discourses. For example, political discourse produces the individual as "citizen," with its consequent images of atomized but equal citizens existing in a common relationship to the state. Legal discourse transforms both human beings and social entities; for example, corporations become "legal subjects." Legal subjects as the bearers of rights and duties are the primary constituents of the "form of law," which will figure large in my subsequent discussion. The creation of legal subjects involves the recognition of "the law" as the active "subject" that calls them into being. It is by transforming the human subject into a legal subject that law influences the way in which participants experience and perceive their relations with others. Thus, legal ideology provides a constituent of what Althusser called the "lived relation" of human actors (Althusser 1969:233). One important implication is that we are encouraged to view law not merely as an external mechanism of regulation but as a constituent of the way in which social relations are lived and experienced. This approach radically changes the role accorded ideology in social life. Ideology is perceived not as a form of consciousness, which is the conventional view, but as a constituent of the unconscious in which social relations are lived. Once this possibility is appreciated, we have in ideology a new and powerful tool for exploring the relationship between "the Law," legal subjects, and social relations.

The Determination of the Content of Ideology

Theorists have been concerned both with the generation of specific elements of ideology and with the patterning or structuring of these elements into more or less coherent and integrated systems that make it possible to employ the concept of "bourgeois legal ideology." Here my earlier rejection of the view that every ideological element has a necessary class designation is important. The class dimension of ideology is not an intrinsic property of words or concepts, but instead arises from the way in which ideological elements are combined and interrelated. Ideologies are not to be treated "as if they were political number plates worn by social classes on their backs" (Poulantzas 1973:202). Therborn expresses this particularly well:

> [i]deologies actually operate in a state of *disorder.* . . . ideologies operate, constantly being communicated, competing, clashing, affecting, drowning, and silencing one another in social processes of communication. (Therborn 1980:77,103)

Thus, an ideology is not a unitary entity. It draws its power from its ability to connect and combine diverse mental elements (concepts, ideas, etc.) into combinations that influence and structure the perception and cognition of social agents. Colin Sumner (1979) expresses something of this approach with his suggestion that ideologies act as grids which select, sort, order, and reorder the elements of thought. This view of ideology is particularly salutary in the field of legal analysis since it counsels us not to assume the coherence and consistency of legal discourse but to search out the resonances of the social, economic, and political struggles that reside behind the smooth surface of legal reasoning and judicial utterance.

The general thrust of the concern with the determination of ideology is the insistence that ideology is a social process that is realized in and through social relations. At the same time ideologies have their own distinctive characteristics, the most important of which are an internal discourse such that the elements of an ideology are not reducible to a mere reflection of economic or social relations. It is this internal dimension of an ideology that semiotics seeks to grasp through the concept of "sign" and its derivatives.

Functions of Ideology

The third important issue within the theory of ideology concerns the *functions of ideology*; attention is directed toward the role of ideology as an essential element in the process of legitimation and hence in the reproduction of the prevailing social relations. This concern is particularly pronounced in Poulantzas, who, building on Gramsci's metaphor of ideology as the "cement" of society, proposes the general thesis that: "Ideology, which slides into every level of the social structure, has the particular function of *cohesion*" (1973:207). Poulantzas is of special significance with regard to the ideology of law because his analysis leads him to the view that juridico-political ideology is the "dominant region" within the dominant ideology within capitalist modes of production. From this he concludes that in capitalist societies law fulfills "the key function of every dominant ideology: namely, that of cementing together the social formation under the aegis of the dominant class" (1978:88). I do not subscribe to the view that to speak of "function" is to lapse into functionalism; rather we must distinguish between function and functionalism and reject the latter. Functionalism assumes that there are necessary functions that must be fulfilled and then proceeds to search for the agency that realizes or fulfills each function. The deficiency of functionalism is that functions are reified. Their existence is assumed and all social practices and institutions must be classified in terms of them. Poulantzas' cement metaphor and his designation of the state as fulfilling "the particular function of constituting the factor of cohesion between the levels of a social formation" (1973:44) come perilously close to functionalism. This danger can be avoided if we treat the metaphor as an hypothesis about the *effectivity* of ideology. The concept *effectivity* seeks to draw attention to the effects or results of ideology while at the same time leaving open the issue of whether or the degree to which a possible function of ideology is fulfilled. Thus, with respect to law, we should abandon any a priori views about its integrative or legitimating functions and treat them as open questions relating to the specific effects or consequences of legal regulation and legal ideology.

Distinguishing among these three different issues within the theory of ideology allows us to identify the significant advances that have been achieved in the recent debate. But these advances have extracted their own price. The most important price has been that in order to establish the "specificity" (distinctive characteristics not reducible to the economic base) of ideology, the Althusserian tradition posited the existence of conceptually distinct "instances" of economic, political, and ideological practices. So pervasive has this tendency been that in many texts these conceptual distinctions are assumed to represent real separations. But there is no location inhabited by ideology; there is no realm of the ideological (Jones 1982). Nor are all social, political, and economic institutions necessarily associated with specific ideological practices. Much more helpful is Althusser's (1971) suggestion of a distinction between "sites" that "produce" ideology and those that "transmit" ideology. Certain institutions such as the media and the university are identified with the ideological realm because they both "produce" and "transmit" ideology, whereas schools, the family, sports, and the like are primarily transmitters of ideology. Applying this distinction to legal systems, we can immediately identify both the creation and dissemination of ideology and proceed to investigate the extent to which these two activities are separated.

A second deficiency within the theory of ideology is the persistence of the *reflection* metaphor, by which I mean the persistent assumption that there exists an objective social world that is "reflected" in thought and in the process is to a greater or lesser extent distorted. This metaphor is ubiquitous as a means of asserting the determination of ideology by material relations and of expressing the divergence between a "real concrete"—that is, some objective ideology-free reality—and its representation in ideology. This imports a dubious epistemology derived from naive materialism. More significantly, the metaphor has its own logic, which leads to notions of ideological "distortion" or, more seriously, "inversion" of the real world. Thus, ideologies are discussed in terms of their truth or falsity, which implies that there is a social reality independent of consciousness and that thought simply corresponds to a greater or lesser extent to this given reality. The dubious nature of the implication is never confronted. While the idea of "reflection" raises the question of how ideology is determined, it does not provide any assistance in pursuing this line of inquiry. As Stuart Hall and his colleagues comment:

> As is often the case in those areas where Marxism is not yet fully developed, the simple formulae are often too simple, too reductive for our purposes. The idea for example, that, broadly speaking, legal norms and rules in a bourgeois society will reflect and support bourgeois economic relations, . . . may provide the first, basic step in such a theory, but it remains, too general, too abstract, too reductive, too sketchy. (Hall et al. 1978:196)

The most important figure in the development of the theory of ideology has been Antonio Gramsci. He has profoundly influenced not only the questions asked but also the general direction of contemporary Marxist discussions. In particular, Gramsci's concern with "hegemony," the processes through which the dominance of capitalist power is secured within civil society, provides both the theoretical and political framework for the ongoing Marxist debate. The issues raised by the idea of "hegemony" go to the very heart of the problems facing the Marxist analysis of law in that this concept poses as a central issue the dialectic of coercion and consent.

The earliest Marxist writings on law, which I have characterized as the "oppositional stage," sought to combat conventional notions of the consensual character of law and strove to demonstrate its repressive or coercive character. In contrast, most contemporary Marxist writings on law have sought to demonstrate and explore the real significance and deep consequences of the dual character of law as coercion and as consent. Not only is this attempt to grasp and to integrate the elements of coercion and consent a central *leitmotif* of Marxist legal theory but, as I have argued elsewhere, its theorization presents major problems. Moreover, if my argument is correct, the same difficulties are encountered by the non-Marxist sociology of law.

THE IDEOLOGICAL DIMENSIONS OF LAW

A concern with the ideology of law is at the heart of all recent Marxist treatments of law. In this section, I shall examine some of this recent theoretical work in the light of the preceding discussion. I hope to show how some of the ideas advanced above have been fruitfully employed, and I shall point to a number of unproductive features that remain. There has, however, been such an explosion of Marxist, neo-Marxist, and critical theory of law over the past few years that I am forced to be selective. I will concentrate my attention primarily on four recent texts.

These are *The Politics of Law* (Kairys 1982), which is especially significant as the first collective presentation of the Critical Legal Studies movement; *Marxism and Law* (Beirne and Quinney 1982), a collection that brings together some of the more important of the previously published contributions to Marxist debate on law; *Reading Ideologies* (Sumner 1979), which is the most closely related to my concerns because it focuses on the applicability of the Marxist theory of ideology to the analysis of law; and *Marxism and Law* (Collins 1982), which sets out to examine the total theoretical field and gives the relationship between law and ideology a crucial role in the attempt to set forth a general Marxist theory of law. As we shall see, a number of the problems that arise are common to all the texts, which in itself suggests the importance of the issues under consideration.

Mystification, Distortion, and All That

The most general feature of ideological analysis is that it starts from the proposition that there is no direct or necessary correspondence between the realm of "knowledge" and that of "the real." As I have already noted, the most pervasive embodiment of the theory of ideology in Marxism is to be found in the metaphor of "reflection." The merit of the metaphor is that it succeeds in combining two central propositions: (1) the known and the real are not identical, and (2) the real is the "object" that produces or determines the "image." The metaphor of reflection captures the most basic feature of Marx's materialist dictum: "It is not the consciousness of men that determines their being, but on the contrary their social being that determines their consciousness" (Marx "1859 Preface"). It is thus not surprising that the metaphor of "reflection" and its derivatives are frequently invoked.

In all four of the texts under discussion a reflection theory of ideology is a dominant motif. The linguistic variants are many, but the most frequently employed are: "mirrors," "distorts," "illusion," "fantasy," "facade," "mystifies," and "reifies." The problem that I wish to highlight is that these terms are used in such a way as to imply a theory about the relationship between knowledge and its object, a taken-for-granted "social reality." Propositions such as "law distorts" and "law reflects" are used as if there were some pregiven relationship between the real and its ideological representation. The alternative I propose is that the nature of the relationship between reality and its ideological representation should be seen as "the problem," or object of analysis, without prejudgment as to the way in which the relationship can be captured or portrayed.

For an example of the limitations of reflection theory, consider the essay in Kairys' collection by Nadine Taub and Elizabeth Schneider (1982) on the role of law in the subordination of women. Taub and Schneider argue that the legal distinction between public and private reflects, in a distorted fashion, an actual distinction between the nondomestic and domestic social realms. In so doing the legal distinction functions ideologically and "camouflages the fundamental injustice of existing sexual relations" (1982:124). This readiness to attribute causality to the legal distinction between public-private leads Taub and Schneider to ignore the question of whether this distortion results from legal ideology or from some other mechanism. For example, no consideration is given to the role of other discourses concerning the family—thus precluding, without discussion, the possibility that the law is largely passive and merely gives effect to an ideological separation between public–private that is produced elsewhere.[4] Now I do not hold any strong view about whether this is the case, but I do wish to suggest that the metaphor of reflection distracts attention from such issues and for that reason should not be invoked as if it were a conclusion.

In contrast, the essay by Peter Gabel on reification in Beirne and Quinney examines the process of legal reasoning in great detail and concludes that "reification" is a result determined by the process rather than a pregiven necessity (Gabel, 1982)[5] In the course of this analysis Gabel makes the important point that we need to distinguish between (1) the processes that create the ideological characteristics embedded in the law and (2) those consequences flowing from law that have a particular ideological content. With this in mind, we can see a hitherto unrevealed distinction in the usages "mirrors," "distorts," etc., which are often used interchangeably. Some terms (e.g., mirrors, reflects, reifies) have as their primary referent the process by which the "real" is transformed into an ideological form (see, eg., Gabel and Feinman 1982) while others (e.g., mystifies, illusion) focus on the results or consequences of the ideological form (see, e.g., Kennedy 1982). Ideological analysis should separate, as distinct methodological and expository stages, the analysis of the production of legal ideology from the analysis of the effectivity of legal ideology.[6]

The Form of Law

It is generally agreed that the ideological character of law can be identified at a number of different levels. I shall specify, at least provisionally, three different levels for analysis since this allows me to explore the interrelationship among them. They are

1. the ideological content of concrete legal norms;
2. the ideological content of what are conventionally referred to, most explicitly by Dworkin (1978), as "principles";
3. the ideological content of the "form of law."

At the core of any attempt to understand ideology is the question of its material determination. Distinguishing these levels allows me to address the important question of whether legal ideology is primarily the resultant of one of them. There is an unexplored and perhaps unconscious polarization in the texts under consideration. It is possible to identify two broadly distinguishable positions.

The first I call *Concrete Determination*. This position argues that the ideological content of law is largely manifest in the content of specific laws, whether judicial rules or specific legislative enactments. This position emphasizes the role of "struggle" in the formation of legal ideology.

The second I call *Form Determination*. This perspective sees in the form of law the key to law's ideological role. The concrete level gives effect to the necessary and inescapably general ideological content inscribed in the form of law.

Frequently, the position taken by an author arises naturally from the object of analysis: where the object of analysis is concrete, as with a specific statute or series of cases, the discussion tends to focus on concrete determination (Kairys 1982a; Horwitz 1982; Tushnet 1982; Klare 1982a; Freeman 1982). Where the interest is at a more general theoretical level, form determination comes to the fore (Gabel and Feinman 1982; Picciotto 1978; Poulantzas 1978; Rifkin 1982). But this is not a simple empirical versus theoretical divide; some of the most powerful work operates at all three levels (Klare 1982b; Hay 1977).

The distinction among the three levels of analysis not only involves important theoretical questions, but it is also related to political differences and debates. Marxists perennially argue over the extent to which law can be harnessed and mobilized to the advantage of subordinate classes or groups, a question that Collins appropriately calls "the radical predicament" (Collins 1982:Ch. 6). Those who give priority to form analysis typically deny that the bourgeois form of law can contribute much, apart from defense, to struggles against the capitalist order. As Mark Tushnet puts it, the form of law "serves as an additional barrier to the organisation of the under-dog to upset existing social arrangements" (Tushnet 1977:102). On the other hand, those who focus their attention on concrete determination tend to see particular legal outcomes as the results of struggles that depend on the balance of forces involved. This issue is at the heart of the important current controversies concerning the "politics of law." There is significant disagreement among "progressives" about the extent to which struggles over the creation and enforcement of legal rights are politically significant and potentially worthwhile. These questions are currently being raised in the internal debates within the Conference on Critical Legal Studies (Hutchinson and Monahan 1984; Munger and Seron 1984; Sparer 1984; Trubek 1984), and they continue to be debated in Britain under the insistent prodding of E.P. Thompson (1975, 1980; see also Adlam et al. 1981; Hunt 1981a).

Leaving aside these broader political questions, I want to focus attention on questions concerning the form of law. An emphasis on the form of law is attractive in that it provides an escape route from the difficulties of instrumentalist versions of Marxist theory, which focus on the law as an instrument of the will of the dominant class. The form of law is seen not as a manifestation of the will of a dominant class but as a necessary and inevitable consequence of the very nature of capitalist economic relations. Hugh Collins (1982) suggests that there exist economistic and class instrumentalist versions of the theory. In my view both the "economistic" and "instrumentalist" trends are inherent within classical Marxism, and they come to the fore with the ossification of orthodox Marxism. The common problem of both variants is that of "reductionism"; the difference is that class instrumentalism merely adds another step in the reductive logic since class relations are treated as directly derivable from and so reducible to economic relations.

The discussion of the form of law in recent Marxist literature is heavily influenced by the renewed interest in the writing of the early Soviet jurist Evgeny Pashukanis (Beirne and Sharlet 1980). Pashukanis' influence has focused discussion on the question of whether a *single* form of law is characteristic of capitalist society (cf. Balbus 1977; Redhead 1978; Hirst 1979; Cotterrell 1980, 1981; Warrington 1981; Picciotto 1979). This discussion has typically proceeded at a high level of abstraction, concerning itself with the general and abstract capitalist mode of production rather than with the situation in actual capitalist societies. Analysis at this level views capitalism as a simple totality of exchange relations and leads to the identification of a single form of law, the bourgeois legal form.

If, however, the level of analysis is changed and we focus our attention on concrete social formations (that is, historically given societies), we need to identify more than a single form of law. Capitalism has undergone massive changes and development. It exists within widely different political and state structures, and its internationalization has profoundly affected the relations among nation states. While mainstream sociology of law has for some time been concerned with the phenomenon of legal pluralism (Galanter 1981), Marxist writers have only more recently paid serious attention to this question (Fitzpatrick 1983). As David Sugarman argues, studies of the contribution of law to the development of capitalism, from Weber (1966) through E.P. Thompson (1975), Atiyah (1979), Horwitz (1977), and others, can lead only to the conclusion that

> there was no single "capitalist" form of law—whether we call it contractual, commodity form or absolute private property. It is more accurate to view each as one of several *forms* of capitalist law which co-existed over long periods, complementing and conflicting with one another. (Sugarman 1983:256)

What remains to be done is to identify systematically the various forms of law and to study the general conditions affecting their interaction.

However, the general trend in the texts we are treating as representative of recent critical and Marxist scholarship is either to assume a simple, single form of law or to slip between the singular and plural. The apparently sophisticated concept "the form of law" tends to be invoked as a rhetorical device that points to some underlying uniformity of legal phenomena that remains unexplored. When the form of law is identified, it is by reference to general values or what Balbus calls "abstract universals" (Balbus 1977:580). But in listing abstract universals, the distinction between form and content becomes blurred. If the concept of "legal form" or "forms of law" is to advance our understanding of the relationship between law and economy, there is an urgent need for conceptual clarification.

My proposals in this regard are modest. I suggest that when we restrict the concept "form of law" at a high level of abstraction to denote the logically necessary characteristics of a legal order within a specified economic or political order, this makes it possible and, indeed, necessary to address the co-existence of forms of law when analyzing specific societies. With regard to law in capitalist societies, the form of law is characterized by (1) "reification" (separation of the juridico-political realms from the economic), (2) legal subjectivity (separation of legal status from political or economic status), and (3) the legal subject (a human or organizational entity vested with legal rights) (Hirst 1979).

I also believe that the form of law has no *necessary* ideological characteristic or content. Instead, certain ideological values have, to borrow Weber's idea, an elective affinity or homologous relationship to the legal form. Hence, values such as individualism, equality, and private property become universal and preponderant values under capitalism and come to function as if they were the form of law itself. The close association between the concept of law and these values means that these values come to legitimate the existing forms of social relationships. Thus, the legitimating potential of law is shared or taken over by values the law only contingently embraces.

I have not included in my definition of "the form of law" the much emphasized element of "formalism." I am uncertain whether formalism inheres in the form of law or is an ideological value preponderantly associated with law in capitalist society. This uncertainty derives from my reflections on Horwitz's work. What Horwitz brings out most powerfully is the essentially contested character of formalism, a contest between impersonal Weberian legal rationality and the class facilitative character of the transformation of American law (Horwitz 1975, 1977).

Treating legal formalism as a problematic feature of the legal form has the virtues of not universalizing the ideological values most characteristic of law in capitalist society and of directing attention to struggles that surround all ideological elements. This approach reminds us that the most pervasive values that may be subsumed under the label "ideological forms of law" (universality, certainty, etc.) are subject to contradiction and interact in complex ways in the course of legal disputes. My approach also reflects reservations I have about following the idealist methodology of starting with legal values and subsequently comparing them to "reality." The viability of this position depends on the questionable assumption that legal values have an existence independent of the concrete legal rules in which they are embedded.

The foregoing analysis of the form of law throws into relief an important problem which I wish to mention but do not have the space here to pursue. The "discovery" of the ideological dimension of law by the Marxist and critical traditions tends towards a conceptualization of law itself as an *ideological phenomenon*. The danger is obvious: the materiality of the law—that is to say, law's real impact on real people and real relations—tends to be ignored. In seeking to establish the extent to which all social practices are suffused by ideology, we must not lose sight, to paraphrase Marx, of "the dull compulsion" of legal regulation, particularly in the spheres where law operates relatively unproblematically to give effect to the existing forms of social, economic, and political relations. If we are to grapple with real world problems, we must not retreat into idealistic theories of ideological determination.

The Function and Effectivity of Legal Ideology

One of the most distinctive features of the contemporary Marxist and critical trends is the powerful historical scholarship that has been its most notable achievement to date. In Britain there has been the major impact of the project that produced *Whigs and Hunters* and *Albion's Fatal Tree* (Thompson 1975; Hay et al. 1975) and *Policing the Crisis*, a "contemporary history" study of the "mugging crisis" of 1972–73 (Hall et al. 1978). The latter work is of particular interest because of its self-conscious attempt to integrate theoretical and historical analysis. And in the United States there has been a similar interest in revisionist legal history, spearheaded by Morton Horwitz. These critical legal histories share a common concern with the effectivity of legal ideology as it operates in conjunction with the material and coercive instrumentality of law. Douglas Hay's powerful analysis of the combined impact of "justice," "terror," and "mercy" is a good example of work that focuses on this conjunction (Hay 1982).

The two most important strands present in this tradition are best characterized by the distinction between "function" and "effectivity." Attention to "function" yields formulations of a general theoretical character about the role of legal ideology at the level of either the abstract modes of production (e.g., Althusser's "ideology secures the reproduction of the social relations of production," 1971:141) or, more concretely, with respect to historical epochs (e.g., Poulantzas' "juridical ideology written into law becomes the dominant area of ideology in a mode of production in which ideology no longer plays the dominant role," 1978:88). A concern for "effectivity," on the other hand, leads to a focus on the causal role of legal ideology in specific historical circumstances; e.g., Klare's (1982a) study of the influence of judicial ideology on the formation of labor relations in the United States before World War II.

The distinction between "function" and "effectivity" rarely appears in pure form. Instead, we frequently find either an oscillation between these foci of inquiry or a conflation of the two levels. This is unfortunate. In the analysis of legal ideology one must keep firmly in mind the different *levels of abstraction* of these relate but distinguishable perspectives. Thus, it is perfectly proper to treat a possible function of legal ideology as an hypothesis to be evaluated through concrete historical investigation and discarded, amended, or qualified in the movement from one level of abstraction to another. It is a mistake, however, to treat a possible function of law as given or proven and to use history to "reveal" the operation of this essential or assumed function. It is equally unacceptable to arrive through concrete historical analysis at a conclusion concerning the effectivity of legal ideology and then to pronounce this a "function" fulfilled by law during a particular historical epoch.

As an illustration of the second of these questionable procedures, consider E.P. Thompson's thesis that "the rule of law itself, the imposing of effective inhibitions upon power and the defence of the citizen from power's all-intrusive claims, seems to me to be an unqualified human good" (Thompson 1975:266). Thompson arrives at this conclusion from his compelling study of "The Black Act" of 1723. The act itself and its enforcement are interpreted as a conflict between the "new" landowning Whig gentry and the customary rights of farmers and forest-dwellers. Thompson demonstrates that in the period after the 1688 constitutional "revolution," when the structures and supports for the legal order were still weak, the rule of law had a significant impact on the manner in which this draconian legislation was enforced. But Thompson moves, without further argument, from his historically specific study to a generalization about the function of legal ideology in modern capitalist society.[7] I have considerably sympathy with Thompson's insistence on the contemporary significance of the rule of law, but not with the means by which he arrives at it, for Thompson ignores important differences in levels of analysis.

Having clarified the different levels of analysis involved in the distinction between "function" and "effectivity," we need to consider the risks inherent in functionalist modes of analysis. One such danger is the temptation to lapse into a naive instrumentalism which posits a single dominating function expressed, for example, in theses such as "law reproduces the social relations of capitalist society" or "law legitimates capitalist social relations." Such single function theses are themselves attributable to the ideological reification of law. In such theories law is presented as "the Law" and is discussed as if it were a totally coherent and integrated process. A valuable corrective against tendencies to see law in this way is found in modern Marxist and critical legal theory: the idea of "contradiction." This concept focuses attention on the limits of doctrinal coherence and on the variable operation of different legal procedures and institutions.

One of the most important contributions of radical legal historiography has been to breathe life and substance into the abstract category of "contradiction." At the outset this enterprise involves distinguishing between *internal* and *external* contradictions. The shift to a more empirical level of analysis, one of the hallmarks of the Critical Legal Studies movement, has allowed scholars to highlight the contradictory character of legal development; and it has helped them to avoid the pitfalls of instrumentalism. There is, however, a tendency within critical studies to focus one-sidedly on either internal or external contradictions. Thus, some work that examines doctrinal development stresses its internal incoherence while another strand emphasizes contradictions arising from the interplay of classes, class fractions, and other social and political forces as they struggle over the creation and practice of law. Both strands of research could be improved if they worked with a more systematic model of internal and external contradictions.

This is not the place to develop such a model, but I want to mention three considerations. First, with respect to both internal and external contradictions different "levels" need to be distinguished. Looking at internal contradictions, for example, we can distinguish among: (1) juridical reasoning and its ideological forms, (2) the ideologies embodied in the policy aspects of doctrine, (3) different legal institutions (e.g., types of courts), and (4) the professional ideologies of different kinds of legal actors. Such distinctions involve no profound theoretical insights, but they do provide a checklist of the sources and forces involved in the ideological determination of law. Second, the internal and external dimensions of legal ideology are not watertight compartments, and the interface between the two is a significant location of contradiction. Models of internal and external contradictions must take this into account and allow for some permeability. Finally, I would stress the practical significance for intervention in the politics of law of a careful analysis of contradictions since these pinpoint areas in which the subordinate classes have their greatest potential for effecting change. This speaks to the political importance of the model-building enterprise rather than to how it should be done.

Thinking about contradictions highlights problems with two widespread features of contemporary Marxist writings. The first is a tendency to overemphasize the independence or autonomy of the internal ideology of law. A clear example is found in Karl Klare's conclusion from his study of the Wagner Act that law-making because of the impersonal, antiparticipatory, suprahistorical forms of thought and procedures involved "is governed by the process of alienation" (1982a:168). This analysis does not give due weight to the pressures and contradictions that constantly press on the judicial process and disrupt the calm of formal judicial logic in ways that Klare's substantive analysis demonstrates. I also question the conclusions that Klare draws from this line of argument. His preferred alternative requires a "quest for justice in each concrete historical setting" and the abolition of the rule of law (1982a:168). In my view the call for individualized justice is not self-evidently a progressive demand. I remain convinced that the most important lesson for legal politics that may be drawn from our experience of "actual socialism" in the Soviet Union and other states is the necessity of retaining formalized and entrenched rights, the core of the rule of law, to protect citizens and social institutions against political usurpation by the state and the bureaucracy.

The second feature of the recent critical literature that my analysis calls into question is what I see as an overemphasis on the autonomy of the general ideological function of law, variously expressed by the legitimating or hegemonic function. Let me take as my example Colin Sumner. His analysis is in many respects parallel to the position I have advanced, but I believe he overstates the general function of legal ideology. "The Law," he argues,

> lies hidden beneath a heavy shroud of discourse, ritual and magic which proclaim the Wisdom and Justice of the Law. . . . Once this shroud is torn into tatters that hegemonic bloc of classes and class fractions which sustain the rule of capital is in trouble because inequality and domination can *only* be justified mystically and that is precisely the ideological function of law. (Sumner 1979:277; emphasis added)

Now if the ideology of "The Law" is as effective as Sumner suggests, it is difficult to imagine how this shroud could ever be "torn into tatters"; this is a case of pure verbal militancy. More important is the contention that legal ideology provides the *primary* justification for inequality and domination. This is, in my view, quite simply wrong. Capitalist systems employ a wide range of ideological justifications which are used (1) differentially over time and (2) in different combinations. These include such important legitimating ideas as "economic efficiency," "freedom," "democracy," and "national interest." The significance of legal ideology lies in its articulation along with other nonlegal ideological bases of legitimation. This point is made by Sumner but then seemingly forgotten.

> The effectiveness of law as an ideological force, as a means toward ruling class hegemony, depends upon its ideological

encapsulation of a consensus *constructed outside itself* in other economic, political and cultural practices. (Sumner 1979:264; emphasis added)

This point is nicely illustrated in *Policing the Crisis* (Hall et al. 1978). The authors show that it was the combination of legal ideology with other elements, including appeals to moral consensus, the nation, and ethnicity, that made the shift to a more authoritarian mode of governance possible. While it is appropriate to stress the importance of legal ideology in contemporary capitalism, we must avoid any tendency to think that law is the only structure other than naked violence that props up the capitalist social order. It follows that our analysis of legal ideology, and its relationship to the production and reproduction of hegemony, must pay close attention to the way legal ideology is articulated in conjunction with economic, political, and cultural ideologies.

CONCLUSION

Martin Albrow in a perceptive but critical review of recent Marxist texts on law expressed doubt as to whether "a general critique of law as ideology can lead into the scientific study of social relations underpinning and generating law, i.e., the sociology of law" (Albrow 1981:127). I hope that the above discussion has gone some way to demonstrate that Albrow is both right and wrong. He is right in castigating a "*general* critique of law as ideology," but he is wrong in suggesting that the investigation of legal ideology cannot contribute substantially to the sociology of law.

Ideology is and will remain a difficult, slippery, and ambiguous concept, and there is little to be gained by searching for a "better" definition. Problems cannot be avoided, for ideology involves issues that go to the heart of the puzzling interrelationship between human subjectivity and social action. Yet, handled with care, the concept "ideology" provides an indispensable and irreplaceable tool of analysis.

If the potential utility of the concept is to be realized, it is necessary that we attend closely to two separate but related sets of distinctions. The first is between the concrete particular and the concrete totality. The transition from one to the other is not a movement from micro to macro levels. This can be illustrated by taking, for example, the methodology involved in the study of a piece of legislation. The concrete particular focuses attention on the immediate or proximate influences, for example, doctrinal developments in that area of law, the particular "problem" addressed by the legislators, or the internal dynamics of the commission or inquiry proposing legislative action. The concrete totality retains the focus upon the legislation itself but seeks to situate that process in the context of wider economic, social, or political determinants. Understanding the relationship between the particular and the totality requires attention to the existence of distinct levels within the legal framework. We need to distinguish, for example, between the ideological elements present in the substance of the legislation, the legal form in which legislation is cast, and the way in which the form and substance of the law relate to the dominant ideological features of the legal system. These levels within the legal system are in turn related to the different levels of social relations, which means that the next step is to investigate the connections between "legal relations," on one hand, and "social relations," on the other. This involves turning our attention from the specific sets of social relations affected by the projected legislation to broader social forces rooted in economic, political, and other practices and to institutions that affect the creation and application of the legislation.

The second set of distinctions that must be maintained is between more abstract and more concrete conceptualizations. The need to distinguish between levels of abstraction is a theme found both in Marx's own methodological writings (Carver 1976) and in the recent methodological debate (Echeverria 1978; Sayer 1979). What follows from this distinction is that concepts must be appropriate to different levels of abstraction. This implies that the unitary conceptions of the "form of law" derived from an abstract conception of the commodity relation are poorly suited to the analysis of the "forms of law" within historically specific legal systems. More generally, when the object of investigation is a specific legal system, more concrete concepts are needed than those that can be derived from an examination of the relationship among economic, political, and ideological practices at the abstract level of "the capitalist mode of production."

The implications of these two sets of distinctions underline one general theme of this chapter: namely, that the ideological analysis of law must be understood as operating at a number of different levels, and that these different levels are both conceptual and empirical.

Colin Sumner suggests a distinction between "ideology" as basic or simple elements and "ideological formations" as complex systematizations of ideologies (Sumner 1979:20). I suggest that we can improve upon this scheme if we define "ideological elements" as the constituents of any text or speech act (for example, a legal norm or judicial pronouncement) but depart from Sumner by insisting that these elements are far from "basic" or "simple." Despite their apparent protean quality they involve already complex determinations. Ideology has no primary units or building blocks, for concepts do not themselves have any necessary ideological content; this is only acquired as they are employed in specific discourses. From this it follows that no word, however sensitive and emotive its connotations, has any necessary class content or implication; "equality," "fairness," "democracy," and the other key verbal labels only acquire ideological characteristics in their use.

I would retain Sumner's term "ideological formation" for those phenomena that link different ideological elements. This use allows for inconsistences and tensions within legal discourse but does not assume any necessary systematization. In a legal system the degree of systematization is an issue for empirical inquiry. Additionally, I suggest the term "ideological form of law" to designate configurations of ideological elements where there has been conscious systematization.

The distinctions that the three concepts defined above allow have a significance with regard to legal phenomena which we can illustrate by contrasting a simple conversation with the judgment of an appellate court. While the former will consist of "elements of ideology," the appellate judgment may either involve an "ideological formation" linking discrete elements or may achieve a more rigorous systematization as "an ideological form of law." This makes the "reading" of legal ideology more complex. In my view it restricts the applicability of semiotic analysis, with its emphasis on discourses reducible to primary units of "signs," because in judicial discourse there is already present a more complex structure derived from the modes of legal reasoning.

The second implication of my classification of legal ideology is that we must be wary of assuming a single function derived from an analysis of the form of law at a high level of abstraction. This means that we should not uncritically accept as proven conceptions of the legal order that seek to identify it in essence as a locus of such phenomena as "mystification," "legitimation," or "alienation." Rather, it is likely that research will disclose a considerable degree of variation in the function and effectivity of different types of legal practice.

The advance of Marxist and critical analyses of law which has been characterized by a special interest in ideological analysis has had a dual impetus. On the one hand, there has been a growing dissatisfaction with the methods and results of traditional legal scholarship and education. On the other hand, there has been a growing consciousness of the need to overcome the limitations and weaknesses of instrumentalist versions of Marxist theory. But the invocation of the concept "ideology" has in its turn necessitated a deepening awareness of both the pitfalls and potential of ideological analysis. This chapter has been directed to an exploration of some problems posed by the use of this concept and to advancing some suggestions for the further development of ideological analysis. In it I have tried to stress the need for a greater theoretical self-consciousness in employing the concept of ideology and at the same time to underline the general shift in critical and Marxist studies towards a more concrete historical and empirical analysis of law.

Finally, to avoid any possible misunderstanding of the nature of my current project, I should acknowledge the importance of issues that I have not discussed. I have had nothing to say about the important questions associated with the investigation of the material or social determination of law and legal relations. Nor have I concerned myself with the other side of the same problem: the extent to which law and legal regulation are themselves constitutive of social and economic relations. The omission of these questions should not be read as denying their importance in the analysis of law. The issues involved in the harnessing of the concept "ideology" to the analysis of law are themselves of sufficient importance to merit the specific focus of this chapter.

CHAPTER 7

THE THEORY
OF CRITICAL
LEGAL STUDIES

"If we, dear, know we know no more
Than they about the law,
If I no more than you
Know what we should and should not do
Except that all agree
Gladly or miserably
That the law is"

(W.H. Auden "Law Like Love," 1976)

A PROGRESSIVE INTERVENTION

Critical legal studies is the first movement in legal theory and legal scholarship in the United States to have espoused a committed Left political stance and perspective.[1] A left-wing academic trend of considerable breadth in the field of law is in itself worthy of attention, but one that has assumed an organized form and has already made a marked impact loudly demands careful scrutiny.

The emergence and growth of the Conference on Critical Legal Studies (CCLS) is to be warmly welcomed. It raises the prospect of generating an impact on legal scholarship that outreaches the impact of Realism in the 1920s and 1930s. It also has the potential of forcing itself on the calm and untroubled world of legal scholarship in such a way as to require the latter to engage in a thoroughgoing debate about the nature and direction of legal scholarship and education.

This chapter sets out to assess the significance and import of the critical legal studies movement. It seeks to do this not by standing aside from the commitment of the movement but adopts and supports its partisanship. The approach adopted is one of committed support for the goals of the critical project; where I am critical I am motivated by a desire to further and advance what is not only a powerful challenge to orthodox scholarship but one whose greatest significance lies in its presentation of an identifiable alternative; an alternative which is not only within legal scholarship but which at the same time has much to say about the politics of law and, more broadly, about the shape and character of a future alternative society.

The critical legal studies movement is too young to require a writing of its intellectual and political history.[2] The present objective will be to identify the distinguishing features of the movement paying special attention to its theory and methodology. The focus on theory and methodology imports an assumption, which should be made explicit, that the long-term viability of the movement and the potential for its application to the politics of law depend on its attaining and sustaining a degree of theoretical and methodology coherence.[3]

The critical legal studies movement in the United States exhibits both homogeneity and diversity. Its homogeneity arises from the distinctiveness and visibility that results from the organization linkages provided by the existence of the Conference on Critical Legal Studies (CCLS). Most critical authors publicize CCLS by carrying an opening footnote which mentions the existence of the CCLS and gives a contact name and address. Conference members display their connectedness rather self-consciously by footnoting their indebtedness to fellow participants in all their writings.[4] The Conference has sought to give itself a public existence and visibility, not only by its own conferences, but through its intervention in other conferences. It has also sought to develop and maintain a public alliance with radical lawyers through its relations with the National Lawyers Guild. The publication of the *Politics of Law: A Progressive Critique* (1982), as a joint venture between the Conference and the National Lawyers Guild, provides a text that comes close to being a manifesto for the critical legal studies movement. This homogeneity is in itself directly and consciously political; it involves the transplantation of "movement" political ideas and lessons into the field of legal scholarship.

The diversity of the critical legal studies movement is just as distinctive. There is a readily identifiable communality of starting point in the critique of liberal legalism and a common awareness of the importance of theory and methodology that is a reaction against the generalized atheoretical character of mainstream legal scholarship. But beyond this point the theoretical inspiration and roots that inform their writing reveals a remarkably wide trawl of twentieth-century radical and revisionist scholarship.[5]

I shall be particularly concerned to address the question of the theoretical orientation of critical legal theory. The problem can be posed in the following fairly stark terms: does critical legal theory achieve new, imaginative, and liberating theoretical syntheses or is its work marred by a jumbled, incoherent eclecticism? In order that the answer to this question should not be prejudged, let me hasten to insist that I do not believe that there is a "one right answer" to the problem of theory. But I am concerned about the preconditions and problems associated with theoretical synthesis.[6] I propose a burden of proof that imposes on the synthesizer the obligation to establish the compatibility of the theoretical elements that are combined. The problems of theoretical synthesis or syncretism involve a recognition that theories exhibit specific incompatibilities that make simple appropriation or fusion of distinct theories impossible. The problem can be captured by the medical analogy of the problems of rejection of tissues from donors in transplant surgery. The success of critical legal studies will be in part determined by the extent to which they succeed in bringing together the diverse theoretical traditions on which they seek to draw.

Lurking behind the question of the theoretical coherence of the critical legal studies movement is the brooding omnipresence of Roberto Unger. His work is widely acclaimed and extensively footnoted by most critical scholars, but I will argue that this is a deferential bow toward a theoretical integration rather than a genuine source of a theoretical inspiration that is systematically explored and deployed to underpin the critical project. Unger himself moved onto the stage of critical legal theory in a typically ambiguous appearance with his lengthy address to the ninth CCLS conference in 1982 (Unger 1982). I will consider the extent to which his intervention should be taken as adequately describing let alone representing the situation of contemporary critical legal theory.

I will follow this discussion of the theoretical and methodological practices of the critical legal studies movement with some proposals designed to offer a general theory and methodology for the critical study of law.

THE CRITIQUE OF LEGAL LIBERALISM

The liberalism against which critical theory directs its critical energies is the liberal theory that has generated the philosophy of legalism and the associated jurisprudence of legal positivism that has so decisively implanted itself in both the academic, the political and the popular discourse of contemporary capitalist democracies. The central features of this powerful doctrine of legalism are (1) the separation of law from other varieties of social control, (2) the existence of law in the form of rules that both define the proper sphere of their own application and (3) that are presented as the objective and legitimate normative mechanism whilst other normative types are partial or subjective, and (4) yield determinant and predictable results in their application in the juridical process. It is the view that Talcott Parson made more historically specific in his formulation that "law when developed to the requisite level, furthers the independence of the normative components of the social structure from the exigencies of political and economic interests and from the personal, organic and physical-environmental factors operating through them" (Parsons 1966:37).

The legal theory of the Anglo-American tradition has exhibited a remarkable degree of continuity. The substance of contemporary debates and controversies exhibits a lineage that can be traced back to the variant models of bourgeois political relations developed by Hobbes and Locke. The interplay and reworking of their differential emphases on the proper relation between state and civil society have been the backcloth against which the repeated play-off between rationalist natural law theory and legal positivism has taken place. It is the persistence of these themes that has so doiminated the terms of debate that it has become increasingly oppressive in the sense that it has colonized the intellectual and political space of discussion about the relationship between law, state, and society.

The sense of excitement and expectation generated by the emergence of critical legal studies is in large part due to the promise it holds out of replacing this dominant tradition of liberal legalism. It explains in no small degree the self-consciousness of the critical theorists of their linkages to the Realist tradition. The significance of Realism for the critical movement is enshrined in the insistence that, after Realism, legal theory could never be the same again.[7] As Elizabeth Mensch argues: "The best of the realist critique, however, cut so deeply into the premises of American legal thought that no amount of enlightened policy making and informed situation sense could ever really put Humpty Dumpty together again" (Mensch 1982:27).

The intervening period between the realism of the 1930s and the emergence of critical legal studies in the late 1970s has been as a series of unsuccessful attempts to recover from the shock of realism some basis for a legal theory that articulates an image of the objectivity of the legal process, even though the explanation offered by postrealism had to be more complex than that provided by a doctrine of rule following. The postrealist revisionism sought to harness the implications of the indeterminacy of legal rules to a legitimating notion of the fluidity and responsiveness of the legal system. The postrealist revisionism provides the immediate focus for critical scholarship. Over a wide range of fields of substantive law the critical scholars take as the starting point for their interventions the manifestations of this postrealist revisionist legal scholarship.[8]

The critique of orthodox legal scholarship draws on a more generalized critique of liberalism and thus constitutes one of the major points of unification of critical legal studies. The core of this critique is the contention that the claim made by liberalism to resolve the persistent and systematic conflict between individual and social interests through the mechanism of objective rules within a framework of procedural justice is inherently flawed. Mediation between conflicting interests at best offers only a pragmatic response to social conflict that can achieve nothing other than a set of results that reflects the unequal distribution of power and resources while claiming to act in the name of a set of universal social values. Critical legal theory thus grounds itself on the critique of the historical project of the Enlightenment, which is perceived as offering a rationalist and consensual solution to the problem of social order.[9] It is in this context that I suggest that we can understand the ambiguous relationship between Roberto Unger and the critical legal studies movement.

Unger provides a general theoretical critique of liberalism while at the same time insisting on the inadequacies of the existing alternatives, the "secular doctrines of emancipation," of which Marxist socialism is the most important. I suggest that sense can be made of Unger's relationship with critical legal studies by recognizing that he provides a coherent critique of liberalism that is widely invoked by critical legal authors. But there is only a very limited acceptance of Unger's own prescription for transcending liberalism. His alternative is itself a "superliberalism" that stands close to the liberal tradition and holds out the promise of realizing the prospect of individual emancipation that liberalism itself has proved incapable of delivering.

Unger himself is explicit; his alternative

> represents a superliberalism. It pushes the liberal premises about state and society, about freedom and dependence and governance of social relations by the will, to the point at which they merge into a larger ambition: the building of a social world less alien. . . . [It] represents an effort to make social life resemble more closely what politics (narrowly and traditionally defined) are already largely like in the liberal democracies: a series of conflicts and deals among more or less transitory and fragmentary groups (1982:602).

It is important to emphasize that it is "liberalism" as an intellectual construct rather than as an historically grounded system of social relationships that is the subject of this critique. Unger himself recognizes that his general critique "treats liberal doctrine as a set of interlocking conceptions whose relationship to society is disregarded. The study of the internal structure of the theory has been pursued at the cost of an awareness of theory's social significance" (Unger 1975:145).[10]

Unger's project is to provide a "total criticism" of liberalism that goes beyond the "partial" critiques of, among others, Marx and Weber. Liberalism is constructed as an ideal type culled from the lineage of Hobbes, Locke, Hume, Spinoza, Rousseau and Kant without it corresponding to the intellectual position of any one author (Unger 1975:8). This ideal typical liberalism is characterized by a series of connected "antinomies" or dichotomies that constitute the "deep structure" of liberal thought. These antinomies revolve around the dualism between "self" and "society," or between autonomy and community. These dichotomies express themselves in equally unsatisfactory liberal psychology and political theory; for example, in psychological theory the primary antinomy of liberalism is that between desire and reason and in political theory that between state and civil society or between the public and private spheres. While Unger himself makes great efforts to hold on to the interrelationship between these various antinomies and indeed to assign priority among them, other critical scholars are more eclectic and, apparently, casual in their adoption of one or more Ungerian antinomies as the organizing focus of their writing.[11]

There is an important problem associated with analysis founded on such dichotomous conceptualization. However useful an analytic device may be for ordering the complexity of legal phenomena, dichotomies have a nasty habit of being self-perpetuating or inescapable. This mode of analysis leads to what Alan Freeman has aptly described as one in which the critical scholar is tempted to "devote great effort to exposing contradictions . . . and then to go home" (1981:1229). Unger's texts are persistently but indeterminantly cited but remain undebated and unquestioned. Ungerian theory is invoked as inspirational source, but a deep silence remains over its relationship or compatibility with the other theoretical and methodological components of critical legal theory.

It is not my present purpose to embark on an evaluation of Unger's relationship with critical legal studies. Such a task would necessitate a consideration of the changes in his position that can be glimpsed in his published address to the CCLS annual conference (Unger 1982). My contention is that we need to understand the role of Roberto Unger as being other than the general theorist of the movement. Rather his significance is that he provides a readily available critique of liberalism that resonates with some of the major themes of the critical writers' engagement with the prevailing orthodoxy in legal scholarship.

What is worthy of comment is that the critique of liberal legalism tends to operate at a somewhat general level. Significantly absent is a direct engagement with the most influential modern versions of contemporary liberal jurisprudence. To make the critique of legal liberalism work more effectively, what is required is a thorough engagement with what may be styled the heartland of modern legal liberalism. The same attention that has been devoted to key figures of early legalism, such as Blackstone, now needs to be directed toward H. L. A. Hart, Ronald Dworkin, and John Rawls. Not only are these clearly powerful and influential embodiments of the tradition, but they also represent significant developments of that tradition in that they seek to overcome some of the criticisms that have been directed against it. Furthermore, to tackle the heartland of contemporary liberal legalism would exemplify that most effective strategy of intellectual engagement, namely, the taking on of one's opponents in their strongest manifestations. The general critique of liberalism needs to be concretized through an interrogation of its modern representatives.

Attention can now be focused on a number of the substantive themes taken up and developed by the practitioners of critical legal studies. The diversity within the movement is such that these themes are represented with differential weight in its exponents. I will start with a consideration of the relationship between critical legal studies and Marxist theory because I am concerned to argue that the absence of a public discussion of this issue has tended to detract from a clear formulation of the theoretical problems with which the movement is seeking to grapple.

CRITICAL LEGAL THEORY AND MARXISM

The conception of liberalism as revolving around a linked set of antimonies is taken up and made operational by critical scholars. Gerald Frug expresses the conception with clarity: "Liberalism is not a single formula for interpreting the world; it is instead, a view based upon seeing the world as a series of complex dualities" (Frug 1980).[12] What is clear in this formulation is that the liberalism under discussion is the philosophy of liberalism. But a distinctive and problematic feature of critical legal studies is that the object of critique, liberal philosophy, slides over into using the same conceptual categories in the critique of liberal capitalist society. What occurs in this process is that the conceptual categories through which liberalism seeks to understand the world become converted into real relations; it comes to appear as if the dualities of liberal thought are sociological categories through which we can make sense of contemporary society. The critique of philosophy is transmogrified into the critique of modern capitalist society. The price that is paid for this slippage from philosophical to sociological discourse is that the categories of liberal thought are taken as identifying characteristics of contemporary capitalism. To understand how this intellectual path has been so willingly trod by critical scholars it is necessary to consider the relationship between critical legal theory and Marxism.

The influence of Marxist scholarship in the United States has been very limited. It is significant for an understanding of critical legal theory to note that just as Marxism begins to have some influence on radicalized intellectuals during the 1970s, this occurs precisely at the time when the Marxist tradition itself is going through its most significant internal upheaval of recent times.[13] The period in which critical legal studies comes into existence is one in which its radical political perspective encounters a bewildering variety of internal variation, differentiation, and sectarianism within contemporary Marxism. This made the adoption of any single strand of modern Marxist theory unlikely, but more importantly, reduced the general attraction of Marxism as the alternative intellectual paradigm. Second, the strand of Marxism that has had the greatest influence within critical legal theory focuses on the processes of legitimacy and of hegemony. This strand, even in its early formulation by Gramsci, and even more clearly in the case of the Frankfurt School of "critical theory," was concerned to search for linkages with other intellectual traditions, the most important of these being with European sociology, especially that of Max Weber. The core concerns with legitimation, domination, hegemony, and consciousness that underpin the critical legal project raise precisely the exciting and challenging theoretical project of synthesizing different intellectual traditions. The implicit theoretical basis of critical legal theory rests on the project of theoretical synthesis or syncretism.

It is a distinctive paradox of critical legal theory that, while sharply distinguishing itself from the apparently atheoretical tradition of orthodox legal scholarship, it has to date only gone as far as practising, what can be labeled, "theoretical adoption." Critical theorists have differentially "adopted" a wide range of available theoretical positions. They have not as yet engaged in any systematic way in the practice of "theory construction," in contrast to "theory adoption." There is little evidence in their published work of any explicit theoretical debate about the merits of any of the adoptions so far proposed. Rather there is evidence, which I shall discuss more fully below, that Duncan Kennedy and to a lesser extent Peter Gabel, who can both be taken as representative of wider trends within the movement, have moved to a more overt hostility toward the exercise of theoretical construction (Gabel and Kennedy 1984). The paradox then is the coexistence of a theoretical self-consciousness, in itself novel in the realm of legal scholarship, with the absence of any real theoretical debate or engagement. While this theoretical paradox characterizes the present situation in critical legal theory, I want to suggest that there is an incipient theorization taking place that has already been given a name, that of "constitutive theory" (Klare 1979:128) but whose development has only been approached circuitously and whose consideration should be postponed until the relationship with Marxism has been explored.

The relationship of critical scholars to Marxist theory, while exhibiting individual variation,[14] has one common feature: critical theorists are agreed on their rejection of "Marxist instrumentalism."[15] The error of instrumentalism or reductionism lies in positing both a necessary and direct connection between class interests on the one hand and either the content of legal rules or the outcome of the legal process. There is less agreement as to whether this objection also includes the more substantial thesis that the connection between class interest and law is not direct but one that asserts itself as a general tendency in the long run or, as it is more generally posed, "in the final analysis" or "in the last instance." This alternative and more sophisticated formulation, which derives from that element of the Marxist tradition that has been much debated within modern Western Marxism under the label of "relative autonomy," does not fall victim to the same criticism as simple instrumentalism.[16] What underlies the critique of orthodox Marxism is better conceived as a critique of economism, which places the primary focus of analysis upon exploring the connection between law and economic class relations (the social relations of production). Positions of this type rest on an assumption of the existence of separate spheres designated by labels such as "law," "society," "economy." This imposes a framework of the form "What is the nature of the causal relationship between law and economy/society?" As Bob Gordon argues: "the big theoretical problem for writers who see the world this way is to work out the secret of that relationship" (1984:57)

Such problematics suppress the more powerful theoretical insight that law is inextricably mixed in the totality of social relations and institutions. The articulation of constitutive theory is confronted with the major problem of finding the appropriate conceptual language to adequately explore the way in which law is imbricated in the social totality.[17]

LEGITIMATION AND LEGAL IDEOLOGY

One of the most distinctive derivations from modern Marxism that characterizes critical legal theory has been the shift of focus from economic relations to the focus on political and cultural relations. Central to this concern is ideology, conceived as a mechanism that forms the consciousness of agents. Underlying this preoccupation with ideology is a concern with the question: how is it that those who are systematically disadvantaged by the existing order nevertheless accept the legitimacy of the institutions and values that perpetuate their subordination? The concept of ideology, and its associates "legitimation" and "hegemony," provides the means through which the persistence of relations founded on inequality and subordination is explored. The initial hypothesis is that law can be fruitfully analyzed as an ideological form, and that "legal ideology" plays some contributory role in the reproduction of human subordination.[18]

The manner in which the concept of legitimation is invoked creates considerable theoretical problems for critical legal theory. It takes the form of a functional theory of legitimation in which the grounding assumption is made that legal ideology is effective in constructing the perception and consciousness of the dominated in contemporary capitalist societies.

The exposition of the legitimation function persistently makes a "leap" of the greatest importance from the realm in which legal ideology is produced, and where it forms the dominant discourse, in courts and law offices, to the realm of the wider society. The leap is made from the legal consciousness of judges and lawyers to the consciousness of those outside the institutional apparatus of law. This "leap" is well caught in a characteristic formulation by Karl Klare. "Legal discourse shapes *our* beliefs about the experience and capacities of the human species, *our* conceptions of justice, freedom and fulfilment, and *our* visions of the future" (Klare 1982:1358; my emphasis).[19] The leap is enshrined in the innocent but problematic term "our"; if "our" refers to judges, lawyers, or legal academics then the formulation is entirely uncontroversial. If "our" is used as the democratic plural to refer to mass or popular consciousness then the claim made is both more important and more controversial. It is certain that Karl Klare neither intends nor would defend a direct causal link between the ideology of judges and that of the labor union members with whom his study is concerned; but what is missing is attention to the problem of mediation through which ideology is struggled over and recombined with other ideological elements.

The formulation of the legitimation thesis in its broadest and strongest sense involves positing a transference of legal ideology from the arena of its production to the level of everyday social relations. This claim raises both theoretical and empirical problems. Theoretically it raises the problem of "mediation," through what processes is legal ideology transmitted from the specialist arenas of legal discourse to install itself in popular consciousness? What changes or transformations does it undergo in the process? Empirically it raises the naive but important question: is there any evidence that the population in general or some particular section, for example, Klare's focus on the labor unions as recipient of labour law ideology,[20] is influenced by the ideological products of the legal process? Now Klare is not unaware of the problem, he footnotes the fact that

> an important limitation of the critical labor law approach is its relative neglect, thus far, of the important task of drawing out empirically the interrelationships and connections between the intellectual history of collective bargaining law and the social history of the post-World War II labor movement. (1981:452)

Presented in this way the problem is reduced to a concern for empirical evidence and, it is hoped, confirmation of the assumption of the effectivity of legal ideology. Conceived in this way the task of establishing empirical corroboration can be safely relegated to a future agenda. But even if the problem is seen as being "only empirical" there is no reason to assume that the evidence is readily at hand or that it will fit into a functional theory of the transmission of ideology. One only has to look at Michael Mann's pioneering study of the consciousness of subordinate classes, which suggests a bifurcation of consciousness in which some general value orientations mingle with more concrete values relating to everyday experience. Mann concluded: "It is not value-consensus which keeps the working class compliant, but rather a *lack* of consensus in the crucial area where concrete experiences and vague populism might be translated into radical politics" (Mann 1970:436).

However, if the problem of establishing the connection between legal discourse and popular consciousness is recognized as being a theoretical problem it cannot be postponed in this way because it goes to the very heart of the issue of whether the legitimation process has been adequately conceived. Rather than presuming a causal relationship between legal ideology and popular consciousness consider for a moment an alternative formulation: legal ideology is itself a product of a dominant or hegemonic political culture that directly produces the forms of mentality or social consciousness of the population. Within such a theoretical account legal ideology does not mediate between a dominant ideology and a popular consciousness; it is itself a more or less accurate replication or reflection of that external process. My intention is not to offer such an alternative theorization but merely to insist that it is consistent with critical theory in every respect other than the assumption of the causal relationship between legal ideology and popular consciousness.

The implications of this discussion of legal ideology and legitimation go to the very heart of the critical legal project. Critical scholars assume, what I will call, the effectivity of legal ideology. But they have not established either an adequate theorization of or an empirical demonstration of the connection between legal ideology and the formation of popular consciousness. I will offer some suggestions as to how this significant gap in the critical enterprise may be filled in the penultimate section.

LEGAL IDEOLOGY AND LEGAL CONSCIOUSNESS

Despite the centrality of the ideological analysis of law for critical theory there are a number of significant but undiscussed differences among critical scholars. But more important than internal differences is the extent to which, despite the sophistication of some parts of critical analysis, in particular with respect to the ideological content of historically changing legal doctrine, this most visible achievement stands on weak and shaky theoretical foundations that require urgent attention if they are to provide a more secure basis for critical scholarship.

The first problem concerns the relationship between ideology and consciousness. The concept "legal consciousness" plays a central role in critical legal scholarship.[21] Its centrality resides in the frequency with which it is invoked in work written under the critical imprint; but I want to argue that the concept has not been rigorously developed. It is employed in two distinct variants and the critical scholars have not shown an awareness of this differential usage nor, consequently, have they discussed its implications.

Legal consciousness is deployed in both a "narrow" and "broad" version. The narrow conception of legal consciousness identifies it with the consciousness of legal professionals, including both judges and practitioners within its ambit. Duncan Kennedy generally adopts a "narrow" position that identifies legal consciousness as "the body of ideas through which lawyers experience legal issues." It is "the particular form of consciousness that characterizes the legal profession as a social group at a particular moment."[22] The significance of the concept for Kennedy is that it provides an alternative both to liberal accounts of judicial reasoning and the equally unsatisfactory instrumentalist view positing a direct connection between legal doctrine and the interests of economically or politically dominant classes. This narrow conception of legal consciousness is very closely related to an analysis of legal doctrine employing a theory of relative autonomy.

The "broad" conception of legal consciousness identifies it as a specific form of consciousness held widely in society; those outside direct contact with legal institutions and processes are nonetheless suffused with legal consciousness. Peter Gabel argues that "Legal domination arises within the consciousness of every person as a sort of legitimating repression. . . . Legal thought originates, of course, within the consciousness of the dominant class because it is in this class's interest to bring it into being, but it is *accepted and interiorized by everyone*."[23]

The two conceptions, "professional" and "universal" legal consciousness, are poles apart and in different respects unsatisfactory. The broad conception of "universal legal consciousness" ignores the difficulties discussed above concerning the effectivity of ideology. In assuming an identity and correspondence between the consciousness of the judiciary and of the remainder of society and, in particular, of subordinate classes it lapses into a naive functionalism and ignores the most important issues about the generation and transmission of ideologies. There is a systematic absence of discussion about the processes of mediation between professional consciousness and the formation of popular consciousness. This is especially important if one holds the view, as I do, that ideologies do not come into existence fully fledged and are not transmitted as complete "systems" into the vacant consciousness of the subordinated.[24]

The narrow concept of professional legal consciousness gives rise to a quite different range of problems. It is employed in order to advance analysis of the development of legal doctrine that on the one hand "takes legal doctrine seriously," by which I mean that it does not seek to account for it through any form of reductionism in terms of class interests. Yet on the other hand it seeks to distinguish itself from orthodox positivist or neopositivist scholarship by identifying the import and significance of doctrinal development as the production of legal ideology to be understood as mechanism of legitimation or attempts to resolve tensions or contradictions which threaten to disrupt the sociopolitical assumptions of liberal theory of law as a "system" founded on a normative coherence of its rules.[25]

The concept of professional legal consciousness seeks to mark out both a new methodology of doctrinal analysis and a new strategy for understanding the connection between legal development and the socioeconomic context. We can examine this process by looking at two related but distinctive applications provided by Duncan Kennedy and Morton Horwitz, respectively.

Kennedy on Legal Consciousness

Duncan Kennedy elaborates both a methodology for the analysis of legal consciousness and an historical application to the formation of classical legal consciousness in his study of Blackstone's *Commentaries* (1979) and in his essay on legal consciousness (1980), which I shall call "critical doctrinal analysis." Legal consciousness is analyzed as a set of concepts and intellectual operations that "evolves according to a pattern of its own" and "has its own structure which mediates the influence on particular legal results" (1980:4). These intellectual practices produce an ordering of myriad elements of law into a systematization through processes of simplification and generalization that function to impose limits, to suggest directions, and to provide elements of a judicial style. What is most significant about these processes is the way in which the elements of consciousness "fit together" to form a "mode of integration" (1980:18). Doctrinal changes are analyzable as the product of historical shifts or changes in the mode of integration employed by the judges.

This model has the obvious and important implication of stressing the realist message of law-making as a process of social construction as something "made" by judges; there is for example no natural concept of "contract," it is constituted by what the judges have decided to include and exclude. The problematic feature of this methodology to which I wish to draw attention is the fact that its explanatory power is limited. It makes possible an account of *how* a doctrinal development occurred but it leaves open *why* it occurred. If the analytic capacity of the method is limited to *how*, it imports a conception of *autonomous* legal development that is precisely one of the primary objections that critical theory raises against orthodox legal scholarship.

However, Kennedy does not entirely abandon the wider and more challenging project but the methodology he employs is, I shall argue, of limited capacity. The method employed links "critical doctrinal analysis," a concept of "fundamental contradiction" and the concept of "motive." This method may be stated in broad and general terms: capitalist society is characterized by the presence of a fundamental contradiction that manifests itself as a problem in the field of legal doctrine, because of the quest for coherence and consistency, it is the "motive" of judges and treatise writers to resolve or dispel the fundamental contradiction; it is this "motive" that reveals the political significance of legal thinking.[26]

A general feature of this theorization of cued motivation should be noted. It does not offer a causal account that proceeds from changes or movement within the social formation to changes within the legal system, rather the causal mechanism is itself ideological since there is no independent guarantee that the "motives" affecting judges are direct or unskewed reflections of changes within the social formation. The consequence is that it can provide only a theoretical justification for a very limited range of causal propositions. This theoretical limitation on the type of result is, of course, not fatal, it merely restricts the heuristic capacity of the theory.[27]

The application of the theory of cued motivation is best exemplified in Kennedy's exhaustive analysis of Blackstone's contribution to the development of liberal legalism. Kennedy's project is "to introduce the reader to a method for understanding the political significance of legal thinking" with the aim of "discovering hidden political intentions beneath the surface of legal exposition" (1979:211). As he makes clear the whole analysis is based on a "premise" about legal thinking that is identified as a "double motive"; on one side to discover the conditions of social justice, while on the other to "deny the truth of our painfully contradictory feelings about the actual state of relations between persons in our social world" (1979:210).[28]

Throughout his discussion of Blackstone, Kennedy tends to employ the idea of "intention" more frequently than that of "motive"; it thus seems clear that his analysis requires the imputation of an explicit or conscious intent to Blackstone in particular, and by inference to legal actors in general. The flavor of this usage of intention is caught by his characterization that it was Blackstone's "intention to vindicate the common law against the charge that it was inconsistent with the enlightened political thought of his day" (1979:234) and later that his "ultimate intention was to legitimate both judicial institutions and the substantive law they enforced" (1979:237). This mode of analysis rests on the imputation of intent that is not substantiated. Yet without the insertion of "motive" the theoretical structure that seeks to move from "doctrine" to the "hidden political intention" is undermined. In other words Kennedy's methodology is not able, without an assumed intentionality, to establish the connection between doctrine and its historical context that critical theory promises.

It is instructive to consider Kennedy's own disclaimer.

> What I have to say is descriptive, and descriptive only of thought. It means ignoring the question of what brings a legal consciousness into being, what causes it to change, and what effect it has on the actions of those who live it. [W]e need to understand far more than we now do about the content and internal structure of legal thought before we can hope to link it in any convincing way to other aspects of social, political or economic life.

He is clearly being appropriately cautious in the claims that he makes. Yet it is far from clear that he remains within his self-denying ordinance, since his theory of legal consciousness does involve claims about what "brings a legal consciousness into being," namely, the motives of its progenitor. These motives are not interpreted at the level of individual psychology but involve political hypotheses about what "needs" to be explained, legitimated, or vindicated in the particular politicointellectual context.

The other feature of his disclaimer that requires comment is that while the desire to "know more" is unexceptionable, what he does not establish is how this accumulation of knowledge will provide the means to address the "bigger" questions of the causation and effectivity of legal consciousness. If critical theory accepts this self-imposed limitation it will be unable to advance beyond the first base of doctrinal analysis. It is the reaction, or perhaps more accurately overreaction, against the charge of instrumentalism that critical theory has focused its attention on doctrinal development without asking the basic methodological question: is "legal doctrine" the best starting point? It should be stressed that this interrogation is of the *methodology* of critical legal studies. It is not intended to detract from what is both one of the most distinctive and one of the most important features of the critical project.

Horwitz on Legal Consciousness

I want to demonstrate that Morton Horwitz's account of legal consciousness, while departing in some details from Duncan Kennedy's, shares significant common characteristics. It is, however, more difficult to approach because as befits a self-declared historian he regards history as something to be done rather than delayed in order to engage in theoretical conjecture. Consequently we find no definition of legal consciousness; it is deployed in a matter of fact manner. His most general formulation seeks to insist on its relative autonomy rather than to provide a positive identification.

> [L]egal consciousness in any particular period is not simply the sum of those contemporary social forces that impinge on law. Law is autonomous to the extent that ideas are autonomous, at least in the short run. In addition, the needs of professional interest and ideology have enabled the legal profession to serve as a buffer or filter between social forces and the law. (Horwitz 1977:xiii)[29]

What emerges clearly is his central concern to link ideology to material interest. His analysis of the transformation of American law that "enabled emergent entrepreneurial and commercial groups to win a disproportionate share of wealth and power in American society" (1977:xvi) is dependent on his ability to establish that there existed an alliance between common lawyers and commercial interests. Once posited, this alliance expresses itself through the development of substantive law that favored or accommodated commercial interests. Ideology reenters the analysis as the intellectual foundation and systematization of this transformed substantive law. Legal consciousness, for Horwitz, is the intellectual apparatus that transmuted economic interests into secured legal rules and judgments; legal consciousness is the cloak behind which the mundane and sordid economic interests of capital were not only secured but legitimated.

We can piece together a general model of the role of legal ideology in translating economic interests into legal form from his account of the history of the doctrine of objective causation in the law of torts (Horwitz 1982). His objective is to provide a causal account of the changing conceptualization of the doctrine of causation that makes sense of judicial formulations that appear unconnected with economic interests. His "politics of causation" argues that the doctrinal debates can be made sense of only in terms that locate them in the context of the material interest of entrepreneurs to restrict the economic costs of capital accumulation and economic expansion. Doctrinal development is explicated as the resultant of the interaction between existing doctrine and policy. It is policy that embodies and gives effect to the legal consciousness of the legal elite of judges and treatise writers. Existing doctrine exhibits a high degree of autonomy such that its development cannot be explained directly in terms of economic interests.

Policy considerations on the other hand are the bearers of more or less explicit economic or political interests. Thus Horwitz places great weight on warnings of "practical communism" and of the destruction of capitalism directed against the doctrine of objective causation. This legal consciousness is formed on the basis of political or economic calculation and gives rise to a perceived need for doctrinal change. Toward the end of the nineteenth century this manifests itself in the quest for an alternative doctrinal principle, in this case a concept of "legal causation" relying on the principle of foreseeability, which could be incorporated into doctrine in such a way as to reduce the rising economic costs of entrepreneurial activity associated with the industrial injuries of factory production. It is thus legal consciousness that is the bearer of economic interests. This contrasts sharply with Kennedy's view of legal consciousness as the systematized embodiment of liberal theory rather than economic interests. Horwitz's account relies by implication on a view of legal doctrine as the pragmatic rationalization of judgments of economic interests. It leads also to a methodology for the analysis of doctrinal development that attaches great importance to the search for the explicitly economic or political utterances of judges and treatise writers for here lies the historical evidence of the connection between legal consciousness and doctrinal development.

The contrast between Kennedy and Horwitz in their application of legal consciousness in no way undermines my earlier insistence on the centrality of the concept "legal consciousness" for critical theory. It does, however, establish that its variant conceptualization and application indicate the degree of the internal variation within the camp of critical legal studies.

THE FUNDAMENTAL CONTRADICTION

The concept of "fundamental contradiction" plays a central role, along with that of legal consciousness, in providing the general theoretical framework of critical legal theory. I want to argue that it fulfils a role in critical thought that is not made explicit by the critical scholars themselves but is nonetheless present. Once brought to the surface it helps explain many of the distinctive traits of this new movement. Its hidden mission is to provide a linkage between the two central intellectual strands on which critical legal theory draws. It provides the linkage between Marxism and modern cultural or interpretive sociology.

I shall set aside, for the time being, Duncan Kennedy's recent recantation of the conceptual armory of "fundamental contradiction" and "legal consciousness" (Gabel and Kennedy 1984). I shall first consider its role in the development of critical legal studies up to the present. Against the objection that there is little point in such a discussion if it has been expunged by its principal architect I will argue that Kennedy's own grounds for conceptual surgery neither justify nor require the elimination of this central concept.

The most general form of the fundamental contradiction is that between "self" and "others." In Duncan Kennedy's words: "The fundamental contradiction—that relations with others are both necessary to and incompatible with our freedom . . . is not only an aspect but the very *essence* of every problem" (1979:213).[30] The presentation of the fundamental contradiction between "self" and "others" is linked to other dichotomies that are either alternative expressions or derivatives therefrom: "subjectivity" versus "objectivity," "public" and "private," and "state" and "civil society."

The concept of fundamental contradiction is central to the methodology of doctrinal analysis pursued by most critical legal authors. The most general form is to seek to demonstrate that with reference to the selected field of substantive law contradictory elements are present. Rules or principles that can be classified under the antithesis between individualism and altruism, or the other variant formulations of the contradiction, are present at one and the same time, existing in a competitive and irresolvable tension.

It is possible to detect at least two variant forms in which this type of analysis is deployed. In the first form the tension between individualism and altruism is ubiquitous. Thus Unger's analysis of contract doctrine identifies a limited number of competing principles, each matched by a competing counterprinciple. (Unger 1982:616–648). A more historicist tendency focuses on doctrinal development and detects a movement backward and forward between the supremacy of one side of the contradiction or the other; this analysis produces a periodization of doctrinal development.[31] However, these two variant applications are not sharply distinguished by critical authors nor are they incompatible.

The general significance of doctrinal analysis in the light of the fundamental contradiction is that it provides an account of the contingency and indeterminacy of the legal process. The existence of competing principles creates the ever-present possibility of judicial choice. Critical scholars have not been much concerned with the exercise that preoccupied the Realists of predicting the resultant of the configuration of contingent factors in particular cases. The critical theorists have generally been satisfied to find evidence for a generalized indeterminacy within the legal process.

There is here an interesting contrast between the critical legal authors and Ronald Dworkin's analysis of the judicial process. He focuses his concern on the "hard case" and repudiates the conventional positivist invocation of the concept of discretion to account for outcomes in hard cases. His insistence on "one right answer" stems from his sociological premise that political communities exhibit a shared set of value commitment that manifests itself in a unitary set of principles that the judges are enjoined to first discover and then apply.[32] We can bring the different conceptual apparatus of Dworkin's analysis alongside that offered by the critical theorists. The latter insist that it is not, as Dworkin argues, that rights are merely controversial, but rather that opposing potential solutions to hard cases express and exemplify the fundamental contradiction between incommensurable values. Since the contradiction between individualism and altruism is unresolvable within legal theory the radical contingency of legal outcomes is an inescapable consequence of liberal legalism.

It is, however, possible to detect a certain ambiguity within critical legal theory concerning the status of the fundamental contradiction. There are two alternative formulations. In the first the fundamental contradiction is itself a product of liberal legalism. It is the very foundation of liberal legalism on the concept of atomized legal subject and the reduction of all collectivities to the individualized status of legal subjectivity that gives rise to the nightmare of the fundamental contradiction. The second version offers a more universalistic view of the status of the fundamental contradiction. It is seen as being a manifestation of the human condition itself. Both variants are in accord in viewing the incoherence of legal doctrine as resulting from the inevitable failure of liberal legalism to resolve the fundamental contradiction. But the two variants diverge about the possibility of overcoming the fundamental contradiction. The former tends to be sympathetic to those utopian perspectives that hold out the prospect of overcoming the self-others conflict. The second variant tends to regard all legal and political strategies as, at best, pragmatic attenuations of a fundamental feature of the human condition.

The presentation of the fundamental contradiction within critical legal theory reveals important aspects of the broader theoretical influences on the movement. In particular it throws into relief the linkage between the more Marxian elements of critical theory and its adoption of elements of a general framework of subjectivist or interpretive sociology. The pursuit of this link is one that is both full of great promise and great danger. Its positive feature is the quest that lies at the heart of the history of contemporary Marxism and of the critical social theory associated with the Frankfurt School. In its more overtly Marxist form it is the path charted out by Gramsci with his emphasis on the processes of the production and reproduction of hegemony and the conditions and possibilities of the creation of counterhegemony. In a different form it is central to the project of the Frankfurt School to embrace the intersubjective reality of social action, hence the concern with meaning, language, communication, and culture.[33] It should be stressed that these different strands of thought all retain a central concern with the analysis of the connection between the processes of economic and class relations and the processes of human consciousness and action. A useful shorthand for identifying these concerns of Western Marxism is that they are all different ways of grappling with one of Marx's most famous and tantalizing aphorisms: "Men make their own history, but not of their own free will; not under circumstances they themselves have chosen but under the given and inherited circumstances with which they are directly confronted" (Marx 1973:146).

The alternative strand, expressed in interpretive or phenomenological sociology, breaks the link between human agency and social determination. Human life is, in Berger and Luckmann's famous title, "the social construction of reality" that takes place in "everyday life" (Berger and Luckmann 1966). In seeking to escape from a reductionist Marxism, critical legal theory has not taken sufficient account of the gulf between these different theoretical traditions.[34] Much of the difficulty revolves around trying to establish exactly which theoretical framework critical scholars adopt. This arises from a tendency to cite the theoretical origins of their positions in a very loose way. Duncan Kennedy, for example, states his object as being to "introduce the reader to a method for understanding the political significance of a legal thinking, a method that might be called structuralist or phenomenological, or neo-Marxist, or all three together" (1979:209). Elsewhere he refers to his theoretical position as "a melange of critical Marxism, structuralism and phenomenology" (1982a:563–564). Mark Tushnet is equally frank about the electicism of the movement's root that he describes as an "unholy trinity of semiology, phenomenology and Marxism." (Tushnet 1979:31).

It must be firmly stressed that to list intellectual influences tells us something about where critical theory is coming from, but it tells us little about what its substantive content is. There is much hard work to be done to move from the listing of influences to the achievement of a coherent and explicit integration.[35] Mark Tushnet proposes a short-cut for the strategy of CCLS "to develop a body of substantive analyses that is guided by the theoretical perspectives afforded by the trinity [semiology, phenomenology and Marxism], whether or not those perspectives are made explicit. . . . But as those contributions accumulate, *they will be seen as presenting a unified alternative*" (Tushnet 1979:31–32). No amount of accumulating substantive work will reveal a "unified alternative"; such a desirable result will emanate only from explicit and rigorous attention to the theoretical and methodological tools employed. My judgment is that it is not so important to aim for a "unified alternative" as it is that there should be a heightened and more self-conscious theoretical debate *within* critical legal studies.[36]

FUNDAMENTAL CONTRADICTION VERSUS EXISTENTIAL ZAP

Now that the role of the fundamental contradiction in critical legal theory has been examined we can consider whether it has any place there. It is necessary to do so because the central focus on "the fundamental contradiction" within the critical legal studies movement has now been renounced by its chief architect. Duncan Kennedy, in his conversational piece with Peter Gabel, "Roll Over Beethoven," declares: "I renounce the fundamental contradiction. I recant it, and I also recant the whole idea of individualism and altruism and the idea of legal consciousness." Peter Gabel joins in the renunciation: "[Y]ou [Duncan Kennedy] tied this tin can around our neck. The entire Critical Legal Studies movement has been dragging around that can" (Gabel and Kennedy 1984:15).

Before considering their reasons for jettisoning the fundamental contradiction and discussing its implications, it is perhaps wise to take stock of what is at stake. I have argued that the concept of the fundamental contradiction has been pivotal for the development of the movement; its centrality stems from the fact that the concept of the fundamental contradiction both grounds and expresses the critique of liberal legalism, and in turn locates the critique of legalism in a wider critique of the tradition of liberal social and political philosophy. The concept of fundamental contradiction is foundational for the demonstration of the tendency to incoherence in legal doctrine; it is also pivotal for the contention that the liberal project of reconciling state and civil society, or of overcoming the dichotomy between self and community is unrealizable. Thus to "recant" the fundamental contradiction does not involve jettisoning of some marginal feature of critical legal theory; rather it goes to the very core of the nascent critical theory.

It is apparent that the renunciation goes beyond the rejection of particular concepts. Beyond the concepts of fundamental contradiction, legal consciousness, and the individualism/altruism dichotomy it is evident that something more of general significance is at stake. The question is what is being renounced?

The form of dialogue selected by Gabel and Kennedy as their vehicle for their revisionist project, whatever its other merits, does not facilitate the clear identification of either the constituent elements of the argument nor the conclusions arrived at. The dialogic form allows the freedom to a participant to formulate positions prompted by the interjection and interrogation of the other. At one stage in the discussion it appears that what is being challenged is the very possibility of theory. But as it moves on it becomes apparent that Kennedy steps back from a root-and-branch rejection of theory as such. But the substance of his amended position is by no means clear. He is certainly clear about his explicit "antagonism to philosophy" (1984:53). But it is by no means clear what it is that is involved in the rejection of "philosophy." I suggest that the concept of "the fundamental contradiction" is rejected by Duncan Kennedy because it is a deficient form of theorization. Since he also associates the repudiation with other concepts, "legal consciousness" and "individualism/altruism," it is not the inadequacy of the specific concepts that is at stake; but rather his critique is directed against the form of theory that employs or produces such concepts. This interpretation is supported by the fact that few if any criticisms of the specific concepts themselves are voiced. Kennedy makes it clear that it is not the "substantive content of the fundamental contradiction which caused right and left deviationists to pursue their deviations" (1984:16). Indeed he goes further and insists that there is a "substantive truth" that the "dead abstraction" of the concept refers to.

The question to be explored is: what deficiencies do Gabel and Kennedy identify in the type or style of theory that had played such a central role in critical legal theory? Peter Gabel's position, as expressed in "Roll Over Beethoven," has not changed substantially; he remains an advocate of a critical legal theory drawing heavily on phenomenology. The sharper "break" is expressed by Duncan Kennedy and therefore in seeking to reconstruct the grounds for his recantation I will focus on the positions he takes up during the discussion.

I suggest that four distinct, but more or less related, critiques of the theoretical enterprise can be identified:

1. Fear of the body-snatchers.
2. Theory as overgeneralized, abstract and "frozen."
3. The impossibility of rationalist philosophy.
4. Against "privileged" concepts.

Fear of the Body-Snatchers

The analogy of the "body-snatcher" and the "pods," aside from attesting to a nostalgia for old sci-fi movies, expresses two critical points. The one to be discussed at this point is an anxiety about the misappropriation of concepts.[37] Concepts, such as "fundamental contradiction," allow "the kind of philosophizing that can be seized on by anyone and anything can be made of it" (1984:15).

I want to argue that this idea provides no grounds for rejecting the type of theorizing under discussion. There can be no personal or corporate property in concepts; rather concepts of any interest or importance are "essentially contested" (Gallie 1955–1956). And it is through this process of contestation that concepts are refined, modified, changed, or abandoned. Anxiety about the way other writers use one's favored concepts is natural, but this anxiety verges on paranoia when prominent participants in a self-consciously pluralistic movement set themselves up as guardians of the movement's theoretical purity. It is perfectly legitimate to criticize the way in which particular authors employ any concept, but Kennedy does not do this. Confronted with a fear of misappropriation, which is not specified or itemized, he seeks to withdraw the concept.

The Frozen Pods

So much for the "body-snatchers." More important is the problem of the "pods," which I take to stand for a concern with the way in which the concept of fundamental contradiction has been used in such a way as to render it "wooden" or "frozen." Thus Kennedy comments that for a period the concept played a useful role "before the body-snatchers turned it into a cluster of pods" (Gabel and Kennedy 1984:16–17). This imagery seeks to express a concern that to seek to encapsulate complex, transient, and contingent reality in intellectual concepts "freezes" that reality and thereby distorts it. The alternative to conceptually frozen reality is identified as "small-scale, micro-phenomenological evocation of real experience in complex contextualized ways which one makes it into doing it" (Gabel and Kennedy 1978:3). To take another example, he insists on the momentary and variable character of human consciousness; once one pins a conceptual label, such as "false consciousness," it "freezes" that reality in the sense that it both distorts and freezes the complex reality which the concept seeks to encompass (1984:43–44).

One facet of Kennedy's concern to stress the indeterminacy and plasticity of individual and social reality leads him to reject all concept formation as reification that "freezes" reality. The other related strand is the strategy of substituting an alternative and radical reconceptualization. In objecting to Peter Gabel's concern to expound a program for realizing "unalienated relatedness" he is objecting to the programmatic project of advancing a single master concept. In its place Kennedy proposes a radical reconceptualization by redefining the general objective as generating "intersubjective zap" or "making the kettle boil." What I take to be behind this flamboyant strategy is to select a terminology that is intentionally incapable of being fossilized into rationalist discourse. Rationalist discourse is seen as holding out the false hope that intellectuals can come to agreement on an exact meaning that the concepts of its discourse shall bear. There is a sense in which we "all know what we mean by" "intersubjective zap" or "making the kettle boil." (But do we? Aren't the "meanings" so situational that outside that context such colloquial phrases become devoid of meaning?) The merit of "zap" and "kettles" is subversive in that their very colloquialism renders the rationalist project both impossible and vaguely ridiculous. A seminar on "alienation" or "unalienation relatedness" is part of the life-style of intellectuals; but you cannot hold a seminar on "the meaning of intersubjective zap." So the rationalist project is disrupted and disallowed.

Against Rationalist Philosophy

It becomes clear that the problem to be addressed is not the merits of particular concepts but the form of philosophical discourse of which they are a part. It is easy enough to get the flavor of what Kennedy does not like about rationalist philosophy, but the nature of his objections to conventional philosophical discussion debars him from marshalling the type of objections to that discourse that intellectuals are accustomed to formulating and debating. His objection rests on "a fundamental, profound disagreement about the possibility of theory" (Gabel and Kennedy 1984:47).

The content of that objection can perhaps best be captured by listing some of the language he employs. "Theory" or "philosophy" is "abstract," "overgeneralized," exhibits a belief that it is possible to settle things "too high up" (i.e., at too high a level of abstraction). His objections thus revolve around the problem of abstraction.

His second concern is with "effective communication." I take it that his concern "to communicate with people" (Gabel and Kennedy 1984:52) stands for "to communicate with people other than professional intellectuals," and that "heavy theory" is a barrier to such communication. If I have understood his position I suggest we can dispense with this issue fairly quickly since it makes only a trivial point that if you want to engage in effective communication you require a situational sense of where the people you are working with and talking with "are at." Speeches or talk full of "heavy" specialized and esoteric theory are ineffective among people who are not professional intellectuals. But who ever said they were? No issue is joined.

The heart of Kennedy's "antagonism to philosophy" centers around the question of the abstract character of theory and philosophy. The objection against abstraction is that distancing and generalization sacrifices the particularity or specificity of reality. Thus, if the objective of thought is to understand and to change reality, "abstraction" is seen as conflicting with this goal. This is what is involved in his criticism that "you can't plausibly describe 'being' except in the vaguest and most general way. You *can* plausibly describe relatively contextualized, nonabstract, rich human situations" (Gabel and Kennedy 1984:48). What is at stake is a familiar debate within epistemology. Kennedy is asserting the view that only those elements of discourse that are capable of participating in "effective communication" are to count as knowledge. This is a perfectly plausible position *within* philosophy, but it neither abolishes philosophy nor does he overcome his primary objection to abstraction. "Effective communication" is not free of abstraction, but rather it privileges those abstractions that are part of "common sense" or ordinary discourse. His proposal that nonabstract communication is possible in terms of "intersubjective zap" and "making the kettle boil," despite the populist style of this language, is not free of abstraction, it simply involves *uncritical* abstractions that are taken for granted and are not experienced as being problematic.

Privileged Concepts

The fourth feature of Kennedy's objection to abstraction stems from the contention that theoretical discourse "privileges" certain concepts. This objection is not to theory as such, but to "bad theory." As I have argued above, all discourse, whether "theory" or "common sense," privileges concepts. "Good theory" requires self-conscious interrogation of the concepts employed, of their underlying assumptions and of their interrelationship. "Bad theory," on the other hand, is distinguished by its mechanical and unreflective deployment of a preexisting litany of concepts.

The foregoing considerations point to the conclusion that the wholesale abandonment and retreat from both the general theoretical strategy and its embodiment in a particular group of concepts are not necessary. It is not necessary in the sense that the concerns and problems that motivated the jettisoning of the fundamental contradiction can be met without the radical surgery. The body-snatchers/concept-snatchers are no problem and can be allowed to return to the world of science fiction. The problems of abstraction, rationalism, and frozen pods can be surmounted through a reflexive view of the role of theory within discourse and a recognition that problems of theoreticism cannot be overcome by a retreat into common-sense discourse.

THE PROBLEM OF RELATIVE AUTONOMY

There are two general theoretical problems that derive from the eclectic character of the theoretical roots of the critical legal studies movement; they emerge as common features of much critical legal scholarship. The first of these seek to develop the focus on the need to explore more fully the connectedness of law to social, economic, and political relations. It is embodied in the theoretically important but sensitive concept of the 'relative autonomy of law'.

It is necessary to be somewhat tentative about the concept "relative autonomy of law" because it does not have a very visible presence in critical scholarship.[38] Rather I suggest that it is implicit as what Gouldner called a domain assumption within critical legal theory. Its presence is the result of the dual opposing positions against which it directs its criticism. On the one hand critical theorists reject all positions that assume the autonomy of legal doctrine and, on the other, differentiate themselves from deterministic positions that present law as a reflection of, and therefore reducible to, economic and political forces.

Between the Scylla of autonomy and the Charybdis of determinism lies the haven of relative autonomy.

Many positions within critical legal theory are reminiscent of Engels' important statement of relative autonomy:[39]

> In a modern state, law must not only correspond to the general economic conditions, but must also be an *internally coherent* expression which does not, owing to its internal conflicts, contradict itself. And in order to achieve this, the faithful reflection of economic conditions suffers increasingly. All the more so the more rarely it happens that a code of law is the blunt, unmitigated, unadulterated expression of the domination of a class. (Engels 1960:400)

The general thrust of critical legal theory is to insist that liberal legalism fails to achieve or sustain this internal coherence, but like Engels to see this attempt as the reason why law does not and cannot directly reflect economic interests. But before pronouncing the twin enemies of autonomy and determinism vanquished we need to enquire whether the intellectual foundations of the theory of relative autonomy provide the desired safe anchorage.

The attraction of relative autonomy stems from the fact that it appears to allow us to hold on to both ends of the chain at the same time; to assert both the specificity of legal doctrine and, at one and the same time, to assert its connectedness to external socioeconomic relations. A very heavy theoretical burden is borne by the concept of relative autonomy. If it is viable it offers a most attractive and compelling solution to a pervasive problem confronting social theory. It is necessary, however, to enquire whether or not it is able to sustain such expectations. Despite the fact that I have over a number of years myself relied on the concept of relative autonomy as the escape route from the dichotomy of autonomy and determinism I am now convinced that it is, at least in the formulations currently available to us, seriously flawed.[40]

The theoretical deficiency of the concept relative autonomy is that unless it is capable of being linked to some account that specifies the boundaries or limitation of autonomy it can only be understood as constantly running the danger of lapsing into the assertion of either autonomy or determinism coupled with an expression of faith that on the one hand autonomy has determined limitations or, on the other, that determination is tempered or postponed.[41]

The idea of relative autonomy is a concept in search of a theory. It requires a theory that is capable of providing the supports for the major claim that it makes of the possibility of specifying connectedness without determinism. The theoretical apparatus for an adequate realization is not available. If this is the case then it follows that the concept of relative autonomy cannot be taken as achieving anything more than pointing toward a desired type of analysis.

The implications for critical legal studies are important. In so far as the general trend of work assumes that such a theory of connectedness without determinism either exists already or at least potentially it has not, as yet, tackled a major obstacle that stands in the way of realizing what is one of its most important claims. This claim is that critical legal studies is developing a theory with the capacity to provide a causal analysis of legal doctrine in its connection with socioeconomic relations without laying itself open to the charge of determinism.

It is in the face of this theoretical difficulty that Duncan Kennedy argues for a much more modest position on the causal capacity of critical legal theory when he insists that "we need to understand far more than we do about the content and the internal structure of legal thought before we can hope to link it in any convincing way to other aspects of social, political or economic life" (Kennedy 1979:221). Before we accept the self-limitation proposed by Kennedy there are two problems, one internal and the other external, with his formulation. The internal problem is that it imports the assumption that greater understanding or knowledge of legal doctrine is the key to the second and most difficult stage of establishing the "link" with external social reality. The difficulty is not an empirical one concerning the state of our knowledge but a theoretical one. Whereas relative autonomy expresses a pointer toward a solution to a theoretical difficulty, Kennedy erroneously reduces a theoretical problem to an empirical one.

There are within Kennedy's formulation indications of a possible theoretical solution. There is a hint of the potentiality of structuralist theory; elsewhere in his writings structuralism is invoked explicitly as a source of intellectual orientation, but it remains tentative and undeveloped. Its presence is marked by periodic references to "hidden structure" and "deeper patterns" and citation of a structuralist theorist, usually Piaget or Levi-Strauss (Kennedy 1979:210, 220, 221).[42] Structuralism offers the possibility of establishing a means of specifying a connection between law, through its form or structural characteristics, and economic or political structures. While it is not an avenue that I wish actively to commend it is clear that Kennedy regards it as having a potential although it is one he does not develop.

The structuralist strand in critical theory connects with another possible theoretical solution to the general problem of establishing the connection between law and the social totality. A theory of "internal relations" similarly provides the possibility that each element or constituent of a social totality in itself embodies the general characteristics of the totality; in other words the part is the microcosm of the whole.[43] This perspective offers the possibility that the study of legal doctrine can in itself be undertaken as a study of the wider social relations within which the legal doctrine exists, just as Ollman, the leading modern exponent of a philosophy of internal relations, argues that the commodity form reveals the dynamics of capitalist society. The problem of connectedness is abolished at a stroke, or at least so transformed that the problems associated with the establishment of causal relations conceived as relations between independent social entities have no further relevance.

Within critical legal scholarship there are occasional passages that resonate with a philosophy of internal relations. Thus, for example, Gabel's view of structure as "a synthesis of elements in which each element is both the complete expression of the whole and a partial constituent of it" is pure internal relations (1977:308). More generally the account of the theory of legal consciousness that I have criticized for importing the assumption of an identity between the consciousness of the legal elite and that of popular consciousness can be reinterpreted. Read in the context of a theory of internal relations, were it to be made explicit and defended, legal consciousness could be examined as embodying a coherent and articulate expression of the dominant ideology of capitalist society. Its stages and changes could then be read as "reflections" of either structural changes at the level of the economy, or mediated through ideology, of the dominant consciousness. I suggest that critical legal scholars are more significantly allied to a philosophy of internal relations than is made explicit in their substantive formulations. If this suggestion can be substantiated it offers not a solution but a different perspective, but one that has to confront the challenge that an internal relations theory is but a sophisticated version of determinism.

The second or external problem raised by Kennedy's general position on the connection between doctrine and the social totality is that by explicitly postponing the question he lays himself open to a strategic objection from within the critical legal studies movement. This criticism from the "Left" is exemplified in Munger and Seron's objection that in abandoning the attempt to establish the link between doctrine and the wider sociopolitical reality, despite all protests to the contrary, Kennedy "reinforces the very assumption that it sets out to demystify, i.e., that doctrine develops autonomously" (Munger and Seron 1984).[44]

Yet it is not self-evident that the significance attached by Kennedy to extending doctrinal analysis necessarily reinforces liberal legalism, but it certainly postpones, and thus possibly impedes, the development of a substantive alternative. The major theoretical consequence of Kennedy's postponement or self-limitation is that it accentuates the concern with the critique of liberalism that takes as its primary focus the project of demonstrating the internal incoherence of liberal legalism. It is thus necessary to consider the part played by incoherence analysis within critical legal theory.

THE PROBLEM OF COHERENCE

One feature more than any other appears to unite the critical legal theorists.[45] They all engage in critiques of mainstream legal thought directed at demonstrating its incoherence. The general form of critical legal writing is that which asserts the incoherence or contradictions of liberal legalism, of specific areas of doctrine, of specific theorists, judges, or treatise writers. Tushnet, for example, seeks to establish the incoherence of the most pervasive styles of judicial reasoning and concludes that it reveals "the potential for destroying liberalism by revealing the institution's inconsistencies and its dialectical instability" (Tushnet 1983:824). It is not made explicit why the demonstration of "inconsistency" cumulatively results in "incoherence," which in turn can lead to the downfall of liberal legalism. The missing step in the argument is that liberal legalism holds itself out as demonstrating the coherence of legal doctrine, which is one plank on which the authority of law, requiring acceptance and obedience, is founded. Once the claim to coherence is demolished both the confidence of liberal adherents and the grounding of the authority of law are undermined. Whilst intellectual systems are vulnerable to successful prosecution at the bar of logic they are points scored in intellectual battles, but it is far from self-evident that the influence of intellectual positions is irretrievably damaged as a result. Indeed I shall argue that incoherence may be an advantage and count in favor of adaptability for a theory.

We need to ask a naïve question: precisely what does it prove to demonstrate an incoherence or contradiction in an intellectual position? It is a well-established feature of rationalist epistemology that the pursuit of internal coherence constitutes a major form of intellectual legitimation. But since critical theory disputes the very claims of rationalist epistemology in its pursuit of logically gapless intellectual constructs, it is puzzling why the shout of triumph should ring out when incoherences or contradictions are demonstrated. At best such findings have a limited audience; they are directed toward the authors of liberal legalism, who holding to the tenets of a rationalist epistemology, may be shaken in their intellectual convictions. Yet it is apparent that critical theorists claim a much more important role for the demonstration of incoherence.

There are a number of overlapping but contrasting claims made by critical theorists for the method of coherence analysis. First, coherence analysis is widely linked to the major strand connecting today's critical scholars to the Realist tradition through the stress on the indeterminacy of the legal process. Judicial reasoning does not and cannot generate determinant results. This denial of the rational determinancy of legal reasoning is an important strand of unity for critical jurisprudence.

Second, the incoherence of legal doctrine is seen as an expression or manifestation of the basic incoherence of liberal political and social theory with its inability to resolve the fundamental contradiction between individual and community. Third, the incoherence of legal doctrine is not merely some deficiency in the intellectual props of liberalism; its incoherence is endemic and attests to the ideological function of legal discourse. Liberal legalism reproduces rather than resolves the basic contradiction; as Hutchinson and Monahan aptly express it legal doctrine embodies the "basic contradiction writ small" (1984:204). To establish contradiction and incoherence challenges the truth-claims of the central tenets of liberal legalism that proclaim the inevitability and naturalness of law, the conflict–resolution function of rule application, and the neutrality of the legal process.

The fourth strand involves a more significant objective that connects the practice of critique to social and political objectives. To expose incoherence creates the possibility of overcoming the diverse ways in which law reifies and mystifies the conflictual nature of social reality. Freeman expresses the critical objective: "for me the task of a scholar is thus to liberate people from their abstractions, to reduce abstractions to concrete historical settings, and, by so doing, to expose as ideology what appears to be positive facts or ethical norms" (Freeman 1981:1236). A more psychologically orientated version is seen in Peter Gabel's proposition that "the law" emerges within our alienated culture as a kind of quasi-religious belief system which simultaneously compensates for our feelings of loss within these alienated groups and conceals these feelings from us" (Gabel 1980:28). As David Trubek remarks "this approach assumes that social actors, like psycho-analytic patients can be freed of the constraints of delusions" (Trubek 1984:610).

A fifth and final form of incoherence argument locates the possibility of a politics that goes beyond the critique of mystification. The contradictions of liberal legalism and the ideology it generates consist of rival social visions. These visions are prefigurative in that they contain the possibility of alternative forms of human association. Most explicit in developing this line of thought is Roberto Unger's deviationist doctrine, which argues that these "conflicting tendencies within law constantly suggest alternative schemes of human association" (Unger 1982:579). His analysis of contract doctrine seeks to demonstrate that alongside the conventional individualistic model of social relations there exists a subordinate and less visible countervision embodying ideals of reciprocity and community. There is an important feature of this strategy which seeks prefigurative alternatives *within* legal doctrine. If well founded it creates the possibility of a "revolutionary reformism" that, rather than envisaging any overthrow of legal doctrine, seeks to accentuate and develop the alternative images of social life until such time as the alternative altruistic or communitarian principles become the dominant element.

The most interesting application of this methodology is provided by Duncan Kennedy's analysis of "motives" in contract law (Kennedy 1982a).[46] The prefigurative motive in contract doctrine is that of paternalism that justifies interference with consensual contract terms on the grounds of an appeal to the interests of one or both parties. He declares himself in favor of a program of advancing paternalism in contract law; "I would favour an adventurous and experimental programme of left-wing compulsory terms" (1982a:629). I have strong reservations about associating paternalism with a necessarily progressive identity. My difference with his position stems from a rejection of his definition of paternalism as "inter-subjective unity of the actor with the other" (1982a:647). My view of paternalism is strongly influenced by the socialist critique of the experience of European social democracy; the paternalism of the societies with histories of social democratic governments has not been one of unity between state and people, but of nonparticipation and lack of identity with "benefits" handed down from above reflecting the state's rather than the recipients' conception of needs and interests. This paternalism is one of separation rather than unity, which reifies the welfare state and its institutions as set apart from recipients who are immobilized when faced with alien bureaucracies. Paternalism involves not unity but a giver–receiver relationship, a relationship of superiority–inferiority.

Kennedy is not unaware of the difficulty that arises from the lack of identity between the professional paternalist separated by a wide gulf of experience and culture from recipients. He seeks to resolve this dilemma by urging the professional paternalist to take on "the task of mobilizing the groups on whose part one may have to act paternalistically" (1982a:649). His model of successful nonalienated paternalism is, as he recognizes, only conceivable in the context of small groups with face-to-face interaction. As a utopian vision it has something to commend it, but it is not one that addresses the big questions concerning the transformation of ever more powerfully aggregated corporate and state power. Like Unger's espousal of face-to-face "organic groups" as the transformative possibility of welfare-corporatism it is a vision of a radicalized community whose integration involves little beyond a tolerance of alternative life-styles.

The other problem with deviationist doctrine in its quest for a prefigurative strategy is that it limits the search for alternative visions to the existing body of legal doctrine. Alternatives that are generated "outside" rather than "inside" legal doctrine are either disallowed or discounted. This issue is closely connected with the problem of paternalism. Perhaps it is precisely because the alternative vision of "community" is found *inside* legal doctrine that it takes the form of paternalism with its nonparticipatory and hierarchical characteristics. The program of prefigurative politics that is opened up by critical legal theory should avoid the invitation proferred by Kennedy and Unger to restrict itself to visions of social alternatives contained within existing legal doctrine.

The Function of Incoherence

One additional dimension of coherence analysis should be noted. The general methodology of critical theory assumes that incoherence is an unambiguously negative attribute of liberal legalism. The general intellectual strategy of liberal legalism has been to hide and deny its own incoherence. Thus the theory of rights, from Blackstone to the present, has been concerned to present itself as an ideal mechanism for the resolution of the conflict of rights. In the contemporary period liberal legalism has, according to Duncan Kennedy, been slowly awakening to the horrible realization that the conflict between self and others is permanent and insuperable. Before we rush to assume that critical legal theory has announced the death throes of liberal legalism we need to ask: isn't it possible that its very internal incoherence and its associated dichotomies are a strength rather than a weakness? Or, to put it more boldly, is incoherence a functional attribute of liberal legalism? The openness of legal doctrine demonstrated by the Realists and reinforced by the critical theorists allows a flexibility in judging, between the competing demands and values generated both internally by legal ideology and by external interests. This process may leave a messy line of precedents behind that can be seized on by lurking critical theorists and pronounced incoherent. Why should this be regarded as a significant defect in the operation of a legal system? The answer to this question will depend on the relative importance attached to the production of "results" in the form of decided cases or to the production of "doctrine." Critical theorists tend to place little emphasis on the "results" of specific legal actions. This, I suggest, is a reaction against a simplistic instrumental theory, of which it is today very difficult to find any adherents, that judges hand down decisions embodying class interests. This is no reason for failing to recognize the argumentative and persuasive role, in particular of the higher appellate courts, in communicating and legitimating specific legal outcomes. The viability and social persuasiveness of these results may be more important than the small price of doctrinal incoherence which is a by-product.

Doug Hay's justly renowned study of eighteenth-century English criminal law can be understood as providing an empirical illustration of the function of incoherence. The incoherencies and inconsistencies of English criminal law, both procedural and substantive, and the consequential space for discretion created thereby, made possible "the peculiar genius of the law" with its interplay of terror, justice and mercy (Hay 1977). Even the resistance to rationalizing reform by the Whig elite can no longer be written off as obscurantism; it takes on a new sense as embodying a distinctive understanding of the eighteenth-century concept of the rule of law, itself significantly different from the formalist conception of the present century.[47]

I have not sought to establish that incoherence is necessarily functional, but rather to reinsert the need to reexamine critical theory's assumption that to demonstrate doctrinal incoherence is to undermine liberal legalism. My question is not new; it was clearly present in the Realist tradition of rule-scepticism. The implications of doctrinal incoherence are not as unambiguous as the critical scholars tend to assume and require a fuller analysis of the effects and consequences of the interrelation of legal decisions and legal doctrine.

THE CONSTITUTIVE THEORY OF LAW

My argument this far has suggested that the critical legal studies movement has, as yet, not developed an elaborated theoretical perspective. It is a trend founded on a level of agreement around a certain style of critique of liberal legalism and more widely of modern society. There is an underdeveloped theoretical strand that offers the possibility of a more coherent and articulated theory. This alternative is provided by an emergent "constitutive theory of law."[48] This theoretical development must be understood against the background of attempts within the Marxist theoretical tradition to free itself from determinism. David Kairys clearly poses constitutive theory as an alternative to determinism. "But the law is not simply the armed receptacle for values and priorities determined elsewhere; it is part of a complex social totality in which it constitutes as well as is constituted, shapes as well as is shaped" (Kairys 1982:5).

Before the problems and potentialities of constitutive theory can be discussed further it is important to emphasize a feature of the critical legal studies movement on which I have not up to this point placed much emphasis. But this in no way detracts from an insistence that a significant strength of contemporary critical legal studies derives from the contribution of the "new legal history" movement. Not only have leading exponents of the new history, such as Morton Horwitz been active participants within CCLS, but equally there has been an important historical dimension to the work of leading CLS activists such as Mark Tushnet, Duncan Kennedy, and Karl Klare. There is here an interesting contrast between Britain and the United States. The work of E. P. Thompson and Doug Hay when they, and others, took up and pursued an interest in the role of the law in eighteenth-century England proceeded in almost complete separation from critical legal scholars. Subsequently the two major texts produced had a profound impact on radical legal academics and that impact later influenced the theoretical development within the critical legal studies movement in the United States.

The importance of the new legal history is not only that it adds an important historical dimension lacking in most orthodox legal scholarship. More importantly, for my present concerns, is the theoretical contribution that is being made to critical legal studies. What is apparent is that the new historians are concerned to address fundamental and sharply posed questions of historical causality. Such lines of inquiry serve to sharpen the focus of the theoretical issues confronting critical legal studies. This is nowhere more important than in Bob Gordon's essay "Critical Legal Histories" (1984). His title is somewhat misleading because his ambit is much broader in that the sustained and powerful critique which he mounts of "evolutionary functionalism" is central to the concerns not only of legal history, but also of the sociology of law and critical legal theory. Further his essay concludes with an important elaboration and development of the constitutive theory of law (Gordon 1984, 104–125).

In considering the interaction of the new legal history and critical legal studies in elaborating a constitutive theory of law it is necessary to consider the way in which this development interacts with debates within contemporary Marxism. It is not simply that Marxism is often the chosen theoretical language, but it is important to recognize that important contributors like Morton Horwitz are explicitly non-Marxist. Rather the interconnection stems from the major questions addressed. These are concerned with exploring the causal interpenetration of legal and economic relations. It is because questions concerning the relationship between economic and noneconomic relationships have been so important within Marxism that the looming presence of Marx hangs over the current debates within critical legal theory.

It is now necessary to return to examine the formulation of a constitutive theory of law. The theses that law both constitutes and is constituted has to be pressed further. In this form it verges on the vacuous. A step forward can be taken by interrogating one of the best known formulations with which Edward Thompson concludes *Whigs and Hunters*. He argues that the daily activities of eighteenth-century English farmers occur "within visible and invisible structures of law."[49] The boundary marker is both the physical boundary as well as the legal object reinforced by ancient boundary ceremonies.

> Hence 'law' was deeply imbricated within the very basis of productive relations, which would have been inoperable without this law. And in the second place, this law, as definition or as rules (imperfectly enforceable through institutional legal forms), was endorsed by norms, tenaciously transmitted through the community. (1975:261)

Thompson's immediate purpose is to reject all instrumental theories of law as reducible to manipulative instruments of ruling classes. What is most important for our present purposes is his phrase " 'law' was deeply imbricated within the very basis of productive relations." Within the canons of Marxist theory he is making the claim that the social relations of production are not logically separable from and independent of the legal superstructure. Rather he argues that the relationships within which productive activity takes place are constituted by legal relations.[50] In addition he is also insisting that the presence of legal elements within the constitution of productive relations has distinctive consequences for the way in which those relations are lived out and struggled over. This point can be illustrated concretely from Thompson's historical material. The English forest peasantry fought tenaciously to defend the customary rights to grazing, timber, etc., not just because they had an economic interest but also because the legal recognition of customary rights was being challenged. Thus not only was their resistance founded on economic interest but it was grounded in legitimations which allowed them, as Thompson demonstrates, to win and mobilize significant allies from amongst the better-off yeomen farmers who became involved in defence of the prevailing customary and legal relations that formed the communities in and around the forest.

A clearly defined theoretical difference can be identified between Thompson's position and that argued by G. A. Cohen who insists that a central tenet of Marx's theory of history is the necessary separability of economic and legal relations (Cohen 1978). The issue posed involves what has become known as "the legal problem in historical material-ism" and centers on the question of whether it is possible to specify "property relations" as economic relations in such a way as to make no reliance upon legal concepts, and thus produce a "rechtsfrei" con-cept of property. Exponents of constitutive theory have not as yet addressed Cohen's argument as fully as it deserves.[51] A test case for the emergent constitutive theory of law will need to engage with Cohen's analysis before it can proceed to grapple with the interpenetration of legal and economic relations.

Karl Klare's initial presentation of constitutive theory involves a conception of the legal process "as, at least in part, a manner in which class relations are created and articulated, that is, to view law-making as a form of praxis" (Klare 1979:128).[52] It is immediately apparent that constitutive theory is closely connected to the concept of the relative autonomy of law; it embodies the aspiration toward an analysis in which law is viewed as both determining (constitutive) and deter-mined (constituted). As a version of relative autonomy theory it en-counters the same range of criticisms that has been considered above. In its role as an attempt to breathe substance into the relative autonomy thesis constitutive theory seeks to identify the effectivity of law. One important feature of constitutive theory that may allow it to overcome weaknesses in presently available formulations of the relative auton-omy thesis is its concern with the effectivity of law.[53] Edward Thomp-son is concerned to insist that the fact that customary practices were embedded in legal *form* had implications both for the way in which claims were mobilized by the forest-dwellers and for how such claims were responded to by both judiciary and the state. Klare illustrates this concern with effectivity (without employing the concept) in his own research on the National Labor Relations Act of 1935. His general conclusion was that the legislation "contributed to defining what the character of capitalism would become and creating the institutional and social relations of the late capitalist workplace" (Klare 1979:131).[54]

This formulation involves a "strong" assertion of the causal role of the NLRA in shaping workplace relations. But just as the relative autonomy thesis provides no means for specifying the "limits" of the autonomy of law neither does constitutive theory provide any account of the causal weight of the legislation's constitutive effects.

One possible response to this objection is to insist that the question of specific causal weight can be resolved only in the context of the study of particular concrete historical situations. The risk inherent in such a response is that of lapsing back into a naive empiricism in which every situation is uniquely the result of the specific causal factors. In its present state of development the constitutive theory of law is an aspiration toward theory that does not, as yet, exist.

A step forward toward this objective can be taken by employing the concept "conditions of existence" that directs attention to the necessary requirements for the existence of a social institution or practice, and the means by which these conditions are secured or provided.[55] The identification of the conditions of existence makes possible the study of both the processes thorough which these conditions are provided and the interaction between the conditions in constituting the social phenomenon under consideration. It we return to Klare's own example of the processes involved in creating the social relations of the workplace, we can identify the part played by labor law in creating specific mechanisms of collective bargaining and arbitration procedures. But we are also enabled to focus on its interaction with the given structure of management and the forms of trade union practice. Within this analytic model we can identify the specific legal regulation of the NLRA not as a single constitutive element but in its interactive relationship with the economic practices within which it is located and on which it has identifiable effects; in this way it is possible to avoid applying constitutive theory as a disguised form of legal monism.

The important question that this suggested theoretical model must confront is whether this is not, dressed up in fancy language, just a simple old-fashioned empiricism in which factors are isolated and assigned some causal weight. This charge can be rejected, not because its object is an empirical enquiry, this indeed is a positive merit, but because it does not employ an empiricist epistemology that insists that an object of knowledge can be provided only by experience. Rather the conditions of existence stand in a logical or necessary relation to the object of inquiry; experimental data are pertinent in requiring the checking of the content or formulation of these concepts. The method allows and facilitates a complex theoretical elaboration that is capable of application to concrete particulars.

This procedure involves the preempirical stage of the analytical identification of necessary preconditions without which the relationship under analysis could not exist. The empirical stage of enquiry concerns the manner and form in which these elements are provided. This stage of analysis will be concerned with the different ways in which, in historically particular circumstances, the conditions of existence are differentially met in comparable circumstances. This can be illustrated by offering a brief reinterpretation of Robert Brenner's analysis of the different trajectories of the peasantry in preindustrial England, France, and eastern Europe.[56] Brenner seeks to explain how it came about that the response to the population decline from the fourteenth century resulted in the intensification of feudalism in the East, the institutionalization of a strong peasantry in France, and the eradication of a peasant class in England. The conditions of existence of a class will involve *inter alia*:

1. the capacity to formulate interests as claims,
2. the means of articulating claims in legitimated form (e.g., claims of right, of custom, etc.),
3. the capacity to mobilize (and to win allies) in advancing and protecting claims.

Brenner's conclusion was that it is not possible to make sense of the course of European feudalism without invoking an analysis of the structure of class relations. In the terms of the methodology here proposed the variant outcomes can be understood in terms of both the degree and the form in which the three conditions of existence identified were secured. In general the capacity of the peasantry to mobilize and thus to secure, protect, and reinforce both customary and legal rights provides the explanatory framework for the divergent fates of the peasantry in Europe.

A methodology of this type has the additional merit of being able to take advantage of some of the insights of structuralist theory. I assume that it is essential to avoid any circularity in the application of structural theory in which the structure is defined in such a way that it provides its own supports or conditions of existence. The most important step is to insist on a dual relationship between the general (structure) and the particular (elements of a structure) by a process that Foucault calls "double conditioning" (Foucault 1978:99–100).[57] Neither a structure nor its elements are understandable on their own. No particular elements of legal regulation or legal practice is to be studied without taking account of its location within the structure of "the Law," while "the Law" has no purchase except through the specific regulations or practices. This interactive relationship is such that neither is reducible to or explainable in terms of the other. This framework is not restricted in its application to the most obvious example employed above of particular legal doctrines situated within a given legal system; it may be employed in such a way as to break free from this common-sense positivist conception of "laws" within a "legal system." Our attention should be directed to its relevance to the analysis of the relationship between different forms of law, thus allowing us to go beyond the general assumption that underlies much critical scholarship of a single form of law as constituting the structure of a legal system.[58] Similarly it helps focus attention on the concern with legal pluralism that is currently playing an important part in a theorization of law that breaks with many of the assumptions of legal positivism (Abel 1982).

The reformulation of a constitutive theory of law that I have proposed is capable of elaboration within a range of different theoretical emphases; it is compatible with, for example, some of the recent advances in Marxist theory, structuralist analysis or Foucault's institutionalism. Further, it is formulated in such a way as to avoid some of the more important problems encountered in the analysis of critical legal theory presented in this chapter. It is compatible with a strong commitment to an emphasis on the connectedness of law and the external social totality without relinquishing a concern with the specific effectivity of legal doctrine. Similarly it seeks to breathe substance into the concept of the relative autonomy of law without falling foul of the indeterminacy inherent in its general formulation. Finally, this theorization seeks explicitly to fulfil the critical theorist's promise of being able to draw on different theoretical traditions. The claim that can be made for it is that it does so by avoiding the "melange" of different traditions, but rather combines them in a form that makes explicit their interconnections and is sensitive to problems involved in establishing such integration.

CONCLUSION

The emergence of critical legal studies is the most important intellectual development in the field of legal studies since the rise of Realism.

It is, of course, significant that it shares many common characteristics with that earlier movement and is conscious of those connections. But to conceive of critical legal studies as little more than a "new Realism" is to underestimate both the distinguishing characteristics of the new movement and its potential.

Critical legal studies takes up a significantly different stance in relationship to the prevailing orthodoxy of legal scholarship from that of the Realists. The Realist disenchantment with legal formalism was pragmatic; orthodoxy did not provide satisfactory answers for the constituency that the Realists sought to represent. Formalism provided no satisfactory guidance for legal practitioners concerned with improving the efficiency of their concern to predict the outcomes of litigation nor an adequate framework for the policy concerns of legislators. Critical legal scholars are not preoccupied by such pragmatic considerations; they do not seek to articulate the concerns of legal practitioners or legislators or, in general, of "insiders" within the legal process. Critical scholars are motivated by a much broader political objective within which it is "the law" itself that is "the problem"; law is not conceived as being capable of resolving the problems that it apparently addresses. Rather law is seen as a significant constituent in the complex set of processes that reproduces the experience and reality of human subordination and domination; thus the wider concern with the conditions and possibility of human emancipation forms the extended political perspective of the movement.

The organizing concerns of the critical legal studies movement are very different and much broader than those of their Realist forebears. Yet it is crucial to an understanding of the potential of the critical movement to take cognisance of their focus on the detailed interrogation of legal doctrine. Other significant precursors of critical legal theory, in particular that embodied in the sociology of law, were concerned with a predominantly "external" perspective on law focusing in on the results and impact of legal institutions and processes. Within these concerns legal doctrine hardly figured. Indeed, insofar as the "sociological movement in law" took up the Realist problematic of "the gap" between legal ideal and legal reality, their focus was, and remains, predominantly with the result or output of legal processes, "the law in action." The critical legal movement runs the risk of omitting the potential of this tradition of research. But this risk of omission stems not from neglect but rather from a preoccupation with the internal processes of legal consciousness, which results in a predominant emphasis on the ideological or legitimatory role at the expense of its regulatory role. Or, to put the same point in the language that has much influenced the sociology of law, to stress the symbolic function of law over its instrumental function.

I detect no impediment, stemming from either a theoretical or a political cause, that will not allow critical legal studies to readjust this balance. The fault, insofar as there is one, has been to overcompensate in their rejection of instrumentalism with an overemphasis on the ideological dimension of law. In this one detects a heavy reliance on a pessimistic view of reification and mystification as the all-embracing reality of modern society. There is less evidence of a more measured attempt to grasp the interaction between instrumental and symbolic, or coercive and consensual dimensions of legal phenomena. Although this thrust does emerge in a number of individual papers, it has not yet received substantive attention and development.

CHAPTER 8

ON LEGAL RELATIONS AND ECONOMIC RELATIONS: A CRITIQUE OF G.A. COHEN

INTRODUCTION

This chapter is concerned with a problem that at first sight is internal to Marxist theory: whether or not a coherent distinction can be maintained between what Marx referred to as the "base" and the "superstructure." This question turns on whether the relations of production that constitute the base can be identified in such a way as not to invoke legal relations since the latter are classified as part of the superstructure. These issues are approached via a critique of G.A. Cohen's defence of Marx's theses concerning the relationship between base and superstructure.

Against the objection that such a project is of relevance only to the exegesis of Marx over which too much ink and energy have already been lavished this chapter has an objective that goes beyond its immediate concern with the examination of Cohen's reformulation of Marx's base-superstructure metaphor. This wider objective involves an exploration of the possibilities for the development of a legal theory that avoids two equal and opposing styles of legal theory. The objective is to avoid the positing of an autonomous conception of law that is characteristic of many versions of liberal legal theory and, at the same time, to eschew the conception of law as dependent or determined, which is characteristic of the version of Marxism defended by Cohen. This chapter is thus a part of a wider project to articulate a third conception, a *constitutive* theory of law. This project may be summarized by the slogan: neither autonomous law, nor dependent law, but constitutive law. In other words it seeks to shift the focus of attention toward issues involved in the formulation of a *relational theory of law* that elaborates a conception of law that starts from a general concept of "social relations" conceived as inescapably cultural phenomena in that they necessarily involve socially constructed meanings, values, and norms. Legal relations are treated as specific forms of social relations and thus likewise involve such socially constructed meanings. As Godelier expresses it, "every social relationship is born and exists at once within thought and outside it" (1978:92).[1]

In seeking the indulgent attention of readers not concerned with the particularities of Marxist theory my contention is that it is in the debates that surround Marxism that one finds in their most developed form explorations of some of the most pervasive problems of determination and causality that confront the whole field of social and legal theory.

"THE LEGAL PROBLEM IN MARX": THE PROBLEM STATED

Marx's exposition of the "guiding thread" for his theory of history involves establishing a distinction between an economic base and a superstructure. Critics have contended that Marx's own formulation fails to establish such a distinction. The key passage appears in the Preface to *The Critique of Political Economy*:

> The totality of these relations of production constitutes the economic structure of society, the real foundation, on which rises a legal and political superstructure . . . At a certain stage of development, the material productive forces of society come into conflict with the existing relations of production, or— *this merely expresses the same thing in legal terms—with the property relations within the framework of which they have operated hitherto.* (Marx 1971:20–21; emphasis added)

Critics (e.g., Plamenatz, Acton) have argued that this passage reveals that Marx held "property relations" to be part of the economic base while more generally in the Preface itself and elsewhere he consistently defines "law" as part of the superstructure. Hence it appears that law is both superstructural and, at the same time, that one of the forms of legal relations, namely, "property relations" is a constituent of the economic base. Thus it seems that the base/superstructure distinction collapses or must be judged to be conceptually incoherent. The issue at stake is no mere terminological issue within historical materialism for as Plamenatz insists "the whole doctrine of economic determinism turns upon it" (Plamenatz 1954:27; Acton 1970).

COHEN'S SOLUTION

G.A. Cohen in his *Karl Marx's Theory of History: A Defence* (1978) sets out to defend the coherence of the base/superstructure distinction. He accepts that the offending passage does lay itself open to the charge levelled by his critics, but he claims that Marx's general thesis can be reformulated in such a way as both to defeat the charge and to provide a coherent restatement of the base/superstructure distinction.

The initial focus of this chapter will be to consider Cohen's reformulation and, in particular, his contention that it is possible to advance a conception of "production relations" that does not involve any reference to legal relations (*rechtsfrei* production relations). I will seek to show that Cohen fails in this endeavor.

Cohen's solution is disarmingly simple: it involves the substitution of the concept of "rights" (which are inescapably tainted by law) by a concept of "powers" (which are law-free). This allows him to elaborate Marx's concept of "production relations" in terms of the powers of economic agents without invoking any concepts that are tainted by law (and thus by a superstructural element). If such a description of "production relations" can be achieved it will again be possible to sustain an insistence on the conceptual coherence of the base/superstructure theory. Once this stage has been reached it becomes, in principle, possible to give an account of legal relations expressed in terms of production relations. It is to this solution that attention must now be turned.

CRITIQUE OF COHEN

It is not part of my project to engage in a general discussion of either Cohen's method or of his version of historical materialism. In particular I propose to consider his defense of the base/superstructure thesis in its own terms. These terms I take to be characterized by his deployment of an analytical method; this method he employs rather than elaborates. It consists of a procedure that treats concepts as standing in a direct relation to the reality that they seek to make comprehensible and that are capable of being "analyzed" in that entities (or "terms") are broken down into their simplest or component elements or parts. These basic elements are treated as standing in external relations to each other. This intellectual strategy involves the construction of formal models of reality as composed of basic or primary concepts that in their additive combination produce access to complex totalities. For reasons that are beyond my present concern I am generally unsympathetic to this intellectual style. What it gains in terms of its analytic rigor and elegance, which his writing undoubtedly possesses, it loses in its capacity to grapple with a reality that I deny can be reduced to atomic components. The many issues associated with this I leave aside and wish only to comment on one particular difficulty.

Cohen's treatment of "relations" involves special problems. For him things, entities, or "terms" have their characteristics or primary qualities inherent to and within themselves; they are thus independent of the relations into which they enter. Relations are external to and independent of the things or the terms related; entities or "things" exist and only subsequently enter into relations. As Cohen expresses it, "the terms bound by relations do not belong to the structure these relations constitute" (1978:35). I find myself unable and unwilling to adhere to Cohen's theory of relations (or more accurately his theory of external relations). I will do no more than state that I hold the opposite view that social reality is constituted by and through relations; there are no things or social entities that have an existence separable from relations. Relations, on this alternative view, are internal to and essential to the nature of all social life. This different view of social relations should be taken into account as providing a wider theoretical context to my criticism of his treatment of both social relations in general and the particular forms of social relations (for example, in the discussion of slavery below) that enter into my discussion.

On "Powers" and "Rights"

Cohen's attempt to produce a clear separation between the economic base and the superstructure requires that he be able fully and adequately to identify relations of production in terms that make no reliance on legal or other superstructural elements. In particular it requires him to eschew any presupposition of any already existing legal relations of ownership and property and any terms that make reference to "rights" such as presume the prior existence of such legal relations. The core of his strategy for the articulation of such a *rechtsfrei* identification of relations of production lies in his claim that it is possible, without loss of substance, to substitute the concept "powers" for all references to "rights."

Now we can transform any phrase of the form "the right to ø" into a phrase which denotes a power by dropping the word "right" and replacing it by the word "power". (1978:219)

The significance of this substitution is that it not only purges all rights-talk but that it involves the claims that (1) the substituted power "matches" the purged right[2] and that (2) "possession of powers does not entail possession of the rights they match" (1978:219). In other words it is possible fully to identify relations of production without reference to rights. My concern is to consider whether he realizes this objective.

A starting point is provided by the interesting exchange with Steven Lukes; Cohen's original formulation of the substitution of powers for rights is challenged by Lukes and defended by Cohen (Lukes 1982; Cohen 1983). The exchange clarifies some of the issues involved. Lukes' challenge is directed against the viability of the nonnormative concept of powers on the grounds that in substituting powers for rights he does not succeed in excluding normative, and in particular legal terms, from his conception of relations of production or, more generally, from the economic base. For present purposes I will assume, as Cohen himself does, that the terms "norms" and "legal" may be used interchangeably. Cohen identifies a power in the following terms, "a man has power to ø if and only if he is able to ø" (1978:220).

For Lukes the ability to do ø cannot be separated from the conditions and constraints that determine the results of such ø-ing. It only makes sense to say "X has the power to do ø" if such a statement includes reference to the conditions and constraints under which X acts. Normative elements necessarily form part of such conditions and constraints.[3] Cohen's reply helps us to restate what is at issue.

My main objection to Lukes' critique is that it is largely an emphatic statement of what I already amply acknowledged. He insists on what I grant, and insist on myself, that powers generally need the support of norms. (1983:214)

Lukes however was well aware of Cohen's "powers need supports" position. What is at issue he identifies as

Cohen's claim that norms can be seen as bringing about and sustaining relations of production *while remaining no part of their content.* (1982:216)

We can make sense of the disagreement if we pose it in the following terms: let us assume that it is agreed that "supports" (normative, legal or other) are external or additional to the exercise of powers; what is at issue is whether one can meaningfully identify a power without reference to its "conditions" as distinct from its "supports." (I will subsequently take issue with this distinction between conditions and supports: see "Powers and Supports" infra). If we consider the simple case of the power of parents to punish their children a "condition" of that power is that the parent is bigger and stronger than the child or that the child cannot yet run as fast as the parent and thus evade punishment. Once a child is larger and faster than the parent then the parent no longer has the "power to punish." A "support," on the other hand, is provided where the child has internalized the parent's "right to punish" or where the police show reluctance to intervene in "family disputes." We can leave aside consideration of supports for the moment since the objection against Cohen is that we cannot specify the content of a "power" without reference to its conditions.

As the case of child-beating indicates these conditions are the relative strength and speed of the protagonists. Lukes' case against Cohen is made if it can be established that normative elements are, along with physical conditions, potential elements of the conditions that specify the content of a power or that except in very limited situations the content of a power cannot be adequately identified without reference to its normative conditions. Cohen, in the course of his exchange with Lukes, is at pains to insist that he does not seek to deny the connection between powers and norms. To amplify this contention he proposes a distinction between a "non-normative concept of power" (which he seeks to defend) and a "concept of non-normative power" (which he suggests Lukes wrongly attributes to him). A nonnormative concept does not deny that norms are relevant to the analysis of powers, but merely that a "concept" can be generated that excludes reference to or reliance on normative elements such that norms are in some important sense external to powers. "What I call 'powers' are not essentially non-normative ... but simply not essentially normative" (Cohen 1983:215).

This response seeks to set up a contest between his preferred "non-normative concept of power" and a "normative concept of power." This formulation, I suggest, evades the issue in dispute. I find no difficulty in conceding that *some* powers can adequately be captured by a nonnormative formulation. Typically I suggest such power situations involve face-to-face contacts exhibiting explicitly coercive features. The gun-slinging "Your money or your life" power can successfully be captured by a nonnormative concept; but such cases are uninteresting and atypical because they lack any temporal dimension or the persistence that characterizes all the most important forms of social relations, including in particular social relations of production. My contention is that Cohen is unable to construct a nonnormative concept of those forms of social relationships, namely social relations of production, which it is necessary for him successfully to represent in norm-free or *rechtsfrei* terms. This can be illustrated if we consider the example of *slavery* which he himself frequently invokes.[4]

Slavery Examined

In constructing his analysis of slavery as a relation of production, Cohen relies on an approach, which, while not denying the pertinence of norms, seeks to externalize them by assigning to them the role of "supporting" or "enabling" powers. His typical formulation is, "the proletarian has the power to withhold his labour power, while the slave does not" (1978:222). My purpose in considering the social relation of slavery is to deny Cohen the entitlement to say that rights and powers are distinct by insisting that rights are only relevant in so far as they provide "supports" but are not themselves constitutive of those powers. Thus he conceives of agents as possessing powers that may be assisted or impeded by independently existing rights.

I shall have more to say below (see "Cohen's Conception of Power") about his conception of power. For present purposes it is sufficient to consider the implication of what Cohen himself insists on, namely, that "powers" are by definition "effective powers"; while we can distinguish between an "effective" and an "ineffective right" there can logically be no "ineffective powers." This is clear in his own formulation that "relations of production involve what people are *effectively able to do*" (Cohen 1983:213).

The concept of "effective powers," and thus of "powers" themselves necessarily includes or embraces an external frame of reference to what it is that makes those powers effective. For present purposes I will retain Cohen's own usage and refer to the "conditions" that generate effective powers. A simple illustration serves to underline this point. We cannot assume that the possession of money makes an agent powerful; it certainly does in a monetary economy but will be irrelevant in a barter economy. Powers then cannot be separated from the conditions that render them effective since without these they are not powers at all. Thus it is necessary to take account of the *conditions* under which an agent operates before it is possible to provide any account of the powers which an agent has. Or, putting the same point in an alternative formulation: to ask the question "Does X have power Y?" can be answered only in the wider social context of the conditions that determine whether the agent has effective power. These conditions are what I will call "fully social conditions" (i.e., they will include both material and normative dimensions). If it can be shown that legal and other norms are constitutive of the conditions that determine the content of an agent's powers then Cohen's attempt at a rigorous separation between rights and powers must fail.

Before offering such a demonstration I shall consider Cohen's defense against this line of argument, namely, that he has never sought to deny and has indeed himself urged that "powers need supports." The admission of the importance of "supports" is no threat to his argument since they are distinct from and external to the powers he seeks to describe. I will shortly challenge the viability of this distinction between powers and supports (see "Powers and Supports" below). For present purposes it is sufficient to suggest that it involves an oversimplified conception of social relations. Powers are not the possessions of agents; rather they are the resultants of the conditions that taken together constitute social relations.[5] It is in this context that we are able to recognize the inherent weakness of his "external" conception of relations pointed to in the Introduction. Since he conceives of agents as external to the relations in which they participate he is obliged to treat power as a possession of agents and not as a characteristic of the relations that are constitutive of the agents themselves.

The problem with Cohen's distinction between powers and their supports is that he treats powers as if they are manifested in the immediate or face to face interaction of parties abstracted from both their material determinants and from the range of meanings, understandings, and beliefs that determine the concrete manifestations of those encounters.[6] In so far as a distinction between the "conditions" and "supports" of a social relation serves any value it is to indicate only a variation in the degree of proximity involved in the encounters between social agents. It is important to keep such usage under close rein for fear that we take literally the spatial imagery of "distance" and "proximity" that we all too readily employ in finding the language to express causality. For present purposes I employ, I hope with due caution, a spatial distinction between "conditions" and "supports" while Cohen falls into error by treating such linguistic devices too literally.

Thus when he addresses himself to the question: "Can a slave withhold his labour?" the answer appears self-evident: "if he does not work he is likely to be killed" (Cohen 1978:222). If master, M, and slave S, were to confront each other on the ubiquitous desert island and we avoid Defoe's common-sensical racism that white men and the "natural" masters of "savages" (significantly this ideology Defoe assigns to both Crusoe and Friday), then whether S must work for M depends on M's physical strength, possession of a superior weapon, or monopoly of some useful resource or skill. But if, for example, S is stronger than M the tables may be reversed (or they might even adopt a nonexploitative division of labor). But in slave societies S's labor for M does not depend on M's superior physical strength. But rather M's power to compel S to work will depend on a range of conditions that gradually moves out from the immediate encounter between M and S, for example, M's possession of a whip, the security of S's shackles, the number of overseers employed, and so on. The conceptual problem is whether each of these conditions should itself be regarded as constitutive of M's power and thus of the social relationship of slavery.

Looked at from S's standpoint whether he submits depends not only on the immediate consequences of refusal but also on the possibility of escape. Not only will he have to free himself from whip, shackles, and overseers but he must also calculate his chances of remaining free. The relevant population, through which S must pass, may fear M's retribution should they assist S's flight. Or, alternatively, they may be under the influence of a religion that legitimizes slavery and will join spontaneously and with enthusiasm the ensuing slave hunt. Or the legal regime may stipulate punitive sanctions for assisting runaway slaves.

As we move further from the face-to-face encounter between master and slave a number of conclusions emerge. First that the power of M over S cannot be understood in terms of the interpersonal encounter; nor is it possible to draw a satisfactory distinction between the conditions (or resources) in which M may draw that are internal to M's power and some other features that are supports, that is, are external to M's power. Cohen's attempt to offer an account of the master's power over the slave looks increasingly unsatisfactory. To understand why this is the case it will be necessary to examine below ("Cohen's Conception of Power") the common sensical concept of power that he employs, but before doing so there is an important dimension of his general solution, namely, the claim that "powers match rights" that must be considered.

The Matching of Powers and Rights

The conceptual distinction that Cohen draws between rights and powers is supplemented by a claim that the powers with which he replaces rights stand in the relations of "matching." It is important to explore the implications of that claim. That rights and powers are conceptually distinct is shown in the demonstration that

> it is logically possible to have a right without the power you have when the right is effective, and to have a power without a right that would make the power legitimate. (1983:214)

In other words the cases of ineffective rights and illegitimate powers establish the conceptual distinction between the terms "rights" and "powers." It is essential to his project to demonstrate that once the conceptual distinction has been established that it is possible to show that the employment of the concept "powers" when used in substitution for "rights" involves no loss of meaning; his term, which designates this claim, is that powers "match" rights; by this he seeks to convey that any rights statement can be rendered syntactically in terms of powers without any loss of meaning or content. His claim is that powers "match" rights but do not provide an adequate analysis thereof. The "common syntax of rights and powers" (1983:217) on which Cohen relies leads Lukes to begin to indicate an objection which I seek to develop; namely, that the common syntax can provide only a "thin *behavioural* description" (Lukes 1982:219) that fails to achieve the "matching" or equivalence that Cohen requires to sustain his solution.

The common syntactic feature on which Cohen's exercise relies is generated by relating both powers and rights to a behavioral focus on "doing": "A power is always a power to do something" (1978:237) This allows him to claim that a "right to do X" matches a "power to do X."[7] The problem with his behavioral definition of power is that it prescriptively excludes legal or other normative elements in that both rights and powers are restricted to an association with external observable or behavioral "doing." Even within the analytic philosophical tradition that Cohen employs it has not proved possible to combine it with a sociological behavioralism on which he now seeks to rely. This is most clearly attested by a consideration of performative speech acts (e.g., promising, naming, willing, and so on).[8] If we employ his method of transcription for "X has a right to promise" it yields "X has a power to promise." This formulation does not succeed in purging normative elements; it is devoid of meaning without reference to concepts of normative expectations and reciprocity. More generally we can object to behavioralism on the more general grounds that it is a form of reductionism that fails to make a full transition from "action" (or "doing") as external behavioral manifestations to "human action," imbued with will, intentionality, and purpose.[9]

These objections suggest that Cohen's "solution" by means of the transposition from rights to powers fails to provide the "match" that he claims. It is only by artificially restricting the range and capacity of rights-talk that he is able to advance a claim that powers match rights. At best powers can never be more than attenuated versions of the rights they seek to replace.

Powers and Supports

One of the major features of Cohen's argument that, up to this point, has not been challenged, must now be brought into question. Recall that the major plank of his defense against Lukes was to insist that Lukes' criticism missed its target because he himself had insisted that "powers need supports." Retaining Cohen's terminology I now want to challenge the distinction between "powers" and their "supports" by insisting that without supports there are no powers or, in other words, supports are not external to or supplemental to powers but rather that they are constitutive of powers. It should be stressed that it is not by purpose to elaborate an alternative account of social power; it is sufficient to insist that such an endeavor must reverse the order of Cohen's treatment in that it would seek to explain the characteristics of social encounters, with which he starts, in terms of the systemic properties of social systems in order to arrive at the means for accounting for the presence of power within particular social encounters.[10]

His conception of "supports" is predetermined by the metaphor that is imported; definitionally that which is "supported" is distinct from its supports, which is as a consequence necessarily external. Thus externality is the semantic result of metaphor rather than of any explicit analysis that might offer criteria of how powers are to be distinguished from those things, in particular normative and legal features, that Cohen seeks to exile to an external or supporting role. For such a strategy to succeed would require him to show that we can provide an adequate account of the mechanisms or properties of powers without importing reference to any of the excluding legal or normative terms. As has been demonstrated with respect to his discussion of slavery he seeks to do this by focusing on interpersonal encounters and by importing a conception of power as a physical property or imbalance within the encounter. Once this reductionist character of his strategy has been recognized it is evident that his analysis cannot account for systematic and systemic power relations. This has already been seen for the case of slavery and can now be demonstrated for the important case of wage-labor.

The power of the capitalist over the worker in Cohen's account results from the conjunction of the capitalist power over productive forces and the free labor that is dependent on the sale of its labor-power such that the capitalist is able to direct and control its application. To have control over productive forces the capitalist has to bring together premises, equipment, machinery and materials. Not only are some or all of these elements dependent on a complex system of legal relations but the power of command over labor that they give rise to is inseparably linked to customary, negotiated, or legal norms (all of which are struggled over and between which the balance shifts in specific and overdetermined forms) about the rate and type of work that can be required. Power is not separable from the network of social and economic relations within which it is located and thus cannot be usefully viewed as an extension of the direct encounter between agents in which one "possesses" more power than the other. Nothing in this account creates any grounds for designating any one feature as a support to a more basic power. This does not imply that we cannot agree criteria for distinguishing between powers and their supports.

The consequence of these criticisms of Cohen's concept of power is that it fatally undermines his claim that the concept "powers" can be substituted for "rights" in such a way that powers can be said to "match" rights. It is the "matching" quality that allows him to approach the exercise as one of *translation* that is where the only term affected is one directly exchangeable and thus involves no other change or alteration while allowing one to say the same thing, that is, to retain the same substantive content. Recall that Cohen's project is to demonstrate that a coherent distinction between base and superstructure can be sustained by "translating" the language in which relations of production are expressed to exclude all superstructural, and in particular, legal content. If my arguments against his substitution of powers for rights succeeds then it follows that he has not established a convincing conceptual separation; at its strongest the powers/supports distinction is purely formal.

Cohen's Conception of Power

The above discussion of "supports" and "powers" discloses an additional ground for rejecting the distinction that Cohen seeks to draw between "powers" and "rights." There is an unexplored connection between "powers" and "power" in which his conception on the former rests on a distinctive but unpersuasive theory of power. There is an elision of "powers" and "power" in his account. His conception of power may be described as a "commodity theory of power"; it assumes that power is a natural "resource" capable of "possession" by agents. His conception of power links two aspects; it is (1) "voluntarist" (the ability to achieve one's goals or exercise one's will) and (2) it treats power as a resource (i.e., as a means of realising goals). The most important implication of this view is that it treats power as something capable of *possession*; it sees power as something one is able to possess and alienate like a commodity. Since it is voluntarist, agents may choose to exercise the power they possess or may abstain from so acting, in which case it may be "saved" for later deployment. This view is analogous to the power of a battery; it is a finite resource capable of being deployed at will but liable to exhaustion unless recharged or replaced.

Before considering the deficiencies inherent in this conception of power it is significant to note that it exhibits an homologous form to the standard concept of possessive rights that Cohen employs. Thus it assists in simplifying his translation from "rights" to "powers" in that they are both presumed to be voluntarist and possessory resources. If his conception of power is successfully challenged an immediate consequence is that it disrupts or even disallows the form of "translation" from rights to powers on which his solution to the legal problem in Marx employs since, as we have seen, this relies upon the simple substitution of "power" for "right" in the phrase "the right to ø."

The objection to the commodity theory of power is that it focuses on the end result of a process that is itself thereby obscured. Our attention is directed toward the moment in which power is exercised and at the same time the presupposition that this occurs within a narrowly conceived relational context between two agents (M exercises power over S) or two groups of agents (for example, slave-masters exercise power over slaves). Within this narrow relational view power, although intensely real and immediate, is somehow mysterious in that although we readily comprehend what it means to exercise power, what it is that constitutes that power is left hanging. This view of power is suffocated by its proximity to unreflective common sense; it is a common sense which is plausible only when applied to face-to-face relations. It is significant that it is such examples that Cohen selects to illustrate his argument. The master stands with ship over the bent back of the slave—that power is present holds no mystery, it is only too material. But slavery is not created in this encounter between master and slave, rather it is the result of the *institution* of slavery that is not reducible to the endless repetition of encounters between masters and slaves.

It is important to stress that the relational aspect of power is not in dispute nor that power is manifested in social encounters. What is omitted is the systemic character of power in which power can be apprehended only by attending to the social conditions of its existence. While the ability to exercise direct control over others is one facet of power, more importantly, power involves the capacity to mobilize both natural and, of key importance for my argument, social resources. Cohen implicitly seeks to restrict his analysis of power to the mobilization of natural or physical resources. Among the many modes through which social power operates is through the shaping of wills and aspirations, the production of subjectivities and of collectivities that are both more typical and more important than the physical control conception of power that Cohen employs. The commodity theory of power abstracts the concept "power" from and wider theoretical or conceptual system that locates power within some social totality. There is an unrecognized empiricism in Cohen's conception of power as if it were something or a property that could be named and over which possession by agents could be asserted without reference to any other features of either social relations or the social totalities within which they have their existence.[11]

Powers and Rights: A Final View

We are now in a position to review the criticisms leveled against Cohen's solution. Its two key features, the rights/powers distinction and the claim that the distinction can provide an analysis in which the substitution of powers for rights can be effected in terms of powers that "match" rights, are both flawed. He fails to establish that it is possible to employ a conception of powers from which all normative and legal dimensions can be systematically eliminated. The fact that this purging can be achieved for a limited number of simple face-to-face encounters does not establish that it is adequate to the task for which it is designed, namely, the analysis of relations of production.

The contention that powers match rights has been shown to rest on limited syntactic characteristics of the sentences that Cohen considers, which in turn are flawed by the behavioralist assumptions that he makes but does not defend. Finally the whole exercise is undermined by an unpersuasive and oversimplified theory of power on which it depends. Cohen, despite the many interesting issues and questions posed along the route, fails to provide us with the promised *rechtsfrei* analysis of relations of production.

Before concluding the discussion of Cohen's substitution of powers for rights it is necessary to consider whether I have succeeded in evading the defense that he readily concedes that "powers need supports" that is a specific application of his general contention that "bases need superstructures" (1978:231). This response suggests that the best that my discussion may have achieved is to elaborate what is relevant to concrete historical analysis, namely, that legal and other normative elements figure significantly in any adequate account of the production and reproduction of power relations. My claim is to have said considerably more than this, in particular by challenging his distinction between powers and supports I have, if successful in making out that case, disallowed the response that he successfully employed against Lukes' criticism. My contention is that his powers/supports distinction is purely definitional in that in setting up a narrow or behavioralist conception of power he thereby permits himself to exclude all unwanted elements from his conception such that they are reduced to the secondary role of supports. I have contended that such a strategy has persuasive power only in the most limited and uninteresting case of face-to-face encounters between agents and cannot be allowed to stand in the central cases to which he addresses himself namely, social relations of production. It remains the case that lurking behind my differences with Cohen is the broader issue of the opposition between theories of external relations and of internal relations that it has been my intention to identify without pursuing in any depth; such a debate concerns his general reading of Marx and is beyond the scope of this chapter.

Thus far my argument has not taken any position on the general issue of the relationship between base and superstructure and its implications for the analysis of the social function of law. Before turning to these substantive issues it is necessary to spell out some further consequences of the failure of Cohen's "solution" by considering two issues with respect to which he offers an account in terms of the rights/powers distinction; the next section addresses the question of the role of contractual relations within capitalist relations of production and the subsequent section considers the account he offers of illegal squatters.

CONTRACT AND RELATIONS OF PRODUCTION

In the course of his exchange with Lukes the issue of the connection between contract (which Cohen concedes is paradigmatically "legal") and capitalist relations of production is posed. Lukes invokes contract in order to make the point that contract is a normative (legal) social institution without which any workable conception of capitalism is inconceivable. Cohen's response is to concede that there is an "important connection" between contract and capitalism but that this does not affect his contention for a *rechtsfrei* conception of relations of production since contract is not itself a relation of production nor does it form part of such relations. In order to stick close to Cohen's argument I shall not pursue the objection that questions the value of a conception of capitalism in terms of relations of production conceived in such a way as to exclude contractual relations (contracts for the sale of labor power and for the sale of commodities) from the primary identification of capitalism.[12] Cohen's defense invokes his rights/powers distinction discussed above that fails if, as I have argued, he cannot sustain the translation solution that hinges on the close proximity of rights and powers presumed by his notion that "powers match rights." Without this "matching" connection his point is trivial since it involves nothing more than the well-established distinction between *de jure* and *de facto* rights or that the existence of rights does not itself secure the conditions for their effective exercise.

His defence involves a new set of issues not so far considered concerning some peculiarities of his conception of "social relations of production." These he defines as "effective powers over persons and productive forces" (1978:63). The issue to be considered is whether this conception of relations of production succeeds in excluding contractual relations. Consider his discussion of Marx's analysis of the gradual subordination of the independent weaver to the merchant that Marx treated as a paradigmatic case of the transition to industrial capitalism. At first the weaver "sells" his product to the merchant. Through a series of stages the merchant comes first to supply the weaver's materials and then to acquire rights or controls over the product that deny the weaver the right to sell to another and next to purchase the weaver's labor power while not affecting the weaver's ownership of the loom as the means of production employed; the final stage involves the separation of the producer from the loom and moving the "proletarianized" weaver into a mill. This process, considered as a whole, transforms the independent producer/merchant relationship into one between proletarian/capitalist. I concur with Cohen's view that the critical stage in this process and thus the most important element in the conception of the proletarian/capitalist relationship is that proletarians sell their labor-power. But I contend that it follows from this consideration that the different forms and stages of contractual relations are constitutive of the production relation conceived as relations between economic agents (or groups of agents). Cohen, I suggest, not only does not but would be unable to give a sufficient account of this process without including reference to the different forms of contractual and other legal relations and the associated rights created thereby. To attempt to reduce the analysis to the exercise of effective powers must fail.

To show that this is the case let us consider in more detail the stage at which the merchant provides (through an act of sale or some other form of assignment) materials on which the weaver works while, at the same time, acquiring by a distinct and separable transaction the product. This process involves (and I claim cannot be understood without) important changes in the legal relation between the parties. At the outset there exist separable contracts (first for the sale of materials and the purchase of the product); the distinctive change comes about when the merchant no longer transfers ownership in the materials to the weaver but where (depending on the further specification of the details of the arrangement, legal relations of bailment or of agency exist, protected by actions for conversion) the retention of ownership is itself an important contribution to the tightening of the connections that bind the weaver to the merchant by denying the former the right to sell his product to another. Similarly the stages (and their variation between different regional and national contexts) that mark the transition by which the weaver alienates his labor-power involve significant changes in the legal form of the relationship. For example so long as the weaver retains ownership of the loom and is paid by reference to the volume and quality of production then he retains some real control over his labor-power to take breaks or to work with varying intensity that is surrendered once the legally significant stage of the wage contract replaces the commodity contract since it brings with it by virtue of the preestablished legal doctrine of the master/servant relationship an intensity of control and supervision absent from commodity contracts.

This account is not undermined by the recognition that the dynamics of this process involve extralegal powers (e.g., where a group of merchants agrees not to buy the weaver's product where the materials are supplied by other members of their combination, which is a relation that may or may not have a contractual expression). The claim is not that legal relations provide a sufficient account of changes in relations of production, merely that no such account can be adequate if it excludes legal relations. We may conclude that an attempt at a *rechtsfrei* account of this process can but be a pale and attenuated version of the production relation analyzed in terms of the coexistence of legal and economic relations.

A further support for this claim for the superiority of a conception of production relations which requires, where relevant,[13] reference to the forms of legal relations involved is provided by one of the distinctions that Cohen is himself at pains to draw. He distinguishes between "material" and "social" relations of production. The core of the distinction is that a "social" relation exists only where the participants fulfil social roles and I want to add that social roles are necessarily on-going, persisting, or reproduced relations. Consider Cohen's example: where X and Y collaborate to carry a heavy object or to operate a two-handed saw; this he insists is a material relation and this remains the case even where they regularly repeat this cooperation (1978:111).[14] Such collaboration he correctly insists could be between slaves, serfs, or proletarians. However, this contention does not end the matter; to observe the immediate cooperation between X and Y is merely to look at work relations through a narrow-angled lens or from a narrowly behavioral stance that prevents us seeing how X and Y receive their income, or their legal relation to the saw and the wood on which they work; in other words his account is of a work relation and not of a relation of production. Now since we deny his entitlement to substitute "powers' for the "rights" it becomes increasingly difficult for him to sustain the claim that social relations of production can be identified without reference to property or other forms of legal relations. With respect to his own "broad" definition of relations of production (as effective powers over productive forces) this difficulty is accentuated by his separation of work relations and social relations of production. We are pushed toward an insistence that unless reference to legal relations is included within the conception of social relations of production they are hazy concepts with little or no content and thus incapable of providing adequate accounts of real historical processes.

THE CASE OF ILLEGAL SQUATTERS

Before claiming any lasting victory over Cohen's project of purging legal relations from the economic structure it is necessary to confront his account of the position of illegal squatters as compared to legal owners of land that provides the most intuitively compelling illustration of the explanatory power of his *rechtsfrei* conception of production relations:

> An illegal squatter on a tract of land might secure his dominion by dint of retainers who use force illegally on his behalf, and/ or by propagating a myth that anyone who disturbs his tenure of the land thereby damns himself to eternal hellfire. The squatter has something in common with a legal owner of similar land whose tenure is protected by the legitimate authorities. Both have the power to use their land. That one employs force (or myth) and the other relies on the law to sustain his position in that production relation is in neither case part of the content of the relation.(1978:224)

Cohen's strongest claim seems to be that although a legal owner has the facility of calling on the "support" of law that in other respects the owner and the squatter are directly comparable in that they exercise dominion over the land since "both have the power to use their land." While this contention seems plausible it is not sustained by his argumentation.

The core of Cohen's argument is that the positions of owner and squatter are analogous in that while one invokes law and the other force or myth, in both cases these are supports and are accordingly, not "part of the content of the relation." In the main this contention merely repeats the previously considered issue of the coherence of the powers/supports distinction, however his treatment here serves to reinforce my previously stated objections (see "Powers and Supports"). If neither rights nor force/myths are part of the content of the relations of production it is far from clear what it is that constitutes the respective relations. Cohen's answer will be both squatter and owner exercise effective powers over productive forces and persons. It seems intuitively implausible that the form in which their respective regimes are secured will not have decisive effects on the production relations *within* their domains. The owner is likely to establish an instance of the general or pervasive relations of production (e.g., feudal capitalist, and so on). But the squatter is unlikely to be able to create an external regime of force and a "normal" internal regime.[15] The institution of an "instance" of the prevailing relations of production requires both internal and external conditions not available to the squatter. Thus there is a very high probability that there will be real differences between the owner and the squatter that are not explainable by reference to external "supports."

It is significant that in the present context he uses "production relation" in a much more casual way than the conception that he develops in the main body of his text (Cohen 1978:31–36). I concede that the squatter may succeed in producing (i.e., establish material relations of production) but deny that it follows from this that there exists an identifiable production relation (unless, that is, the pattern becomes institutionalized and adopted or imposed on other units of production—but then legal/normative relations will have crept back in). In this respect the position of the owner and the squatter are different in a way that again cannot be reduced to differences in their "supports."

Note that the context of Cohen's discussion of squatters is directed to defeating the objection that his theory of powers is merely an instance of the "force theory" rejected by Engels in *Anti-Duhring*. The success of his defense depends on it being true that the squatter's position remains the same whether he relies on "force" or on "myth," namely, that he has the same powers since neither force nor myth form part of the *content* of the production relations that result. It seems implausible to imagine that a regime externally established by force will not find it necessary to rely on force over those compelled to work thus creating production relations that differ significantly from those that will exist in circumstances structured by the necessity to reproduce the myth that establishes the squatter's capacity to extract surplus value. Thus, although it is important to the persuasive capacity of his argument to suggest that the squatter's position remains the same whether production relations are founded on force or myth he offers no defense for such a claim and I can see no reason why we should accept this improbable assumption. A more satisfactory account would need to explore the consequences that flowed from whether the squatter's regime derived respectively from force or from myth.

I conclude that Cohen's assertion of the analogous power situation of legal owners and illegal squatters cannot be sustained and that this is the case even if we accept his separation between powers and their supports. In undermining Cohen's most attractive illustration of his translation program we may comprehensively insist that he has failed in his project to expel the unwanted presence of legal relations from the identification of social relations of production.

SOME REFLECTIONS ON METAPHORS

Social theory employs different figurative styles but metaphor is perhaps the most readily identifiable and widely used tropological figure. Metaphors are a mixed blessing; they light the path of investigation but they have a nasty habit of forcing it into channels determined by the metaphor deployed.[16] The most frequently recurring species of metaphor that invade social theory are the topographical (the relation between components, elements or instances within a space, e.g., higher/lower, nearer/further, and so on), the architectural (e.g., base/superstructure), and the organic (e.g., birth/death, functional interdependency and specialization of organs). The first two forms emphasize spatial separation and linear conceptions of causality while the latter focuses on the connections between parts and wholes. The base–superstructure distinction is merely one of the better known metaphors and is unashamedly architectural.

Recent Marxist scholarship has become more conscious of the metaphorical status of the base–superstructure distinction.[17] This recognition involves identifying both the limits inherent in metaphors but also their positive attributes, in particular, their capacity to "focus" or direct our attention. Althusser captured better than anyone else the close connection between the base–superstructure metaphor and what it is that has made Marxism powerful and attractive force. Particularly in view of his recent fall from favor it is worth recalling his perceptive observation in some detail:

> The great theoretical advantage of the Marxist topography, i.e., of the spatial metaphor of the edifice (base and superstructure) is simultaneously that it reveals that questions of determination are crucial; . . . and that, as a consequence, it obliges us to . . . think what the Marxist tradition calls conjointly the relative autonomy of the superstructure and the reciprocal action of the superstructure on the base. (Althusser 1971:130)

Cohen is, of course, not attracted to the second feature (relative autonomy) that Althusser suggests our metaphor renders "visible"; he is preoccupied by the first issue, that of determination; it is for this reason that we can appreciate his specific concern with the limitations of the metaphor that seems to assign a "static" role to the base in the sense that the foundations of a building merely support the superstructure. There is a sense also in which its imagery flies in the face of Cohen's concern to vindicate the determination of the superstructure by the base in that a given architectural foundation allows, within certain specifiable limits, a great variety of different possible superstructures to be constructed; a foundation provides only limiting conditions but is not literally determinant of the superstructure.

In addition the architectural metaphor fails to provide an adequate imagery for the thesis that he is concerned to defend, namely, that while bases determine superstructures that nevertheless "bases need superstructures."

> This seems to violate the architectural metaphor, since foundations do not normally need superstructures to be stable. (Cohen 1978:231)

Accordingly he offers an alternative architectural imagery designed to capture the thesis that "bases need superstructures."

> Four struts are driven into the ground, each protruding the same distance above it. They are unstable. They sway and wobble in winds of force 2. Then a roof is attached to the four struts, and now they stay firmly erect in all winds under force 6. Of this roof we can say: (i) it is supported by the struts, and (ii) it renders them more stable. There we have a building whose base and superstructure relate in the right way. (1978:231)

While this figure illustrates that superstructures contribute stability to bases, it omits to note that if too heavy or otherwise ill-designed they can bring the whole lot down! Cohen's more contrived model loses some of the plausibility of Marx's original; the idea of four posts (why four? What, if anything, do the individual posts stand for or represent?) sacrifices any sense that the metaphor "represents" reality. It does, however, capture some flavor of his wider project in that it retains a sense of the primacy of the base while at the same time capturing some sense of causal interdependency between base and superstructure.

It is tempting to conclude that the only sensible approach is to eschew metaphors, but we are unable to escape the figurative nature of the language available to us. The best that we can do is to be self-conscious about both the strengths and the limitations of the metaphors we employ. The real problem with both Marx's version of the metaphor and Cohen's is that at one and the same time it simplifies to the extent of oversimplification while not being able to sustain the causal claims that are the source of its metaphorical attraction. We can, I suggest, conclude that we are unlikely to make any further progress with our inquiry into the causal connections between economic and legal relations by further manipulation of the base–superstructure metaphor.

Instead I propose to consider Cohen's substantive claim that legal relations can be explained in terms of the requirements generated by the production relations.

THE EXPLANATION OF LEGAL RELATIONS BY PRODUCTION RELATIONS

It is necessary to recall that Cohen's "translation programme" is not an end in itself; having developed the claim that it is possible to express production relations without reference to legal relations he insists that "the point is that one could dispense with them, not that one should" (Cohen 1978:224) and then turns his attention to a more ambitious project. He seeks to demonstrate that having generated *rechtsfrei* descriptions of production relations, it can be shown that production relations, so described, can explain or otherwise account for property relations. Specifically he sets out to defend the thesis that "property relations change in order to facilitate or . . . to ratify changes in production relations" (Cohen 1978:226). He illustrates such a process by a standard example, Case I, in which we are asked to envisage a set of circumstances that favors the formation of production relations forbidden by existing law with the result that the law is broken (or otherwise circumvented) and the new production relations become established and only later is the law changed to bring it into line with this new reality. In his second illustrative case, Case II, the circumstances again favor new production relations but this time the law is "too strong" with the result that new production relations do not arise until the law is changed.[18] These cases illustrate the propositions that economic change may *cause* legal change, while law can only *impede* economic change.

The contention that I will seek to uphold is that Cohen simply misses the most difficult and important issue, namely, whether there are some circumstances in which changes in production relations can only come about when the conditions (or the conditions of existence) of such a change are provided by some relevant legal change. The problem with his treatment is that it assumes the thesis that it seeks to defend and thus fails to consider the possibility of "law led" changes in production relations. I readily concede that Case I is historically an important source of explanation of legal change. But to dispute Cohen's explanation of legal relations by production relations does not involve denying that this form of causality never occurs; it is necessary merely to show that some changes in production relations cannot be explained without reference to some necessary or prior change in legal relations. This possibility I now proceed to consider.

My first case is significant because it was one that Marx himself drew attention to, although he did not comment on its theoretical implications. In Chapters 27 and 28 of *Capital* Vol I Marx analyzed the processes whereby the most important precondition of the development of industrial capitalism was formed, namely a "free proletariat," doubly free in so far as, unlike serfs or slaves, they were not themselves part of the means of production but neither did they have access to the means of production. The significance of Marx's analysis is that it illustrates a dual process. The first corresponding to Cohen's Case I whereby the peasantry was illegally expelled from the land. But the second aspect involves a proposition incompatible with Cohen's thesis, namely, that legal changes, in particular legislation, created the conditions for this transformation. Marx's formulation was that, after the Stuart restoration:

> the landed proprietors carried, by legal means, an act of usurpation, effected everywhere on the Continent without any legal formality. They abolished the feudal tenure of land. (Marx 1961:J, 723)

Cohen himself cites this passage but rather surprisingly passes over it by treating it as an illustration of Case II, where the law impedes economic change, thereby avoiding its more important implication that law either caused or provided the necessary conditions for economic change. Since he assumes the inevitability of the economic change it follows definitionally that law (or any other potential causal agency) is limited to the role of either assisting or impeding this process. Within such a closed framework it is not possible to consider a more complex model of historical causation. My point is not to replace an economic determinism with a legal (or any other) determinism, but to establish that Cohen's argument admits of only one possible answer whereas Marx's own historical analysis was more complex than the version that Cohen attributes to him.

Marx's major point, however, was to stress that the separation of the agricultural population from the land was not itself sufficient to create an industrial proletariat; what was necessary was to create the economic and moral discipline for the development of widespread wage labor. The major mechanism for this process, which Marx unambiguously described in his chapter title as "Bloody legislation against the expropriated," was the legislation against vagabondage.

Thus were the agricultural people first forcibly expropriated from the soil, driven from their homes, turned into vagabonds, and then whipped, branded, tortured by laws grotesquely terrible, into the discipline necessary for the wage system. (Marx 1961:I, 737).

This I take to illustrate a paradigm case, ignored by Cohen, in which economic processes and legal change combine in such a way that both provide the necessary conditions for the resultant socioeconomic change.

It is worth considering a more complex and contradictory case that Marx also discusses that bears on our present concerns. He stresses the important role played by legislation governing wages and other aspects of work from the fourteenth century onward. With the expansion of manufacturing in the eighteenth century the strength of capital is such that legal regulation becomes unnecessary:

Only at a certain stage of the development of capital does the exchange of capital and labour become in fact formally free. One can say that wage labour is completely realized in form in England only at the end of the eighteenth century, with the repeal of the law of apprenticeship. (Marx 1969:770)

From this stage onward Marx presumed that the capitalist regulated his factory by "his private legislation," although with hindsight we note that *laissez-faire* wage regulation proved to be a relatively short-lived phenomenon and that for most of its history the capitalist–wage relationship has existed within a complex of legal and nonlegal forms of regulation. The important issue on which I wish to comment is the extent to which it is the existence of a state–law framework that makes these apparently private mechanisms effective. That this was the case in early nineteenth century England is nicely made when we notice the different remedies available to the parties; a battery of criminal sanctions was available to employers to enforce their "private legislation," while workers had to rely on a combination of legal actions, taking the form of "private" actions, and trade union activity heavily encumbered by legal restrictions.

There is much more that could be said about the process whereby modern wage labor comes into being, but enough has been said to indicate that such a fuller analysis could not proceed successfully within the framework provided by the limited models proposed by Cohen. It is the complex interaction of public legal regulation, private ordering and economic power that provides the only satisfactory basis for the exploration of the extent and the manner in which legal relations entered into the constitution of economic relations. Edward Thompson catches this complexity well with his insistence that " 'law' was deeply imbricated within the very basis of productive relations" (Thompson 1975:261).[19]

In addition to this injunction to examine in historically specific detail the causal interaction of legal and economic forces there are other important cases in which legal relations provide the distinctive form within which production relations develop in such a way as to decisively influence both the form and the content of economic relations. To take just one further example, consider the processes whereby the share came to be the distinctive form of corporate capital in England. In the early joint-stock companies of the sixteenth and seventeenth century the "share" was literally conceived as a proportionate interest in the assets of the company with the result that the assignability and alienation of shares were severely limited. The requirements of capitalist development called for the bringing together of finance and industrial capital to provide the capital necessary for the ever larger capitals required for such projects as railway development. Through a long and tortuous line of cases and legislation the legal form of the share is transformed until it achieves between 1825 and 1840 the status of a form of property in its own right, no longer tied to corporate assets, with the result that the form taken by capital is transformed (Ireland et al. 1987). Such a form of property is incapable of translation or separation from its legal form and thus not reducible to a set of nonlegal powers. As a result, the relations of production must be understood as being shaped by their legal form or, to put the same point another way, the legal relation is itself constitutive of the relations of production.

The important question is: what bearing, if any, does this sketch of one aspect of the development of the legal form of capital have on Cohen's claim that it is possible to explain the development of legal relations by production relations? If we start cautiously we can suggest that any such legal development might be useful or facilitative for a capitalist economy; but we press beyond caution when we suggest that the development of capital *required* new and more fluid forms for bringing together industrial and financial capital in the period of the great expansion of British capitalism. It is this caution that is, in general, thrown to the wind by Cohen's advocacy of a Marxist variant of functionalism that like other forms of functionalism suffers for the inherent defect of presuming that economic processes can provide for their own developmental requirements.[20] But if we employ the caution that I commend it is possible that such developments could have occurred without any change of the legal regime or, more likely, that some other legal developments could have proved functionally equivalent. Even if we think that some legal change was likely, this recognition does not provide an explanation of whether such a set of legal mechanisms would be created nor, perhaps more importantly, with what form and content such mechanism would be endowed. This consideration reveals a serious omission in Cohen's account in that he has nothing to say about the mechanisms or mediations by which production relations provide their own legal (and other) requirements. His account would seem to rest on the presupposition that the existence of the "need" is self-realising. A second dimension of this weakness lies in its failure to consider whether the specific form or content of such a mechanism can and does have a causal effectivity for the subsequent course and rate of economic development.

There are a number of available alternative models that can be employed in addressing such issues while retaining some or all features of a determinist account. Since my present purpose is not to debate the merits of such alternatives, but merely to indicate their possibility, they can be briefly sketched. (1) A political analysis, emphasizing the links between a dominant economic class and a ruling political class, posits the political class as motivated by the economic interests of the class that they represent or support and that provides by legislation or other means the legal requirements that are conducive to those interests. (2) An Althusserian model in which it is the economic base that determines which "instance" or component of the superstructure is dominant during any specific historical period. (3) A third possibility posits a "dominant ideology" that functions in such a way as to secure correspondence between production relations and legal relations (Collins 1982:87ff). While all of these models bring with them their own problems and deficiencies they do have the advantage over Cohen in that while they strive to retain some notion of determination by the economic, however attenuated, they do address the absence of any consideration of mediation between the economic and the legal that marrs Cohen's treatment.

LAW AT EVERY BLOODY LEVEL

Edward Thompson reflecting on his own historical studies of eighteenth-century criminal law concluded:

> I found that law did not keep politely to a "level" but was
> at *every* bloody level; it was imbricated within the mode of

production and productive relations themselves (as property-rights, definitions of agrarian practice) and it was simultaneously present in the philosophy of Locke; it intruded brusquely within alien categories, reappearing bewigged and gowned in the guise of ideology; it danced a cotillion with religion, moralising over the theatre at Tyburn; it was an arm of politics and politics was one of its arms; it was an academic discipline, subjected to the rigour of its own autonomous logic; it contributed to the definition of the self-identity both of rulers and of ruled; above all, it afforded an arena for class struggle, within which alternative notions of law were fought out. (Thompson 1978:288)

Thompson's strongly figurative language provides a compelling descriptive summary; it resonates with our intuitive sense of the complexity of the social world. But before we cast our votes for Thompson in preference to Cohen we should pause to consider what it is that is being compared. We are confronted with two very different projects that cannot be directly contrasted. Cohen operates at a higher level of abstraction and his fault is that he seems to believe it is possible to directly employ these abstract categories in the study of specific historical situations. Thompson, on the other hand, is clearly impatient with philosophical debates about determination and appeals directly to (untheorized) notions of "experience" and "culture" to serve as the "middle terms" that create a bridge between theoretical categories and the lived reality, the knowledge of which must be the purpose and justification of inquiry. Yet since "experience" and "culture" are complex empirical categories and are the result of many determinations they can never provide the link, however valuable they may be as reminders of why we find it necessary to engage in theoretical work in the first place.

The contrast between Thompson and Cohen is but one illustration of a set of tensions that has come very close to paralyzing not only Marxism but all forms of theory that make claims to deal with issues of determination and causation. The proper and laudable desire to emphasize the inevitability of complexity had led by a series of short steps to an emphasis on indeterindeterminacy and contingency. The very authors whom Thompson savaged as adherents of an arid theoreticism had even before the publication of his attack on Althusserian Marxism passed him in the fast lane and had taken up positions that had dismantled or rejected great swathes of the orthodoxies of Marxism that Thompson was only then accusing them of reifying. The controversies within Marxism parallel disagreements over a wide field of intellectual and political debate about the possibility of theory and of causal analysis. My purpose here is merely to signal this wider context rather than to engage with it. My objective has been realized; I have argued that Cohen's solution to the "legal problem in Marx" fails and that his attempt to explain legal relations by production relations cannot be sustained. In an obvious sense my objective has been negative in that it has been concerned to mount a criticism of Cohen, but I lay claim to a more positive if not yet substantive conclusion. The problems generated by the attempt to elaborate a determinist relationship between production relations and legal relations does not necessitate the retreat into the descriptive approach employed so effectively by Edward Thompson. The possibility exists for the elaboration of a constitutive theory that retains a concern with issues of determination and causality but sets itself the task of employing a conception of causality that is not unidirectional and that can grapple with questions posed in terms of the mediation between legal relations and economic (and other forms of social) relations. That project is the conclusion enjoined but not realized by this study.

CHAPTER 9

THE CRITIQUE OF LAW: WHAT IS "CRITICAL" ABOUT CRITICAL LEGAL THEORY?

INTRODUCTION

Critical legal theory is the *enfant terrible* of contemporary legal studies. It delights in shocking what it takes to be the legal establishment.[1] Its roots lie in a deep sense of dissatisfaction with the existing state of legal scholarship. These dissatisfactions and grievances are many and varied; some are more concerned with the state of legal education, others with the political conservatism of legal education, while others experience frustration at the failure of orthodoxy to grapple with what they see as the real problems of the role of law in the contemporary world. Advocates of critical legal studies may not all share the same rank ordering of dissatisfactions but are all reacting against features of the prevailing orthodoxies in legal scholarship, against the conservatism of the law schools and against many features of the role played by law and legal institutions in modern society. These reactive roots explain why the development of critical legal theory has taken the forms of "movements," albeit loose and unstructured in character (Conference on Critical Legal Studies in the United States of America, *Critique du Droit* in France and Critical Legal Conference in Britain) that predate the emergence of any clearly formulated and generally agreed theoretical position. The situation of the critical legal studies movement is not too dangerously distorted if one puts the point polemically; it is a movement in search of a theory, but at the same time it is a movement that has not agreed that such a theory is either possible or desirable.

This chapter explores the question: does critical legal studies have the potential to go beyond its reactive origins and develop a viable alternative theorisation that is capable of providing a new direction for legal scholarship? I will offer an account of the distinguishing characteristics of the critical movement and then make some suggestions about the possible direction of its development.

BEYOND THE REACTION
AGAINST ORTHODOXY

At the outset it is important to appreciate that the reactive aspect of critical legal theory signifies something more than the mere youthful debunking of orthodoxy. It fulfils two important roles. First, it insists that there is an orthodoxy that needs to be and can be challenged and that the debates and disputes that take place within legal scholarship are arguments within a more or less monolithic tradition. One important part of the critical project is the need for continuing debate about both the nature of orthodoxy and how much of it should be jettisoned. A second function of reactive scholarship is to draw attention to the very real difficulties involved in mounting a challenge to a well-established orthodoxy. A primary characteristic of critical legal theory lies in the insistence that it is both possible and necessary to think differently about law.

The aspiration to think differently about law raises a set of issues about the choices involved in seeking to specify that "difference." The project of critical legal studies is marked by diversity. Some of this diversity may indicate substantive intellectual and political differences between participants. But this diversity also attests to a less conflictual source of divergence, namely, the mutual recognition that the problems encountered in both imagining and then articulating an alternative require a considerable degree of experimentation in the construction of such an alternative.

The question of whether it is either possible or desirable to construct a "general theory" is a major source of tension among critical scholars. One trend insists that the very project of "general theory" should be abandoned (Hirst and Jones 1987; Rose 1987). This argument is strongly influenced by recent debates, in particular, in modern pragmatist philosophy, deconstruction, and poststructuralism (Gabel and Kennedy 1984). Others continue to see value in seeking to elaborate an "alternative general theory." The issues involved here are important and provide much of the general terrain of controversy within critical legal studies. I will return in the next section to take up these issues.

Another important dimension of the search for an alternative revolves around what I will call "the problem of politics." The relationship between politics and legal theory exhibits a number of different but related aspects. First, many proponents wish to espouse an explicit political commitment in that their work seeks to contribute towards some political goal. A typical formulation expresses commitment to overcoming "domination" and "hierarchy."[2] This concern involves a rejection, on the one hand, of the prevalent apolitical stance of much legal scholarship founded on the belief in the possibility of value neutrality that portrays the lawyer as a technical expert. The concern with politics within critical legal studies involves a commitment to some conception of "praxis," of the interaction of theory and practice. Finally, there exists a generalized commitment to activism in general, and legal activism in particular, with the objective that the committed legal academic can and should be able to contribute to the activist struggles of the day. Yet at the same time there are significant differences over the possibility and role of such activism. These dimensions lead to a general concern with "the politics of law."

So far I have suggested that a number of the distinctive characteristics of the critical legal studies movement flow from reactions against the prevailing orthodoxies. But the movement has now been around sufficiently long that it must soon pass beyond the stage of debunking and trashing orthodoxy; it is having to grapple with the problems of advancing a distinguishable and working alternative. Such an alternative, even if it resists the self-description of being a "theory," must include such general features as a conceptualization of its object(s) of inquiry and some statement of the inquiry procedures or methods which it employs. But, as I hinted above, there is a strand within the critical tradition that has considerable reservations about this attempt to give a generalizing statement of the critical project. They see it as self-deception and likely only to reproduce, albeit in radical guise, the errors and mistakes of those theories that it rejects. So, before advancing an argument that outlines the elements of a critical theory of law, it is necessary to consider this tension within the movement more closely.

ON THE POSSIBILITY OF THEORY

In confronting what is perhaps the most important controversy within critical legal studies I should make clear my objectives. I want to comment on one of the big intellectual issues of our time and quickly make clear that I have no original contribution to make, but I do want to suggest a way in which critical work can continue without pushing aside or ignoring the "big" metatheoretical issues. Much hinges on how these issues are posed since this in turn determines how the lines of battle are drawn. What follows is an attempt to sketch the issues making use of a metaphor.

As we approach the end of the century we are sitting anxiously on the edge of a glacier aware of its ultimate fate but impressed by its endurance. The seemingly solidity of the main face, called the Enlightenment, continues to hold to the possibility of objective knowledge realisable through natural and social scientific procedures. Piling up behind and threatening to displace this long-standing and already factured edifice is a complex intermeshing set of newer glaciers, each having its own distinctive origins. They have many and varied names: linguistic philosophy, phenomenology, poststructuralism, deconstruction, pragmatism, and relativism to name but a few. They are all expending some part of their energy pushing in roughly the same direction. They insist that the Enlightenment created a myth of science that held out an evolutionist and progressive image of accumulating knowledge giving access to reality. These newer glaciers challenge the most basic tenets of the Enlightenment beliefs. They insist, traumatic though it may be, that the glacier Enlightenment will and must collapse soon, and in turn they concede that whatever post-Enlightenment way of thought emerges will in its turn be displaced by glaciers whose shapes and names we cannot envisage.

How does this sketch link up with critical legal studies? The critical school is self-consciously engaged in confronting a very profound intellectual challenge to the conventional methods and preoccupations of legal scholarship that have been generated through the attempt to come to grips with contemporary developments in philosophy, sociology, and literary theory. The central issue stems from pressing to their most disturbing implications the consequences of accepting the culturally constructed nature of social existence. The need to pursue this path has come about because of a deep disenchantment with all those intellectual traditions since the Englightenment, which claim to offer the possibility of access to a verifiable truth. The challenge requires us to explore the implications of the fact that our very capacity to pose such issues, namely language, is the paradigm case of cultural construction. Can we sensibly claim to go beyond the socially constructed languages or discourses that we can deploy to reach a reality that is not itself constrained by language/discourse? Or does language provide not only the content but also the barriers to what we can communicate about? We are challenged to renounce the reassuring belief that our discourses stand in some relation of "correspondence" to a reality independent of consciousness. We are not asked to surrender our working assumption that such a reality exists but rather to give up the complacent assumption that our thought and talk can arrive at some verifiable or objective access to that reality. It is this central intellectual challenge and its ramifications to which critical legal studies is currently seeking to respond in the arena of legal studies.

The challenge outlined above comes in many different forms and from different disciplinary sources. I will focus attention on the recent flurry of work that represents a newer and deeper engagement between relativism/pragmatism and realism. I will single out just one strand that is not only the most accessible but that is also having a significant impact on critical legal studies in both the United States and Britain and is personified in the writing of Richard Rorty (1979; 1982).[3] Rorty's critique of the Enlightenment project is directed against the pretensions of its theory of knowledge (epistemology). He declines to present an alternative epistemology because he rejects its very premise that we can find a way to make our thought and theory "correspond" to reality. His antiepistemology insists on the "contingency" of language and that all we have available are different conversational strategies or language-games for talking about the things that interest us. None of these can have any privileged status by which we can claim that they provide a "right answer" in the sense of providing a correspondence to reality. He denies that this argument involves a relativist claim that any language-game is as good as any other. We can and do make choices between alternatives and indeed our social history is significantly influenced by major shifts in the language-games that people employ such as the abandonment of the theological language that was the great achievement of the Englightenment; where that intellectual movement went wrong was in erecting reason or science as the substitute for theology. The crux of his position, as it affects my present concerns, is that when we choose between alternative language-games we can make no stronger claim for our choice than that "it works," and not that it is true.

What he does not, in my view, satisfactorily address is whether there is an important distinction, as I believe there is, between the claim that "Language-game X works for me" (that is, relativism) and "Language-game Y works for us." "Working-for-us" allows the possibility of a sociology of knowledge that can seek to explain the sequence of language-games that have played major roles for whole communities across significant periods of time and to show that these have made it possible to say and to do what was not possible before. This, I suggest, leads back to the major controversy because it requires us to confront the question: do different language-games merely allow us to say different things or can we claim that one rather than another makes it possible for us not only to say something different but to *say something more* or to *understand more*? Claims of this sort are inherently controversial because they necessarily appeal to some criteria of "more" that is external to each language-game. The trouble with Rorty is that he rejects both of these choices while failing to elaborate any third-way account of what the claim that "it works" might mean.

To return to the issue as to whether the critical school should pursue the project of developing a theory is to pose the choice between "theory" and "conversation." To renounce theory in favor of conversation is seen as avoiding the pitfalls of unwarranted claims to truth and correspondence to reality. The counter to this objection is that the renunciation of theory can only have the result of either importing an implicit theory *via* the concepts used in the conversation since there can be no concepts that are theory-free, or by relying only on common sense or idiomatic language of rendering the conversation dependent on intuitive understandings between participants. We cannot evade theory since theory is nothing more than the positing of connection/interconnection between two or more concepts. There is no escape from theory; no conversations can be free of it. The best that we can do is to be as self-conscious as possible about the assumptions and connections that we bring into our conversations.

While the philosophical debate proceeds we should not let its heat obscure the extent to which there is also an important area of consensus within critical legal studies. While critical theorists disagree among themselves about whether "reality" is the goal of inquiry there is agreement that reality cannot be approached directly, that there is no royal route to knowledge and that there can be no claims to absolute knowledge. Similarly, there is a general agreement around the necessity of an hermeneutic approach, broadly conceived, which insists on the social/cultural construction of social life and that enquiry must embrace the meanings of social contexts for their participants. It may be that we can embrace the hermeneutic and linguistic shift in contemporary thought without endorsing the wholesale exclusion of the extraconversational context of the physical, environmental, and technological conditions of social life. The positions adopted by individuals within the critical camp will continue to be influenced by the position that they espouse on the general philosophical issues but there is no barrier to a fruitful exchange even if some feel that the use the label "theory" may seem to claim more than they believe to be possible or desirable.

The danger of purporting to abolish theory is that it implies that a troublesome problem has been avoided. But it cannot be so easily escaped; we must recognize that the best we can do is to engage with the contestable character of all theoretical enterprise. Thus, for example, we cannot abolish abstraction from our conversations, but we can debate the appropriate form and level of the abstractions that we employ.

We are still confronted by the concept of law. This remains more rather than less important as we come to recognize and explore the diversity or pluralism of the phenomena designated by the concept "law." Until such time as we are persuaded to renounce the very concept itself we are constrained to pursue its theorization, that is, to explore different ways of formulating and explicating both its internal and external connections. We are required by our own conversation to accept that there can be no escape from the project of theorizing law.

INTERNAL OR EXTERNAL THEORY?

If it is only possible but, as I have argued, desirable and necessary to pursue the objective of advancing a general theory of law, it is necessary to consider what kind of theory we should be seeking to develop. Critical legal theory must first confront the problem posed by the choice between an internal and an external theory of law. The dominant tradition of contemporary legal theory is epitomized by H. L. A. Hart and Ronald Dworkin, who despite their other differences insist on the adoption of an internal perspective, I want, first, to criticize the conventional internalism of Hart/Dworkin legal theory. I will then consider whether this criticism leads critical legal theory to adopt an external perspective or whether we can avoid this unsatisfactory either/ or choice.

Internal legal theory is "internal" in a number of different but related senses. At the most general level it sees law through the eyes of judges and lawyers. Thus, for example, the questions that it addresses are those that concern or perplex lawyers; hence the preoccupation with how judges either do or should carry out their judicial function narrows or restricts the scope of "legal theory" to little more than the theory of the judicial decision. This approach goes hand in hand with the adoption of the standpoint or perspective of judges or lawyers as defining the field of inquiry for legal theory. Nothing that passes as legal theory has ever, to the best of my knowledge, adopted a victim or defendant perspective.[4] Internal theories exhibit a predisposition to adopt the self-description of judges or lawyers as primary empirical material; their stated views on what they do and why they do it are treated as direct evidence about the nature of legal practices. There is thus a naive acceptance of legal ideology as legal reality.

Internal theory is simply *too close to its subject matter*. This proximity to law and its privileged participants gives rise to normative consequences, either implicit or explicit, through the adoption of the values of legal professionals. This is especially evident in Ronald Dworkin's commitment to "law as integrity" in order to provide "the best justifications of our legal practices as a whole" (Dworkin 1986:vii). Given this explicit commitment and partisanship it is astounding that when he turns his fire on critical legal studies, after expressing the hope that some within the movement can be harnessed to the aim of law as integrity, he attacks an alternative partisanship:

> But others [unspecified] may have a different and converse goal. They may want to show law in its worst rather than its best light . . . to move towards a new mystification in service of undisclosed political goals. (1986:275)

There are two important differences between the liberal and the critical project revealed by Dworkin's formulation. First, it is perfectly proper for him to take issue with the "political goals" of others but these are no more undisclosed than his own. As I have argued, it is a characteristic of the critical school to take a stand in favor of commitment/partisanship in scholarship. There remains much that the critical movement needs to do in clarifying its objection to "illegitimate hierarchies" or to "alienation." But Dworkin's imputation of "undisclosed political goals" has a very unsavory ring about it. There is something frustrating about liberalism's smugness about its own commitments while being dismissive about alternative commitments. It is significant that Dworkin avoids or refuses this engagement with radical or socialist positions and engages only with conservative or neoliberal positions.

Second, it is a travesty of the views of the critical school to allege that their project is to show law in its worst light. A distinctive feature of critical scholarship is *a deep perplexity about law*. We perceive law as involving *both* negative and positive characteristics. There are many ways of formulating this tension but one expression of it is that we recognize the attractiveness of the rule of law and its aspiration to rational and consensual social ordering, but at the same time we insist that in societies exhibiting systematic socioeconomic inequality the espousal of the rule of law buttresses and legitimates those inequalities. I conclude that the differences between the partisanship of liberal and critical legal theory justify a claim for the superiority of the latter. Critical scholars are genuinely undecided about a whole series of major questions about law such that, without renouncing their partisanship, they can come closer to realizing classical academic standards of objectivity (even while having well-founded doubts about the possibility and desirability of such universal standards fashioned outside of current intellectual and political engagements) than their liberal rivals.

There is one further objection to the internal perspective: the adoption of such a position seems to lead its proponents to posit a clear inside/outside distinction in a manner that erects law as an autonomous field of inquiry; law is treated as sufficient to itself. Even with the mild socialization of legal theory during the twentieth century it has relied on an inside/outside imagery within which law is both influenced by and influences the "external world"; this way of conceptualizing law is deficient because it retains the assumption of law as an autonomous field.

If "internal theory" is deficient does this commit the critical school to the adoption of an "external theory"? It certainly does not if "external" is treated as involving the adoption of a detached behavioralism that self-consciously chooses to ignore the meanings associated with the consciousness of legal actors. Behavioralism is but a sociological variant of the most rigid legal positivism. The concern with meaning, legal language, and interpretation is common ground between much modern liberal legal theory and critical theory.

There are also problems with the adoption of an external perspective that disclaims interest in "lawyer's problems" and focuses on the impact of law on the wider society. The history of sociolegal studies and the sociology of law has been dominated by this response that has had the practical result of establishing an intellectual division of labor between itself and legal theory that hold each other at arms length. One of the most distinctive features of critical legal studies has been that it has joined battle with liberal theory in a way in which the various trends within the sociological movement in law failed to do. Critical approaches are centrally preoccupied with legal doctrine and with judicial decision making. Expressed as a slogan the critical movement has insisted on *taking doctrine seriously*. This leads them also to follow Dworkin in taking rights seriously even though their work reveals rights to be ambiguous and problematic. My argument appears to point toward the rejection of external theory, but I want to hold back from that conclusion because there is at least one version of externalism that deserves to be defended.

It is important to defend the necessity of critical theory distancing

itself from the assumptions and taken-for-granted attitudes and preju-
dices of legal professionals. This does not involve, as Dworkin quoted
above suggests, a choice between being "for" or "against" law. It
simply insists that what judges and lawyers think and feel about law,
how they explain and legitimize their various practices must also be
subject to a scrutiny that preserves a critical distance between itself
and those whose practices the theory seeks to understand. There is
one important and very visible difference between liberal and critical
theory: critical theory employs the concept "ideology," a concept systematically absent from liberal theory.[5] Once we dispense with a crude
version of ideology as falsity it becomes clear that what the concept
"ideology" provides is precisely a way of problematizing the attitudes,
beliefs, and values of legal actors. It makes it possible to ask questions
about the formation of the consciousness of legal actors, about the
internal relations between the constituents of their beliefs, and also to
make the consequences that flow from these beliefs a central focus of
legal theory.

There is a related but more general sense in which a critical perspective needs to defend a more complex version of external theory. Critical
theory must be external in the sense that it seeks to overcome the
closures or silences generated by internal theory. The drawing of the
conceptual boundary of law and the hoisting of the flag of legal theory
over that terrain is not an innocent act. The manner in which the
boundaries are stipulated determines both the set of questions with
which the inquiry is concerned and, at the same time, it excludes or
silences other issues. Given the long predominance of liberal legal
theory, it is difficult to make the first steps in marking out an alternative
theory for each of us is deeply imbued with the influence of that
tradition. It is, therefore, necessary to self-consciously explore the
closures or exclusions effected by the dominant tradition since the
effect of closure is not merely that of absence but rather is to render
other issues invisible.[6] Perhaps the most important closure produced
by liberal theory is the result of its theoretical and ideological adherence
to the doctrine of the separation of powers. The closure that results is
the radical separation of state and law that takes the form of the
absence of the concept of the state entirely or the employment of a
naive theory of the state exemplified by Dworkin's equation of state
and community in which officials are merely servants of the community
carrying out public duties.[7]

These considerations enable me to offer a solution to the question
of whether critical legal theory favors an internal or external perspective. My answer is, first, that the style of theory must be external in

the sense discussed above of maintaining a critical distance from the self-conceptions of legal professionals. But, second, it is able to refuse the choice between internal and external perspectives because through its reconceptualization of the field of inquiry, illustrated for present purposes by the aspiration to embrace the law–state complex, it has so redrawn its boundaries that the problem is no longer relevant.[8] This boundary changing aspect of critical legal theory accounts for some of the hostile reactions it has encountered since it does involve a challenge to the form in which law is currently constituted as an academic discipline.

FROM CRITICISM TO CRITIQUE

The account of critical legal theory offered thus far has portrayed it, in the first instance, as reactive against orthodoxy and, subsequently, as being engaged in exploring the creation of an alternative theory, the first stage of which is the search for alternative starting points, different boundaries, and conceptualizations of the object(s) of inquiry. At this stage the project advances more ambitious and controversial claims that involve going beyond "criticism" to the pursuit of "critique" as the approach or methodology of a critical theory of law. I will consider the nature of "critique" and then examine some of the controversies and difficulties that surround such a project. It should be noted that I will employ the idea of "approach" rather than "method" because the latter carries with it the implication that it is both possible and desirable to stipulate general procedural rules for the conduct of inquiries. The search for an "approach" is intentionally agnostic concerning the possibility and desirability of prescriptive methodologies.

By "critique" I understand an approach that starts with internal criticism of existing theories in terms of their own criteria and then proceeds to generate the conceptual equipment necessary to overcome the deficiencies and closures discovered in the theories examined, and at the same time to understand the social origins of the influence wielded by the theories criticized. It is thus concerned to understand the historical nature of these theories and the conditions that affect the possibility of the emergence of an alternative theory. This concern to locate the historical context makes it possible to advance claims about the development of "better" theory in the sense of serving to address historically generated questions that a prior theory either failed to address or was unable to address satisfactorily. While we cannot ignore the linguistic and cultural constraints on the production of our ideas we can, through critique, aspire to push our language and our theory beyond the substantive and historical limits of the theories with which we engage.

Consistent with my stated intention of avoiding the temptation to erect a stipulative methodology I will avoid suggesting that critique involves any sequential stages of inquiry; instead I will examine in more detail the different elements that together make up the critique approach. It is an important characteristic of critique that it does not seek to engage immediately with the "reality" of its object of inquiry.[9] Rather criticism is directed, in the first instance, at *theories* of law. This internal criticism or immanent critique of theory in its own terms permits debate about the appropriate style of criticism. One of the most common forms practiced by critical legal studies is to examine the internal consistency of the theory, a characteristic conclusion being one that concludes that liberal legal theory is contradictory (Kennedy 1979:205). It should be stressed that in itself this form of criticism is practiced in most forms of scholarly debate. Another style focuses attention on extracting the assumptions that underly the theory in question. In critical legal studies this has often taken the form of identifying the assumptions that liberal theory makes about the notion of the legal subject, or about the forms of human association. Associated with one or both of these styles of criticism and beginning to mark out a distinction between criticism and critique is the search for what may be called the social origins of the theory and thus to locate it in its historical context. In general the concern is to understand why it was in the specific historical context that some particular theory was proposed and to account for its influence.

An additional characteristic style of criticism is that of ideological critique. Closely connected with the explorations of the social origins of theories, it explores the ideological presuppositions, the taken-for-granted and commonsense knowledge on which the theory relies. There is another variant of ideological critique that is often confused with the search for the ideological content of the theoretical text. To make this distinction we may talk about the ideological practices of a social group such as lawyers and judges; such an investigation explores the ideological content of the beliefs and justifications of the nontheorist. While textual ideology and ideological practices are distinct, the examination of their interrelationship can contribute significantly to the quest for the social origins and role of the theory under consideration.

Another element of critique again starts with the examination of particular theories but this time focuses attention on that which the theory excludes and on how conceptual barriers are created which divide the object of inquiry internally, for example, by deploying a

classification scheme. Critical legal studies has thus paid much attention to the pervasive effects of the public/private distinction in legal
theory and doctrine (Collins 1987; Horwitz 1982a; Olsen 1983). The
quest for silences, barriers, or closures has an important constructive
significance because it begins to point the direction toward a reconceptualization that removes these impediments so as to allow what was
previously invisible to become part of the reconstructed theory. For
example, the critical project has identified the fact that the concept and
reality of "power" is invisible to liberal jurisprudence and is thus led
to explore how power is to be inserted as a major focus within its
alternative perspective. The project of developing an alternative or
reconstructed theory thus flows directly from the internal or immanent
critique. Reconstruction flows from criticism in the sense that the latter
points toward the new or additional concepts, or more generally to
new ways of thinking and talking about the object of inquiry that hold
out the prospect of transcending the deficiencies and closures of the
existing theories. The final selection of concepts and their elaboration
into an alternative theory involves the selection of some explicit normative criteria that express the goals of social transformation through
which critique seeks to link theory and practice. The elaboration of
these criteria also provides a further dimension to the criticism of
existing social conditions as well as providing objectives for the social
transformations that it aspires to participate in. It is in this context
that critical legal theory must be concerned to clarify its normative
commitments. The internal pluralism of critical legal studies is revealed
by its widely varied normative projects that range through varieties of
libertarianism, radical liberalism, and humanistic socialism. There are,
for example, wide differences over what role should be envisaged in a
future society for law as a principle of social organization. It is an open
question as to whether critical legal studies can and will sustain its
cohesion, given the considerable variation in the objectives of its transformatory project.

The view developed above is one that holds that critique does not
involve a single prescriptive methodology but rather involves a combination of some (but not necessarily all) of the elements that have been
identified and distinguished. The treatment is by no means exhaustive
but I do want to comment on one important and neglected problem:
what part, if any, does prescriptive or empirical evidence play in critique? The work produced to date by the critical school has been light
on and even dismissive of the deployment of empirical evidence.[10]
But empirical study is already inescapably present within the critical
project; for example, the ideological critique that seeks to establish the

link between the content of legal theory and the ideology of legal professions is an empirical question, and a complex one at that.

Empirical evidence has another and more general role within the critical project. It facilitates the identification of deficiencies within legal theory because it brings to the surface features that are ignored or unsatisfactorily explained by the prevailing theories. For example, liberal legal theory offers little or no account of the widespread ambivalence toward law of the great bulk of the population. I suggest that social ambivalence toward law reveals deep tensions that exist between the different principles of social ordering that coexist within contemporary societies. My present concern is not to substantiate this argument but to use it to illustrate the contention that empirical evidence has an important role in the critical project through its ability not only to alert us to deficiencies in existing theories but also to open up constructive lines of enquiry and conceptualization that may contribute to a more satisfactory understanding of those elements of our experience of law.

TOWARD A RELATIONAL THEORY OF LAW

A relational theory of law sets out to generate a reconceptualization of the field of inquiry of legal studies. It proposes an analysis that posits the existence of a number of different forms of legal relations that interact in varying ways with other forms of social relations. Its project is one that takes "law" as its object of inquiry but that pursues it by means of the exploration of the interaction between legal relations and other forms of social relations rather than treating law as an autonomous field of inquiry linked only be external relations to the rest of society. Relational theory proposes an approach that is both functional and critical. It poses the question: what part, if any, do legal relations play within any selected area of social relations and under what conditions can that role be transformed? The approach thus draws on a sociological model of analysis but it differs from the conventional approach epitomized by the sociology of law since its emphasis on the variety of forms of legal relations captures the significance of the diversity of legal phenomena (legal pluralism) by insisting that the exploration of the internal interconnections between different forms of legal relations will provide important insights into the role of law. The approach outlined can be described as an holistic approach without importing any Hegelian inferences of a metaphysical unity of social phenomena. Rather it is holistic in the sense that it insists that law as an object of enquiry can be be approached by focusing on the interaction between legal and other forms of social relations.

Considered as an abstract model relational theory starts from "social relations" as the general form of sociality. Different types of social relations may next be identified; for illustrative purposes these can be limited to economic, political, and legal relations.[11] Any concrete social relation will be likely to involve a specific combination of these abstract categories. For example, employment relations involve economic, legal, and other forms of relations. When we focus our attention on legal relations, relational theory makes the important claim that the forms of legal relations can and should be linked back to the primary types of social relations. Schematically we may identify economic–legal relations (concerned with access to and control over economic resources), political–legal relations (concerned with the distribution of authority), etc.; thus all legal relations involve the presence of other forms of primary or abstract social relations. To take an obvious but important illustration: the social institution of marriage involves a number of different forms of social relations (legal, economic, gender, sexual relations, etc.); such a conceptualization makes it possible to explore questions about the role that law plays in the development and change of this and other social institutions and practices.

It would be possible but not very helpful to elaborate a much fuller classificatory model; relational theory should not, I suggest, seek to develop a grand classificatory scheme. A better approach will be to gain experience through engaging with more concrete analysis of specific forms of legal relations by employing classifications that appear pertinent. On the basis of such an approach issues and controversies will inevitably arise about the most fruitful classifications to be employed and how they are to be conceptualized. I have in mind that it is very much easier to identify classificatory types that stand in a direct connection with institutions; more difficulties are involved in the classification and characterization of affectual and interpersonal relations.

The merits of relational theory can be established only through their application; other than the general claim to provide a holistic capacity that does not artificaly separate legal from other forms of social relations, relational theory facilitates the recognition and exploration of the degree and forms in which legal relations penetrate other forms of social relations. This point does not just involve the well-known thesis that modern law increasingly reaches its regulatory arm into more and more social relations. It also embraces the idea that the "presence of law" within social relations is not just to be gauged by institutional intervention but also by the presence of legal concepts and ideas within types of social relations that appear to be free of law. For example, ideas of possession and of contract penetrate many forms of interpersonal relations. Another line of thought stimulated by relational theory draws attention to the differential combination of legal and nonlegal relations present within particular types of relations that leads to the suggestion that this affects and possibly determines different *forms* of legal relations depending on the social practices and institutions to which they relate. Employing an approach similar to that outlined above, Boaventura de Sousa Santos distinguished between four distinct forms of law (domestic, production, territorial, and systemic law), which are in turn associated with corresponding mechanisms of power and forms of rationality (Santos 1985).

It follows that if we direct our attention to the forms and mechanisms whereby legal relations penetrate social relations we must also focus attention on the reverse process. The field of legal relations is not autonomous and is marked by the penetration of extralegal relations. For too long the study of judicial decision making has been preoccupied by the quest for distinctive and exclusive forms of legal reasoning. A relational approach should examine both the presence and the source of other discursive and rhetorical forms that are not simply variant forms of legal reasoning but derive their significance and their legitimating capacity from the forms of social relations from which they originate. Thus the controversy over the place of policy analysis in legal thinking can be pursued by drawing attention to the interaction between legal and bureaucratic decision making characteristic of the administrative state.

This chapter has explored what is involved in the critical legal studies movement realizing its critical objectives. I have urged that the critical school cannot avoid the challenge of elaborating a distinctive theory of law. I have argued in favor of a distinctive approach of critique. I have also argued that it must be transformative in that it should strive to contribute to some specified goal(s) of social change. Finally, I have suggested that a relational theory of law has potentially the greatest capacity to fulfil these aims. The major claim that can be made for a relational theory of law is that it overcomes the divide, discussed above, between internal and external theories of law or to put the same point a different way, to overcome the divide between jurisprudence and the sociology of law. It gives an important place to the traditional concerns of liberal legal theory but, at the same time, makes it possible to pursue the critical objectives that mark the distinction between critical legal theory and liberal legal theory.

CHAPTER 10

RIGHTS AND SOCIAL MOVEMENTS COUNTERHEGEMONIC STRATEGIES

DILEMMAS IN THE POLITICS OF RIGHTS

The question "Can rights contribute to the realization of progressive social causes?" has given rise to an extensive debate. This chapter argues that using the Gramscian concepts of hegemony and counterhegemony makes it possible to advance a positive evaluation of the place of rights strategies within progressive politics without succumbing to illusions about what Stuart Scheingold called "the myth of rights" (Scheingold 1974).

The rights debate continues to run and to produce an energetic opposition between "pro-rights" and "anti-rights" positions. These positions are as far apart as ever. I have no illusion that it would be possible to bridge the gulf between the important intellectual and political issues at stake. But I will start with an attempt to restate in the most basic form what is at stake and divides the positions.

A diverse range of positions has warned against illusions that the quest for legal rights and their realization through litigation can achieve substantive gains for progressive social movements. These voices have taken the form of both general theoretical critiques of rights (Tushnet 1984; Gabel 1984) and conclusions derived from the study of the experience of particular social movements (Handler 1978, 1988; Brodsky and Day 1989). In their most general form the core of these criticisms consists of a warning against the illusions generated by the liberal faith in rights. The liberal "myth of rights" is the view that those suffering disadvantage should seek redress by striving to have their grievance protected by securing legal recognition of their claim as a right. Once a right is recognized, whether by constitutions, legislation, or judicial decision, all those whose rights are threatened or denied may approach the relevant court and have their rights enforced; as Scheingold puts it: "The myth of rights is, in other words, premised on a direct linking of litigation, rights, and remedies with social change" (1974:5). Faith in the instrumental value and utility of rights forms the political common sense of the age.

The critics of the myth of rights have not had the argument all their own way. The main thrust of liberal legal theory has taken the form of an extensive and powerful defence of rights (Dworkin 1978, 1986). A defense of the relevance and value of rights struggles has also come from self-consciously progressive or radical opinion (Thompson 1975, 1980; Campbell 1983; Bowles and Gintis 1986; McCann 1986; Bartholomew and Hunt 1990). These writers have advanced a case for the political pertinence of "rights without illusions"; they all, in varying degrees, reject the myth of rights while nevertheless claiming that rights are a significant, yet not exclusive, vehicle for realizing the goals of progressive social movements.

This chapter will first explore Gramsci's concept of hegemony and then fill out his much less developed concept of counterhegemony. These concepts, and the implications drawn from them, will then be used to take a new view of the rights debate. The main objective of the chapter will be to advance an unambiguously positive case for the role of rights-based strategies in the struggle for social change. I will advance and defend the thesis that to achieve the project of counterhegemonic political strategy requires the transition from the "discourse of interests" to the "discourse of rights." I will challenge the objection that rights are problematic because they allow both sides in each dispute to marshal contending rights-claims; this feature does not condemn rights, but rather praises them.

GRAMSCI: INTRODUCTORY REMARKS

There has been surprisingly little explicit attention paid to the implications of Gramsci's theoretical and political thought for the understanding of law.[1] Gramsci's unique contribution to Marxist theory stems from his criticism of the economistic versions of Marxism that had become institutionalized by the beginning of the twentieth century. This led him to a central concern with ideology. The most distinctive feature of Gramsci's account of ideology was the break with Marx's conception of ideology as "Ideology," that is, as a *Weltanschauung,* a coherent world-view, intellectually developed and at the same time informing the consciousness of active social classes.

The work that Gramsci does on Marx's concept of ideology is fivefold. Focus is shifted from the intellectual plane of philosophical systems to the formation of popular consciousness of common sense. Second, there is less emphasis on ideology as "system," as integrated or coherent. Third, ideological struggle is viewed, not as titanic struggles between rival *Weltanschauungen,* but as practical engagements about shifts and modifications in "common sense," or popular consciousness. Fourth, is the emphasis on ideologies as active processes that " 'organize' human masses and create the terrain on which men [*sic*] move, acquire consciousness of their position, struggle, etc" (Gramsci 1971:377). Fifth, his conception of ideology is positive while Marx's was negative. For Marx ideology blocked and distorted, while for Gramsci it provided the very mechanisms through which participation in social life was possible.

HEGEMONY: FROM IDEOLOGY TO POLITICAL STRATEGY

The far-reaching implications of Gramsci's development of the concept of hegemony is that, on the one hand, it makes it possible to grasp the connection between the ways in which social consciousnesses are formed and the exercise of political (or class) rule under conditions of high level of popular consent. On the other hand, it provides the key to the strategy of revolutionary political change in "the West."[2] Gramsci's concept of hegemony was developed as he grappled with this dual project of elaborating the mechanisms whereby modern capitalism succeeded in securing its continued role under conditions of relative social stability, while he searched for appropriate political strategies capable of securing the opening up of a transition to socialism under these characteristic conditions of capitalist rule in "the West."

Hegemony is the process that generates

> the 'spontaneous' consent given by the great mass of the population to the general direction imposed on social life by the dominant fundamental group [historical bloc]. (1971:12)

Hegemony is thus an active process involving the production, reproduction, and mobilization of popular consent. But it should be noticed that Gramsci's focus is on the securing of "leadership" and "direction" by the dominant bloc rather than upon the more passive idea of consent itself.

The hegemonic or historical bloc[3] can never constitute its leadership by simply articulating the immediate interests of its own constituents. One of the most important corollaries of Gramsci's conception of hegemony is that for a hegemonic project to be dominant it must address and incorporate, if only partially, some aspects of the aspirations, interests, and ideology of subordinate groups. This "incorporative hegemony"[4] creates the opportunity to move away from the sometimes narrow class-reductionism of Marx's account of politics (that is, the ruling class conceived as deploying the instrumentality of state and law to advance, impose, and protect its own class interests).

A number of quite distinctive mechanisms are involved in the processes whereby "incorporative hegemony" installs the presence of subordinate interests within the dominant hegemony. First, a successful hegemony needs to incorporate values and norms that contribute to securing the minimum standards of social life. Second, the process by which, as a result of actual struggle or the apprehension of it, a dominant bloc engages in a more or less self-conscious "compromise" to incorporate some element of the interests of a subordinate group. Frequently a "compromise" is inflected toward the interests and values of the dominant bloc. An important example of this process is the way in which the institutionalization of welfare provisions has been incorporated not in the form of generalized or universal rights, but in forms that tend toward the degradation of the "client" who is transformed in minute ways into a supplicant.

A third and more complex process is the way in which a dominant hegemony will articulate values and norms in such a way that they take on significant trans-class appeal. While, for example, the content of law in capitalist societies protects and legitimizes property relations, it is of considerable significance that the most visible form of property law, in the criminal law of theft, provides both protection and legitimation for the widest form of "private property" in consumption goods. The effect is not only to obscure the fundamental distinction between capital and consumption goods, but even more importantly, it valorizes property in the most general form in which it is held by the whole population.

Gramsci identified a number of different stages or levels of hegemony. These have special relevance with respect to the formation of counterhegemony, that is, the process by which subordinate classes challenge the dominant hegemony and seek to supplant it by articulating an alternative hegemony. The most salient aspect is that subordinate groups will tend to articulate only their immediate interests. His most important illustration was that trade unions tend first to succeed in gaining influence over the immediate circle of those sharing common circumstances of work; in so doing they articulate a "corporate consciousness" that focuses on their shared interests, but this may coexist with the presence of a rivalry against some other group of workers (for example, maintenance of wage differentials *vis-à-vis* some other group, or men over women, or skilled over unskilled, and so on). An important feature of Gramsci's antieconomism was his insistence on the political and intellectual limitations of corporatist consciousness.[5] While Gramsci was at pains to stress that the "stages" that he identified were not simply sequential or developmental, his second stage, "class economic-corporate," widened the scope of consciousness to focus on the common interests of the class and thus required deliberate strategies to overcome sectional interests.

The most important and distinctive stage is that of "hegemonic consciousness" whose key characteristic is the emergence of political and ideological projects that seek to develop the capacity to integrate purely class aspirations with the achievement of leadership over other subordinate groups by taking up and integrating the interests of those other groups and classes along with those of the working class, which was his primary point of reference. Such a project implied the necessity of foregoing or at least varying immediate class interests in order to bind in more closely other social forces. Illustrations of such hegemonic practices would be the need to challenge long-established trade unions' chauvinist practices, which excluded or marginalized women workers, or to restrict wage demands in order to construct alliances with consumers or with other classes. The general characteristic of hegemonic practices is the increasingly conscious projection of a subordinate class to aspire to national leadership by seeking a common articulation of popular interests and of popular culture; for this project Gramsci coined the concept of the "national-popular."

Gramsci's treatment of hegemony is premised on his traditional Marxist preoccupation with the primacy of the working class and the concern with the Leninist problematic of "the Party" as the agent of hegemonic transformation. I want to suggest that the concept of hegemony remains pertinent even when one displaces the traditional Marxist unitary agency of the class/party. A contemporary politics oriented toward social transformation through a more pluralistic conception of agency will still require expression at the level of the nation/state through the medium of political parties even though one conceives of such a party representing hegemonic projects forged within civil society and constituted through alliances and coalitions of social movements. This displacement of the unitary conception of party/class suggests that it may be valuable to make use of a concept of "local hegemony." This is a potentially useful "new" concept specifying the construction of some hegemonic project within some particular area or region of social life. For example, one could readily envisage the realization of a radically transformed sexual division of labor as a hegemonic project of women's movements, but one that is not necessarily linked to any specific form of political transformation.

WHAT IS COUNTERHEGEMONY?

One of the more important themes that marks more clearly than any other Gramsci's theoretical (if not political) rupture with the Marxism of both Marx and, more significantly, of Lenin is the contention that in "the West" the working class must first become "hegemonic" in the sense of securing a generalized leadership over a decisive majority, including classes and social groups outside the working class.[6] Gramsci identifies the conditions under which hegemony is attained when

> one's own corporate interests . . . transcend the corporate limits of the purely economic class, and can and must become the interests of other subordinate social groups. This . . . marks the decisive passage from the structure to the sphere of complex superstructures . . . bringing about not only a unison of economic and political aims, but also an intellectual and moral unity, posing all the questions around which struggle rages not on a corporate but on a 'universal' plane, and thus creating the hegemony of a fundamental group over a series of subordinate groups. (1971:181–182)

I will return below to elaborate on Gramsci's suggestion that the achievement of hegemony requires a transition from the posing of issues in "corporate" terms to their transformation onto a "universal" plane.

It is important to stress that counterhegemony is not some purely oppositional project conceived of as if it were constructed "elsewhere," fully finished and then drawn into place, like some Trojan horse of the mind, to do battle with the prevailing dominant hegemony. Without such an understanding the quest for counterhegemony can only be a continuation of that which the concept seeks to displace, namely, the search for a unitary political subject that needs simply to achieve consciousness of itself to be able to challenge the dominant hegemony.

The alternative to this scenario is a conception of counterhegemony that has to start from that which exists, which involves starting from "where people are at." Such a conception of counterhegemony requires the "reworking" or "refashioning" of the elements that are constitutive of the prevailing hegemony. Gramsci himself made this important point in the following way:

> [I]t is not a question of introducing from scratch a scientific form of thought into everyone's individual life, but of renovating and making 'critical' an already existing activity. (quoted in Larrain 1983:84)

This is real, practical activity that involves a number of different elements whose mixture can only be identified concretely, but some of whose characteristics can be sketched. One step is to "supplement" that which is already in place; to add to or extend an existing discourse.

Beyond this first step, characterized by the paradox that it is necessary to struggle to achieve that which is already proclaimed within the hegemonic discourse, is the importance of opening up its "silences." The struggle for votes for women attests to both the difficulty and the importance of the opening up of the discourse of "manhood" suffrage that dominated so much of the nineteenth century to the exclusion of half the population.

The most significant stage in the construction of counterhegemony comes about with the putting into place of discourses, which while still building on the elements of the hegemonic discourses, introduce elements which transcend that discourse. The struggle for trade union rights is a classical exemplification; starting on the terrain of traditional elements of individual rights (of speech and association) this struggle inserted the transcendant presence of social and collective rights. And this example serves to illustrate another very important issue. A Leftist reading of counterhegemony often involves strategies that are directed at negating or reversing the existing hegemony; for example, in the rights debate one encounters the opposition between individual and collective rights in a form in which "individual rights" are opposed in order to replace them by "social" or "collective" rights. The emphasis on counterhegemony as a transcendant project involves a line of thought that does not negate that which exists, but strives to construct, in Gramsci's terms, "good sense" from "common sense" and in this way to prioritize or valorize those elements or features that are "new." The effect of such a process ends up with the dying away or exhaustion of elements once dominant. In the eighteenth century and through the first half of the nineteenth, the connection between the franchise and property constituted the common sense of the dominant political discourse; the struggle for the extension of the franchise created a context in which any attempt made today to reestablish a link between the right to vote and a property qualification would seem entirely anachronistic and to fly in the face of common sense.

The insistence on the *contested* nature of hegemony applies with even greater force to counterhegemony. It follows that the process is never either incremental or evolutionary, but it involves both changes of direction, that is, advances and retreats, as well as changes in pace. Gramsci effectively displaces the notion of "crisis" from the economic realm and redirects attention to the importance of "hegemonic crisis." The political and theoretical significance of this innovation is that capitalism is no longer conceived as having any necessary economic tendency to "break down"; in its place, attention is directed to the circumstances under which a dominant bloc may experience a "hegemonic crisis" either as a result of some circumstances internal to its own project or as a result of a rapid advance of counterhegemonic forces that has the result of undermining the previously secured leadership of the dominant bloc such that it is no longer able to rule in the old way.

It is probably necessary to go beyond Gramsci's own account of hegemonic crisis and to suggest another possibility. The contest of hegemonic projects can result in circumstances in which they "block" each other.[7] One form of such a blockage could be the kind of circumstances in which no historical bloc is able to achieve hegemony and which thus opens up the opportunity for the kind of exceptional outcome that Gramsci labeled "Caesarism." But another scenario could be where one element of the dominant hegemony may be of such paramount significance that it blocks or inhibits change and development within the dominant hegemony itself. For example, the priority within Catholic theology of the injunction against birth control impedes any process of doctrinal modernization over the whole range of reproductive and familial policies. Alternatively the strength and near fixity of some element in the dominant hegemony may have such wide-ranging repercussions as to block the development of a counterhegemonic project; for example, the centrality that Islam accorded to gender segregation may have succeeded, for the present at least, in blocking the modernizing and secularizing thrust unleashed during the overthrow in 1979 of the Shah in Iran.

This consideration of "blocked hegemony" leads to the suggestion that one possible objection to the pursuit of a rights strategy, at least in the United States, is that the association established within the dominant hegemony between "liberty" and "rights" has such a central role so as to block the extension of a discourse of rights to the kind of broadening that would encompass social and collective rights and thus to impede significantly, if not block, a progressive rights strategy. These reflections on "blocked hegemony" are tentative and for this reason I will not pursue this potential objection further, save to suggest that it may be worthy of future consideration.

Although neither hegemony nor counterhegemony is a concept used by Foucault, a Foucauldian approach can be helpful in emphasizing the "small" or microconstituents that constitute "shifts" in the dominant hegemony or in a developing counterhegemony. Where I suggest Foucault is lacking is in his almost complete failure to address the strategic question of the cumulative connections between the elements of micropolitics that are essential if a counterhegemony is to succeed in displacing an existing hegemonic bloc. For Gramsci the realization of counterhegemony is necessarily a "project" involving intention and agency on the part of specific social actors. This role he assigned to "the Modern Prince," his coded reference to "the Party." There is no necessity that this role be attributed to a single party nor to make any particular assumptions about the relationship between parties and classes. But what is important is the contention that political parties exemplify a "strategic" capacity; it is for this reason that this chapter concerns itself with "counterhegemonic strategies." Strategies involve the idea of a special role for social agents that sustain a commitment to a self-conscious reflexivity about the conditions and possibilities of transformative politics.

One of the most important features of any such strategic project is the concern to find ways of going beyond the limited expression of the immediate interests of social groups, Gramsci's "corporate stage," such that they connect up with and find ways of articulating the aspirations of wider constituencies.

GRAMSCI: LAW BETWIXT STATE AND CIVIL SOCIETY

It is not my intention to embark on a consideration of Gramsci's suggestive but tantalizingly underdeveloped comments on law. Rather my present concerns are to comment on a number of its features that are pertinent to a consideration of the connection between hegemony and rights strategies.

The first feature to be noted is the location that Gramsci attributes to law within his social topography. He locates hegemony at the intersection of state and civil society. This is precisely the location in which he places law.[8] Law combines coercion and consent or persuasion. Law is closely tied to the processes of securing an equilibrium between "state" and "civil society"; on the one hand, law lends authoritative legitimations to the norms and projects through which the state seeks to govern civil society; but, on the other hand, law has a degree of responsiveness to civil society where state law provides a facilitative framework for private transactions and those dimensions of public law that provide mechanisms of public accountability and surveillance.[9]

One of Gramsci's most distinctive motifs is the connection that he points to between "law" and "education." He suggests that law "renders the ruling group homogeneous" (1971:195). The leadership of the hegemonic bloc is never automatic, but rather it constantly needs to secure its own coherence and unity. Legal norms, and the values that underlie these norms, are not only mobilized and reinforced, but they are linked and connected in a way that helps to secure their coherence. Gramsci gives a different inflection to the educative role of law when he refers to the idea that law serves the role of "assimilating the entire grouping to its most advanced fraction" and that it results in a "social conforming" (1971:195). This is a more conventional sense of education since it involves the idea of transmission from an originating subject, from the hegemonic bloc to its allies. This I suggest is exactly the same process that Foucault calls a "discursive formation"; it puts in place a set of values, renders them coherent, but most importantly, they become *material* in providing an active framework in the sense that what law proscribes as self-evidently "wrong" and what it valorizes tend to become perceived as how things should be.[10]

The feature of Gramsci's comments on law that connects most closely with my present concern is the very specific way in which he envisaged the "struggle over law" developing in the struggle for socialism. He conceived the struggle for the control of law as involving the need for subordinate classes to become "legislators" by achieving authoritative, norm-creating capacity (1971:265–266). What is needed in order to develop this line of thought is not so much the focus on the struggle for substantive law reform, but rather to focus on the connection between law as an arena of struggle and the development of hegemonic structures in which law reform has a part to play. The remaining sections of this chapter seek to contribute to just such a strategic line of enquiry.

THE CRITICISMS OF RIGHTS RECONSIDERED

This section of the chapter is devoted to taking a fresh look at some of the more important criticisms that have been leveled at rights strategies. My purpose is to assess these criticisms in light of the foregoing discussion of a Gramscian theory of hegemony. My general thesis is that viewed through the prism of hegemony the standard criticisms of rights either dissolve on their impact is significantly restricted: my objective is thus to persuade those who are committed to a range of projects of social transformation, first, that rights strategies do not involve the handicaps and dangers that they presently perceive. More ambitiously, the second strand of my argument is to persuade rights skeptics that there is substantial merit in the conscious pursuit of rights strategies.

For my present purposes I define rights strategies as any political strategy that deploys one or more dimension of rights discourses. My first step is to consider the most pervasive concern that rights strategies necessarily lock social movements into the dangerous and paralyzing embrace of litigation. My general concern here is to disaggregate "rights" from "litigation" by arguing that the espousal of a rights strategy does not necessarily imply the espousal of a litigation strategy. The deployment of litigation is one possible—but certainly not a privileged—feature of a *counterhegemonic rights strategy.*

RIGHTS STRATEGIES AND LITIGATION

The rights debate is dogged by an important misunderstanding. Those who are hostile to rights-based strategies tend to conflate "rights" with "litigation." My advocacy of the politics of rights accords no special importance to litigation. I view litigation as nothing more than one of the *tactics* to be deployed within a much broader conception of an essentially political, rather than legal, strategy. But because the controversy over litigation goes to the heart of the differences that surround a politics of rights it is important to explore in more detail both the limits and the possibilities of litigation.

Does Litigation Atomize Social Struggles?

An obvious starting point revolves around the objection that litigation atomizes issues in a way that impedes the visibility of their political substance. The conflict of interests, for example, between landlords and tenants, it is contended, becomes obscured when it is reduced to an issue about what maintenance was done, when, and by whom. What needs to be identified at the outset is the significant tension that surrounds the discourse of legal rights: on the one hand they are "social" in that they are assigned to generic legal subjects (for example, citizens, tenants, and so on), but they are always invoked or "cashable" by specific legal subjects (typically citizens or corporations). The degree of this disjuncture between the range of subjects covered by each legal right and those legal subjects that happen to initiate litigation varies according to jurisdictional practices concerning the admissability of class actions and test cases. An important feature of the modern politics of law has been the emergence of more self-conscious selection and pursuit of test cases that marks out one of the important characteristics of the "public interest law" movement. On the one hand, this makes possible the pursuit of the most representative cases that thus resonate more closely with the wider themes pursued by social movements. But, on the other hand, the high investment of resources and commitment can serve to focus attention on the particular case at the expense of that which it represents. This would seem to lend some support to the criticism leveled at rights-oriented movements.

The force of this criticism is, however, significantly undermined by the insistence I want to develop that a most important feature of contemporary social movements is that they rarely, if ever, take a single organizational expression. Even the most cursory view of three of the most important modern social movements, the civil rights movement, the women's movement, and the environmental movement, shows that they are characterized by their multiplicity of organizational expressions. There seems to be a discernible pattern of organizations focusing to a greater or lesser extent on litigational activities while other bodies pursue a wide range of alternative tactics. This general characteristic raises some interesting issues that are deserving of more detailed study than they have received so far about the articulation of the different components of social movements. One of the questions that interests me is the implication of this "multiple agency" for the possibility of hegemonic strategy.

The multiple-agency character of modern social movements raises the interesting problem of whether hegemonic strategy is a relevant or possible consideration. The worst-view scenario is that multiplicity and the consequent competition produce outcomes that are the chance result of complex and unpredictable actions. The more interesting suggestion is that a generalized hegemony, in the sense of a general dominant conception, emerges that is shared not only by activists but also by a wider constituency, but that is not the product or property of any unitary agency. Only detailed empirical study could confirm the possibility of this "local hegemony" without the existence of a unitary agency such as "class" or "party."

The real world of social movements is to be found in the combination of both different sorts of "organizations" and different forms of "action," and, perhaps more important, but much more difficult to tie down, in the dispersed areas in which transformations of consciousness and action affect a large penumbra of a diverse set of constituencies beyond the organizational nuclei of a social movement. For example, Gusfield demonstrates the importance of understanding the dynamic of social movements by looking at their impact on the private sphere where incremental but profound changes in both practices and consciousness occur among those not directly connected with movement organizations (Gusfield 1981:317).

Does Litigation Produce Only Hollow Victories?

A second group of criticisms of the rights-litigation nexus focuses on the results of litigation. The general contention is that the results secured even by "successful" litigation do not justify the reliance and investment that social movements make in litigation. What has first to be addressed is the question of how "success" is identified. If the contention is that litigation does not change the world then there is no issue of substance since this argument is only effective against the "myth of rights." It is precisely the significance of Stuart Scheingold's first intervention that it opened up the question of the criteria of success (1974). I take his focus on "mobilization" not simply as a wider conception of "success," but as pointing to the need to develop a more holistic view of social movements. What is needed is the exploration of the articulation of litigation along with the other components of the strategies pursued by social movements.

Beyond questions concerning the criteria of "success" there is another and perhaps more fundamental problem with the existing studies of the use of litigation by social movements. There is a failure to distinguish between the very different types of social movements that have been studied.[11] What is missing is a concern with what I propose to call the "hegemonic capacity" of social movements. In a first approximation the distinction can be drawn between "single issue" movements and those whose goals would constitute a wider set of social changes than their immediate objectives. But this approximation requires further refinement because some movements that are apparently single issue have extensive ramifications. The abortion rights movement, while superficially focusing on a single issue, has ramifications extending beyond the immediate question of women's right to control their fertility. The abortion rights movement is a prime example of the concept of "local hegemony." Such a movement is not directed to the kind of global hegemony that Gramsci had in mind with his focus on the role of the revolutionary party. But movements directed toward local (or regional) hegemony can only be adequately judged in their capacity to transform a wide range of social practices and discourses. For present purposes I suggest that, in addition, the environmental movement and the civil rights movement also serve as my example of movements of "local hegemony" in that while focused on a set of specific demands, their realization would both necessitate and occasion wider structural changes. The most immediate implication is that their "success" is not a matter of securing some immediate interest. It follows that to evaluate the role of litigation for such movements necessitates that focus be directed to the articulation between the elements that make up the strategic project of the movement.

My suggestion is that a key feature of any such assessment revolves around their capacity to put in place a new or transformed discourse of rights that goes to the heart of the way in which the substantive issues are conceived, expressed, argued about, and struggled over. My more controversial suggestion is that the immediate "success" or "failure" of specific litigation has to be approached in a different way that requires that we take account of the possibility that litigation "failure" may, paradoxically, provide the conditions of "success" that compel a movement forward. In current struggles over wife abuse, all those cases in which judges impose derisory sanctions are contexts that drive the movement forward because they provide instances of a dying discourse in which women "deserve" chastisement by their husbands. Such judicial pronouncements become more self-evidently anachronistic and in this inverted form speak of a new and emergent discourse of rights and autonomy. The implications of this line of thought are that the whole question of the success or failure of litigation and its connection with transformative strategies is far more complex than our existing attempts to measure "success" and "failure" admit.

A more far-reaching criticism of litigation is that, rather than helping, "law," conceived variously as litigation or legal reform politics, is itself *part of the problem*. This line of argument is at the root of Kristin Bumiller's study of the civil rights movement (1988). This strand of the anti-rights critique is, I want to suggest, even if unintended, a form of "Leftism" whose inescapable error lies in the fact that it imagines a terrain of struggle in which a social movement can, by an act of will, step outside the terrain on which the struggle is constituted. Here a hegemonic strategy must insist that it is precisely in the engagement with the actually existing terrain, in particular, with its discursive forms, that the possibility of their transformation and transcendence becomes possible. To refuse this terrain is, in general, Leftist because it marks a refusal to engage with the conditions within which social change is grounded.

RIGHTS AND COUNTERHEGEMONIC STRATEGY

As we saw above, Gramsci identified hegemony as

> posing all the questions around which struggle rages not on a corporate but on a 'universal' plane, and thus creating the hegemony of a fundamental group over a series of subordinate groups. (1971:182)

Let me now defend the thesis that to achieve the shift from the "corporate" to the "hegemonic" *counterhegemony requires the transition from the discourse of "interests" to the discourse of "rights."*

Gramsci's suggestive, but undeveloped, insight is that the project of counterhegemony requires a shift from the plane of the "corporate" to the "universal." He identifies the counterhegemonic project as involving

> the concrete birth of a need to construct a new intellectual and moral order, and hence the need to develop more universal concepts and more refined and decisive ideological weapons. (1971:388)

By the concept of the "corporate" Gramsci refers to the level of "interests" conceived as specifying those circumstances that benefit the group. Thus, for example, I share with my academic colleagues an interest in securing a higher salary. The critical point is that the existence of this interest discloses no reason why any other social group should support my claim. The forms of legitimation that support and justify the myriad of "corporate" interests are legion. The discourse of rights provides a key exemplification of the movement to the plane of the "universal"; rights are contestable and comparable, and they are capable of articulating social norms that are general and capable of sustaining legitimation.

Rights discourses operate at a number of different levels; without attempting a complete classification, it is desirable to distinguish between rights-claims, institutional-rights and legal-rights. Rights-claims are interests interpellated into the normative language of rights that embody some claim to legitimation by analogy or extension from other rights; for example, my salary claim expressed as a right may express an entitlement to comparability with some other group. An institutional-right exists where as the result, for example, of local bargaining an agreement has been secured for an annual salary review. A legal-right is a rights-claim or an institutional-right that has secured legal recognition that involves a capacity to mobilize public resources for its assertion or defense. Once secured as legal-rights they achieve the distinct status of being prelegitimated claims. Legal and constitutional rights mark out those social claims and demands that have already, as a matter of political fact, been adopted by the legal system and that have available some access to legal resources for their enforcement. It should be noted that this does not involve any assumption about the efficiency or the effectiveness with which particular political systems protect legal-rights.

It is now possible to spell out the radical implications of my contention that rights are significant precisely because they function at the "plane of the universal." This claim is significant precisely because it is a direct inversion of the most persistent objection against rights, articulated most fully in the critical legal studies movement's critique of rights, namely, that it is precisely the universalistic *form* of rights that embodies their abstraction and thus manifests their inherent reification.

These differences can be explored by considering Mark Tushnet's objection to rights on the grounds that both sides can structure their discourse in the typically abstract form of legal-rights (1984). This, he argues, entails the "troublesome consequence" of raising the problem that the claim, for example, to exercise a free speech right by political demonstration pushes one toward conceding that others have the same rights with respect to causes that we find repugnant.

Let us face it directly; in perhaps its most dramatic form it is the problem of "rights for racists." Legal-rights are never absolute; they always clash with competing rights. This, rather than being a disadvantage, is a distinct merit in that it makes it possible to compare rights-claims at the most relevant level of generality. Presumptively the general right to free speech should be protected; the problem posed by racists is to determine whether some other right (for example, to personal security in black neighborhoods) is infringed to such an extent as to justify the denial of free-speech rights to some particular category of persons. Whether the test applied be that of "clear and present danger" or some other test is not my present concern; my contention is that there is real merit in needing to provide some overriding consideration, itself couched within a discourse of rights, before denying to any group, however unpleasant, one of the most basic of political rights. The need to provide and to struggle for such a justification is a central feature of democratic politics.

The objection that rights are problematic because they allow two (or more) sides to marshal contending rights claims is not to condemn rights, but to praise them. This remains true even where competing rights are raised against some valued right that has been secured only after long and arduous struggle. The abortion issue provides just such an illustration. There are many voices from the women's movement that are equivocal about the discourse of rights now that we are confronted with the emergence of "the backlash" of claims articulated in terms of "father's rights." I want to suggest that all who support the right of women to control their fertility should welcome this challenge.

The pro-choice movement has seized the high ground, both ideologically and legally, in making significant, though never secure or final, advances over the last two decades. A challenge, couched in terms of "father's rights," provides the terrain within which women will need to continue the struggle to secure social recognition (both legal and ideological) of the relevance of "difference" in biological reproduction that necessitates the according of priority to women to control their own fertility.

The issue becomes more controversial when I suggest that this should not lead to the conclusion that men have *no* rights. Rather, I suggest that the grounds on which putative fathers should be denied rights is that the nature of their connection is too distant if their claim is nothing other than that they claim to have provided the sperm. But let me pose a hypothetical situation: assume a female and male living together and intending to continue that association; the woman becomes pregnant by her partner and learns that the fetus she is carrying is female. The woman is particularly anxious to bear a male offspring and therefore decides that she will have an abortion. In these circumstances my contention is that since the issue is not a matter of whether the woman is prepared to bear a child, the father has a justiciable claim. I do not claim that he should be accorded some legally entrenched right to block the woman's intended course of action, but merely that in the circumstances specified the issue is contestable.

While all hypotheticals suffer from their essentially contrived character, we should never fail to recognize that the developments in reproductive technology are likely to proceed more rapidly than changes in cultural values surrounding the priority accorded to preferred sex of children. Once sex-determination techniques become widely available major social policy issues will be posed about their demographic consequences since many, if not all cultures, to a greater or lesser extent, valorize male offspring. My contention, about which I feel uncomfortable and which is undoubtedly controversial, is that I could countenance legislation that made sex determination a prohibited ground for therapeutic abortion.

Since I am treading on controversial ground I should make clear that the primary purpose of my argument is to show that rights discourses have as one of their most distinctive virtues that they can never be absolute. To concede a rights-claim is to invite a counterclaim. The achievement of real social change requires the securing of what I have termed "local hegemony," that on grounds of political contestation, ethical justification, and legal recognition, some claim that at one time was controversial and contestable becomes self-evident and thus secure. Such claims become secure when they achieve hegemonic status, that is, they become a component of "good sense." Even in the present climate of neoliberal reaction against collective provision nobody (to the best of my knowledge) is arguing for the privatization of domestic sewage disposal. It is "self-evident," a matter of "good common sense," that under conditions of urban life public resources are allocated to sewage disposal. But we do need to remember that it was not so very long ago that such claims were controversial. Abortion rights are in the most basic sense about securing the "good sense" of our respective cultures that women have a primary entitlement to secure control over their own fertility. But we should not confuse the entitlement to a "primary" claim with an "absolute" claim.

The foregoing discussion of the contestability of rights claims illustrates another important feature of hegemonic struggles around ideas or values. Even more central is the contention that rights struggles are ultimately always struggles about social *practices*. These struggles ultimately come down to how people lead their lives and how institutions behave. During the contested phase of hegemonic engagements ideological contests between competing rights-claims take center stage; the ultimate test lies in the field of social and institutional practices. All such struggles are uneven and outcomes are rarely stable or guaranteed. The struggle over access to effective contraception is a case in point. The primary struggle for the generalized "right to contraception" is behind us; in the most general terms the ideological battle has been won. But at the same time it is true that local resistance remains strong and there are major regional variations. Hegemonic struggles, whether for local or societal hegemony, are about securing basic shifts in the center of gravity of contested issues; struggles to anchor and secure such victories almost inevitably involve the most microscopic struggles around individual and institutional practices.

The implications of my position can be illustrated by comparing it with Mark Tushnet's argument that the discourses of rights lack political utility. In place of rights discourses he argues the case for a political discourse grounded on interests and demands. He argues that

> people need food and shelter right now, and demanding that those needs be satisfied . . . strikes me as more likely to succeed than claiming that existing rights to food and shelter must be enforced. (1984:1394)

Tushnet's claim seems counterintuitive. Starting from a shared concern that the hungry get fed, it is necessary to make some judgment about how that objective is to be secured. In struggles over the distribution of resources each interest pressed must, as a minimum step, advance and sustain some legitimation of the claim. Why should the hungry be fed? Why do they have some claim against the resource of the community? It is a key requirement of the discourse of rights-claims that it provides an appropriate and socially persuasive rationale or justification for any "demand" advanced.

The "demand strategy" advocated by Tushnet singularly fails to provide the required legitimation. The interests of the poor are not self-legitimating. If that were the case, such interests would not be politically controversial. A "demand strategy" makes no sense. If when asked why a demand should be satisfied we merely reply "Because we demand it" we fail to answer the challenge. Social claims, especially new ones, require legitimation. The deployment of the discourse of rights has a special and distinctive role in the historical process of the legitimation of social interests.

RIGHTS AND THE DISCOURSES OF THE POWERFUL

Another significant objection that can be leveled against rights strategies is that they require social movements to restrict or accommodate themselves to the discourses of the powerful and thereby limit the movement and, even worse, may result in the "cooptation" of the movement within the orbit of dominant interests. There is no doubt that cooptation is always a possibility. But this is only one of the practical manifestations of the social consequences of the real world of hegemony. What needs to be stressed is that *all struggles commence on old ground.*

Ideology needs to be understood, as I have argued, not as the competition between fully developed and mutually opposed systems of thought (Ideology), but as the protracted process of the *articulation* of discrete discursive elements into new configurations. Such a process has both positive and negative dimensions. On the one hand, it involves the "reworking," that is, doing "new work" on old materials; here it may appeal to and mobilize elements that already exist. Since rights discourses are already in place, its appeal is to that which is familiar, to a taken-for-granted form in which entitlement-claims are already in place. One sees this most readily in the general field of political contestation, which revolves around a reworking of, that is a rearticulation of, elements already present in popular discourses: democracy, freedom, equality, liberty (and a few other key symbols) constitute the whole territory of political discourse. What is decisive is the way in which concrete political discourses generate and mobilize *recombinations* of these well-tried elements.

To understand the point, it is essential to insist that no discursive symbol has a *necessary political content*. This point is easiest to illustrate if we put it in terms of traditional Marxist analysis; in this context we may make the same point by saying that no political symbol has what Poulantzas called a "necessary class belonging" (1973:75). Take the example of "nationalism": nationalism is neither progressive nor reactionary, neither petty-bourgeois nor proletarian. Nationalism manifests itself, for example, in central America, in the authoritarianism of Noriega, and the radicalism of Ortega. Whether the figurative discourse of nationalism takes a progressive or reactionary form depends not on some essentialist concept of "nationalism," but rather on the way in which it is articulated with other discursive elements.

To recap: my general thesis is that discourses deploy concepts and symbols that are already in place. New discourses are not invented but rather transform already existing elements and it is generally within this context that "new" or original elements are added and, conversely, old elements are excised—as today we are conscious of the gender implications of our language. What determines the substantive content of discourse is not the result of intrinsic properties of the symbols themselves but their articulation with other discursive elements. Litigation produces paradigmatically contestable outcomes. Because "victory" or "defeat" is nothing more than a particular combinatory articulation of a common set of discursive elements that is necessarily unstable, the next case, making only small shifts in its rhetorical structure, could produce quite a different configuration and thus have quite different political implications.

Litigation thus involves not only contests in the traditional sense, but is, more importantly, contestable. Rather, my analysis suggests a model of advance and retreat leading cumulatively, occasionally, and even possibly exceptionally, to shifts in the discursive fields. It is thus important not to overstate the ramifications of litigation. The ideological output of the courts does not implant itself directly into popular discourses. Judicial reasoning can and does make a difference without in any sense being determinant. There do occur decisive changes in which the consolidation of key figurative elements, once in place, alter the terms of the future conduct of the discursive field in question and thus come to influence the terms of debate.

CONCLUSION: RIGHTS IN THE CONSTRUCTION OF HEGEMONIC PRACTICES

Rights take shape and are constituted by and through struggle. Thus, they have the capacity to be elements of emancipation, but they are neither a perfect nor exclusive vehicle for emancipation. Rights can only be operative as constituents of a strategy of social transformation as they become part of an emergent "common sense" and are articulated within social practices. Rights-in-action involve an articulation and mobilization of forms of collective identities. This does not imply that they need to take the form of "collective rights," but simply that they play a part in constituting the social actors, whether individual or collective, whose identity is changed by and through the mobilization of some particular rights discourse. They articulate a vision of entitlements, of how things might be, which in turn has the capacity to advance political aspiration and action.

In exploring the connection between hegemony and rights discourse, my major aim has been to argue for the need to displace two types of questions that have distorted the rights debate. The first is the essentialist question which, in its simplest form, is "Are rights bourgeois?" I have devoted only limited attention to this question because I have recently dealt with it extensively elsewhere (Bartholomew and Hunt 1990). The second question is more practical in its thrust and its simplest form is "Do rights work?" With respect to this second question, my case is that what is wrong with this way of posing the question is that it has the effect of isolating the problem of the effectivity of rights from the surrounding conditions that constitute the politics of law. I have been concerned to interrogate the part that rights discourses can play within the construction of counterhegemonic practices. The implication of this thrust is that the more rewarding questions to pose need to focus on the way in which rights discourses and political discourses are mutually articulated. Put in its simplest form, my answer to that question is: we are more likely to arrive at a positive evaluation of rights strategies if we see them as part of the wider field of hegemonic political practices. While rights-in-isolation may be of limited utility, rights as a significant component of counterhegemonic strategies provide a potentially fruitful approach to the prosecution of transformatory political-practice.

The great potential of the line of inquiry that Gramsci opens up is to provide a way of linking the most general concerns with the strategy of political change with the micropolitics of the way in which the constituents of social discourses are articulated. My position is unashamedly Gramscian in another sense: I am motivated by the view that whatever limitations we need to recognize in our roles as professional intellectuals, that we can and should strive to make a contribution, as what Gramsci called "organic intellectuals," by seeking to explore the strategic possibilities hidden within the concrete particularity of issues and movements. It is in this sense that I have argued a case for "rights without illusions" as holding out a vision, not only of a possible future, but as providing an outline of the means to its realization.

CHAPTER II

MARXISM, LAW, LEGAL THEORY AND JURISPRUDENCE*

THE OBJECT OF MARXIST THEORY OF LAW

Theories may be distinguished from one another in two major respects: they ask different questions and they employ different concepts. There are no "correct" questions or concepts. The questions we ask and the concepts we use are determined by what we decide is "important" or "significant" about our object of study.

Marxist theory of law asks: what part, if any, does law play in the reproduction of the structural[1] inequalities of class, race, and gender that characterize capitalist societies? If law participates in the reproduction of capitalist relations, through what mechanisms and processes does it realize this effect?

It is not my intention to write a history of the complex and interesting shifts that have occurred as Marxists have attempted to come to grips with the phenomenon of law.[2] Instead I will identify a number of themes that have been developed and have also been reworked into new and variant combinations. On the basis of this review I will, in the section below, present an outline account of a version of Marxist theory of law that seeks both to integrate these major themes with the tradition and to provide a theory adequate to the task of understanding democratic capitalist law.

In summary form the major themes that are present in Marx's own writing and in subsequent Marxist approaches to law are

1. Law is inescapably political or law is one form of politics.

---

* This chapter has been edited to eliminate repetition of material addressed in earlier chapters.

2. Law and state are closely connected; law exhibits a relative autonomy from the state.
3. Law gives effect to, mirrors, or is otherwise expressive of the prevailing economic relations; the legal form replicates the forms of economic relations.
4. Law is always potentially coercive or repressive and manifests the state's monopoly of the means of coercion.
5. The content and procedures of law manifest, directly or indirectly, the interests of the dominant class(es) or the power bloc.
6. Law is ideological; it both exemplifies and provides legitimation for the embedded values of the dominant class(es).

These six themes are present in Marxist writings on law in a variety of different forms and, in particular, with very different degrees of sophistication and complexity.

The six themes are not mutually exclusive; rather they frequently overlap and interconnect. No single theme is intrinsically more important than the others, nor is one of them a privileged route to a "correct" Marxist theorization of law.

The themes identified above raise issues excluded or ignored in orthodox jurisprudence. Some of these themes simply add to the agenda of jurisprudence; for instance the focus on the connection between law and politics or between law and class interests either adds to or redirects the concerns of jurisprudence. Other Marxist themes have more wide-ranging implications for legal theory. For example, the insistence on the ideological nature of law involves an entirely different way of looking at the texts, discourses, and practices of law. Such a point of departure disallows a straightforward or positivist acceptance of legal rules and doctrines as the primary reality of law that is taken for granted.[3]

This brings us to an important dimension of Marxist theory of law. It is not a project that occupies the same field or scope as orthodox jurisprudence; its agenda is necessarily different. Thus it cannot simply replace elements within liberal legalism in order to produce an alternative or competing theory. However, this very different character of Marxist theory of law itself raises problems. If it is so radically different in its agenda, methods, and concepts then there will be no real possibility of comparing it with liberal legalism. If it forms a different project then it will be unlikely that Marxist theory of law will be able to provide solutions to any of the questions that motivate orthodox jurisprudence. It is to this question that attention will next be directed.

OUTLINE OF A MARXIST THEORY OF LAW

What follows is an outline of a Marxist theory of law that concentrates on achieving an integrated theoretical structure from the main themes present in its diverse versions. It is not an attempt to offer a precis of Marx's own writings on law; neither Marx nor Engels produced anything that could or should be called a theory of law; law was never a sustained object of their attention, although they did have much to say about law that remains interesting and relevant (Cain and Hunt 1979).

My account makes no claim to represent a "correct" interpretation of Marxism. What I do claim is that it provides a comprehensive framework for a Marxist theory of law. The selection of a starting point is the most important step in the development of any theory. Accordingly I propose to offer both an explanation and a defense of the starting point that I have selected, and to indicate how it differs from alternative candidates.

A RELATIONAL THEORY OF LAW

The law is a specific form of social relation. It is certainly not a "thing," nor is it reducible to a set of institutions. Law as a social relation provides the starting point most in keeping with Marxism because the focus on "people in relations" is what makes Marxism so strongly and distinctively social—more rigorously social than most sociology. In one of many similar passages Marx stated his relational approach in the following terms:

> Society does not consist of individuals, but expresses the sum of interrelations, the relations within which these individuals stand . . . To be a slave, to be a citizen are social characteristics, relations between human beings A & B. Human being A, as such, is not a slave. He is a slave in and through society. (1969:265)

It is important to stress that Marx does not abolish or ignore the individual. What he does do is to avoid adopting a theoretical humanism that starts from the individual endowed only with native capacities and will (Robinson Crusoe is the classic embodiment of such a humanist approach). The relational approach insists that it is only through living life within a complex of relations that individuals come to be formed and to act with purpose and intention. Life within social relations is the general form of the human experience.

In an important and complex sense social relations are objective. My life and your life are located within sets of relations (of work, politics, domestic, and so on) that are gendered, hierarchic, subordinating, and empowering in ways that (although we may affect their impact) are set up or predate our individual involvement; thus in some important sense they are external or objective. But social relations are not objective in any sense that implies that they are not a lived part of life within a culture, constructed and lived in and through language and forms of consciousness, as well as sets of objective conditions and sets of social practices. This point needs emphasizing to explain why a relational starting point is chosen rather than either of two other influential approaches, namely those provided by the concept of "base and superstructure" and by "the commodity form" theory of law.

MAPPING RELATIONS

The relational approach to law posits relations as the general form of sociality that are exhibited in a general and undifferentiated category of "social relations." Each social relation is constituted as a complex of a variety of different types and forms of relations. For example, the social relation of the family involves, among others, economic, sexual, gender, and legal relations. It is not my intention to suggest a full typology of the varieties of social relations. In the context of Marxist theory of law I will limit my account by assuming that only the following varieties are involved: economic, political, legal, class, and gender relations; gender relations are included not only as an important category in their own right, but also because they do not form part of the received Marxist tradition. This preliminary classification is posited at a fairly high level of abstraction. Nowhere do there exist "pure" economic or political relations; workplaces may exhibit predominantly economic relations, but political relations (embodied in the command structure of management or in trade union–employer relations) and gender relations (sexual division of labour) both play their part.

Each concrete relation involves a complex of relations; this is made clear if we adopt the terminology of calling a concrete relation a relation-set. The characteristics of each relation-set are identified by the relative predominance of its constituent relations and, in particular, by whether any pattern of dominance exists. Thus the specificity of a relation-set should be specifiable in terms of patterns of interaction between different relations identifying whether they supplement or conflict with each other.

Before leaving these general conceptual considerations something needs to be said about the problem of power. Despite the expenditure of considerable intellectual labor no usable conception of power is available. We can, however, identify some conceptions of power to be avoided; power is not a "thing," some property capable of being owned, possessed, or wielded. Nor is power a zero-sum game, in which each increment on one side is balanced by a diminution on the other. Power is quintessentially relational; power is the capacity of social actors to realize aims in a relation of oppositions and resistances to others. It is preferable not to speak of "power relations" since this implies that there exist some relations without a power dimension; on the contrary even in affectual relations, relations of personal attachment, the participants can never be entirely free of the power capacity of the wider social relations in which their relationship is located. Thus in every type of relationship particular characteristic forms of power are discernible; hence it makes good sense to speak of economic power (constituted by access to and control of economic resources), political power, etc.

It is, however, important to avoid such an all-inclusive conception of power that power is everything and everywhere. Foucault's accusation that Marxism equated power with the state is unjustified in the light of Marxism's emphasis on noncoercive economic relations as the primary source and location of power in capitalist societies (Foucault 1980:122). But Foucault is helpful in directing our attention to the dispersal and localization of power. What is missing, and is of special importance in the theorization of law, is to grasp how the particularistic and localized powers and disciplinary techniques coalesce or are aggregated at the level of institutions and of the state. To make comprehensible law's dispersed effects, its penetration of many and varied social relations, it is important to grasp that these "local effects" are made possible or are facilitated by the concentration of the legal system and its proximity to the monopolized coercive capacity of the state. While law cannot be reduced to the commands of some political superior or sovereign, it is nevertheless wrong to lose sight of the command capacity of the centralized legal institutions. It is the mutual reinforcement achieved through coercive capacity and ideological legitimacy that is the key to the understanding of legal power.

These brief comments on power lead to the need to stress the distinction between different dimensions of social relations. Power is one of the most important dimensions. Just as the idea of power relations has been resisted so it is proposed that it is better to speak of an "ideological dimension" than to speak of "ideological relations" since this implies the existence of nonideological relations. It is suggested that it is more fruitful to explore the power, ideological, and discursive dimensions of social relations, to examine their form and content and to study their interaction.

The proposed conceptual scheme is represented in Table 1.

Table 1

Relations	Dimensions of Social Relations			
Type of Relation	Power	Institutional	Ideological	Discursive
Economic				
Political				
Legal	X	X	X	X
Class				
Gender				

LEGAL RELATIONS

Legal relations are first and foremost a variety or type of social relation that are identified by a specific set of characteristics that separates them from other types of social relations. First, legal relations are interpellative in the sense that they can exist only through calling into existence or play social actors as "legal subjects." The legal subject does not coincide with the natural person; thus until relatively recently women were either not legal subjects or were constrained within a specific legal status that imposed duties while granting few rights. Similarly children are not full legal subjects and, as the present concern with child abuse highlights, it is not self-evident that either parents or the welfare state can be presumed to be capable of representing their interests. The current controversy arising from the abortion debate over the status of the fetus is another instance of this process whereby legal subjects are constructed or refused. It should be noted in passing that there is an important connection between "legal subject" and "citizen" that is neither homologous nor opposed and that has important implications for our understanding of politics, democracy, and participation.[4]

The most simple instance of the legal subject is that of the adult person recognized by state, courts, and other agencies as the bearer of rights, able to initiate litigation and owing enforceable duties to others (such as having to pay taxes, support dependants, and so on). One important consequence of the point that legal subjects are not coextensive with natural persons is that a variety of groups and social aggregates are endowed with legal subjectivity (or, as it is usually termed, "legal personality"); the corporation as legal subject is probably the most important example. It is also important to emphasize the wide variety of legal statuses into which people and groups are interpellated; "defendants" in criminal trial may be held in detention, subjected to bail restrictions and debarred from their normal activities. "Witnesses" are literally interpellated or summoned in being called before a court. Trustees, beneficiaries, states, agents, owners, and a host of other legal statuses are also summoned into being.

In one important set of instances this legal interpellation is itself constitutive of the social relation, as in the case with the formation of a corporate entity or with the creation of a trust. In these and other instances law is performative (where some legal act of speech, writing or signing changes the positions of the parties). Generally this creative role of law does not create a relation *ab initio*, for example, to form a legal partnership will probably serve only to formalize an existing economic relationship. It is, however, important to stress that significant actual or potential changes are effected by changing the positions, capacities, and obligations of the parties. In a much wider number of other circumstances the legal interpellation does not create a social relation but rather it affects the terms, conditions, and limits under which that relationship is lived out and struggled around. It is in order to keep this general primacy of social relations in mind that in elaborating a Marxist theory of law it is desirable to adhere to the methodological injunction; start with the social relationship before proceeding to examine the legal relation involved.

LAW AND MODES OF REGULATION

A legal relation always generates a potential mode of regulation; it is "potential" in the sense that many legal relations may be wholly or largely passive as the legal dimension of the relation may play no part at all in the way the concrete social relation is lived out. One obvious but important illustration of this is the fact that a legal relation often becomes significant only when a dispute or some other problem arises.

Law provides a wide variety of modes of regulating social relations. Generally a different mode is associated with different types of social relations. In many instances this is directly apparent in the conventional classification of types of law; thus criminal law employs different agents (like police) and imposes different sanctions (for instance imprisonment) from those techniques associated with private law (such as the individual initiation of litigation, monetary damages as primary remedy). The concept of a mode of regulation serves to focus attention on law as a continuing set of practices that contributes to the reproduction and transformation of social relations. It is not the frequently idiosyncratic outcomes of litigation that are significant, but rather the permanent processes that serve to normalize and stabilize the dynamic of struggle, conflict, and competition which characterizes relations within class society.

The major ingredient of a legal mode of regulation is the form that flows from the attribution of rights to interpellated legal subjects. The discourse of rights needs to be understood as consisting of a bundle of rights/duties distributed between legal subjects located within social relations. Both rights and duties embrace a variety of different types of attributions, whose significance is that they not only provide a relatively unified legal discourse that can handle a range of different social relations, but that also overlap with wider normative and moral discourses. This interface of legal and moral rights provides for both the authoritative determinations of rights/duties in litigation, a meta-discourse that provides legitimation and also a setting for contestation and change in which new or variant claim-rights are articulated and asserted.

The significance of the rights-grounded discourse is that it provides an integrated field within which all forms of social relations can be made subject to a common discursive apparatus. This is not to suggest that rights discourse is or can be fully coherent or free from internal tensions or contradictions. Indeed one of the major contributions of contemporary critical legal studies (CLS) has been to highlight the internal incoherence and contradictions within the discourse of rights. But this critique ignores the significance of rights as providing a comprehensive discursive field. It is worth noting that rights-discourse figures in other forms of dispute handling that are outside litigation, including negotiation and public debate.

LAW AS A DISTRIBUTIVE MECHANISM

Law and the legal process have the potential to change the relative positions of legal subjects within social relations; in this basic sense law is a distributive mechanism. Again it is necessary to stress "potential" since it does not follow that a change in legal capacity necessarily affects positions within concrete social relations. This is particularly obvious where law "fails," for example, in not achieving an adequate mechanism to enforce child support payments by divorced or deserting fathers. The general process of legal distribution is that interests and claims are transcribed into rights-discourses, and in that process the capacities of legal subjects are confirmed or varied. Law is rarely involved in the direct distribution of resources, but it is a major distributive process in the sense that it operates to vary the relative positions and capacities of the participants in social relations.

The intimate connection between law and politics is revealed clearly when it is recognized that a major instance of this process of affecting capacities is, particularly in our contemporary age of legislation, to alter the boundary between "political regulation" and "market" or "economic regulation." For instance the existence of legislation governing unfair dismissals from employment expands the sphere of political regulation of economic power. Thus one important dimension of legal regulation is that it regulates the boundaries or spheres of competence of other modes of regulation. This process frequently manifests itself in the never-ending process in which legal discourse invokes and redraws the boundary between the public and the private. The criticism leveled by CLS points to the inability of legal doctrine to sustain a coherent public/private distinction. While valid in its own terms, the inconsistency criticism misses the point that one of the major legal distributive mechanisms is located precisely in the fact that these boundaries are constantly drawn and redrawn.

It is important to emphasize that I do not suggest that the quest for consistency in legal doctrine is unimportant. Engels formulated the issue clearly in his letter to Conrad Schmidt:

> In a modern state, law must not only correspond to the general economic conditions and be its expression, but must also be an internally coherent expression which does not, owing to internal conflicts, contradict itself. (Cain and Hunt 1979:57; Marx and Engels 1975:399; original emphasis)

Two important points follow. First, it explains why law is rarely if ever the direct instrumental expression of the interests of a dominant class.

Second, it is the persistent quest for coherence, rather than its realization, that is significant. Indeed a necessary tension between competing versions of legal boundaries, such as that between the public and private, ensures the flexibility and responsiveness of law to changing contexts and pressures.

The theoretical framework developed above is intentionally abstract; it is also consistent with a range of different social theories and political perspectives. Its distinctively Marxist character can be developed by returning to the persistent themes and questions that have motivated it. Theories distinguish themselves by the questions they ask and the conceptual tools used in supplying the answers. I take Marxism's central concerns to be to explain the relations of subordination or domination that characterize particular historical epochs, to account for the persistence and reproduction of these relations, and to identify the conditions for ending relations and realizing emancipated social relations. The method and content of a Marxist theory of law will necessarily be concerned to explore the role of law in these three areas.

ECONOMIC RELATIONS AND THE LAW

A core question for Marxist theory of law is: what part does law play in the production and reproduction of the class relations that are characteristic of capitalist societies? While it is emphasized that there is an interactive connection between economic and legal relations, the focus adopted here will concentrate on the contribution of law to the reproduction of economic relations.

In the first instance a number of key legal relations form part of the conditions of existence for capitalist economic relations without which they could not function or would be able to do so only in a temporary or fragile manner. Law provides and guarantees a regime of property. In the discussion of ideology above attention was directed toward the universalization that characterizes the property relations of contemporary capitalism; the trajectory has been away from a unitary regime of individual legal owners exercising direct control over production, epitomized by the classical imagery of the factory owner standing by the gates of "his" factory, selecting the workforce and organizing the productive process. The expansion of the forms of capital, and their complex routes of circulation, requires a regime of property that recognizes and protects multiple interests that fall short of an absolute right of ownership.

The development of the modern regime of property has given rise to the recognition of a complex of legal rights that coexists between multiple interests. It is necessary to consider the nature of law's contribution to this modern property regime. One possibility is that law does no more than give retrospective recognition to those economic relations that develop spontaneously in the course of economic change and innovation. If this is the case, law would have no causal significance and, in principle, might even be largely redundant, merely giving formal expression to already existing normative practices.[5]

This view of the legal relation as simply reflecting economic change is misleading; it assumes that informal normative mechanisms operate in the same way and with the same results as legal regulation. Heavily dependent on the idea that all that law adds is a slice of formality (it merely formalizes that which already exists), this view ignores the extent to which legal relations have distinctive effects. The most important of these is the extent to which legal relations actually constitute economic relations. The most significant example is the formation of the modern corporation with limited liability; this is a legal creation in the important sense that it is precisely the ability to confer a legal status limiting the liability of participants that makes the relationship not only distinctive, but also a viable vehicle for the cooperation of capital drawn from a range of sources.

There is, too, a more general context in which law, while not creating or constituting an economic relation, makes it possible for a social relation to exist in the complex form necessary to support and sustain its contemporary economic role. There are undisputed connections between the modern commercial contract and the simple act of barter. There is thus a superficial plausibility to the view that law merely reflects the prerequisites of economic life. However, this anthropological extrapolation breaks down in the face of the degree of specialization of modern exchange relations, which involve a degree of complexity that could not be sustained within informal normative mechanisms. The modern contract must embrace contract planning for a wide range of potential variables. The same consideration affects the expansion of issues embraced in collective agreements between labor and capital, which necessitates a level of detailed specification that cannot be sustained within traditional notions of custom and practice.

It is essential to stress the complex interaction that exists between legal and economic relations (see Chapter 8). Some of these features can be briefly indicated. First, for any set of economic relations to operate with any regularly it must do so within conditions of a reasonable and sustainable degree of social peace and security. In general, law plays an important but not exclusive role in providing the general condition of personal security that allows us to get on with life in general and to participate in our economic roles as employees, consumers, and so on.

Second, legal doctrines and processes must make provision for the interrelations of capital, through commercial law, insurance, banking, and other financial services. One traditional way of identifying these activities is to speak of the conflict-resolution role of law. But it may be wise to avoid this formulation since it focuses too narrowly on litigation and the courts. It is probably more helpful to think of these mechanisms as background conditions that constitute the framework within which economic relations are conducted, that is as providing a mode of regulation.

Third, as has already been mentioned in the discussion of legal ideology, law provides the central conceptual apparatus of property rights, contract, and corporate personality that plays a double role in both constituting a coherent framework for legal doctrine and providing significant components of the ideological discourses of the economy. In speaking of legal ideology it is important to avoid any suggestion that judicial rhetoric does, save in exceptional circumstances, directly enter the field of public debate. This does not imply that legal ideology and judicial rhetoric are unimportant. Their significance is that legal conceptions and frames of reference have come to play an increasingly central part in the public discourses of the media, politics, and culture. Conceptions of rights, duties, responsibility, contract, property and the like, are persistent elements in public discourses, and the interpenetration of the legal and nonlegal features of these discourses plays a significant part in explaining the reach and purchase of legal conceptions on popular consciousness.

LEGAL RELATIONS AND CLASS RELATIONS

Another of the core questions for Marxist theory of law is: what contribution, if any, does law make to the reproduction of class relations? "Class" is a disputed concept within Marxism. Put simply, the controversy centers around the question of whether classes are a strictly economic category, or whether some element of consciousness on the part of class members is involved. To avoid the need to debate this issue I will adopt the strategy of distinguishing between two overlapping conceptions of class, the "immediate relations of production" and "general class relations," dealing with each in turn.

Immediate relations of production center on the connection between labor and capital embodied in the contract of employment. The legal relations of employment exhibit the characteristics of a distinctive form of law that, on the one hand, embodies the general features of contract doctrine (universality and individualization) and, on the other, comprises a significant specialization that in most modern legal systems marks off the contract of employment as distinct from other contractual forms. The individualizing element of general contract doctrine represents the presupposition of a voluntary relation between formally equal legal subjects, whereas the specialization of the contract of employment allocates distinctive sets of rights and duties to employer and employee. It is this combination of identity and difference that demonstrates the practical and ideological significance of the legal relation of employment. It constructs an apparent coherence within a framework that both denies and confirms the underlying inequality of the labor relation.

The regulation of the contract of employment, perhaps more than any other field of law, reveals the directly political character of law; labor law epitomizes an integrated field of law and politics. This politicization is apparent if we consider the legal response to trade unions as the distinctive form of organization of labor in capitalist economies. There are two salient consequences of the development of trade unions. The first provides one of the most important illustrations of the way in which law expresses the historically changing balance of forces between labor and capital. From periods of simple illegality to times when legislation imposed recognition of trade unions on employers, the content of the law has expressed the complex and shifting balance of forces. The second feature reveals the tension within legal doctrine. The classical individualistic core of contract doctrine presumes that the bargain is struck between individual employee and employer; yet the economic reality increasingly strips these parties of any significant role in determining the content of the labor contract, because the locus of bargaining has shifted to the collective agreement between trade union and employer. The complexity of labor law doctrine manifests the unstable tension between the form of law and its substantive content.

Aside from providing a basis for understanding the complex development of legal doctrine, this framework for analysis also discloses the difficulties associated with working out a political practice in this central arena of class relations. One illustration should indicate the complexity of political strategy in this field. The legislation of the British Conservative government since 1979 has been explicitly directed at weakening the position of the trade unions and reversing the gains made by organized labor since 1945. One important feature has been the imposition of legal controls over the internal procedures and democracy of trade unions; an example of this was the imposition of ballots prior to strike action. These proposals were bitterly resisted by the majority of unions on the grounds that the legislation infringed the self-governing autonomy of the unions. However, the imposition of ballots has had the paradoxical effect of providing increased legitimacy for strike decisions taken after ballots. It is thus arguable that from the outset trade unions should have moved prior to legislation to incorporate ballots and other mechanisms that increase membership participation into their own procedures.[6]

Turning to the role of law with respect to general class relations involves a shift of attention to the wider impact of law on the broad pattern of social inequality and subordination (though it is important to stress that focus on "class" does not exhaust the forms of inequality/ subordination). Two general theses will be defended:

1. The aggregate effects of law in modern democratic societies work to the systematic disadvantage of the least advantaged social classes and groups.
2. The content, procedures, and practice of law constitute an arena of struggle within which the relative positions and advantages of social class are changed over time as a result of the interplay of struggles within the legal arena and those outside it.

The important point to be stressed is that these two theses are neither incompatible nor contradictory; they are both true at one and the same time. The first thesis, that law disadvantages the disadvantaged, operates at all levels of legal processes. I will assume that these unequal consequences are either self-evident or so well-evidenced in empirical studies as not to require support here. Substantive inequalities disadvantaging the working class (and other subordinate groups or classes) are embedded in the content of legal rules. The procedures of law, the discretion of legal agents (in particular the police), the remedies and sanctions of law, the accessibility of legal representation, and many other dimensions all manifest unequal social effects. To produce a complete analysis of law's capacity to participate in and to reinforce the reproduction of social inequality it would be necessary to trace the detailed interaction between the different processes involved and, at the same time, to provide an analysis of the ideological effects and resonances of these processes.

The second thesis, about law as an arena of struggle, involves the outlines of an account of the historical trajectory of law as providing evidence of shifts and changes that are to be understood by reference to the play of social interests (material, symbolic, and ideological) within a field of social struggle of which law and legal relations are a component. The class analysis of legal doctrine requires some means of registering and establishing the connection between economic interests and the categories of legal doctrine.

An adequate theory of the dynamics of law and class needs to focus on how interests and claims are translated and transformed through the discourses of law. It is here that Marxist theory of law must come directly into contact with the concerns of liberal jurisprudence about the nature of judicial reasoning. Yet this does not involve a simple adoption of jurisprudence's problematic.

The difficulty to be confronted in developing a Marxist approach to judicial law-making is to avoid any assumption of the direct transposing of social interests into legal rights. Rather it needs to attend to the manner in which social interests are translated into rights-claims, and the degree of "fit" between those claims and the prevailing form of law expressed in existing legal rights. Analysis of this type generates hypotheses such as claims capable of translation into a discourse of individual rights and those interests congruent with existing rights categories are more likely to succeed than claims not matching these characteristics. This line of enquiry is fuelled by empirical evidence that suggests that different social movements of the disadvantaged meet with markedly different success when pursuing social change through law. The exploration of such issues fits well with the general concern of Marxism that its theory should be able to generate political strategy.

GENDER RELATIONS AND LEGAL RELATIONS

The connection between legal and gender relations exhibits an interesting paradox in that it is marked by both persistence and variability. The persistence is to be found in the near universality of gender inequality being expressed and reinforced through legal rules and procedures, while the form and content of that inequality exhibit great variation in the forms of disadvantage that law inscribes in the relations between women and men and between particular categories of women.

Marxist theory has exhibited considerable difficulties in coming to grips with gender relations. Marxism played a historically progressive role in its early recognition of the persistence of the subordination of women. It sought to provide a general historical explanation of the origins of oppression through focusing on the connection between property relations and unequal gender relations (Engels 1970). On the other hand Marxism's tendency to accord priority to economic relations has persistently submerged the specificity of gender relations under the general primacy accorded to class relations. This tension attests either to an as yet incomplete theoretical project of understanding the interconnection between gender and class—a project that has been taken up by socialist feminism. Or, alternatively, it may be that Marxism is incapable of resolving this theoretical tension—a conclusion pressed by radical feminism.

The uncertain condition of Marxism with respect to gender seriously handicaps the capacity of Marxist theory of law to offer a developed account of the connection between gender relations and legal relations. The comments that follow should therefore be regarded as very tentative. They are motivated by an attempt to understand the paradox referred to above concerning the persistence and variability of the law–gender connection.

One route to making sense of this paradox stresses the importance of a continuing attempt to identify the origins of the subordination of women. The significance of the quest for the origins of oppression stems from the suggestion that whatever these originating circumstances may have been, subsequently the oppression of women has been ideologically reproduced and has persisted beyond the socioeconomic conditions that generated it. The emphasis on the ideological reproduction of the subordination of women has two important consequences. First it suggests that it is precisely this ideological reproduction that is the reason for the very diversity of the legal forms this oppression has taken. Second it suggests the political conclusion that the primary arena of the struggle against oppression is ideological and revolves around the multiple and complex processes through which gender difference is socially constructed. This emphasis on ideology should not be understood as denying or marginalizing the role of economic and political struggles; rather it suggests that material issues around, for instance, pay equity or child care, are manifestations of the ideological construction of gender.

It follows that the connection between gender relations and legal relations can best be understood as exemplifying a situation in which legal relations are the bearers of ideological determinations, where these legal relations play a significant but prescribed role in their constitution and legitimation. In its simplest form this suggestions is that, with regard to gender, law plays a narrowly ideological role. For example, while the institution of marriage is a legally constituted relation it also exemplifies the role of law as a distributive mechanism assigning differential rights and duties between the parties. Yet the distributed benefits and burdens do not originate in legal doctrine but rather reflect the prevailing ideological construction of gender relations. At the same time the legal form imposes definite limits on the content that can be borne by the legal rules. The general trend of legal relations toward universalization produces a pressure toward formal equality. This process is by no means automatic as is witnessed by the resistance from most legal jurisdictions to the recognition of marital rape. This predisposition to favor formal equality, however, suggests that struggles around the legal reform of gender relations are likely to favor those reforms whose content most closely approximates formal equality. Conversely, legal reform is likely to lend itself less effectively to programs of affirmative action or substantive equality that conflict with the presuppositions of formal equality.

The tentative nature of these observations on the connection between gender relations and legal relations underlines the absences and uncertainties with which Marxist theory confronts the field of sex–gender relations.

CONCLUSIONS

This chapter has been concerned to outline a general framework for a Marxist theory of law. There are inevitably issues that have been omitted or passed over. Most significantly I have had almost nothing to say about the history of Marxist work on law, whether of Marx or of more recent Western Marxism. Consequently I have had little to say about how the position that I argue relates to the wider currents and themes within the ever-growing body of Marxist theory. But in default of addressing these issues I do need to make it clear that my position is contestable and would not be acceptable to many shades of opinion within the Marxist tradition.

There is one other omission that I do want, albeit briefly, to comment on; it concerns the relationship between Marxist theory of law and orthodox jurisprudence. The agendas of Marxist theory and jurisprudence overlap but do not converge. Marxism gives prominence to issues omitted or marginalized within jurisprudence, such as the repressive role of law and its fundamentally political character. In these and other respects Marxism can provide a much needed supplement to jurisprudence by its stress on the rootedness or connectedness of law with social, cultural, and economic relations. It provides a powerful source of resistance to the prevalent tendency within orthodox jurisprudence to treat law as disconnected, even autonomous, as being capable of study in and of itself. Marxism further refutes the timeless or ahistorical quality of much liberal jurisprudence. Marxism insists that the role and place of law are always consequences of a concrete and historically specific dynamic of the interaction of institutions and practices.

If Marxism supplements jurisprudence, it should not simply seek to negate or displace orthodox jurisprudence. The pervasive jurisprudential issues—such as the grounds for the obligations of citizens to obey the law, the means of determining the proper limits of state action and the conditions under which it is permissible to restrain the conduct of citizens—are also important questions for Marxism. Not only are these issues important questions within modern capitalist democracies, but history is currently teaching us most forcibly that these issues are ones that should have been on the agenda of Marxism's political project of building socialism. The contemporary revolutions in Eastern Europe hold many important lessons; one of the more important is that the renewal of socialism requires not the withering away of law, but the realization of a legal order that enhances and guarantees the conditions of political and economic democracy that facilitates democratic participations and restrains bureaucratic and state power.

The implication is that a Marxist approach to law will be concerned not only with characteristically jurisprudential issues, but also with the potential contributions of legal strategies to achieving effective political strategies for the social movements that reflect the Marxist political and ethical commitment to the poor and the oppressed.

CHAPTER 12

FOUCAULT'S EXPULSION OF LAW: TOWARD A RETRIEVAL

FOUCAULT'S EXPULSION OF LAW

Amid the great stir caused across a wide range of intellectual inquiry by the writings of Michel Foucault surprisingly little attention has been paid to the implications of his work for an understanding of the role of law in modern society.[1] This chapter engages with Foucault's writings on law; it is a partial engagement in that I attempt no exhaustive exegesis of Foucault's writing on law. My project is to draw attention to and to problematize one of the most distinctive features of Foucault's account of the historical emergence of modernity, one that I will term his *expulsion of law from modernity*. By "expulsion of law" I designate his metahistorical thesis that law constituted the primary form of power in the classical or premodern era, for although law lingers on, especially in the doctrine of sovereignty, it is undermined and even supplanted by the discipline(s) and government as the distinctive manifestations of power in modern society.[2]

Foucault's expulsion of law is a direct result of his pervasive concern to break with two closely related ways of posing the problem of power, both of which he views as endemic to Marxism. The first treats power as primarily a question of state-power and the second equates state-power with repression.[3] The expulsion of law is an effect of Foucault's strategy; his own intention was to resist the privileging of law that is characteristic of many modern political discourses.

Foucault's expulsion of law is exemplified when he writes: "We shall try to rid ourselves of a juridical and negative representation of power, and cease to conceive of it in terms of law, prohibition, liberty and sovereignty. . . . We must at the same time conceive of sex without the law, and power without the king" (Focault 1978:90–91). His most general formulation of the expulsion of law is the following:

> In short, it is a question of orienting ourselves to a conception of power that *replaces the privilege of the law* with the viewpoint of the objective, the privilege of prohibition with the viewpoint of tactical efficacy, the privilege of sovereignty with the analysis of a multiple and mobile field of force relations, where far-reaching, but never completely stable, effects of domination are produced. The *strategical model* rather than the *model based on law.*[4] (Foucault 1980:102; emphasis added)

My project is to move beyond criticism of Foucault (although there is, as I will argue, much to criticize) to propose an exercise in *retrieval,* in particular a "retrieval of law," to recuperate much in his thought that is suggestive and illuminating for our understanding of the complex role of law in the constitution of modern society. I will argue that in place of some generalized opposition between "law" and "discipline," through which Foucault seeks to characterize that which is distinctive of modern society, a better grasp of the modern can be secured by positing that "law" and "discipline" compliment each other and combine in the ubiquitous presence of "regulation" as the mark of the modern condition. I will argue that an appreciation of both the quantitative and qualitative *expansion of law* is a necessary precondition to an adequate grasp of modernity.

Since much that I have to say will be critical of Foucault I want to start by entering a caveat: I do not wish to be read as mounting an attack on Foucault. My purpose is to use, or even exploit, Foucault to help sharpen my formulation of an alternative understanding of the place of law in the project of modernity. This alternative is not an exercise in unreconstructed positivism that believes that it is possible to get law "right." Rather I seek only to throw a different focus on the interpenetration of law, discipline and regulation than that offered in Foucault's original expulsion of law. It is central to my strategy that I will deploy Foucault himself as a major component of the "retrieval" that I propose. In brief, there is a "later Foucault," one who passes beyond the preoccupation with the disciplines to focus on an expanded conception of "government" and "governmentality." I will make use of this strand in Foucault's own work and relocate it within a focus on "regulation," which while not part of his own theorization, is compatible with his concerns.

Foucault's work, like all important social theory, is marked by an attempt to hang onto both structure and agency, and as a result there is a certain oscillation toward one or the other of these poles. This expresses itself in a tension between, on one side, his radical relativism with its bleak succession of forms of domination and, on the other side, his political concern to ground an alternative emancipatory project that his relativism always tends to undermine (Dews 1989). One expression of this dilemma is exemplified by his aphorism: "My point is not that everything is bad, but that everything is dangerous" (Foucault 1982:231). My own view is that these tensions within Foucault's work are not resolvable, but far from undermining his significance, they rather attest to his emblematic significance as an expression of the intellectual and political angst of the late twentieth century.

My immediate interest is to explore Foucault's treatment of law. It is important to stress that I make no claim to "discover" a Foucauldian "theory of law" because law was not one of his explicit objects of inquiry. Nevertheless he had a very considerable amount to say about law. The question of law not only figures significantly but persistently returns in his texts. Law comes to the fore in a group of major texts from the late 1970s.[5] It forms a central motif during that stage of his work, which is marked by the shift that takes place within what should be read as his unified project from "power," via "discipline," to the "subject" that occurs between *Discipline and Punish* (1977) and *The History of Sexuality* (1978).[6] Indeed law plays such a key role in *The History of Sexuality* that it would not have misdescribed this work had its English translation been "The History of Law," the text being, in important respects, as much about law as it is about sexuality.

There is a third key text that explicitly engages with law. The second of his "Two Lectures" is centrally preoccupied with the distinction that he wishes to sustain between "law" and "discipline" (1980). When I first read "Two Lectures" I was struck by certain pronounced echoes of Marx's famous 1859 "Preface," the text in which he summarizes the "guiding thread for my studies" and proceeds to give the much quoted condensed summary of what came to be called historical materialism (Marx 1971:20–21). Both pieces are self-reflective and offer overviews of their respective positions; Marx's "guiding thread" is mirrored in Foucault's "guiding principle" and "methodological imperatives." (1980:94). Foucault, the otherwise skeptical critic of all metatheories, comes closer in this text than anywhere else to laying out an overarching conceptual framework and philosophy of history.

In setting out to interrogate Foucault's treatment of law, one quali-fication should be entered; although for convenience I will refer throughout to "law" and "the law" in the singular, I do not take the unitary character of law for granted; on the contrary I hold to a general conception of legal pluralism which posits a plurality of legal forms over which state law persistently, but never with complete success, seeks to impose a unity (see Chapter 10). Further I want to insist on the importance of avoiding any essentialist conception of law as if it were an entity independent of its specific forms of existence that embod-ies either a universal or even a general essence. To speak of "law" or "the law" always runs the risk of falling into one or other of these traps; however to speak of "law" is simply easier on both the writer and the reader!

OF LAW AND MONARCHS: ESCHEWING THE MODEL OF LEVIATHAN

In his overview of the rise of modernity Foucault's starting point is a "Classical Age," stretching from the late sixteenth century through to the second half of the eighteenth, characterized by a monarchical state constructed around the integration of "law" and "sovereignty." "Law was not simply a weapon skillfully wielded by monarchs: it was the monarchic system's mode of manifestation and the form of its acceptability. In Western societies since the Middle Ages, the exercise of power has always been formulated in terms of law" (Foucault 1978:87).

His most distinctive thesis is that it was not just that law and sovereignty constituted the "juridical monarchy" but that law and sovereignty have remained central to modern forms of state power despite the passing of the monarchies.

> At bottom, despite the differences in epochs and objectives, the representation of power has remained under the spell of monarchy. In political thought and analysis we *still have not cut off the head of the king*. Hence the importance that the theory of power gives to the problem of right and violence, law and illegality, freedom and will, and especially the state and sovereignty. . . . To conceive of power on the basis of these problems is to conceive it in terms of a historical form, that is characteristic of our societies: *the juridical monarchy*. (1978:88–89; emphasis added)

Thus Foucault installs a problematic of law, characterized by sovereignty and the juridical monarchy, as essentially *premodern.*

This account of the classical era characterized by the figures of law, monarchy, and sovereignty is supplemented by a conception of "right" conceived as providing the discursive cement of the premodern era.

> The essential role of the theory of right, from medieval times onwards, was to fix the legitimacy of power; that is the major problem around which the whole theory of right and sovereignty is organized. . . . My general project has been . . . to show the extent to which, and the forms in which, right (not simply the laws but the whole complex of apparatuses, institutions and regulations responsible for their application) transmits and puts in motion relations that are not relations of sovereignty, but of domination. (1980:95–96)

This conception of "right" is rooted in notions of the divine right of kings and in an imperative conception of law; the king's right is his right to command. But in the passage quoted above, Foucault effects an unexplored shift; a shift from "right" to "rights" that has the effect of locating the modern or bourgeois discourse of "rights" as synonymous with the imperative notion of "right" of the juridical monarchy and to bind them close by attributing to rights a general function of legitimation.

One of Foucault's most pervasive concerns is with the enigma of modern power. In the Classical era power was transparent, epitomized by the command power of the king, but in modern society power becomes diffused and its location becomes almost mysterious. This shift is epitomized by the visibility of political power and the often veiled reality of economic power. The result is that the tracking of domination, its strategies, techniques, and technologies, comes to form a central concern of both scholarship and political practice. "The problem for me is how to avoid this question, central to the theme of right, regarding sovereignty and the obedience of individual subjects in order that I may substitute the problem of domination and subjugation for that of sovereignty and obedience" (1980:96). Despite Foucault's concern to distance himself from Marxism it is noticeable that here he comes close to returning to Marxism's concern with the mechanism of domination and its tendency to counterpose coercion to consent.

Modernity for Foucault is marked by the emergence of "government" and "governmentality": "the instruments of government, instead of being laws, now come to be a range of multiform tactics.

Within the perspective of government, *Law is not what is important"* (1979:13; emphasis added).[7]

In a key passage he presents the rise of disciplinary administration as the "dark side" of law.

> Historically, the process by which the bourgeoisie became in the course of the eighteenth century the politically dominant class was masked by the establishment of an explicit, coded and formally egalitarian juridical framework, made possible by the organization of a parliamentary, representative regime. But the development and generalization of disciplinary mechanisms constituted the other, dark side of these processes. The general juridical form that guaranteed a system of rights that were egalitarian in principle was supported by these tiny, everyday, physical mechanisms, by all those systems of micro-power that are essentially non-egalitarian and asymmetrical that we call the disciplines. . . . The real, corporal disciplines constituted the foundation of the formal, juridical liberties. (1977:122)

Alongside this vision of law as playing the role of masking domination and as thus being an ideological phenomenon, there is a trace in his discussion that views law as, in some important sense, constitutive of the new forms of modern power. Law in this guise expresses the paradox of modernity. Confronted by the rise of the new disciplines, which are themselves exterior to law, the response of law is to seek to control or "recode them in the form of law" (1978:109). It is this trace that will contribute to the proposed retrieval of law to which I return below. Yet despite this suggested "recoding" of the new disciplinary mechanisms of power, Foucault is unwilling to grant any significant effectivity to law. The operation of disciplines "is not ensured by right but by technique, not by law but by normalization, not by punishment but by control" (1978:89).

Thus there is a dual impulse that impels Foucault away from law. The first, as we have seen, is his historical analysis of the central role played by law in the emergence of monarchy–law–sovereignty. The second motive that leads him to displace law is methodological. It stems from the reversal he advocates for the study of power and involves a shift of emphasis from state-power to local or capillary power. His project of redirecting the study of power has the effect of displacing law.

[T]he analysis . . . should not concern itself with the regulated and legitimate forms of power in their central locations. . . . On the contrary, it should be concerned with power as its extremities . . . with those points where it becomes capillary. . . . [O]ne should try to locate power at the extreme points of its exercise, *where it is always less legal in character.* (1978:96–97; emphasis added)

From this injunction to seek out power in its less legal manifestations it follows that research on the nature of power should be directed not toward the juridical edifice of sovereignty and the state apparatuses, but toward domination and the material operators of power in their dispersed and localized sites.

We must eschew the model of Leviathan in the study of power. We must escape from the limited field of juridical sovereignty and state institutions, and instead base our analysis of power on the study of the techniques and tactics of domination. (1980:102)

This methodological move presents Foucault with a serious difficulty: how to secure a focus on localized power without at the same time ignoring the indusputable significance of state power and other forms of centralized and institionalized power? This issue is probably the single most important theoretical and political weakness in Foucault's whole project, since without attention to the aggregation or condensation of power in centalized sites, the resistance that power engenders is forever doomed to remain localized and fragmented, forever repeating the cycle of single-issue struggles which resists particular manifestations of power without ever being able to mount a wider transformatory politics. I will return later to a more detailed consideration of this problem.

For Foucault history is always a "history of the present," but this concern may disadvantage the treatment of the past. My contention is that Foucault's derivation of law from monarchical power eliminates a more adequate history of law as emanating from dispersed sites of royal power, popular self-regulation, customary rights, competing specialized jurisdictions (ecclesiastical, guild, commercial, etc.), local and regional autonomies, and other forms of law. It was within this reality of legal pluralism that royal power, reaching its zenith in the absolutist state, fought a never ending and never entirely successful battle to subdue and unify. The equation of law with negative proscription involves the acceptance of an ideological conception that came to form the conventional view of the monolithic unity of state and law—a view that, paradoxically, Foucault is prepared to accept in launching his own critique of the presumption of a monolithic state power.

A similar reductionism is present in Foucault's treatment of sovereignty. All forms of sovereignty are conceived as derived from the particular form associated with monarchical power. While his evocation characterization of modernity's failure to cut off the king's head captures the limited forms of popular sovereignty that were secured during the course of the nineteenth century, there is a deeper sense in which he sees the very project of sovereignty as necessarily tied to the juridical monarchy.

His tendency to treat "right" as synonymous with monarchical power and to regard rights as mere ideological legitimations results in his paying little attention to some of the key doctrines that emanated from the period of the "juridical monarchy." Habermas is correct in his contention that Foucault ignores the real progress achieved through the "rule of law" in securing the constitutionalization of political relations and in winning guarantees of liberty and legality which were to have some, albeit varying, practical signficiance (Habermas 1987:338–340). Law's project of coordinating and unifying the new technologies of power requires further attention, and I will return to it below in discussing the relationship between law and discipline.

It is important to stress that Foucault's conception of his project requires that the repressive hypothesis be replaced by some other historical story line.[8] Here we encounter the postmodern Foucault, one who is deeply suspicious of all metatheories. But the modernist Foucault reasserts himself by launching a wider interrogation of the relationship between power and knowledge in the constitution of modernity in which the history of sexuality serves as an exemplary incidence of the rise of a distinctively new form of power, that he variously labels biopower or disciplinary power. Biopower refers to the emergence of new objects of power, epitomized by the emergence during the eighteenth century of a concern with population, its numbers, health and productivity. Disciplinary power focuses on the methods or, as he prefers, the techniques of power.

Foucault's thesis that modernity is characterized by a transition from law to disciplinarity and normalization bears a remarkable and paradoxical resemblance to the very "repressive hypothesis" he himself sets out to displace. This similarity lies in the fact that he relies upon a metahistory that invokes a general process of the rise and subsequent displacement of law as a repressive mode of social governance. Thus

Foucault ends up reinventing the repressive hypothesis that he had set out to displace.

FOUCAULT MEETS MARX

A central feature of Foucault's project lies in the distinctive form of his engagement with the legacy of Marx.[9] As is so often the case with debates with the "ghost of Marx," they occur tangentially and in fragments. This is certainly true in Foucault's case. While he insists on the impossibility of undertaking historical scholarship without taking serious account of Marx, most of his other scattered comments are more negative (1980:52–53). What Foucault does is to "use" Marx to set up a negative pole against which he seeks an alternative. The Marx that emerges is somewhat one-dimensional: rigid determinist, economistic, with a narrow conception of power as repression, and viewing the state as a unitary agent and the instrumental bearer of the interests of the ruling class.

The other, and more interesting, facet of Foucault's treatment of Marx is the conscious avoidance of both Marx's concerns and his concepts. This he does not because he rejects these concerns but rather to avoid being trapped within the terms in which they have been debated within the Marxist lineage. Foucault's relationship with Marx can best be understood as a self-conscious avoidance of Marx, but it is an avoidance that should not be mistaken as ignoring Marx. By "avoiding" Marx we should understand that Foucault seeks to open up new and unencumbered ways of addressing both new and classical problems. For example, Foucault self-consciously avoids dealing with the question of the state. "I don't want to say that the State isn't important; what I want to say is that relations of power . . . necessarily extend beyond the limits of the state" (1980:122). Similarly he avoids Marx's concept of ideology for fear that it leads to the espousal of an opposition between truth and falsity; thus Foucault's variant of the concept of discourse fills some part of the space vacated by the concept ideology. One fruitful way of interrogating Foucault's work is to understand his strategic reasons for *avoiding Marx*.

However, there is a heavy price to be paid for this concern to circumvent a negative conception of power. His critical step is the equation and conflation of negativity with repression; the result is that to avoid a negative conception of power, he first expels repression and elaborates an account of modern power founded on nonrepressive forms of domination. To secure this objective, he sets out to purge all those elements that are associated with negativity and repression. This has two fateful results. In the first instance he displaces the question of the state because he views the Marxist problematic of the state as inescapably bound up with the equation of class power and repression. Second, having already reduced law to an adjunct of sovereignty and centralized coercion, it is necessary that law be displaced or expelled from his analytics of modern forms of domination.

The important question is whether it is possible to retain Foucault's emphasis on the productivity of power without lapsing into the neglect of the state and of the condensation of power relations that occurs around it without repeating his expulsion of law. There are strong grounds for believing this retrieval to be possible, and I will attempt such an exercise later.

I have argued that Foucault's concern to focus on localized or capillary power exposes him to the objection that he ignores the significance of the state and other forms of centralized and institutionalized power. But the problem is more than just a matter of achieving an even-handed treatment of two different species of power. My sense is that there is a broad post-Foucauldian consensus that any adequate social or political theory has to take account of what we may loosely describe as "big power" and "little power." The really difficult question is to find an adequate way of grasping their mutual articulation and interaction. The weakness of Foucault's project is that in putting "little power" onto the agenda, he appears to ignore or to understate the importance of the processes that aggregate or condense power in centralized sites. This weakness manifests itself not only in a descriptively inadequate theory but also impedes the generation of adequate political strategy. As Poulantzas expressed it, "one can deduce from Foucault nothing more than a guerrilla war and scattered acts of harassment of power" (1978:149).

It is far from clear whether Foucault himself recognized this problem. It is possible to offer reasonable accounts for the view that he did address this issue and also for the view that he never came to grips with it.[10] Jessop's exemplary comparison of Poulantzas and Foucault provides a useful starting point; he argues that "Foucault increasingly emphasized the need to examine how different micro-powers are invested, realigned, and integrated into a global strategy of class domination by the state"[11] There is no doubt that Foucault recognized the existence of major or global dominations; for example, he suggests that micropowers "form a general line of force that traverses the local oppositions and links them together. . . . *Major dominations* are the *hegemonic* effects that are sustained by all these confrontations" (1978:94; emphasis added). This view makes use of the metaphor of a "diagram" along the lines of a simple model of a parallelogram of forces, as used in elementary mechanics, in which a number of autonomous forces act in such a way to produce a resultant (or aggregate) force acting in a direction different from any of the originating forces. The great attraction of this model for Foucault is that the forces/powers that act remain autonomous and there is no implication of intentionality or purpose which underlies or explains the directionality in which the resultant force/power operates.

In the important essay "The Subject and Power" he seems to recognize that he has perhaps gone too far in stressing the diffusion of power. "[W]hat makes the domination of a group, a caste, or a class . . . a central phenomenon in the history of societies is that they manifest in a *massive* and *universalizing form, at the level of the whole social body,* the locking together of power relations with relations of strategy and the results proceeding from their interaction" (1982a:226; emphasis added). Elsewhere he describes as a "methodological precaution" the need to "conduct an *ascending* analysis of power, starting, that is, from its infinitesimal mechanisms . . . and then see how these mechanisms of power have been—and continue to be—invested, colonized, utilized, involuted, transformed, displaced, extended, etc., by ever more general mechanisms and by forms of global domination" (1980:99). One index of his failure to grapple either theoretically or politically with the condensation of power is the gap created by the virtual absence of the concept "hegemony" (or any equivalent). He does use the word *hegemony* occasionally but only in a descriptive sense (1978:93, 94, 126, 127; 1980:156).

Foucault's most significant attempt to grapple with the condensation of power emerges in his development of a radically new, perhaps even bizarre, conception of "strategy." In a very characteristic formulation he argues that

> domination is organized into a more-or-less coherent and unitary strategic form; that dispersed, heteromorphous, localized procedures of power are adapted, re-enforced and transformed by these *global strategies* . . . [H]ence one should not assume a massive and primal condition of domination, a binary structure with "dominators" on one side and "dominated" on the other, but rather a multiform production of relations of domination that are partially susceptible of integration into *overall strategies.* (1980:142; emphasis added)

This approach has yielded valuable insights into the way in which two or more technologies of power interact to produce resulting forms of power that cannot be deduced from the individual techniques; thus, to cite just one example, the combination of law and medicine results in a distinctive regulation of women's bodies (Smart 1990). But this emphasis on the combination of techniques of power does not necessarily offer an account of how the diffuse techniques of power relate to and are aggregated in the massive institutional presence of state, military and economic apparatuses. The most fertile opening that he provided is to be found in his illusive concept of "strategy" and, in particular, in his deliberately ambiguous interest in the idea of strategy without positing the existence of any strategist—strategy without strategist. "Power relations are both intentional and nonsubjective. . . . [T]hey are imbued, through and through with calculation: there is no power that is exercised without a series of aims and objectives. But this does not mean that it results from the choice or decision of an individual subject" (1978:94–95). But what he does here is to conflate "tactics," the multiple wills and intentions of agents, with the suggestion that the aggregation of these tactics manifests the existence of a "strategy."[12] But we should not allow him to take advantage of this argument, because the claim can only make sense if we reintroduce some privileged agent, for example, the agent he is especially keen to banish, "the ruling class." The most that can be allowed, and this is sometimes Foucault's usage, is that "strategy" denotes a regularity or pattern of effects. Although he refers to the notion of the "strategical integration" of discourses, he never returns to develop this theme. In fact the idea of "strategy" is rendered redundant; the concept "effects" or "results" is sufficient (1978:102).[13]

The limitations of Foucault's treatment of "strategy" stem from his insistence on the diversity of power relations while, at the same time, he rejects both structural determination and the logic of (objective) interests. The result is that he is left with no means of accounting for the aggregation or globalization of power. To talk of strategy is to imply some explanatory principle for the historical patterns of power relations without providing the means to offer an explanation of their specific manifestations. Theoretically Foucault denies himself the capacity to explain why, for example, the medicalization of the discourses of sexuality should be succeeded by the dominance of psychiatric discourses. Thus despite his invocation of "strategy," his general theoretical stance prevents him from providing any but the most gestural account thereof.[14]

Poulantzas offered a far more adequate approach to this idea of "strategy without strategists." In countering the conception of a unitary, omniscient, omnipresent "Power-State," he was at pains to insist that the state is potent and ubiquitous, yet at the same time he drew attention to the prodigious incoherence and chaotic character of state policies. Strategy only emerges ex post facto through the collision of mutually opposed tactics in which the general line of force is conceived as the complex resultant of the balance of forces involved when the specific tactics of social movements and classes clash and compete (Poulantzas 1978:33, 135–37). Foucault's superficially similar thesis that "the logic is perfectly clear, the aims decipherable, and yet it is often the case that no one is there to have invented them, and few can be said to have formulated them" (Foucault 1978:95) says much less. He sustains only the worthwhile, but hardly novel, view that social action produces consequences that are not intended by the participants.[15] What he fails to provide is the capacity to generate explanation of the directionality of change and the explanation of the success of specific tactics and discourses.

Foucault offers another formulation which suggests a recognition of the problem of condensation of power within state and other apparatuses "[I]t is doubtless the strategic codification of these points of resistance that makes a revolution possible, somewhat similar to the way in which the state relies on the institutional integration of power relationships" (1978:96). The question is whether he provides himself with any means to adequately deal with the condensation of power. He might simply have replied that this was not a major concern. He consciously selects just such an *alternative problematic*: "what were the most immediate, the most local power relations at work?" (1978:97). And only then should one ask: "How were these power relations linked to one another according to the logic of a great strategy?" (1978:97).

What Foucault fails to pursue Stuart Hall provides with his concept of "constituted points of condensation" that borrows the Foucauldian notion of power but refuses Foucault's absolute dispersion (Hall 1988). Hall argues for the need to distinguish between "lateral power" (multiple sites of power in civil society) and "vertical power" (state apparatuses) (1988:52). This approach begins to provide an approach that while consistent with Foucault, goes a long way toward overcoming Foucault's relative neglect of this critical issue.

THE DESTINY OF LAW

[I]t is part of the destiny of the law to absorb little by little elements that are alien to it. (Foucault 1977:22)[16]

As we have seen Foucault's impulse toward the expulsion of law from modernity involves a view that assigns a relatively marginal role to law in contemporary society. This tendency to marginalize law contrasts sharply with positions that invest law with an increasingly significant role in modern society. Such views cover a wide spectrum of recent social and legal theory; a thesis that posits the increasing centrality of law can be attributed to such diverse figures as Weber, Poulantzas, Dworkin, and Luhmann, to name only a few. The diversity of the accounts that attribute increasing significance to law reveal the radical revisionism that typifies Foucault's work.

Foucault's account of the decline of law does not involve a thesis that suggests that law might wither away; rather his position can be characterized as allocating to law an increasingly subordinate or support role within contemporary disciplinary society. "I do not mean to say that law fades into the background or that institutions of justice tend to disappear, but rather that the law operates more and more as a norm, and the judicial institution is increasingly incorporated into a continuum of apparatuses (medical, administrative, and so on) whose functions are for the most part regulatory" (1978:144). Here he suggests two distinct tendencies. The first tendency is a version of the widely held view that counterposes law and regulation, seeing the rise of administrative and technological regulation as signaling a decline or demise of law (Hayek 1973). What, for Foucault, distinguishes the new forms of power is that they function primarily by means of surveillance. For reasons that he does not explain he views law as not having the capacity "for the codification of a continuous surveillance" (1980:104). This view ignores the evidence of developed forms of legal rationality present in premodern societies of the kind (discussed, for example, by Raeff) that were already evident in late-medieval Germany (Raeff 1983).[17] He does, however, offer a suggestion that highlights the idea of law as a component of regulatory practices; this version will provide an opening for my proposed retrieval below.

The second tendency presents law as functioning increasingly as a "norm." Foucault does not develop this suggestion save for an insistence that counterposes "norm" and the "juridical," associating the later with monarchical law. François Ewald has provided an extended examination and extension of Foucault's thesis about the normativization of law (Ewald 1990). The norm is to be distinguished from the rule, rather it identifies general standards, not in the sense of "principles" as used by Dworkin, as meta-rules, but rather as a set of standards; perhaps one way of grasping this idea is to extend Foucault's own notion of a discursive formation, to say that would imply that Ewald thinks that what Foucault had in mind was a "normative formation." Ewald illustrates this idea by exploring the popular contemporary theme that late modernity is characterized by the rise of the risk or insurance principle (O'Malley 1990; Simon 1987).

Ewald may well have succeeded in capturing Foucault's intention, but if he has, then he reveals the deficiency in the normativization thesis. Because the contention that we are witnessing a pervasive enlargement of the insurance principle points not to a change in either the form or concept of law, but rather to an extralegal development that displaces rather than transforms law. Law enforcement authorities are no longer able to provide protection in metropolitan areas against petty housebreaking; thus we witness the emergence of insurance companies insisting on the installation of alarm systems in private households as a condition of issuing or renewing policies. The implication is that we are forced to accept that housebreakers do not get apprehended and that we must rely on monetary compensation via insurance claims. This process is, I suggest, not to be understood as an advancing normativization of law, but rather as the emergence of a new "limit of law." The general evidence that Ewald advances is consistent with that element in Foucault which seems to suggest a "displacement" of law. But his account fails to add either substance to or confirmation of a thesis about the advance of the "norm."

The more persuasive response to Foucault's account of law in late modernity suggests that the trajectory of law is far more complex. Briefly, a more adequate account would need to stress a persisting plurality of the forms of law. Only one facet of this process is characterized by the rise of substantive justice and discretion, epitomized in welfare legislation. This trend is matched by a persistent increase in the range, scope, and detail of legal intervention that produces a general movement towards an expanding legalization and juridification of social life.[18] Also suggested is an increase in the particularistic character of law as laying down detailed rules for a host of specialized areas of activity, for example, in detailed provisions concerning welfare provision, construction standards, product safety, credit transactions, and so on. Alongside these developments, exhibiting features of both the above trends, is the complex phenomenon of the advancing constitutionalization expressed in many and varied extensions of both the forms and types of entrenched rights that go far beyond the classical political and property rights of the constitutionalism of the eighteenth and nineteenth centuries. In short, Foucault's account is simply inadequate to grasp the complex trajectory of both premodern and modern law.

In general Foucault's image of modern law is one of a mechanism that is ineffectual and generally epiphenomenal, confined mainly to providing legitimations for the disciplinary technologies and normalizing practices established by other mechanisms (1977:222).[19] Thus in discussing the incarceration of juveniles he observes that while legal principles have increasingly forbidden imprisonment outside the law, yet incarceration continues to increase under the auspices of the new disciplines of medicine and psychiatry. But the question that needs to be posed is: what does the evident and undisputable fact that law is relatively ineffective demonstrate? It is too weak merely to reply that law is ineffective. What we need to ask is: how is law implicated within different social relations? In particular we need to direct our attention to some of the persisting questions of classical jurisprudence about the capacity of legal control of diverse social practices, whether of the new disciplines or the "old" disciplines implicated in political and economic power. The adequate pursuit of these questions requires the abandonment of jurisprudence's assumption of legal effectiveness, but it also requires the rejection of Foucault's presumption of legal weakness. Again we need to recognize that fruitful inquiry requires that we focus on the interaction of law (conceived as a range of different forms) and other disciplinary practices. Only then is it possible to distinguish between the different forms of legal effectiveness and to explore our intuitive judgment that there is considerable variation in the effectivity of law. This allows us to return to those classical, but still important, questions about the capacity of law to check nonlegal forms of power.

One persistent feature of Foucault's reflections on the destiny of law is the contention that there is some fundamental incompatibility or tension between the legal form and the new forms of power.

> For this is the paradox of a society which, from the eighteenth century to the present, has created so many technologies of power that are foreign to the concept of law: it fears the effects and proliferations of those technologies and attempts to recode them in forms of law. (1978:109)

> We have been engaged for centuries in a type of society in which the juridical is increasingly incapable of coding power, of serving as its system of representation. Our historical gradient carries us further and further away from a reign of law that had already begun to recede into the past at a time when the French Revolution and the accompanying age of constitutions and codes seemed to destine it for a future that was at hand. (1978:89)

This emphatic position receives a characteristically Foucauldian treatment. Over time he offers a series of alternative formulations wtihout offering a more elaborated treatment; elsewhere he describes the fate of law in the following terms: "the procedures of normalization come to be ever more constantly engaged in the colonization of those of law" (1980:107). His terminology changes, but I suggest that "absorbing" (1977:22), "recoding" (1978:109], "incorporation" (1978:144), "colonization" (1980:107), and "reorganization of right" (1980:107) are each attempts, none entirely satisfactory, to specify the character of the engagement between law and the new disciplines.

Modern power characteristically employs the discourses of law, but Foucault is concerned to suggest that this is a surface phenomenon, even an ideological phenomenon—although, as we have seen, he avoids this term. His point, I suggest, that he wants to insist on some basic incompatibility between the form of law and the new disciplines. This incompatibility only arises from his own insistence on the unbreakable link between law and sovereignty and the command model of law that it generates. The connection between law and the new disciplines is much less troubling and involves no necessary tension or contradiction the moment we abandon his unitary model of monarchical law. A more adequate conception of law must start by conceding that, like all other social relations, law is subject to both change and variation in form. Once this simple, but fundamental, point is made, we can represent the problem in a more manageable and fruitful way. The question now becomes: how is law articulated with the new disciplines? Or, more accurately: how are the shifting forms of law articulated with the new disciplines? It is this reformulation of Foucault's problematic that makes possible the retrieval of law that is pursued below, but first it is necessary to consider his notion of disciplinary society in more detail.

BEYOND THE DISCIPLINARY SOCIETY

There is a deep ambiguity, maybe even a contradiction, between Foucault's stress on the productivity of power and his bleak imagery of oppressive "disciplinary society" in which the individual "finds himself caught in a punishable, punishing universality" (1977:178). This ambiguity is echoed in his stress on the negative, prohibitive visage of law and the negative productivity of disciplinary power.

At the heart of Foucault's expulsion of law lies his conern, manifest in all his interventions about power, to identify the emergence of distinctively new forms of power that characterize modernity. His account of the transition to modernity posits a series of displacements, starting in the seventeenth century, in which it is assumed that centralized monarchical power is consolidated during the course of the eighteenth century so that by the second half of the nineteenth century we find in place a distinctive new form of power—disciplinary power that, in contrast to the unitary form of state power, is constituted through the play and interplay of a plurality of disciplines.

In charting the rise of disciplinary society, Foucault employs a tactic that is characteristic of much of his work. To clear the space for a new thesis, he displaces or contradicts the existing common sense, a strategy epitomized in his rejection of the "repressive hypothesis" in the history of sexuality (1978:45). It is in this context that we should understand the way in which he counterposes disciplinary power to juridical power. "This new type of power, which can no longer be formulated in terms of sovereignty, is, I believe, one of the great inventions of bourgeois society. . . . This non-sovereign power, which lies outside the form of sovereignty is disciplinary power" (1980:105). It is in this sense that he describes the disciplines as being a "counter-law" which operates "on the underside of law" (1977:223). It is from a concern to highlight the distinctiveness and novelty of the disciplines that Foucault is led to counterpose them to law. But it needs to be firmly insisted that, contrary to Foucault, disciplinary power is not opposed to law, but rather that law has been a primary agency of the advance of new modalities of power and constitutes distinctive features of their mode of operation.

To bring out the distinctiveness and novelty of the "new disciplines" Foucault emphasizes the difference between law and discipline. The operation of these new mechanisms of power, he argues, is ensured "not by law but by normalization, not by punishment but by control" (1978:89).[20]

A significant but elusive feature of his treatment of the rise of the disciplines is the emphasis he places on the role of "norms." Discipline, rather than being constituted by "minor offenses," is characteristically associated with "norms," that is, with "standards" that the subject of a discipline must internalize or manifest in behavior—for example, standards of tidiness, punctuality, or respectfulness. These standards of proper conduct put into place a mode of regulation characterized by interventions designed to correct deviations and to secure compliance and conformity; normalization is thus counterposed to a prohibition—punishment model. The "norm" is implicit in surveillance in that it provides the criteria that the gaze invokes (e.g., deference is translated into a sequence of behavioral signs) and deviance involves the infraction of the norm. It is through the repetition of normative requirements that the "normal" is constructed and thus discipline results in the securing of normalization by embedding a pattern of norms disseminated throughout daily life and secured through surveillance. It should be noted that although the concept "norm" is present, it is underdeveloped and plays only a minor role. It is as if the articulation of a norm were the by-product of the routinization of the normalization process; the norm itself has no history. It is perhaps for this reason that the normative content articulated in legal rules does not attract his attention.

Yet for Foucault law is paradigmatically a system of universal norms. One dimension of the distinction between law and disciplines is that between universal norms and the particularity of the disciplines. "[W]hereas the juridical systems define juridical subjects according to universal norms, the disciplines characterize, classify, specialize . . . [T]hey effect a suspension of the law that is never total. . . . Regular and institutional as it may be, the discipline, in its mechanism, is a 'counter-law'" (1977:223).[21]

Foucault's account of the difference between law and discipline is at its sharpest where he draws this contrast between universal law and "counter-" or "infralaw." "At the heart of all disciplinary systems functions a small penal mechanism" (1977:177), an "infra-" or a "micropenality" that takes possession of an area left empty by law, providing regulation for diverse types of behavior; these micropenalties involve such "offenses" as lateness, untidiness, disobedience, and insolence. His point is that these wrongs are, on the one hand, so trivial as to be beneath the attention of law but, on the other, are the very stuff and heart of the modern disciplines. There is no doubt that he makes an important point that regulation is not synonymous with or bounded by law. Yet he misses the more important point that state law is always involved with, if not preoccupied with, the task of either exercising control over or exempting from control the different forms of disciplinary regulation. For example, historically law ceded family discipline to the patriarchal father and this site has more recently become a major field of regulatory contestation. A more adequate account starts from the idea that the whole field of social regulation involves an ongoing process of expansion and contraction of the sites of regulation and the advance or withdrawal of the different regulatory techniques. It is within this framework that the issue of the role of law, of its advances and retreats and the changes in its active forms, can be more rigorously posed than is allowed by Foucault's counterposing of law and discipline.

For Foucault another important difference between the disciplines and law is marked by their characteristic forms of punishment. In the place of the corporeal punishments of the old criminal law, "exercises" and the repetition of tasks characterize the disciplinary model of bio-power. In turn these new forms of sanctions exist side by side with a greatly extended range of "rewards" (e.g., ranks, grades, prizes, badges, privileges). Thus the contrast he draws is between "standards," which lay down general targets or criteria of judgment (such as attitude, demeanor, etc.), and "rules," the legal form that he continues to conceive of as negative and prescriptive ("Don't do X; if you do the punishment will be . . . ").

> Another consequence of this development of bio-power was the growing importance assumed by the action of the norm, at the expense of the juridical system of the law. . . . But a power whose task is to take charge of life needs continuous regulatory and corrective mechanisms. . . . Such a power has to qualify, measure, appraise, and hierarchize, rather than display itself in its murderous splendor. (1978:144)

It is, of course, only by virtue of his "command theory" or police conception of law as a mechanism of orders, which focuses on its murderous splendor, that Foucault can sustain these contradictory formulations in which law is both equated with norms and distinguished from them. Once this conception of law is abandoned, then the mechanisms that "qualify," "measure," "appraise," and "hierarchize" provide a more than adequate characterization of the capacities of modern legal processes. At best he can only conceive of law playing a minor or supporting role by providing legal justification of normalizing discipline by contributing to the "normalization of the power of normalization" (1977:296).

Thus Foucault's reading of the new disciplines works only when law is thought of narrowly in terms of a system of commands or prohibitions. Once we abandon that conception, we find not a separation or distance between discipline and law, but rather an interplay or even interpenetration of law and discipline; and it is the explication of this connection that needs to inform the project of retrieving law.

As we have seen, much of Foucault's account invokes a general opposition between disciplinary and juridical power, but just occasionally he insists that this is not his intent. "We must . . . see things not in terms of the substitution for a society of sovereignty by a disciplinary society and the subsequent replacement of a disciplinary society by a governmental one; in reality we have a triangle; sovereignty-discipline-government, that has as its primary target the population and its essential mechanism apparatuses of security" (1979:18–19).[22] But despite formulations of this type, his predominant tendency is to counterpose the disciplines to law, that is conceived as antithetical and "absolutely incompatible" (1980:106). "The discourse of discipline has nothing in common with that of law, rule, or sovereign will. . . . The code they come to define is not that of law but that of normalization" (1980:106).[23]

What sense should be made of his determined separation of law and disciplines followed by partial retreats? In the first place, Foucault separates these concepts primarily to give emphasis to the multiple origin of the disciplines in dispersed social practices, in particular, those emanating from the "human sciences." On the other hand, he recognizes that law has not disappeared or withered away. Since law does not constitute an object of inquiry for Foucault he has no special interest in exploring one rather obvious, but nonetheless attractive, hypothesis, namely, that associated with the rise of the disciplines there has occurred a change in the form of law. I will return to explore this possibility in the concluding section.

Perhaps the central deficiency that permeates Foucault's treatment of discipline is the lack of any explanatory mechanism whereby the dispersed and plural "disciples" are aggregated into his pessimistic and negative utopia of the Gulag that is "disciplinary society." To identify such a strategic unification would tend to suggest the existence of some far-sighted and malevolent "ruling class," but this Foucault explicitly refuses as one of the major grounds for his break with Marxism. And yet, without some mechanisms of unification or aggregation, the dramatic imagery of the disciplinary society is undermined.[24] The resort to this tactic on Foucault's part is a manifestation of the problems that are inherent in his general thesis of "strategy without strategists."

It is only by invoking a globalized conception, the disciplinary society, that he is able to sustain the idea of the displacement of the law-sovereignty complex. But this globalization comes into conflict with his pervasive and forceful insistence on the dispersal of the sites of power and the plurality of the disciplines.[25] Do the modern disciplines and normalizing practices have any unity? And, more important, if so, where does this unity come from? How are the mechanisms of normalization orchestrated?

Foucault attempts to resolve this difficulty by an inspired, but ultimately unsatisfactory, move; he insinuates unification by positing a unifying mechanism whose manifestation takes two well-known forms—"the gaze" and the Panopticon. Both of these devices are significant in that they imply a process of unification or centralization of diverse practices without the need to posit a unifying agent. In *Discipline and Punish* the metaphor of the Panopticon plays this role of imposing unity in that he treats the Panopticon as the essence of modern disciplinary power. This claim lays itself open to two objections. The first is the sociological challenge that whatever significance we might be prepared to accord to the Panopticon (and in passing it may be suggested that he greatly overemphasized the historical significance of what was never more than an unrealized project), there is no evidence to suggest that the other forms of normalizing discipline were motivated by the same global aspirations. It is similarly apparent that there is no unitary "gaze"; for example, psychiatrists, social workers, and prison guards all deploy distinct and fragmented gazes.

A second set of difficulties surround Foucault's persistent, but elusive, identification of discipline with surveillance and "normalization." He paints a set of vignettes of the "discovery" of new sites of disciplinary intervention. For example, he contends that a moral panic surrounded the "discovery" of juvenile masturbation that brought into play a heightened level of surveillance over the bodies of children and an objectification of sexuality through moralizing medical discourses. His texts are full of the "discovery" of the multiplication of disciplines that have their beginnings in "little places" and that extend their range of operation. Much of the reason for Foucault's very considerable influence is that—in the most general and untheorized sense—the picture that he is taken to have painted is of ever extending and ever more intrusive mechanisms of power that insert themselves into every nook and cranny of social and personal life. There is no doubt that this strikes a chord of intuitive recognition and resentment in the self-consciousness of the late twentieth century.[26] This picture fuels not only the antiauthoritarianism of the Left, the innumerable projects of escape from modernity, but also the projects of the escape from the constraints of overregulation on the part of neoliberal conservatives. Now, of course, this story line is not new, but Foucault's version of the undramatic but cumulative impact of the disciplines connects with contemporary sensibilities. However much we may empathize with this general orientation, it should not blind us to the fact that Foucault is far from convincing in establishing the massification of the dispersed disciplines into "the disciplinary society."

Foucault's thesis concerning the rise of normalization as a new form of power should not be allowed to obscure the long history of normalization that predates the rise of the modern state. In premodern society wide arenas of conduct were subject to strict surveillance, discipline, and legal control through the regulation of consumption and the ordering of appearance (Lofland 1973); these regulatory mechanisms were later abandoned or defeated, but new sites of normalization became the subject of contestation. To take just a few examples: the strict regulation of dress codes enshrined in the sumptuary laws of the early New England colonies (Demos 1982), the speech and eating codes of medieval knights (Elias 1978), or the regulation of "excessive" consumption by German peasants at weddings (Raeff 1983) each attests to the pervasive role of normalization and discipline in premodern society. Normalization, discipline, and regulation are not new and, of course, Foucault knows this perfectly well, but in the search for the distinctive novelty of the modern he tends to obscure our vision of the regulated pasts.

The really interesting questions that need to be posed concern the shifts and transformations that mark the changes characterizing the genuinely novel mechanisms Foucault has done so much to chart. These issues provide fertile avenues for research because they involve complex articulations of self-control, confessional techniques, legal regulation, and disciplinary processes. And, significantly, these shifts involve different modalities of the participation of law in these processes.

Foucault's overemphasis on the novelty of disciplinary and normalizing power also creates the risk of undermining the significance of his own account of modernity. While he often returns to suggestive ideas about modernity understood as manifesting the reconstitution of elements already in place and developing interstitially in the old order, his tendency to succumb to the "big sweep" as epitomized by his counterposing of law-sovereighty to discipline-normalization does much to undermine this potential.[27]

If we are to take seriously, as I believe we should, the shift of attention that Foucault proposes toward the microphysics of power, doing so implies that this shift disallows any assumption that these dispersed powers form any kind of unity. On the contrary, the serious pursuit of Foucault's concerns should lead us to pose a different set of questions. How should we approach the study of the forms of articulation of the dispersed disciplines? How are they combined? How are their competitions resolved? Down this route lies a fruitful line of inquiry that focuses on the role of both law and state, marginalized by Foucault, with respect to the coordination and condensation of the forms of power.

The implications of this line of inquiry are of considerable importance; while we can go along with Foucault's rejection of the unitary class state, we are brought back to engage with some of the more important problems that classical Marxism first posed. One shorthand answer is that the state apparatuses and state law are continuously driven to pursue *projects* of the unification of power, but the success of these projects is always partial, limited, and incomplete.

FROM DISCIPLINE TO GOVERNMENTALITY

One of the most significant contemporary intellectural paradigm shifts has been toward a focus, captured by the notion of *governance*. It is, of course, Foucault who has provided the major intellectual impetus, although he prefers the term "government," a term that for me has a rather too institutional ring to catch the concern for what might well be described as the history of the "ideas of government."[28] This attention to governance opens up a space that allows us to think of government as process rather than as institution and to break with the common-sense perception that only governments govern. When Foucault proposed his notions of government and "governmentality," he conceived government as having "as its primary target the population and its essential mechanism [is] apparatuses of security" (1979:18–19) and the distinctive mentality, "governmentality," the forms of knowledge and administrative imperatives that emerge with the governmentalization of society. This set of concerns emerges only in Foucault's later work. In the earlier version he started from the contention that *political power* is, in some important and distinctive sense, *legal* whereas both *pastoral* and *disciplinary power* were in some significant sense *nonlegal.*[29]

Foucault constructs his later account of modern governmental rationality by contrasting it to the form of rationality that characterized the European experience from the sixteenth through to the eighteenth century. This form of rationality that precedes modernity is difficult to name. Foucault uses the label "reason to state" and sometimes "police state."[30] The latter, while accurately reflecting his conception, is perhaps best avoided to prevent confusion with the conventional equation of "police state" with modern authoritarian regimes. Although it is far from satisfactory I will use the label "cameralist reason," which, although not used by Foucault, is consistent with his intent, to capture a governmental style that emphasized a commitment to the necessity of the positive regulation of an expanded conception of the polity and economy through a project of policing that knew little of the modern dichotomy between the public and the private.[31] The role of cameralist government was conceived as that of educating people to a discipline of work and frugality (Oestreich 1982:157).

It is in contrast to cameralist reason that Foucault constructs a picture of the emergence of governmental reason. His reflections on this question were fragmentary and largely unpublished; for this reason I shall rely on Colin Gordon's reconstruction (Gordon 1991). The particularly insightful idea that Gordon advances, and that goes significantly beyond Foucault's own account, is that we should understand Foucault as coming to grips with what Gordon calls "real liberalism." Real liberalism is contrasted with the more abstract and ideological construct of "laissez-faire" that overemphasizes state abstentionism. To focus on "real liberalism" allows us to direct attention on the actual mechanisms of regulation and governmental conduct rather than on this presumed abstentionism. Gordon suggest that Foucault's sketch of modern governmental rationality is to be found in the combination of "security" and "liberty."

The emergence of a concern with "security" forms, according to Foucault, a dominant component of modern governmental rationality. It is embedded in the shift from a view of indivudals as "subjects" to one in which they are conceived as the bearers of "interests," that is, they are economic subjects: subjects or "subjects of the state" considered only insofar as the state requires to regulate their conduct or to demand performance from them (military conscription and imposition of taxes being two central instances). The individual considered as a bearer of interests requires the state to take cognizance of those interests, in their multiplicity and complexity. "Security" functions not by negative prescription or refusal but rather through the specification of a range of tolerable variation. Thus liberalism constructs a complex governance within which political, economic, and juridical instances of subjectivity are dispersed.

The association of "security" with "liberty" marks not merely the rise to prominence of rights discourses but involves the idea that the systematic realization of political and juridical rights is an essential condition of good government, itself a precondition for the persistence, stability, and prosperity of both economic and political government. Gordon succinctly captures this governmental role of rights. "[D]isrespect of liberty is not simply an illegitimate violation of rights, but an ignorance of how to govern" (1991:20). This concern with rights and the conditions of prosperity can be seen as reaching a high point in Keynesian economic strategy in which the attempt to master cyclical economic crisis and to secure its emblematic goal of full employment are conceived as preconditions of both economic prosperity and of political stability. The "security-liberty" characterization of liberalism poses the question: *What part does law play in modern governmental rationality?*

Foucault's account of the place of law in the transition to modern governmental rationality involves a distinct and significant shift from some of his earlier positions associated with his expulsion of law discussed above. As demonstrated in his major texts published between 1975 and 1977 [*Discipline and Punish* (1975), *History of Sexuality*, Vol. 1 (1976), and *Power/Knowledge*], he equated law with sovereignty and the juridical monarchy. As we have seen, he had been at pains to stress not only the dispersion but the privatization of disciplinary power.

However, there are in this group of texts hints of a different conceptualization, one we can locate as the retreat from a transition from "law to disciplines" to a new focus on "law and regulation." One of his key formulations posits this historical shift from law to regulation. This transition occurs when he suggests that law does not "fade into the background" (1978:144). It is this insight that is developed in the "late Foucault," the Collège de France lectures of 1978 and 1979,[32] the papers "Governmentality" (1979) and "Omnes et Singulatim" (1981), and, more generally in his concern with the "government of the self" (1988). In this phase of his work the earlier expulsion of law from modernity is significantly modified. Now his conception of law focuses on the purposive rationality of the legislative output of representative legislatures. He emphasizes the increasing particularism of regulatory instruments. The previous conception of law as a totalizing and transcendent unity is superseded by historically specific production of regulatory devices that mediate between state and civil society and between state and individual. It is this line of thought that forms the basis of my proposed "retrieval" of law.

RETRIEVING LAW

The criticism of the most visible surface of Foucault's treatment of law, in particular, of those elements that I have argued amount to an expulsion of law from modernity, creates the possibility of a fertile reconstruction. Such a reconstruction does not dismiss Foucault but rather will draw heavily on him to provide a richer understanding of the place of law in modernity. Just as it is necessary to discard his expulsion of law from modernity, so it is even more important not to lapse into, what I have elsewhere called "legal imperialism" (Hunt

1992). Legal imperialism is the view that sees law as becoming the predominant factor in the coordination and regulation of the complex of subsystems that establish modern societies.[33] In its most pervasive form legal imperialism marks a distrust of democratic politics and sees law as the primary agency for the restraint of political power. The project of retrieval is thus located as the quest for a "third way" between Foucault's expulsion of law from modernity and legal imperialism's faith in the autonomy and effectivity of law.

The position that I want to develop is to elaborate on the theme first enunciated by Poulantzas that law is "a constitutive element of the politico-social field" (1978:82–83). This thesis establishes the claim that law does more than merely reflect or encode existing social relations. In its simplest form a constitutive theory of law draws attention to the fact that law actually constitutes certain economic relations.[34] A more general contention is that law constitutes or participates in the constitution of a terrain or field within which social relations are generated, reproduced, disputed and struggled over, the most important implication being that within such a field, which Foucault would designate as a discursive formation, the legal discourses in play both place limits of possibility on social action and impose specific forms of discursive possibility. One of the clearest and most important illustrations of this is the way in which rights discourses both impose limits on but also generate possibilities for the form and content of social struggles (Bartholomew and Hunt 1990).

While Foucault would almost certainly have refused this line of argument, there are traces in his position that are compatible with it. The most fruitful connection with or appropriation from Foucault draws attention to the way in which legal discourses and institutional practices increasingly incorporate or are themselves incorporated into the interpenetrate with a continuum of other discourses and apparatuses (medical, administrative, and so on) (Woodiwiss 1990:117). One interesting line of exploration of these issues is opened up by Tony Woodiwiss's revisionist Foucauldian reading of the intrinsic technologies of law which he explicates by using the concept of "transpositioning" to identify a major feature of legal effectivity. Transpositioning identifies the distinctive role of law in being able to change the social positions of social objects and agents (e.g., the way in which divorce proceedings change the positions of the parties with respect to economic assets). Woodiwiss's point can be extended by noticing that not only is the position of parties changed by and through law but that one major dimension of this process is the access that is opened or closed to the mobilization of both cultural capital and institutional resources; for example, a spouse's claim to economic resources is not only legitimated by the issuance of a court order but, depending on the jurisdiction, a variety of institutional apparatuses may be brought into play, with varying decrees of effectiveness, to pursue their interests.

One important general conclusion can be stated. I suggest that no specific directionality should be implied with regard to the way in which law mobilizes cultural capital or institutional resources. We should not assume either that law dominates or incorporates other discursive and institutional practices or, conversely, that law is subsumed by other disciplinary discourses or practices. Directionality and causality must always be questions of specific historical and contextual investigation.

These themes also invite an appropriation of Foucault's notion of the proliferation of discourses (1978:48), every social field is traversed by a series of incommensurate but not necessarily contradictory discourses. No single discourse generally achieves exclusive dominance but borrows from, incorporates, and makes concessions to other coexisting discourses. However, one important correction needs to be made to Foucault's idea of the proliferation of discourses; he tends, particularly in his work on the discourses of sexuality, to posit an expansion of discourses over time so that modernity is characterized by a numerical increase in the number of discourses. This is seen in its simplest form when, as we have noted, he contends that the unitary discourse of the "juridical monarchy" is displaced by the multiplicity of the modern disciplinary discourses. It is important to insist on the fundamental tenet of legal pluralism that law has never been a unitary discourse but has always involved a range of discourses connected to and competing with a range of extralegal discourses. Foucault was perhaps too ready to accept the "truth" of the claims of state absolutism to provide the ruling discourse that succeeded in eradicating the dispersed discourses of premodernity.

The theme of the proliferation of discourses does not simply imply the existence of a multiplicity of coexisting discourses. Two considerations need to be stressed. First, the historical shift from one epoch to another involves a displacement or marginalization of some discourses and the enhancement or creation of new discourses (for example, the displacement of religious discourses and the rise of the scientific discourses). The identification of such shifts involves, among other features, the movement from one constellation of discourses to another.

Second, what is missing from Foucault's proliferation of discourses thesis is explicit attention to the means of explaining how one discursive formation[35] comes to be predominant. Foucault's epistemological wariness led him to avoid pronouncing on causality in his historical studies, thereby incapacitating himself from providing a satisfactory account of how specific discourses arose or how they came to prevail over rival discourses. For example, he suggested both a tension and a competition between medical and psychiatric discourses with respect to criminality, but he was reluctant to commit himself to a causal explanation of, say, the shifts in these discourses and their connection to the changing legal doctrines about criminal insanity. He never succeeded in fully expunging causality, but his causal pronouncements were implied rather than defended. Thus it seems clear that he explained the rise of modern government and governmentality as resulting from the emergence of the interconnected concern with "population" and "policing" (in his broad sense), the numerical expansion of populations, and the exigencies of modern warfare; but he rarely, if ever, committed himself to causal pronouncements on such matters.

Those who are concerned, as I am, not to relinquish a concern with causality, even if we share Foucault's quite proper refusal of the evolutionist tendencies of the social sciences, must add to our conceptual apparatus. As I have already suggested, my suggestion is that some version of the Gramscian concept of hegemony offers a necessary supplement (see Chapter 10). In the present context the concept of hegemony focuses our attention on how it comes about that a specific discursive constellation comes to be predominant at a given historical juncture.[36]

Powerful though the concept of hegemony is, it has at least one important limitation; it tends to focus attention on the end result of securing loss of hegemony by some constellation of social forces or power bloc. It has had less to say about the process through which different discursive elements are put together in constituting hegemony.[37] Hegemony requires a supplement. The supplement I will explore is provided by the concept of "structural coupling," a concept that comes from the systems theory of autopoietic theory of Niklas Luhmann via the neo-Marxist capture effected by Bob Jessop (1990). Since my debate is with Jessop rather than the autopoietic theorists, I will comment briefly only on the part that the concept plays in their work. Autopoietic theory posits social differentiation and the emergence of radically autonomous systems as the defining characteristic of modernity. The autonomy of each system is the result of the self-referentiality of the system's communicative mechanism that produces "closure" or separation between different systems that are conceived as providing the "environment" within which each specific system functions. One important form of interaction between two or more systems occurs through the coevolution that links or harnesses the systems by processes of uncoordinated mutual evolutonary adaptions.

The key significance offered by the concept of structural coupling that Jessop sets out to appropriate is its capacity to provide an attractive account of the connections and interaction between law, state and other discursive-institutional entities that, on the one hand, sustain an emphasis on their autonomy while, on the other, keeping alive the strong Marxist concern with causality embodied in the preoccupation with "determination." In seeking to escape the trap of attributing any necessary causal priority to economic forces, Jessop, following in the footsteps of Althusser and Poulantzas, in searching for a more complex theorization of the connectedness of social instances that will avoid the dangers of a structuralism that implies a self-activating social totality, society.[38] His borrowing of structural coupling is drawn from the unlikely tradition of Luhmannian social theory.

What we need to ask of the concept of structural coupling is, what does it contribute to an understanding of the linkages or connections between two or more systems? I will explore one rather obvious case of the codetermination of closely related institutional mechanisms, namely, that between courts and the police. The two institutions stand in a close connection that creates a mutual dependence. I use this example to develop the important extension of the structural coupling idea that it may take either positive or negative forms (and in principle exhibit a mixture of forms of positive and negative coordination). As a positive form of structural coupling, the courts and the police offer much to one another. Courts provide major legitimations for police jurisdictional claims and a wider social recognition that in general police practices can count on reinforcement from the courts. On the other side the courts depend on the police to provide some positive evidence of their effectiveness; offenders arrested by the police provide socially visible evidence of legal effectiveness as offenders are brought into court and are taken after trial and sentence to the penitentiaries.

The closeness of the interdependence of courts and police also makes them vulnerable to negative structural coupling when the pattern of interaction operates in such a way too undermine the "proper" functioning of their interaction. Thus courts rely heavily on the police as professionalized providers of objective evidence. The reliance of the police on this preferential treatment itself creates the conditions under which the doctoring of evidence occurs, but at the same time produces the conditions that undermine the special police–judiciary relationship. Periodic crisis over police malpractices threaten to disrupt this mutual dependence. This unstable interdependence is exemplified in the recent

British cases in a major series of illegitimate convictions, wrung from courts in the face of terrorist actions by the IRA against civilian targets, have been overturned. The reversal of these highly publicized convictions threatens to disrupt the mutual police–judiciary dependence. The judiciary's much treasured independence and neutrality is undermined when disclosure suggests that they have placed an unwarranted confidence on fabricated evidence; from the other side, the police jeopardize the evidentiary privilege on which they normally rely. Once the normally cooperative relations between judges and police (i.e., the positive structural coupling of courts and police) are put in doubt, then both subsystems face a level of mutual suspicion that disrupts the normal pattern of their interaction. Judges increasingly view police as threatening their public legitimacy, while police no longer experience confidence in the regular support of the judiciary on which they have come to rely.

From a theoretical perspective, this brief consideration of the structural coupling that exists between the police and the judiciary suggests the following conclusion, that pervasive patterns of interdependence are threatened by the emergence of patterns of a destructive or blocked interaction in which the normal hegemonic preconditions of both institutions are undermined.

The case of police–judiciary relations serves to suggest important limits on one essential ingredient of autopoietic theory, namely, an unwarranted confidence in the self-referentiality of systems and subsystems. In systems theory terms, police and judiciary provide a whole series of inputs, both practical and ideological, for the system of the other. Their functional interdependence is of such a high order that the presumption of self-referentiality and autonomy that systems theory makes is unwarranted. It can be seen as an ideological variant on the hallowed doctrine of the separation of powers. But it is an inherently unstable dependence, because once the structural coupling of law and police is put under strain, there is a potentially disastrous loss of cultural capital and legitimacy. It follows that the theorization of structural coupling that is proposed is significantly different from that offered by autopoietic theory. The mutually supportive structural coupling between the systems, while having important practical and ideological advantages for both, is inherently unstable and always vulnerable to demonstrations of undermining counterfactual experiences.

This discussion of the potential offered by the idea of structural coupling facilitates the exploration of the formation of hegemonic discourses. It is necessary to bring into play, and to distinguish, the concepts, "strategy" and "projects."[39] Strategy needs to be purged of Foucault's attempt to suppress its association with purposive or intentional action because to admit the normal sense of strategy does not necessarily imply, as Foucault fears, the existence of historical agents (e.g., "ruling class") with preformed strategies; it involves nothing more than the view that social agents inscribe, but not necessarily successfully, purposes on their practices. The critical ingredient that Foucault resists is that of "interests"; it is not that interests exist outside of discourse, for they are always articulated within discourse, but rather that they are not reducible to discourse. Thus "strategy" is the purposive pursuit of interests through discursive practices that necessarily implies that social agents can be more or less successful in securing these interests.

"Projects" can be distinguished from strategies in order to provide us with a way of capturing the consequences that stem from the institutionalization of discourses; a project is a set of institutional imperatives. It is this that makes it possible to speak of the project of science, or medicine, or law without succumbing to the reification that the personification of science, medicine, and law implies. The concept also suggests the idea that institutional projects involve some compromise between competing sectional interests. My major substantive claim is that the project of state law that traverses premodernity and modernity has been that of the unification of laws, legal discourses, and legal institutions into "the Law." The distinctive supplement of modernity that is added to law's project, which is captured by the concept of the rule of law, is that of policing the boundaries of the political and securing the constitutional unity of the nation state. In brief the project of law is the unity of law and state through the doctrinal separation of law and state and of state and civil society.

These reflections on strategies and projects make it possible to address the question that Foucault avoids: how does one strategy and its associated discourses come to predominate over other coexisting discourses? It is in addressing questions of this type that the absent concept of hegemony can provide an understanding of the complex processes that secure and reproduce the predominance of particular strategies, projects, and discourses. For those concerned with transformative politics this is especially important, for it provides the starting point for the generation of counterhegemonic strategy. The problem with Foucault, in brief, is that his conception of power lacks a conception of either ideology or hegemony.

This revised approach to the dispersion of discourses lays the basis for a better understanding of the role of law. Instead of positing, as Foucault does, a quasievolutionary opposition between "law" and "discipline," we should focus our attention on the shifting patterns of combination and recombination between law and the disciplines of which the discussion above of the structural coupling of courts and police is one example. In place of the opposition that he sets up between law and discipline, this line of argument suggests that one of the features of modernity is the increasing interaction or even integration of law and discipline. What is happening in late modernity is not simply "more law" and "more regulation," as suggested by the various versions of the juridification any more than it is captured by the Foucauldian thesis of the displacement of law by the new disciplines. Rather there occurs a more extensive and probably more intensive set of structural couplings between a set of semi-autonomous patterns or modes of regulation.[40] Law has become a primary agency of the advance of new modalities of power and provides one of the distinctive methods of operation of the new technologies of power.

In addition, once we take account of an older lineage of the disciplines than Foucault tends to recognize, our quest for the distinctive shift that marks the profound, but never clearly visible, transition from the premodern to the modern makes it easier to identify a new relationship or combination between laws and disciplines. This quest can be pursued by considering whether or not there has been a shift from one "mode of regulation" to another where regulation has been conceived as a set of discursive practices that involves some combination of law and discipline. It is not my intention to attempt such an analysis but rather to claim that it holds out the prospect of a retrieval of law that, while declining Foucault's expulsion of law, does not simply reverse it by indulging in an exercise in legal centralism that assumes that law becomes everything in modernity.

Thus, rather than counterposing law and disciplines we can now make more sense of Foucault's comments about the connection between law, norm, and normalization. This has a strong family resemblance to his idea of the carceral continuum that "provides a communication between the power of discipline and the power of law" (1977:304). This theme can be extrapolated to suggest a significant role for law as a mediating mechanism—law as the bearer of the normative framework of the normalization worked on by a diversity of disciplinary practices. Discipline, normalization, and law share persisting linkages and connections that can be fruitfully pursued through the idea of structural coupling. But before rushing to the conclusion that we confront an era of superdisciplinarity, I want to suggest that we hang on to the recognition that the integration between the different discourses, practices, and projects of regulation is rarely, if ever, complete. My emphasis is rather on the idea of the always incomplete project of legal discourses to "supervise" the other disciplinary discourses.

It is in this context of the interpenetration of the discourses of law and of discipline that it is necessary to reopen the problem of sovereignty. As was noted earlier Foucault recognizes a shift during the nineteenth century toward democratic sovereignty.[41] Despite his resistance of Marx's concept of ideology, he views this democratization process in rather conspiratorial terms as a means of disguising domination (1980:106). What is required if we are to carry through a retrieval of law is to take serious account of the significance of the democratization of political sovereignty. This does not require that we take constitutional doctrine at face value nor that we should have any illusions about the limitations of the mechanisms of representative democracy. Foucault failed to provide any means of assessing the potential of the varying forms of political sovereignty that have come into being over the last two centuries. What he does provide is the important notion of "government" and "governmentality." What needs to be done is to link these concepts to an analysis of the sites of democratic politics that has definite consequences for the limits and restraints on governmental power. Only then can we make more positive use of his idea of "resistance" that, as has been argued, will remain forever doomed to be localized and reactive unless it is linked to an analysis that takes as its explicit political objective to understand both the limits and the possibilities of democratic politics and the politics of law. Such a project must not simply reverse Foucault's omissions by concentrating on the fields of democratic and legal politics to the exclusion of all the other fields of resistance to disciplinary power. An alternative politics must ground itself in the project of working through the linkages between multiple fields of struggle that Foucault's crucial insight into the dispersal and proliferation of the sites of power makes possible. The retrieval of law from the expulsion to which Foucault subjects it is one of the important components of such a project.

CHAPTER 13

LAW AS A CONSTITUTIVE MODE OF REGULATION

STILL TRYING TO GET BEYOND THE MODEL OF RULES

The modern history of legal thought can be understood as a series of attempts to escape the iron grip of the model of rules. This model conceives "rules" as the distinguishing feature of law, captured in Lon Fuller's aphorism of law as "the enterprise of subjecting human conduct to the governance of rules" (Fuller 1964:106). It is associated with the normative attitude, identified by Judith Shklar as "legalism," that attaches positive value to the project of the governance of rules (Shklar 1964). The equation of law with rules is significant in that it captures the common sense, not only of judges and lawyers, but— and this perhaps more than anything else explains its vitality and longevity—it also resonates with a widely shared common-sense characteristic of modernity. Law is, first and foremost, conceived as an extensive collection of rules that is applied by specialized personnel (lawyers) in specialized institutions (courts) that impose sanctions that are ultimately backed by the coercive capacity of the state. Versions, whether simple or complex, of this conception of law form the normal science or dominant paradigm within which most, if not all, discussion of law takes place.

The model of rules has formed the dominant preoccupation of Anglo-American jurisprudence. It is epitomized by H.L.A. Hart's sophisticated version of the model of rules that sought to go beyond a narrow focus on the negative or prescriptive dimension of law and to embrace the positive or facilitative character of law (Hart 1961). Hart concern typifies the preoccupation of the model of rules with accurately describing the most general characteristics of legal rules, his contribution being to introduce the distinction between primary and secondary rules that served to place greater emphasis on both the procedural and the private law dimensions of the corpus of legal rules. While this version of the model of rules has come under increasing criticism the form taken by the contemporary jurisprudential debate has been preoccupied with identifying what supplement needs to added to the model of rules in order to provide an adequate conception of law. Thus, Hart's major challenger remains Ronald Dworkin, who seeks to direct attention toward an underlying essence of law that is embodied in a deep core of legal "principles" that constitute a realm of "integrity" (Dworkin 1986). Even though Dworkin insists that his move is characterized by a displacement of rules to a new focus on law as interpretation, it is apparent that this does not displace "the model of rules," but rather that rules remain the presupposition because it is, of course, rules that are the object of interpretive activity.

The history of modern legal studies can be understood as an ongoing engagement between the jurisprudential model of rules and the aspiration of the "law and society" movement to found a successor tradition. It is important to ask: How does the 'law and society' tradition position itself with respect to the presuppositions of the model of rules? The assumptions underlying the model of rules are not displaced, rather the focus of attention is shifted to the results or outcomes of legal processes. This feature is nowhere more explicit than in the varieties of both new and old legal realism that seek to capture the "reality" of law. In the powerful imagery of O.W. Holmes the project of legal theory is to capture "law in action," to "tell it how it really is" in contrast to the idealized realm of "law in books." It is this imagery of "telling how it really is" that provided the central motivation of what I have called "the sociological movement in law" (Hunt 1978). The central preoccupation of this wide and diverse body of scholarship has been one of descriptive accuracy. It starts from the simple idea that there exists a social phenomenon called "law" and the task of legal theory is to provide an economical descriptive account of that phenomenon. This tradition involves a semaphore view of theory in which the signs employed (the concepts or conceptions) serve to both distill and to order the inescapable complexity of the real world. The project of these accounts conceives the task of legal theory as being to provide the most economical or condensed encapsulation that captures "the truth of law." The inherent limitation of this strategy has two closely related dimensions. First, it perpetuates the view that the task of legal theory is fulfilled when the phenomenon of law itself is identified. Even though twentieth-century jurisprudence has moved beyond the idea that it is enough to "define" law it has retained the core assumption of such a definitional strategy, namely, the preoccupation with the self-referentiality, that law can be adequately specified by reference to itself.[1] The related defect of the search for a self-referential treatment of law is that it tends to import both descriptive and normative claims about the autonomy of law that has been such a central theme of all varieties of liberal legal theory.[2]

The controversies that have traversed legal theory since the nineteenth century (if not earlier) can be understood as an ongoing and ever-shifting engagement between self-referential theories of law and those that insist that if we wish to understand law it is possible to do so only through the project of tracking law in its interrelationships with nonlegal social phenomenon. For the moment I leave the designation of the alternative to self-referentiality deliberately broad for reasons that need to be explained. One simple version of the alternative that has been widely deployed is to specify the alternative as "sociological," indeed this is a position that I have adopted and is epitomized in the contest between jurisprudence and the "sociological movement in law" (Hunt 1978).[3] The reason for avoiding this counterposing of jurisprudence and sociology is that it involves a mechanical reversal or negation. One version of this opposition is found in the controversy that presents itself in terms of the counterposing of "internal" and "external" perspectives in legal theory.[4] Here the core of the controversy relies on the analogy with visual inspection; whether it is better to position oneself inside law so as to take account of the meanings and intentions of legal participants (and this usually means the perspective of judges and lawyers) or whether it is better for observers to "distance" themselves by adopting some position "outside" of law itself. My resistance to this way of setting up the debate is that an external perspective can be as fixated on the self-referentiality of law if, to press the visual observation metaphor, it looks at law as one might watch goldfish in the proverbial bowl. Conceived in this way neither an internal nor an external perspective is able to attend to the connnectedness of law or what is better expressed as a relational concern that insists that to study any social phenomenon must ensure that its general perspective is focused on its connectedness to other social phenomena. Law is to be understood not in itself, through the introspection of self-referentiality, but rather from addressing the connectedness of law, from viewing law in its location interacting with and interpenetrating other social processes.[5] My project will be to argue that a position, designated by the label "constitutive theory," can achieve a sustainable break with self-referentiality while not falling into the trap of seeing a simple reversal as itself providing an adequate or attractive alternative.

Contemporary legal theory is still haunted by the ghost of realism. It arose as the most powerful challenge within Anglo-American legal scholarship to the self-referentiality of legal positivism or analytical jurisprudence. But the question to pose is: did legal realism break with self-referentiality? I want to suggest that the significance of the project of realism epitomized by the American legal realism of the interwar years can best be grasped as involving a dual thrust, the elements of which have never been fully integrated. These two dimensions of realism have in the current period bifurcated and have each formed the organizing paradigm, on the one hand, of the law and society movement and, on the other, that of the critical legal studies movement.

Realism's first feature is epitomized by the realist's focus on the gap between "law in books" and "law in action"; the "truth of law" was not to be found in its expository tomes that portray a complacent realm of doctrinal harmony. The aim of capturing "law in action" required focus to be directed toward the outputs or results of law. Realism's second face was the critique of doctrinalism that insisted on the necessary incompleteness of any project that grounded itself on the claim that the autonomy of law can provide a system of adjudication that secures a coherent derivation of decisions in individual cases from rules that can itself provide a sufficient grounds for the legitimacy of those decisions as securing the requirements of justice. It is the first feature that has grounded the law and society movement and the second that has provided the organizing paradigm for critical legal studies. There is a considerable interchange and cross-fertilization between critical legal studies and the law and society movement as the two intellectual currents that have explicitly sought to supersede the model of rules. Each of these traditions has made important contributions toward a more adequate understanding of law. However, both can provide only a partial critique of the dominant intellectual paradigm provided by the model of rules. This is because they take one feature of that paradigm and simply reverse or negate it; an external perspective is substituted for an internal or a coherence conception of legal reasoning is abandoned in favor of an incoherence model.

Here we come to the heart of the significance of breaking away from the model of rules: the necessity of abandoning the presupposition of legal autonomy. The models of rules and legal autonomy are, if not the same thing, so closely intertwined as to continuously reinforce one another. Legal autonomy is grounded in a belief in the severability of law from other related social phenomena. It is an ideological position that sees in the doctrine of the separation of powers the most powerful ambition of liberal legal theory, namely, to ground and to secure a firm separation between law and politics.

Do we really need another legal theory? It is not just that the different versions of the model of rules are wrong or inadequate and that some other theory can provide a better descriptive distillation of legal reality. Rather the case for yet another theory of law has a different objective; it seeks to facilitate a quite different project. First is an explicit rejection of the currently influential reaction against the very possibility of theory. What undermines this denial of the possibility of general theory is that the quest for a new theory does not aspire to descriptive adequacy, but is driven by a different motive. What is at stake is an attempt to start from a general statement of the preoccupations that motivate contemporary controversies around law and to use this as the basis on which to generate the conceptual tools that specify the "field" within which these controversies are located. Conceived in this way theory does not aspire to tell some truth. Its objective is more modest; it is to provide the means of addressing our contemporary concerns. This implies the grounds for the criticism of other theories, not because they are wrong, but because they impede or otherwise frustrate the engagement with our current agenda.

If there is a need for yet another theory of law then it is because we find the available theoretical frameworks less and less adequate because they are largely reactive to the dominant paradigm of the model of rules. I want to suggest that we are in the midst of a sea change in the problematic within which we interrogate law. There are rarely revolutionary ruptures in intellectual agendas; many of us get stuck burrowing in long worked-out furrows; over time the swing to new agendas and problematics asserts itself, but only becomes visible long after the shift has already occured.

The paradigm shift in which we are currently participating is a move toward a focus on *governance*. The term "governance" is useful in that it marks a departure from the term "government," a concept that is too tarnished with its long-standing association with state–government and state–constitutionalism and thus impedes our recognition of the distinctiveness of our contemporary concerns. The focus on "governance" opens up a space that allows us to think of government as a process rather than as an institution and to break with the habits long instilled by the dominance of the nation–state in our experience that only governments govern. The term "governance" helps us to think of government as a process and to focus on the many dimensions of the experience and consequence of being governed.

Being governed means being under police supervision, being inspected, spied upon, directed, buried under laws, regulated, hemmed in, indoctrinated, preached at, controlled, assessed, censored, commanded, . . . noted, registered, captured, appraised, stamped, surveyed, evaluated, taxed, patented, licensed, authorized, recommended, admonished, prevented, reformed, aligned, and punished in every action, every transaction, every movement. (Proudhon quoted in Oestreich 1982:272)

It is through the elaboration of the concept of "governance" that one of the most significant intellectual landmarks of the paradigm shift has been articulated.

Central to this conception of "governance" is the idea that government is not only the work of "Governments"; central to the projects of government are the key institutionalized professions—such as the medical profession—that stand between Government and the population. Or to put it in different terms, this conception of "governance" traverses the distinction between state and civil society; it is to be found on both, not just on one side, of this evocative dichotomy. Foucault himself rapidly moved even further away from a traditional sense of state–government in the preoccupations in his last works with the "care of the self" (Foucault 1985). The radical thrust of Foucault's thought is perhaps best captured by the oxymoron "the government of the self" that undermines our common-sense equation of "government" with external or top-down imposition.[6] My goal will be to explore this general field of governance in a way that will make use of an expanded conception of law as a significant component of these processes.

I have argued (in Chapter 12) for the need to break with Foucault's imperative conception of law. In its place we neeed a conception of law that is compatible with a perspective that conceives of law as a complex of varied forms that provides some of the major mechanisms through which governance is effected. One preliminary way of approaching this conception is to contrast it with its most important precursors. If Austin's definition of law tended to the equation of law with criminal law (Austin 1954), then its successor, as expressed by Hart and then Dworkin, has been a reversal whose conception of law gives priority to the model of private law.

If the first instance the model of law as regulation can be seen as a shift toward public law that focuses on the varied means whereby extensive fields of social life are made subject to regulatory intervention. But this view requires an immediate modification to our conventional conception of "public law." Rather than being bounded by the activities of territorial states whether national, provincial, or local, the conception of the "public" that we need must embrace the regulatory activity of territorial states, the enormous regulatory productivity of quasistate institutions, professional and institutional agencies, and the regulatory activity of economic agencies. It is by grappling with the range and diversity of these activities that two main effects should be noted: first, that the pertinence of the distinction between the public and the private can be maintained only by problematizing its complexity (Friedmann 1972; Unger 1976). One response to the limitations of the public/private dichotomy has been a revival or interest in the distinction between state and civil society with the advocacy of an apportionment of powers to a multiplicity of public spheres between state and civil society (Keane 1984).

Much of the recent debate on the characterization of modernity has been preoccupied with the implications of the proliferation of the regulatory complex for the fate of the rule of law. This debate has taken a variety of forms, but perhaps its most general form is one in which the passing of "autonomous law" is viewed as being supplanted by increasingly bureaucratic regulation (Hayek 1973–1979; Kamenka and Tay 1978; Posner 1987). Others have adopted a less pessimistic response and have seen positive potential in the diversification of the forms of legal regulation (Nonet and Selznick 1978; Luhmann 1985; Teubner 1986). I want to suspend any evaluative judgment on these different visions of the trajectory of modern law; instead I want to focus attention on their implications for a more modest role for legal theory conceived as seeking to provide the conceptual tools for understanding a complex process in which our existing concepts have become impediments to understanding. My project is to articulate a conception of law that starts out from an interrogation of the law as a mode of regulation.

At the heart of this endeavor is a concern to give full recognition to the lessons of legal pluralism, that we should recognize the diversity of legal phenomena and avoid falling into the presumption of a unitary entity "the Law," while at the same time to give due recognition to the importance of both the state as a political agency and to state–law. On the one hand law exists as an increasingly detailed and particularistic regulation of ever more specific situations and relations in which any boundary between law and nonlaw is difficult is not impossible to identify. On the other hand this important recognition of the diversification and pluralization of law and regulation should not lead us to forget about the role that law plays as the medium of an ever-expanding state. These spheres of diversification and of centralization exist in complex tension. Provisionally we can express the role of the central state–law apparatuses as being continuously engaged in the "project of regulatory unification"; this project is pursued with varying vigor and commitment; it is never more than partially successful. In some periods, most recently in the political projects of neoconservatism, there was a surprisingly unsuccessful attempt to restrict the scope of this unification project. The unificatory project is always present and must inform our theorization of law just as must our recognition of the reality of legal pluralism.

The rediscovery of legal pluralism has been an important feature of recent legal studies.[7] In challenging a unitary conception of state–law and drawing attention to the diversity of legal orders there has been a tendency to displace attention from the distinctive significance of state law. I am concerned to retain the insights of legal pluralism without losing sight of state–law. The general form of the importance of state-law (and more generally of state power) on which I want to insist is to take account of the capacities, never fully realized but as ever-present projects, for unification, concentration, condensation, and globalization.

My concern is to develop an account that makes it possible to retain the insights of legal pluralism and the focus on "governance," the new forms of dispersed and localized power, with a continuing appreciation of the significance of state–law. To pursue this line of inquiry I will pay particular attention to the work of Boaventura de Sousa Santos because, although I have some differences with his position, his is the most theoretically sophisticated pluralist theory that retains an emphasis on state–law. My major focus will be on his paper "On Modes of Production of Law and Social Power" (Santos 1985). I will use his work as a starting point from which to advance an alternative theorization that overcomes some of the minor limitations that I will identify in Santos' own position. I will articulate an account of law as part of a system of "modes of regulation." I hope to demonstrate that to theorize law in this way makes it possible to retain a continuing focus on the proximity of law and state, and their respective importance within contemporary societies, while facilitating the identification of a plurality of ways in which law is implicated in the processes of governance and social regulation.

BEYOND THE UNITARY STATE: FROM STATE TO GOVERNANCE

One unambiguously positive contribution made by the emergence of Marxist strands within the field of legal studies was its insistence on the importance of the connection between law and the state. However, this may seem it is important to reflect on the fact that the texts of jurisprudence and of the sociology of law before the late-1960s were devoid of any consideration of the state. It is undoubtedly true that when "the state" first appeared in debates about law it did so in the form of a unitary conception of the state ("the State"), conceived as both a unitary political subject and also as forming a unity in the sense of expressing and giving effect to the interests of a dominant class such that the state is conceived as providing the link between the capitalist class and the capitalist state. Although there exists today a tendency to chide Marxism with proposing a crude theory of the unitary state this forgets in the enormously significant work of Poulantzas, Offe, and others in articulating a much more complex and analytically powerful account of state institutions and practices. It is not by present concern to reexamine that work, rather to suggest that we need to remember its existence.[8] In the meantime as significant shift of intellectual and political attention has occurred that has focused interest on the dispersal of social power and the localization of politics and, more generally, on the significance of "civil society" and "everyday life." Foucault, one of the pioneers of this major shift of intellectual focus, as I argued in the previous chapter, displaced the whole question of the aggregation and condensation of power in and around the state. My contention is that working through the problematic of governance will encourage and facilitate the bringing together within the same conceptual and political agenda the politics of everyday life and the condensation of power in and around the state. If everyday life is full of the importance of strategy and tactics, as Bourdieu shows, for example, in "knowing" how to play the serious game of making marriage arrangements, so to do governments have to know how to govern. To focus on governance offers the prospect of joining the circle and thus of breaking out of seeming to be required to make an either–or choice between the local and the global, between state and civil society.

The conceptual shift that Foucault effects is epitomized by his neologism "governmentality," by which he designates a new set of preoccupations and dispositions, literally a new mentality of government that marks a crucial stage in the birth of modernity (Foucault 1979). It is expressed in his distinctive notion of "police" and "policing" used to refer to an ensemble of mechanisms serving to ensure order, regulating economic activity, and preserving the size and health of "the population." The health and physical well-being of the population comes to figure as a political objective from the end of the ancien regime.[9] What "governmentality" seeks to capture is, in the first place, an historical thesis that the transition to modernity, that accelerated during the eighteenth century, witnessed the rise of a new "mentality" of "government" that manifested itself in the rise of a conscious concern to secure the purposeful administration of social life through the pursuit of social policy; no longer could a system of power protect itself by laying down negative rules backed by coercive sanctions. To achieve positive results rather than negative prohibitions an entirely different conception of government had emerged. The process of the "governmentalization" of the state not only involved a qualitative expansion of state institutions and their range of activities, but also required new forms of connection between state and nonstate institutions. There never has been a clear or simple distinction between state and civil society, but from this period forward this distinction becomes ever more complex.

For these reasons I am not inclined to follow Santos in abandoning the state/civil society distinction. He argues that the distinction is ridden with internal contradictions and is in permanent crisis. Although he perhaps overstates the difficulties we should concede his general criticsm, but this should not lead use toward rejectionism because there are some important features on which the distinction helps to focus our attention. What I have to say goes also for the public/private as well as for the state/civil society distinction. There is a central preoccupation within the liberal tradition of political and jurisprudential theory with the proper limits of state action and within the socialist tradition with the limits of public economic power and its connection with the state. But perhaps more importantly the events in Eastern Europe have confirmed the importance of those spheres of social life that are in some important, if never absolute, sense spontaneous, voluntary, and optional; since there is no other label we need to retain the concept of civil society and to sustain political commitment to the respect that a viable civil society is an important criteria of the health of a social formation (Keane 1984; Cohen 1982).

Most significantly governmentality comes to focus on the economic life and well-being of "the nation," and the order, health, and prosperity (or lack of it) of its citizens. The "national economy" and "the population" become the key targets of calculated administration; one of its most important intellectual manifestations is the invention of political economy (Tribe 1978).

The concept of "governmentality" ties in with Foucault's concern with the role played by the "human sciences" in the formation of modernity. The projects of rendering economic and social life governable were generated by an ever-expanding body of experts and professionals who produce not only new bodies of knowledge, but also an array of policies, strategies, programs, and technologies. In brief, governmentality invokes not only a mentality of government but a mentality that is dependent on the production and deployment of knowledge of which the advent of censuses and other forms of gathering of statistical data are key features not only of state formation but also of the advance of governmentality.

It is possible to identify a number of major themes in this discussion of the state, government, and governmentality.

1. The boundary between state and civil society not only becomes blurred, but also becomes permeable; government comes to involve complex networks of interaction between officials, experts, and professionals, within and without the state, generating new targets and new technologies of administration.

2. There is a shift of focus from "state action" to a broader field identified by policies, programs, strategies, projects, and tactics; the "practices" thus generated extend well beyond the traditional boundaries of the state apparatuses. Increasingly the production of knowledge comes to form a crucial focus of attention. We are alerted to the wider implications of this process by Foucault's evocative "power/knowledge" couplet.

3. Social action increasingly revolves around and is directed toward the collection, classification, collation, compilation, calculation, and circulation of information. Some care is needed in characterizing these practices. Foucault himself, despite his general stress on the need to take account of the positive and creative role of power, tends to treat information practices as negative; terms such as "discipline" and "surveillance" have generally negative connotations and are closely linked to the problematic of "social control" in which the otherwise free subject is constrained by "society." That there has been a significant expansion of information, surveillance practices is not in issue. It is, however, important to avoid a one-sided assessment. This can best be achieved by ensuring that alongside the recognition of the disciplinary practices that attention is paid to what may usefully be termed "constitutive practices"; these are positive practices that play some part in

creating, constituting, or directing some social practice. This approach has the merit of fleshing out the power/knowledge concept and of retaining both positive and negative dynamics.[10] Even overt surveillance produces both positive and negative results; judgments about the balance between these features can only be a matter of concrete political judgment: for example, video surveillance on subway platforms and in shopping malls is certainly an extension of surveillance; it may reduce the incidence of attacks on users, but it is also possible that it simply displaces or diverts the location of such attacks.

4. The sites of power are dispersed. There is a move away from a "top-down" conception that pictures the state as the locus and source of power, the site where power may be "possessed" and "wielded." Rather power is to be located as a characteristic and component of all social relations; it exists even where the trappings of coercion are absent. Power is local; power is capillary. The only problem is that this intentional decentering of power tends to ignore consideration of state power. It should be stressed that this expulsion of the state is only a "tendency"; there is another strand, in which Foucault recognizes the significance of the globalization of power.

> I believe the at the manner in which the phenomena, the techniques and procedures of political power enter into play at the most basic levels must be analyzed; . . . but above all what must be shown is the manner in which they are invested and annexed by more global phenomena. (1980:213)

It therefore remains important to attend to the continuing significance of the role of the state in the condensation or concentration of power relations. This recognition does more than simply apply a necessary corrective; it also facilitates a more positive means of grasping the significance of the very current of thought that has drawn attention to the dispersal of power. My suggestion is the desirability of focusing on the articulation between the different forms of power.[11] In embracing the pluralization of power it is essential to retain attention on the state as a site of special significance for the condensation and concentration of power, but to do so without importing any assumption about pre-given mechanisms of that articulation.

Since I attach considerable importance to this issue of avoiding the omission of state power let me say something more about the risks attendant on the current preocupation with the plurality and dispersion of power. In reorienting the focus of attention toward the plurality of power and to the signfiiance of local and capillary power there is an unwelcome, but avoidable, tendency to *expel the state*. Without derogating from or evading the significance of the plurality of power it is essential to "bring the state back in."[12] But the state needs to be brought back in without at the same time expelling local or capillary power. Aside from the self-evident sense in which the state is important, my substantive grounds for retrieving the state is to draw attention to one pervasive feature of government, namely, the persistence of projects of unification and centralization. The focus is on "projects" in order to link the idea of strategies to that of practices, but with the important implications that projects compete, that they are rarely, if ever, realized in the form envisaged, and that unintended consequences rule. The project of "unification" is not only a state project but has a special significance with regard to law where the quest for "the Law" is of more than passing ideological significance.

5. My interest revolves around the implications for the theorization of the place of law in contemporary societies of the shift of attention from state-power to the exploration of capillary power coursing through the diversity of social practices. As I demonstrated in the previous chapter, one important, but by no means inevitable, consequence was Foucault's expulsion of law. If we are able to avoid this move, rather than counterposing law and disciplinarity, we can focus attention on the question of the interplay of law and discipline.

6. The seventh, and final, theme ushered in the shift of focus from state to government is the movement away from a concern with "interests" (classically in the Marxist tradition, with class interests), conceived as objective categories that provide the grid through which the play of social, economic, and political life can be made intelligible. There is, however, an ever-present risk of slipping into the vice of teleology. It is an all too easy move from talk of strategies to the attribution of purposes to collective agents and institutions. My own argument will run perilously close to this fault line of social theory (for example, in arguing that state–law pursues projects of unification). There is no simple "cure" for teleology; a retreat into an empiricist focus on behavior would obliterate the proper concern with the role of social agency. The best that we can ensure is that by posing the problem and by keeping it in sight we avoid unintentional lapses into teleological explanation.

POWER/LAW/KNOWLEDGE

I propose to lend emphasis to the focus on the connection between state, law, and power by conceiving the process of governance as significantly revolving around *regulation*. The immediate attraction of a focus on regulation is that it avoids, or more accurately refuses, the coercion/consent opposition. The regulation approach does not need to take sides in this old debate; regulation encompasses modalities that transcend the coercion and consent dichotomy.

Yet the proposed focus on "regulation" remains close to the concern with the linkage between power and knowledge in its emphasis on the role of information, expertise, policies, and strategies. These features can be captured by expanding Foucault's own suggestive linkage of power and knowledge by offering a schematic definition of regulation as *power/law/knowledge*. Regulation involves the deployment of specific knowledges encapsulated in legal or quasilegal forms of interventions in specific social practices whose resultants have consequences for the distribution of benefits and detriments for the participants in the social practices subject to regulation.

A further feature of regulation should be stressed in order to avoid falling into a purely technicist or instrumental conception of regulation. Every instance of regulation must be understood as encompassing *moral regulation*.[13] Moral regulation is not simply a variety of regulation but it is a more less significant dimension of all regulation. The idea of moral regulations is most fully developed by Corrigan and Sayer who demonstrate that each stage in the process of state formation is associated with a distinctive form of moral regulation. They emphasize the dual character of moral order as being both externally regulative and internally constitutive and as such has impact not only on social practices, but also on the formation of identities and subjectivities (Corrigan and Sayer 1985:194). By extension it follows that all regulation involves the suppression, marginalization, or repudiation of alternative ways of being, while "encouraging" other realities. This view of regulation is diametrically opposed to any technicist view of regulation.

Just in the same way as power is productive, so regulation may be productive and should be freed from any negative connotation. But my linking of power/law/knowledge, as if they formed a triptych, suggests that they are not merely linked but that they exhibit a certain symmetry.

In approaching theory construction that makes use of the concept "regulation" it is important to stress that this term plays a part in a number of diverse fields of debate and inquiry. I want briefly to distinguish my usage. It is wider than the legalistic usage of the term "regulatory law" that treats regulation as a branch of public law concerned with the control of nongovernmental economic agencies. In my usage "regulation" is not a subspecies of law, but rather it is a distinctive type of social process with respect to which legal aspects may or may not be present. In a somewhat broader usages "regulation" refers to a specific style of purposive, instrumental, and policy-oriented mechanisms of control that avoid negative or prescriptive imposition of rules in favor of regulatory negotiation that makes the regulated agent play some part in the process of both the development and implementation of those processes of control (Harrington 1988). While closer to my usage this version still presumes a too specific and distinguishable type of connection between law and regulation. I do not make any assumption about the existence of a "regulatory crisis" as a currently fashionable way of engaging with the wider contemporary agenda of the politics of law (Reich 1984; Teubner 1984).

Finally, there is no necessary connection between my use of the concept regulation and the "regulation school" of political economy. In arriving at an interest in regulation I approached with interest this body of work, associated in particular with that of Lipietz and Aglietta (Aglietta 1979; Lipietz 1985; Boyer 1990). It is striking that although "regulation" is used as a self-description and a new concept, "mode of regulation," is proposed, this body of work reveals a distinct absence of any substantive discussion either of regulation in general or of modes of regulation in particular. I suggest that the adoption of the term "regulation" has a symbolic function for the regulation school in that it marks its break with the "productionism" of orthodox Marxism. My only connection then with the work of the regulation school is that I will freely borrow their concept "mode of regulation."

I want to suggest the importance of making a distinction between "regulation" and "control." There is a tendency to think of "control" as the result or outcome of regulation: my point is simply that this runs the risk of prejudging the outcome of regulatory processes by assuming that regulation leads necessarily to control; such a view has widespread currency and projects a rather bleak scenario of social life being ever more circumscribed by an ever-expanding system of surveillance, disciplines, and control. Outcomes are more open; circumvention, deflection, rechanneling, and avoidance of regulations are just as likely. The results of the regulatory process are a matter for empirical investigation.

WHAT IS REGULATION?

It is now time to look more closely at regulation. I will sketch the elements of a general concept of regulation, a mode of regulation. Regulation is always intentional (even though its results may be unintended); thus the first step is the constitution of an *object of regulation*.

There are no natural or ready-made social objects and hence no ready-made objects of regulation. Their existence is always the outcome of some active process that creates that which is to be regulated. Foucault provides a key insight in his demonstration that today's taken-for-granted objects of regulation (e.g., "the economy" or "population") had first to be created, in specific historical contexts, as objects of regulation. Regulatory interventions are frequently responses to the "discovery" of some social problem and this is turn is often closely connected with the collection of information not previously available (or, if available, not recognized). The recent "discovery" of child abuse is just such an example where the recognition of a connection between parental violence and sexual abuse has radically changed the agenda; one of the most obvious implications is to shift attention from a presumed threat from strangers, "child molesters," to recognition that the contemporary crisis of the family is internal (Campbell 1987). It follows that if objects of regulation can be created, then they can similarly be dismantled and abandoned.[14]

The selection and deselection of objects of regulation can often constitute primary sites of political contestation. Contemporary struggles over abortion, gay rights, and drug testing, to name but some of the more obvious, are all struggles about the creation of particular objects of regulation. The struggle over whether to regulate some social relation or social practice is frequently of central importance and this significance is underlined by the way in which the apparently simple question "To regulate or not?" comes to be the bearer of major symbolic dimensions whose ramifications extend far beyond the immediate object of regulation.[15] Thus the struggle around the regulation of abortion is at the same time a wider engagement that extends beyond abortion as a object of regulation to encompass symbolic engagements with the ideology of patriarchal control over women's fertility and over the medicalization of reproduction.

A second general feature of regulation is that it always involves the designation, identification, or creation of *regulatory agents* who are charged with a range of functions ranging from the collection and recording of information, inspection, surveillance, reporting, initiation of enforcement action, and a host of other activities. The significance of regulatory agents can be readily seen in terms of H.L.A. Hart's well-known distinction between primary and secondary rules, where primary rules are rules of conduct directed toward individuals (or other legal subjects) associated with the object of regulation requiring some behavioral conformity. Secondary rules, as "rules about rules," are rules directed broadly toward officials, in this case to regulatory agents, establishing the content and range of their jurisdiction and authority, the procedures they are to use, and much more besides. Secondary rules form a very considerable proportion of most regulatory legislation; even where behavioral norms are specified these should perhaps be best understood as specifying the standards that regulatory agents are charged with enforcing.[16]

The third general feature of the regulatory process revolves around the production of *regulatory knowledge*. The identification, acquisition, and deployment of knowledge are central features, in the first instance, of the construction of objects for regulation. Only after some social phenomenon or social practice has been constructed in such a way that it can be studied, quantified, and measured does it become possible for it to be treated as a suitable candidate for regulation. The collection of knowledge plays a central role in formulation of regulatory policies and strategies; and once some regulatory mechanism, is in place then further collection and manipulation of data are important in the assessment and evaluation of the regulatory instrument.

The processes through which regulatory knowledge is produced reveal a complex interplay between official and unofficial mechanisms. One of the characteristic features of modernity is the rise of the quest for objective knowledge that replaces reliance on the unsystematic knowledge through personal impression that is characteristic of the aristocratic production of knowledge of premodernity. Independent scholarly research, initiatives of social movements, interventions by "reformers," and most important of all, the data collection and processing agencies of the state and quasistate institutions all play their part in the production of regulatory knowledge. In general a key feature of this process is the emergence of organized social science and the complex process of transition from "amateur" to "professional" social science that occurs in the second half of the nineteenth and early twentieth century. There is an interesting connection between the professionalism of regulatory knowledge and the growth of systematic regulatory activity.

It should also be noted that regulatory knowledge can and does take on a life of its own. Knowledge projects frequently go far beyond any possible "useful" knowledge in the sense of being capable of translation into governmental action, and indeed often come into conflict with the pragmatic political considerations of governments. Involved at the core of the practice of "government" is the existence of the necessity for at least two processes to be at play; on the one hand between a "desire to regulate" and, on the other, the "regulatory knowledge" that makes this possible. The importance of the desire to regulate is most apparent when some new regulatory project is the subject of current controversy. For example, in the long-running debates over the regulation of prostitution what has separated the "regulationists" from the "repealers" has generally been quite small—a different inflection to and prioritization of a remarkably common field of signifiers (Walkowitz 1980; Stansell 1982). Yet small as these differences have been they determine whether there is a desire to regulate; only when this has been established do questions about the technologies and techniques of regulation arise.

These processes are worthy of more detailed attention and probably justify distinctions being made between different "modes of production of knowledge." However, my present purpose is served if I stress the increasingly significant role that is played by law in the process of the production of knowledge. Not only is access to and deployment of regulatory knowledge increasingly governed by legislation (e.g., freedom of information legislation), but the forms and procedures for the collection and storage of knowledge are similarly subject to legal controls (e.g., data protection, census legislation). Additionally, law also plays a significant part in the formation of the institutional mechanisms for the collection of regulatory knowledge; in addition to the creation of standing data collection agencies (e.g., censuses, statistical bureaus and departments, medical returns, and school attendance records) there are the specifically constituted "legal inquiries," "royal commissions," "committees of inquiry," "environmental impact studes," etc. In general law enters the processes of the production of knowledge more and more commonly, and this applies to state, public, and private agencies that are increasingly organized around the collection of systematic regulatory knowledge. Legislation both stipulates and ordains the knowledge to be collected and prescribes the parameters of the knowledge to be collected. And again it is important to note that these parameters and boundaries are frequently the subject of political and administrative contestation, for example, over whether an inquiry should focus on a single incident of police action or should explore whether there is a pattern of police racism that the particular incident illustrates.

There is another interesting aspect of the politics of the official production of knowledge. Decisions about the type of knowledge-gathering mechanism to employ are themselves political questions: for example, does the establishment of an official enquiry signify delaying tactics by the government or that the state takes the problem under scrutiny seriously? These and many other questions indicate the political dimension of the choice of the means for the production of regulatory knowledge.

The production of "regulatory knowledge" serves to link the creation and constitution of "objects of regulation" with a third important aspect of the regulatory process, namely, the formation of *regulatory strategies*. Not only is knowledge "produced" but it must also be transformed into a form that is capable of being expressed as a regulatory policy or strategy, which in turn is capable of being incorporated into legislative form. I use the term "legislative" broadly to refer to any process that "transforms" regulatory knowledge into the form of procedures, ordinances, rules, and statutes, whether in public or private institutions. The production of a regulatory mechanism involves some definite limitations on the strategies that may ultimately find legislative expression. It is important to stress that there is frequently some potentially significant disjunction between regulatory strategy and its legislative form; one obvious example is that much state regulation is a form of taxation or other fiscal measures while different policy objectives condition the discourse of the legislative instrument itself; for example, tobacco taxes and duties have long being instruments of revenue with a loose veneer of public health policy.

A feature of the merit claimed for a regulation approach to theorizing law is that it locates law within a wider context. Regulation has a distinctive form (the *form of regulation*) that has a least five significant features: identification of object(s) of regulation, conferment of powers on regulatory agents, specification of decision-procedures, identification of policy objectives, and the stipulation of rewards or sanctions. These remarks do not purport to offer an exhaustive analysis of the regulatory form, but merely serve to lay the basis for distinguishing between "legal form(s)" and "regulatory form," for example, by reference to its distinctive personnel and its decision-procedures. Of special importance in order to locate legal forms within the orbit of regulation is the focus of attention on mutual interaction of the different forms of regulation and, in particular, with respect to the regulation of regulation. In conventional positivist theories of law priority is accorded to law by virtue of its presumed hierarchical authority over other forms of social ordering. The regulation approach adopts a more sociological approach by assuming only that forms of regulation compete and conflict, but refrains from assuming any a priori ranking. Rather it reserves as a matter of historical and empirical investigation the outcomes of these interactions and the extent of the relative autonomy of each regulatory form. To take policing as an example, police activities interact with other regulatory practices; for example, their capacity to intervene depends in part on the degree of jurisdiction secured by other regulatory agents. If we consider different forms of public space there are significant distinctions between types of public space in which police intervention varies, for example, between the streets (that are subject to only informal and unstable alternative regulation) and university campuses or shopping malls where more formally constituted regulatory regimes are in place. Similar considerations relate to the types of conflict being regulated and their temporal and spatial location; the practical reach of policing is not exhaustively specified by formal legal rules. Again we can note the crucial, but always shifting and contested, importance of the public/private distinction.

The regulation approach invites us to ask: What are the distinctive relations that are constituted as the "objects of regulation"? What are the means or mechanisms of regulation that are selected? In general the regulation approach commends a focus on the correspondence between the "regulatory project" and the "regulatory form" that is selected or otherwise linked to that project. A provisional conception of a "mode of regulation" can be identified as the institutional ensemble and set of practices and norms that function to secure social reproduction despite the unstable and contradictory character of capitalist relations. The regulation approach thus focuses attention on social ordering as the outcome of the interaction between multiple modes of regulation. Its persistent focus as a contribution to the theorization of law is to pose the question of the form and manner of the legal component of any field of regulation in such a way that foregoes any assumption that the role played by law can satisfactorily be understood by reference to its own rules as satisfactorily specifying its relation with other modes of regulation.

One important consequence is that a regulation approach systematically denies the possibility of grounding a theory of law in the assumption of legal autonomy; in this respect the approach is at variance with most traditional jurisprudential models. It also departs in significant respects from the currently influential theories of autopoiesis or of self-referentiality (Luhmann 1985; Teubner 1988) that fail to allow sufficient space for the unruly clash and competition between different, regulatory mechanisms.

REGULATION AND LEGAL PLURALISM

Thus far my argument has been concerned with establishing and marking out "regulation" as a characteristic feature of modern life and to insist that law is not synonymous with regulation. In the course of this argument I have treated law almost as if I had in mind the singular "the Law." Now I want to explore what it means to take account of legal pluralism.

The problem with legal pluralism is that it is difficult to give it more than lip-service. There always seems to be a return to the taken-for-granted and ever-present reality of state–law. Legal pluralism seems plausible and, more importantly, usable when we are concerned with specific contexts. If, for example, we are considering business relations then it is not difficult to take account of Stewart Macaulay's classic study of noncontractual relations (Macaulay 1963) or if we are concerned with the internal order of the factory to take on board what Stuart Henry calls "private justice" (Henry 1983). What is much more difficult is to find an adequate way to express the general and pervasive sense in which it is true that state–law never has a monopoly and is always in competition with other forms of legal ordering.

An important feature of the weakness of the case for legal pluralism has been that it has never had an adequate theoretical grounding that was able to offer a general model of coexisting legal systems. It is by filling this gap that makes Santos' work interesting (Santos 1985). His general thesis is a standard legal pluralist position:

> [T]he legal regulation of social relations is not the exclusive attribute of any [one] form of normative order, it is rather the end result of the combination of the different forms of law and modes of production thereof. (1985:307)

His key step is to associate the different forms of law with a provisional social map composed of four clusters of social locations or places: these he labels householdplace, workplace, citizenplace, and world-place. Each of these locations is characterized, inter alia, by an institutional form, a mechanism of social power, and a form of law. The potential advance over more orthodox forms of legal pluralism achieved by Santos is to suggest an explanatory device to account for both the source of and the characteristics of each legal form. Taking the "householdplace," for example, the institutional form is marriage, the mechanism of power is patriarchy, and the resulting form of law is "domestic law."

What I am interested to explore is whether Santos is able to show how the characteristics associated with his social locations provide a satisfactory account of the associated forms of law. But before tackling that question directly there are two specific problems with Santos' theory that need to be noted. His social mapping raises the unexplored question of its incompleteness; why, for example, is the marketplace excluded? The answer is that Santos is probably guilty of a certain reductionism: economic relations are reduced to production/workplace relations and, similarly, gender relations are reduced to marriage and/or family relations. These difficulties can in principle be overcome by devoting closer attention to the social mapping that is to be employed.

A more substantial problem concerns the conception of law that Santos employs. In what sense is "production law" (the law of the workplace) and "domestic law" (the law of the household place) law? The former raises few problems; we are familiar various versions of the models of private ordering of the workplace that provide operative systems of regulation by rule and, more or less regular, procedures. It is unproblematic that the factory codes, that Marx described so eloquently, constitute multiple systems of private law

> in which capital formulates like a private legislator at his own good will, his autocracy over his workpeople, unaccompanied by the division of responsibility, in other matters so much approved by the bourgeoisie, and still unaccompanied by the still more approved representative system. (Cain and Hunt 1979:106)

The subsequent development of the juridification of factory rules is well known; mechanisms of "appeals" to higher levels in management structure, the right of representation, the use of standardized penalties and rewards are all part of the development of specific systems of "company law" (Edwards 1979; Henry 1983).

The case of domestic law is more problematic. There are general and pervasive patterns that govern the sexual division of labor, there exists widespread social legitimacy and material supports for the patriarchal powers wielded by men over women and by parents over children, and there are socially recognized rewards and sanctions whereby patriarchal power enforces and reproduces itself. But the other side of the picture is that "households" exhibit considerable variation in form and composition, and correspond less and less to the stereotype of the monogamous heterosexual "family." Accordingly, relations between participants reveal marked variations to such an extent that it is doubtful that anything of the level of generality and visibility that would be necessary before the label law seemed appropriate. In whatever way we might decide to describe the mechanisms that sustain regular and unequal relations within the "householdplace," law is probably not a pertinent designation for the majority of these processes. For example, while males earn more than females how this income is divided is subject to wide variation. Again while the use of physical coercion by males over females is endemic there is extreme variation in its form, its frequency, and its incidence; in particular it should be noted that there is considerable variation across class, cultural, and ethnic boundaries. Rather more systematic is parental rule over children, the right to issue commands, to enforce obedience, and to employ coercive sanctions are, while not universal, at least pervasive. It is then a mute point whether the notion of "domestic law" does not oversimplify both the form and content of domestic power relations.

The status of domestic and production law becomes clearer when they are considered in their connections with state–law. Both of these are illustrations of state–law recognition and reinforcement of private regulatory regimes. There is, of course, a complex story to be told about the variation of and shift in the boundaries between the private and the public through which legal intervention or nonintervention is determined (Horwitz 1982a; Klare 1982d; Olsen 1983). It is not that recognition and reinforcement by state–law create domestic and production law, but rather that these lend emphasis to the pluralist contention of the relative autonomy of different and dispersed legal orders. This classification assists legal pluralism to successfully meet the objection that it, albeit unintentionally, is guilty of a certain sleight of hand, namely, of linking by the use of the term 'law' widely different social practices and thus of implying that connections exist between the different kinds of ordering or mechanisms of power that manifest themselves in very different social relations.

What is missing from the account of legal pluralism thus far is any attention to the way in which the dispersed sites of local regulation are articulated, that is, the specific connections and their mechanisms, with state–law in regulating the social relations and institutional practices in the home and in the workplace. Santos advances a general thesis that the reproduction of capitalist relations is the result of "the complex articulation between four different modes of production of political power and law" (1985:319). But unfortunately he does not have anything to say about the characteristics of this "complex articulation" nor, in particular, about the role of state–law in either reinforcing or subverting the local normative regulation of domestic and economic life. Any adequate treatment of legal pluralism must address the specific articulation between state–law and non-state–law.

A THEORY OF MODES OF REGULATION

It should now be possible to bring together the two lines of inquiry that this chapter has pursued. The discussion of the nature of regulation and of legal pluralism points to the possibility of their combination. That the concept of "modes of regulation" provides a potentially fruitful way of thinking about the complex mechanisms of social ordering and their interaction. It further allows us to explore the particular contribution made by specifically legal mechanisms. The most important benefit is that it facilitates an account that remains sensitive to the variation in modes of regulation and of local power, while at the same time allowing attention to be retained on the role of state–law in the concentration and condensation of power relations.

The first step is to depart from Santos's approach that links distinct forms of power to particular types of social relations, which, in turn, give rise to specific forms of law. In its place I want to propose the idea that there exist distinct "modes of regulation" that are *relatively autonomous* in the sense that the type of regulation that exists is not directly determined by the type of social relation that is the object of regulation. One important exemplification of the argument in favor of the relative autonomy of modes of regulation is that it allows us to take account of changing historical forms of regulation. The example that has been most extensively studied is the regulation of labor. What is clear from the history of labor relations is that the form of regulation has varied significantly over time and that the major determinant of that variation from coercive command power of capital through to collective bargaining and grievance procedures is the relative power of labor and capital (Henry 1987; Tomlins 1985; Woodiwiss 1990a).

We can now consider one of the most interesting features of Santos's analysis. He offers a reinterpretation of the much debated case of the English Factory Acts of the mid-nineteenth century. The point he makes is that to provide a full picture it is important to take account of the mutual interaction or articulation of citizenplace and workplace. His thesis is that factory legislation marked an absolute gain for workers at the level of the political system, opening up the road to securing working-class political representation. This advance was balanced by the advantage accruing to capital in the workplace where it secured greater control and intensification of the labor process.[17]

What is significant about this analysis is that it draws attention to two related but distinct features. On the one hand it stresses that different regulatory systems interact and should not be considered in isolation, just as Gusfield and Edelman remind us to consider both the instrumental and the symbolic dimensions of all regulatory practices (Gusfield 1963; Edelman 1971). On the other hand it introduces a new dimension of considerable importance, namely, the role played by law in drawing and sustaining boundaries. There is a literal sense in which law, and most explicitly property law, demarcates and enforces boundaries; but this notion of boundary maintenance has a wider significance. In the case of the workplace boundaries have a special import precisely because of the critical significance of the division between work and politics within capitalist economies; it is here that there is the distinction between the incorporation of the working class within the polity while excluding workers from full participation in the workplace (Renner 1949). Considerable ideological significance flows from the sustenance of the apparently natural exclusion of workers from the same participatory rights within the enterprise that the struggle for the franchise secured in the political realm; indeed the struggle for democratic participation rights in the enterprise has become an important element of modern radical politics (Abrahamson and Brostrom 1980). It is not that law creates this boundary but rather that once in place it is protected and reinforced by both legal ideology and legal practice. This suggests a broader thesis, namely, that one characteristic feature of the connection between law and regulation is that law serves to demarcate and secure the boundaries between distinct fields of regulation such that their relative autonomy within their specific fields is reinforced.

The potential of the regulation approach is that it encourages attention to both the positive and the negative dimensions of power. To grasp the full potential of the regulation approach it is important to eradicate the pejorative sense of regulation as simply negative control. Regulation needs to be understood as making possible and facilitating certain forms of social relations while discouraging and disadvantaging others. It is in tracking these processes of material and discursive construction that a firm sense of the play of power relations, as shifting sites of the condensation of power, institutionalizing the dominance or subordination of specific social forces and their historically unique combinations, thereby deepening the analysis with the shifting modalities of social domination.

LAW AND REGULATION: A DYNAMIC RELATION?

To urge that the study of law be pursued by first locating its object of inquiry within a wider realm of "regulation" has four implications that require exploration and development.

The first is that the proposal to treat law as an aspect of regulation invites the objection that to do so runs the risk of losing sight of the specificity of law. To locate law within a wider field of regulation might simply miss that which is distinctive about law. It may possibly not very be different than what early sociological jurisprudence did when it proposed to study law as the most specialized form of "social control" (Pound 1942). While there remain important limitations to the social control perspective (Hunt 1978:22–36) it is significant to note that, far from being an abandonment of the quest for the specificity of law, it sought to pursue that objective by making use of the potentially fruitful research strategy of seeking to distinguish law from those social mechanisms that are the most similar to it. The regulation approach differs in important respects from the law as social control perspective. It does not claim that law is one form of some broader category, "regulation," nor does it seek to compare law with other varieties of regulation. Such an approach might well have some heuristic value, but it is not the approach that is here being commended. The regulation approach is not an exercise in such a comparative methodology. Instead it proposes the deployment of a conceptual model (of regulatory objects, agents, etc.) designed, in the first instance, as has been argued, to break out of the pervasive grip of the model of rules that reduces the phenomenon of law to one primary characteristic, namely, that of being a system of rules.

To effect the disruption of the self-evidence imported by the model of rules the regulation approach proposes the adoption of a quite different strategic direction. It starts out from the suggestion that law be approached as itself, being a set of social relations that stands in some definite connection with other forms of social relations. This initial starting point is immediately modified to avoid the implication that there exist self-standing and unidimensional social relations (legal relations, economic relations, etc.). Instead the model suggests that social relations are necessarily complex sets of connections between social agents that exhibit a range of potential dimensions. Thus rather than "legal relations" and "economic relations," the claim is that social relations exhibit, among other potential dimensions, legal and economic dimensions. The significance of this standard sociological strategy is that not only does it break with the model of rules, but it makes the strong suggestion that what is interesting and should serve as the focus of research activity is the forms of connection that exists between the different dimensions of social relations. What is significant for this project is the range of issues that flows from the question: How is the legal dimension related to the economic, political, gender, and other copresent aspects of social relations?

This approach is unapologetically concerned with notions of causality. It leads unavoidably to the pursuit of questions about what effects or consequences result from the legal dimensions of social relations for the way they are lived and struggled over. This concern expressed in abstract form the strong ambivalence that I, and I hope others, experience about law. "Does law matter?" and "does law make any difference?" are questions that I remain puzzled by and undecided about. It remains important, because of the inflated self-aggrandisement of legal discourses, to chip away at the myth of legalism and not to assume that because most social relations have legal dimensions that it follows that law makes much difference to lived relations. In other words, it is strategically important to adopt a stance that is always ready to deflate legal imperialism.

Yet there is always another side, one that sees law as contributing to an explanation of some of the most persistent problems of social being about how people not only do manage to live within complex social connections and about how they might live better. These concerns go to the "big" questions of political theory about democracy, rights, and freedoms. And in these contexts law always figures ambiguously and problematically; it is at one and the same time a mechanism that contributes to both the mechanisms of social domination and to the potential for human emancipation. Now it may be that the theoretical paradigm that is proposed within which to address these questions is simply evidence of a paralyzing refusal or inability to take sides. The more affirmative claim insists that such a paradigm is a necessary feature of any serious inquiry, that it is a positive virtue of the approach that its starting point is self-consciously undecided. Whether law is a "good thing" or a "bad thing" is quite deliberately left open. It is left open, however, in such a way as to encourage the pursuit of such evaluatory or normative questions. In this sense it openly both encourages and espouses engagement with a "politics of law" as being the proper end result or conclusion of the kind of scholarship that is here commended.

A second implication of the regulation model for legal studies serves to extend the widely rehearsed "law and society" critique of orthodox legal scholarship. That criticism resists the prevalent internalism of forms of scholarship that not only accept the model of rules, but that also assume that law conceived as rules can and does provide all the necessary resources in order to understand what law is and to answer normative questions about what it should be. The regulation project goes an important stage further by *relocating* the domain of law. It shifts attention away from the self-evident and unquestioned focus on courts and lawyers. It does not refuse significance to courts and lawyers, but insists on the merits of starting elsewhere by suggesting that we best engage with law by starting with "lived experience," with the pervasive and manifold varieties of social relations through which people in their diversity and complexity lead their lives in home, work, political, familial, and gendered relations. In other words, its starts with relations that from the standpoint of the pervasive model of rules seem to be "distant" from the conventional scenario of courts, judges, and lawyers.

An approach that starts with lived social relations invites the question: What part, if any, does law play in social life? This paradigmatic question can contribute to the revitalization of the project of the "law and society" movement. Law and society studies have inhabited an institutional space on the fringes of institutional law and its practitioners have, despite their best endeavors, continued to play out a role of what I have described as "intellectual subcontractors" to orthodox legal scholarship (Hunt 1978:145). The most obvious consequence of this role is that law and society scholars are forever dragged back into the vortex of court and litigation–centered issues. To break with this subservience is not easy. The case I make out can be read as an alternative scenario to David Trubek's continuing attempt to redirect the "law and society movement" (Trubek 1990). It is not that I disagree with Trubek's espousal of a revitalization of the commitment of law and society scholars to the empowerment of the disadvantaged and to fundamental social change through a more explicit commitment to alliance with the new social movements. I share those commitments, but my contention is that such ethical commitments do not in themselves provide the intellectual resources to effect the much needed revitalization of the movement.

I take up that element of Trubek's agenda that remains underdeveloped, namely, how the theoretical perspective adopted connects with progressive normative commitments. In this respect Trubek remains unusually noncommittal; he quite understandably wants to hang on to a commitment to concrete interventions through what he has called "critical empiricism" (Trubek 1984b; Trubek and Esser 1989). At the same time he wants to capture the significance of discourse theory, but his proposal for a "discursive science" is more tentative and underdeveloped. I put aside my reservations about the label "science" that, for me at least, has too many reminders of the positivist roots of the social sciences to offer any attraction; I find only relief in giving up on claims about science. My suggestion is that the theoretical program I advocate can contribute significantly to the kind of program that Trubek espouses. What is necessary is that we be as self-conscious about what shifts or ruptures from the received tradition of the law and society movement are necessary.

A third implication of the regulation perspective that contributes to such an undertaking involves a shift away from a pervasive institutionalist perspective that associates law with its institutional expressions. In place of an institutional perspectives that focuses on courts and professions, the alternative commends that attention be directed to the study of law in everyday life. To grasp how this relocation is to take effect it is necessary to attend to the decisive role that conceptions of social space play in both social and legal thought. All social thought operates through some selection of the appropriate spatial metaphor with which to work. Any attempt at a treatment of law that seeks to do more than undertake a purely internal enquiry that assumes the radical autonomy of law must adopt some view on how law is to be conceptualized in relation to the nonlegal. The treatment that follows resists and refuses the notion of "legal system," whether it be the commonsense usage of legal professionals or the more theoretically sophisticated usage in systems theory, for example, as developed by Luhmann. The objection to "system" is that it reproduces the assumption that the legal system transforms itself according to its own internal or self-referential mechanisms. Related objections rule out the use of notions of "legal region" or "legal field" on the grounds that the common usages (geographical and agricultural) of the terms suggest a bounded space.[18] The deployment of any spatial concept to refer to social phenomena imports a strong suggestion that that phenomenon has a spatial location; it stimulates the suggestion that there is some specific place or places where that phenomenon is located. Now there is, of course, an obvious sense in which this is true. Law is to be found in a particularly condensed fashion in law courts or lawyers' offices; in the same way economic phenomena are associated with stock exchanges or factories. But focusing attention of the spatial or institutional location of social phenomena stimulates the inference that those phenomena are not present in other locations. And it is this inference that must be challenged by encouraging shifting attention to the presence of law outside the courtroom, to law in everyday life.[19] This reorientation is not simply a matter of attending to the effects or outcomes of law; although it should be stressed that such studies, particularly those that are attentive to the unintended and unanticipated consequences of legal interventions, have an important contribution to make. There needs to be a broader thrust, one that extends the discussion of legal ideology initiated in Chapter 6 to develop the idea of the plurality of legal ideologies.[20] It is not simply a matter of commending attention to the impact of law on behavior or on the formation of identities and social consciousness; this has long been a focus for law and society studies, and for Realism before that. The feature to be emphasized is that law rarely, if ever, functions alone, but in combination or connection with other regulatory mechanisms. This is perhaps the most important reason why the sociology of law must be fully integrated within the general field of social theory. Thus in contrast to Foucault we should not be content to pursue an analysis of power into arenas that are "less legal," but rather into contexts where law is intermingled with other processes. This is not, however, to advocate some very general thesis about the social construction of reality. Rather it is to commend a research strategy that adopts a perspective that employs the idea that all forms of social relations are subject to processes of governance. This does not involve any claim that this exhausts all that can be said about these relationships, but merely that it provides a fruitful vantage point for the study of the mechanisms of power and the part played by law in those processes.

There is a fourth implication that flows from treating law as a mode of regulation. It concerns the question of whether such a theoretical move involves (intentionally or otherwise) any developmental thesis of the kind that conceives of the late twentieth century through the imagery of regulation, bureaucracy, and its associates. For much of the present century there has been a strand of thought that has been predicting the imminent demise of law. It is significant to note that this response has come from both those who would deplore and those who would welcome such an outcome. It is not my concern to debate the "end of law" thesis—a debate it may be noted that seems to recur with a certain regularity.[21] My present concern is to consider the related but narrower thesis that the rise of regulation involves the replacement of law or that law loses its autonomy and becomes subservient to regulation. Thus, for example, Unger sees the rule of law being undermined by the growth of policy-driven state intervention (Unger 1976:192). A similar thesis, as seen in Chapter 11, is that advanced by Foucault, where he envisages "the judicial institution is increasingly incorporated into a continuum of apparatuses (medical, administrative, and so on) whose functions are for the most part regulatory" (1978:144).

While Foucault sometimes counterposes law and regulation, this formulation is indistinguishable from the thesis that I have been exploring that views law and regulation as standing in a complex symbiotic relation. But what is at stake and is precisely posed by Foucault are two questions: (1) Does the center of gravity of the general processes of social control shift away from law toward a relatively autonomous realm of regulation? (2) Is there a discernible change in the role played by law *within the law-regulation* complex?

Bourdieu can be harnessed to explore these questions. It should be noted at the outset that he employs a set of concepts that is not entirely congruent with those of the regulation model and, consequently, the issues arise in a somewhat different context. He sketches a developmental theory of modes of domination that suggests a sequential shift from a premodern reliance on "overt violence" to one organized around "symbolic violence," what he calls "the gentle hidden form" (Bourdieu 1977:196). Then he suggests a more recent stage in which symbolic violence has progressively withered away as "objective measures came to be constituted that, in rendering superfluous the work of eumphemization, tend to produce the 'disenchanted' dispositions their development demanded" (1976:196).[22] This unmasking of symbolic violence and the barrenness of the world of formal bureaucratic rationality paradoxically generates a return to new forms of symbolic violence that operate through the dissimulation of the mechanisms of domination.

Of this most recent phase he gives two examples; the first is redistributive social policies and the role of private funding of "disinterested" projects and foiundations. Bourdieu does not illustrate these strategies, but the following examples are probably consistent with his usage. Assimilationist educational policies in multicultural societies serve to illustrate the role of symbolic violence in social policies, while the role tobacco and beer companies as major funders of prestigious sporting events illustrates the potential for symbolic violence through private funding. This second strategy is more obviously cynical, but assimilationist educational policies are more complex manifestations of symbolic violence because they have frequently been motivated by genuinely humanist concerns on the part of their originators and practitioners. Yet such policies have operated to impede and even to extinguish significant ethnic and cultural identities and have thus contributed to the reproduction of mechanisms of domination.

One of the features of Bourdieu's ideas that is worth further reflection is his use of the idea of "dissimulation" and "euphemization." I want to consider their applicability to advancing our understanding of the role of law. "Dissimulation" involves the concealment or disguise of some social phenomena under a feigned appearance, while "euphemization" conjures up some process of substitution in which a more palatable term is used to replaced something that is more explicit or more accurate, as in the common euphemization imposed on the language of children for body parts and bodily functions.

Does law dissimulate and euphemize social relations and their attributes? Does the use of such terms developed into concepts allow us to go beyond the more conventional terminology of "legitimation"? I want to make the suggestion that dissimulation and euphemization supplement but do not replace "legitimation." The power of the idea of legitimation lies in the connection it establishes with a normative context that provides not only justification, but also positive affirmation. The appeal to "fairness" and "justice" as conventional tropes of legal discourses serves to provide not only a metadiscourse that links the multitude of particular rules into a presumed normative coherence, but to provide an ongoing link to pervasive social values. Dissimulation and euphemization are operative as components of the discursive techniques of law, but it is important to remember that they coexist with another side of legal discourses, those of "censure" (Sumner 1990). Censure as the "hard side" of law stigmatizes specific forms of conduct as socially subversive and dangerous as in the resonances carried by such labels as "conspiracy" and "treason" when applied to "normal" politics.

Returning to dissimulation and euphemization it is suggested that these concepts provide useful description of features of the tropes deployed in both legal discourses and social policy discourses. They provide the means of grasping the normalizing and naturalizing properties of legal discourses. This is nowhere more apparent than with respect to the discursive construction of economic relations. As the recent preoccupations with "insider dealing" reveal the uncertain boundary line between legitimate entrepreneurial conduct and fraudulent misuse of privileged knowledge. In constructing and reconstructing that boundary we find that prohibited conduct is censured while the noncriminalized is euphemized. In general the procedures of euphemization always exist in their connections with the dark side of censure. These techniques, while not exclusive to legal discourses, are nevertheless particularly highly developed. Analyses conducted in these terms offer a particularly fertile way of exploring what may be called the technologies of legitimation.

Returning to consider the developmental connection between law and regulation there is no dispute about the expansion of regulation. What is more controversial is whether the expansion of regulation occurs at the expense of law. Theses that counterpose law and regulation rest on a misapprehension of the role of law that is rooted, where this chapter started, with the illusions that have for so long surrounded "the model of rules." The simple presumption is that *"law rules through rules,"* that primary rules of conduct are, or at least once were, law's medium. It is only when we specifically break with the common-sense perception of law as orders backed by coercive sanction that we can readdress the question of regulation. To adapt a slogan from the debate about the relationship between family law and divorce mediation, what we have is the prevalence of "regulation in the shadow of law" where law casts a very long shadow. The significance of the case that I have advanced for a theoretical perspective that starts from the general problematic of law conceived as a mode of regulation is that is facilitates the exploration of this dynamic articulation between law and regulation and avoids the counterposing of law and regulation.

We should, however, hesitate before accepting any simple developmental thesis that posits a general transition from law to regulation that, as Peter Fitzpatrick neatly observes, is an "over-heralded event" (Fitzpatrick 1992). My advocacy of a regulation approach as a starting point for the theorization of law provides, as a minimum, a corrective to any overdramatic scenarios about the fate of law. More positively is has the potential for providing a framework in which law can be viewed in its location as a component to a general and persistent process of social regulation that secures general patterns of social domination and points toward an understanding of the conditions of possibility of counterhegemonic strategies that can challenge existing forms of domination.

ENDNOTES

Notes to Chapter 1

1. I was struck while rereading some of the retrospectives produced by participants in the law and society movement of the risk involved, however unintended, of creating an impression of a world of "insiders," who on occasions such as the giving of inaugural addresses when the author is inducted to some well-deserved office in an academic association, creates also the "outsider," who has not been a participant in the triumphs or the defeats that are described.

2. The link between sociology of law and the jurisprudential tradition is less fully represented in what follows than might otherwise have been desirable for completeness because this engagement lay at the heart of my *The Sociological Movement in Law* (1978) and, more recently, was the focus of *Reading Dworkin Critically* (1992b).

3. The literature of the engagement with Marx from the perspective of its implications for the theorization of law is by now voluminous. The following are some of its more comprehensive contributions: Cain and Hunt (1979), Collins (1982), Fine (1984), Hirst (1979), and Sumner (1979).

4. In my own case it was in *The Sociological Movement in Law* that I undertook an engagement with Durkheim and Weber, and in the collaborative work with Maureen Cain, *Marx and Engels on Law* (1979), that the engagement with Marx was pursued. The general position that I derived from these explorations bore the clear imprint of Gramsci; it was a theory emphasizing the primacy of law as a mechanism of ideological domination and as a significant contributor to the hegemonic process that finds its expression in Chapters 2 and 6. This perspective remains an active component, although I have been at pains to avoid treating Gramsci as a general theoretical resource.

5. The recognition of the "inherent right to self-government" of native peoples in the 1992 round of Canada's constitutional settlement is a significant example of such a struggle.

6. This classification of rights borrows from T. H. Marshall's classic descriptive model of stages of citizenship (Marshall 1963).

7. This concern with the weight to attached to liberty and equality is epitomized by the work of John Rawls and Ronald Dworkin (Rawls 1971; Dworkin 1981).

8. For the distinction between individualism and individuation similar to that employed here, see Abercrombie et al. (1986).

9. A more modern illustration of this clash of regulatory strategies is analyzed in Harrington (1985).

10. I use the concept of "project" to suggest institutional goals that not only serve as ideological legitimation but objectives that are always never fully realized.

11. Here I allude to Hobsbawm's powerful thesis that traditions are not so much bequeathed from the mists of antiquity, but come to be laid down through active processes of "invention" (Hobsbawm and Ranger 1983).

Notes to Chapter 2

1. In Britain judicial appointments are made on the initiative of the Lord Chancellor, himself a member of the Cabinet and as such a directly "political" appointment. In the United States the political character of judicial appointments is even more apparent.

2. For details on the use of law in Northern Ireland, see Boyle et al. (1975).

3. For a concise history of trade union law, see Wedderburn (1965).

Notes to Chapter 4

1. This chapter revises and extends the argument developed in Chapter 3, which stressed the basic unity in the sociology of law of the 1960s and early 1970s.

2. Referred to by Trubek as "the stifling debates between instrumental Marxism and liberal legalism" (Trubek 1977:553).

3. For the present purpose "normative integration" is an equivalent designation to that more commonly referred to as "liberal legalism"; the former is preferred insofar as it designates a theoretical core rather than provides a politico-theoretical description (Hunt 1979).

4. It would be a fruitful area of enquiry to examine the range of different postulations of a crisis of law and order in order to establish the characterization given to this crisis.

5. In the case of Britain the process whereby law becomes invoked in the resolution of "hegemonic crisis" is extensively invoked in *Policing the Crisis* (Hall et al. 1978). With reference to the United States the same process is central to the thesis of Balbus (1973).

6. Note the contrast between Black's position in *The Behaviour of Law* (1976) and that in his earlier essay (Black 1972).

7. See Winkler (1975) and Jessop (1977).

8. Unger (1975:7); his orientation to these competing paradigms is not dissimilar to that earlier advanced by Dahrendorf in which both are recognized as grasping different aspect of reality.

9. I refer to a "tendency" within Marxism toward instrumentalism because Marxism has a certain openness in its formulation by Marx, which allows a range of emphases in interpretation and elaboration. This range of

positions within the Marxism of Marx and Engels was demonstrated with respect to their treatment of law in Cain and Hunt (1979). The reduction of Marxism to an instrumentalist theory of law and state can claim some very real textual authority and it has continued to exercise a persistent influence that has important correlates with the wider politico-strategic debates that have occurred within Marxism since the death of Marx and Engels but that are beyond my present concerns.

10. Paul Hirst makes a similar point in commenting on the two types of Marxist theory of law although he locates the differentiation with respect of an emphasis on two different function of law (regulation of relations of possession and the regulation of the struggle between classes (Hirst 1979:96).

11. See the most explicit use of "the iron fist and velvet glove" imagery in the study of the American police by the Center for Research on Criminal Justice (1975).

12. For many years the only available translation, and that a very defective one, was in Hazard and Babb (1951). More recently two very useful and much improved translations have become available: Beirne and Sharlet (1980) and Pashukanis (1978).

13. See the following for important aspects of the Pashukanis debate: Balbus (1977), Arthur (1977), Redhead (1978), and Hirst (1979a).

14. See the discussion in Beirne and Sharlet (1980) and Redhead (1978) on the "interpretation" of Pashukanis' "self-criticisms." Although the criticism of his positions became more vociferous after 1927, he remained a very powerful figure well into the 1930s. I am inclined to accord status to his writings up to about 1932; although after that his writing degenerate and are completely incompatible with his general theory.

15. There is in this regard an illustrative parallel between Pashukanis and Durkheim. It is the most distinctive feature of Durkheim's sociology of law that his treatment of criminal law is reduced to a theory of punishment; this is most clearly evident in his "Two Laws of Penal Evolution" (1973), in which he sought to modify the earlier counterposing of mechanical and organic solidarity. It is precisely the absence of a theory of the state that led Durkheim to slide from criminal law to punishment in his analysis. In Pashukanis' case it is the contradiction between his commodity theory of private law and his Marxist–Leninist theory of the state that results in his slippage from criminal law to punishment.

16. An interesting line of comparison is suggested by the striking similarity in emphasis on the divisibility of punishment and its association with conceptions of "responsibility" that are to be found respectively in Durkheim, Pashukanis, and more recently in Foucault (1977).

17. Exactly the same thesis was advanced by Poulantzas, "The centre of legitimacy shifts away from the sacred towards legality" (1978:87).

18. Thompson's method of criticism of his opponents is fraught with problems; the "some Marxists," "structural Marxists," and "theoretical illiterates" that haunt his waking hours, and from the intensity of his polemic, probably his sleep hours as well, are disembodied creatures whose actual positions are never addressed. Rather these figures do service as leaden caricatures to be ridiculed through his splendid polemic. For example, I am very fond of his dig at Althusser: "When I close my eyes and think of what an 'ideological state apparatus' might look like I can only think of Robin Day

[British TV interviewer]." Dashing though the polemic is, it intrudes to such an extent that it violates the principle of taking one's adversaries seriously. I do not see it as my task to defend Thompson's adversaries, but to note its limiting effects on his argument.

Notes to Chapter 5

1. The call to "take seriously" is becoming a pronounced theme in both socialist and liberal politics. It extends from Dworkin's concern for "taking rights seriously" (Dworkin 1978) to renewed concern among socialists with problems of democracy and legality.

2. The classic treatment of the symbolic dimension is Gusfield (1963); while Scheingold (1974) attributes primacy to the mobilizing potential of legal rights.

3. Much of the recent debate has been given a particular inflection as a result of the enthusiastic rediscovery of the writings of the early Soviet legal theorist Pashukanis (Beirne Sharlet 1980; Pashukanis 1978). For discussion of Pashukanis see Fine et al. (1979) and Hirst (1979).

4. These processes have been much focused on in the literature of deviancy theory and of media studies as analyses embodying and expanding on the title of Stan Cohen's book *Folk Devils and Moral Panics* (1972).

5. The National Council for Civil Liberties (NCCL) has a long tradition in this field and of more recent origin is the Legal Action Group (LAG) and the journal *State Research*. A much more recent trend has been the appearance of a number of Left studies that take seriously the politics of law (Thompson 1975, 1979a, 1980; Hall et al. 1978; Young 1979).

6. The multiplicity of elements I perceive in Left responses may result from lack of sufficient detailed scrutiny of the press and publications of the Left; here is a field in much need of more detailed research to examine what I am conscious is lacking in my discussion, that is a sense of historical change or development in positions taken up by the Left.

7. It is to make this general point about the dangers of deductions from general theory that recent Marxist literature frequently invokes Lenin's definition of Marxism as "the concrete analysis of concrete conditions" (Lenin 1960–70 CW 31:66).

8. A sophisticated version of this "dry run" theory is advanced strenuously, despite rather limited evidence, in Baldwin and Kinsey (1980).

9. Significantly this thesis still underlies much of the official criminology of Eastern Europe.

10. For an interesting attempt to establish a critique of the movement away from imprisonment in terms of the imperatives of capitalist economic and political requirements (Scull 1977).

11. There has been sharp internal controversy within the NCCL over the demand for bans on marches and meetings of "far right" organizations.

12. The Schwendingers make precisely such a case for the criminalization of capitalism itself and come very close to the legitimation of "normal crime" (Schwendinger and Schwendinger 1975:165).

13. It should perhaps be pointed out that while it in no sense invalidates Thompson's conclusions, the historical origins of the jury lie not in a demo-

cratic inspiration, however much it may have become suffused with that tradition, but in the system of collective criminal responsibility that the Norman monarchs and barons imposed on an obdurate and resentful populace.

14. The importance of "rights" in political mobilization is stressed by Scheingold (1974). He argues that mobilization remains even though "the myth of rights" has often resulted in an overestimation of the progressive capacity of legislation to secure specific rights.

15. Even when there is legal recognition of group or collective entities, and they are deemed to have rights, it is significant that the notion of "legal personality" endows the collectivity with the attributes of the individual legal subject.

16. For example, the controversy between Dworkin and Rawls as to whether "liberty" or "equality" is to be given priority as the basis of the theory of rights involves competing ontological views.

17. That is a position that defines law as being restricted to the rules laid out in the existing legislation (whether formulated by parliament or the judiciary); in its simplest form, the law is the rules laid down by the lawmakers.

18. My argument against the positivist definition of rights is consistent with the position argued with great vigor in the name of radical liberalism by Ronald Dworkin (1978). It is not necessary to apologize for invoking a liberal defense of "rights against the state." The real problem that follows is the nature and extent of the divergence between the concrete rights that liberals and socialists seek to promulgate.

19. The issues touched on here are complex both with respect to the interpretation of Marx's text and their intellectual location; for a useful discussion of Marx's treatment of justice and its implications from a number of contrasting positions see M. Cohen et al. (1980).

20. The worst excesses of the libertarian phase were particularly evident in "the new criminology" and its offshoots subsequently labeled by Jock Young as "left idealism" (Young 1979).

21. It should be noted that these issues concerning legal apparatuses in important respects parallel the more developed area of concern with "policing the police" and it may be that the issue posed of popular and political "controls" on official apparatuses offers a point of entry for the consideration of transforming and democratizing legal institutions.

Notes to Chapter 6

1. For my present purpose I distinguish "Critical Legal Studies" as a trend of analysis that, while drawing significantly on the Marxist tradition, is primarily identified by the political project of intervening in the scholarship and practice of legal education.

2. This chapter does not discuss the concept of "symbolism" further. It is, however, important to note the existence of important strands of work that, drawing on the symbolic-instrumental dichotomy, have brought the focus on the symbolic dimensions of law into increasingly close proximity with the concerns of ideology analysis. Such an exploration would require an extended discussion of such diverse authors as Foucault (1977), Ignatieff (1978), and Habermas (1976).

3. To undertake this task systematically would require a thorough study of the historical development of the Marxist theory of ideology. Much of this work has already been undertaken with a greater or lesser degree of success; of particular interest is the work of the "Birmingham Group" (Centre for Contemporary Cultural Studies 1977), Ernesto Laclau (1977), and Larrain's wide-ranging history of ideology theory (1979). The decisive intervention of Althusser is to be found in his major texts (Althusser 1969, 1971) and has been the subject of critical analysis by Hirst (1979) and McLennan et al. (1977). The impact of semiology on the theory of ideology is investigated by Coward and Ellis (1977) and Sumner (1979).

4. For a stimulating discussion of the public–private dichotomy as it relates to family law (Olsen 1983), which has the great merit, in contrast to "reflection" approaches, of isolating the complex and shifting boundary between the public and private and, consequently, its tortuous history in legislation.

5. In the case of reprinted papers, reference is to their reprints in the Beirne and Quinney collection (1982).

6. Note that the reflection theory of ideology is not the only one available within the Marxist tradition. Another version is that derived from Marx's application in *Capital* of the essence/appearance distinction. We should be cautious about assuming a simple continuity between reflection theory and essence/appearance theory. Frequently, these two approaches are conflated in the texts under consideration. The further exploration of the ideological dimension of law requires attention to the issue of Marxist epistemology and the need to challenge the simple empiricist model of both reflection and essence/ appearance that characterizes much of the recent discussion of the ideology of law (Hindess 1977; Cutler et al. 1977).

7. The historical studies in the two collections of texts are peppered with less serious and less controversial examples. Genovese in his otherwise very convincing account of the role of law in the slave states asserts, as a given, the hegemonic function of law (Genovese 1976). In so doing he comes perilously close to the functionalist circle of specifying a necessary function and then showing it revealed in practice. Janet Rifkin (1982) in advancing an abstract, necessary connection between law as hegemonic ideology and the ideology of patriarchy, similarly builds an unnecessarily functionalist account of the rule of law in perpetuating male dominance.

Notes to Chapter 7

1. Duncan Kennedy defines critical legal studies as "the emergence of a new left intelligentsia committed at once to theory and to practice, and creating a radical left world view in an area where once there were only variations on the theme of legitimation of the status quo" (Kennedy 1981:506). In characterizing this "legal leftism" Kennedy elsewhere insists that "our methodology is linked, however obscurely, to our Left politics. We're trying to do radical legal scholarship" (1981a:1275). The movement is "a full frontal assault on the edifice of jurisprudential writing and thought" (Hutchinson and Monahan 1984:199). "There is, at long last, a 'left' in legal academia, equipped with nascent theory" (Sparer 1984:509).

2. A sympathetic analysis of the genesis and trajectory of CLS is provided in Livingston (1982); a more critical account is provided by Allan Hutchinson and Patrick Monahan (1984); see also Trubek (1984).

3. The quest for theoretical and methodological coherence is not a call for theoretical and methodological uniformity. It is clear from the most preliminary reading of critical legal texts that there is a considerable degree of diversity in both method and theory. The question is rather whether there exists a degree of compatibility that allows for development through internal dialogue. Others have already arrived at the conclusion that the internal differences are such that "the divergences within the group are so fundamental as to demand their disbandment" (Hutchinson and Monahan 1984:24).

4. It is not entirely flippant to notice that a preliminary test of whether an article or book is to be regarded as falling within the critical legal studies movement is whether it carries an attribution to Duncan Kennedy!

5. The inventory of theoretical acknowledgement is wide and varied; the more frequently cited are Habermas, Sartre, Marcuse, Piaget, Freud, Levi-Strauss, Lukacs, Gramsci, Althusser, Poulantzas, and Foucault.

6. For some cautionary strictures see Hunt (1981).

7. Critical authors present a range of positions in assessing the degree and intimacy of the relationship to American realism. Thus, for example, David Trubek with his prior commitment to a neo-Realist model for the sociology of law (1972a) stresses the continuity between realism and critical theory. A similar emphasis on the realist connection is found in Livingston (1982). Alan Freeman presents his defense of the method of "trashing" as "a continuation of the Realist project" (1981:1230). Tushnet is more ambivalent; on some occasions he stresses the link with Realism (1981:625), while elsewhere he stresses the inherent limits of the Realist project (Tushnet 1979).

8. Some of the best examples of this critique of postrealist legal scholarship are Brest (1981), Freeman (1982), Gordon (1981), Kelman (1981), Kennedy (1982a), Klare (1982a), and Tushnet (1979a, 1983).

9. Unger's influence within CLS is primarily through his earlier text *Knowledge and Politics* (1975), while his apparently more immediately relevant work *Law in Modern Society* (1976) has attracted very little interest from critical legal scholars.

10. Unger seeks to remedy this admitted deficiency, but his attempt to establish the relationship between the theoretical construct and social reality has little of the brilliance and perceptiveness of his critique of the theory itself.

11. For example, Duncan Kennedy organizes his analysis of legal formalism through the dichotomy between rule making and rule applying (Kennedy 1973). Kennedy's later analysis of Blackstone is more Ungerian in its focus on the "fundamental contradiction" within which "relations with others are both necessary to and incompatible with one's freedom" (1979:215). Olsen's impressive study of contemporary family law is organized around the antimony of the private and the public (Olsen 1983), whereas for Mark Tushnet the major contradiction is, respectively, between objectivity and subjectivity and between sociality and individuality (1981a:120).

12. Frug lists the major dualities of liberal thought: reason/desire, fact/value, freedom/necessity, self/community, civil society/state (1980:1075).

13. This upheaval has many dimensions but for present purposes we can

identify it as the split between orthodox and western Marxism and between Soviet communism and Eurocommunism.

14. Some CLS activists have a closer connection than others with debates and developments in Marxist theory; thus Karl Klare was associated with the Marxist humanism of the journal *Telos* during the 1970s and Mark Tushnet with the short-lived journal *Marxist Perspectives*, while for others Marxism has played a much less significant role in their intellectual formation, e.g., Morton Horwitz and Duncan Kennedy.

15. The critical theorist who comes closest to adopting, but not espousing, an instrumentalist position is Morton Horwitz who significantly is the critical scholar least concerned about the question of their connection with Marxism.

16. Problems associated with the theory of relative autonomy have not been widely canvassed in critical legal literature although they were discussed in Karl Klare's influential essay (1979) and by Mark Tushnet (1978).

17. One major task that confronts constitutive theory is to critically examine the most sophisticated version of economistic Marxism advanced by G. A. Cohen in *Karl Marx's Theory of History* (1978); Chapter 8 seeks to contribute to such an undertaking.

18. Alan Hyde has provided a powerful critique of the way in which the concept of "legitimation" has been deployed in recent sociology of law and critical legal studies. It is possible to agree with the substance of his critique without adopting his conclusion that the concept of "legitimation" should be abandoned; rather I suggest that the problem is not the concept itself but rather the functional theory of legitimation within which it is invoked (Hyde 1983). I have discussed the application of the concept of ideology in legal analysis, and made some suggestions for overcoming some of the weaknesses identified by Alan Hyde, in Chapter 6.

19. A much more assertive view of the necessary effectivity of legal ideology is put forward by Peter Gabel: "Legal thought originates, of course, within the consciousness of the dominant class because it is in this class's interest to bring it into being, but it is accepted and interiorized by everyone because of the traumatic absence of connectedness that would otherwise erupt into awareness" (Gabel 1982:26).

20. As David Trubek notes, "Klare assumes that the justificatory messages in this elite literature [of labor law doctrine] have a direct influence on worker and union decision-making, he is able to assert that there is a relationship between the creation of a labor law ideology and the relative passivity of American unions in the post-War period" (Trubek 1984b:611).

21. David Trubek goes even further and characterizes the concept as "the central tenet of the critical legal studies creed" (1984b:592).

22. Kennedy (1980). In a similar usage Elizabeth Mensch identifies legal consciousness in terms of the intellectual schema employed by "jurists," referring to appellate judges and treatise writers, that is those who employ a conceptual elaboration (Mensch 1982).

23. Gabel (1980:26; emphasis added). David Trubek gives a similarly broad definition of legal consciousness as "those aspects of the consciousness of any society which explain and justify its legal institutions" (Trubek 1984b:592).

24. I present an argument for a view of ideology as "contested," which insists that the formation of popular consciousness cannot be deduced from

an elite ideology but is also subject to concrete historical determination in Chapter 6.

25. I intend the distinction between positivist and neopositivist scholarship to capture the differentiation between a closed system that posits the existence of a finite system of legal reasoning through which rules are handled and manipulated and a more open system, best exemplified by the Realist tradition, which seeks to embrace a view of doctrinal development as contingent.

26. At this stage I shall postpone discussion of how this fundamental contradiction is identified and whether this concept has any continuing role in critical legal theory.

27. An alternative theorization of legal consciousness is offered within critical legal theory by Al Katz, which though distinct in its formulation has precisely the same theoretical structure as that advanced by Kennedy. Human consciousness, and therefore legal consciousness, is constantly confronted by contradictions (the nature and origin of contradiction remain unspecified) with respect to which there are a limited number of possible responses; these can be analyzed in terms of two types of boundaries, "vacuum boundary" (which allows only an either/or choice) and "live boundary" (which allows the possibility of mediation or compromise). Now although the concept "motive" is not utilized by Katz, his account can be readily translated into such terms; the "motive" that makes sense of the areas of doctrinal development that he considers to illustrate his boundary theory is the ubiquitous search for the "middle ground" that purports to resolve the dilemmas and contradictions. Katz's theory is thus of the same general form as Kennedy's; as a consequence I do not intend to examine it separately (Katz 1979).

28. Kennedy is explicit that his paper is concerned only with this second motive of apology or denial, "but I don't want to be understood to deny the first utopian aspect." I do not think he should be allowed to evade the problem quite so simply. If the premise of "double motivation" is taken seriously then it must mean that the two motives coexist and find expression in work written under their sign and that the tension, conflict, or contradiction between the two motives must find expression in the substantive analysis. Let us assume that Duncan Kennedy finds time to return to Blackstone and exhaustively analyzes his writings from the standpoint of the first motive. There would then be a need for a third article considering the most interesting question of how these motives interact; this is the most interesting question because historically important scholarship is unlikely to have been motivated exclusively by apologetics but will always be found to contain positive insights into the quest for justice alongside or, more accurately, embedded in, its apologetic features.

29. The fusion of economic and political interest is epitomized in Horwitz's account of the resistance to and ultimate subjugation of arbitration as an alternative to court handling of commercial disputes at the beginning of the nineteenth century when "an increasingly self-conscious legal profession had succeeded in suffocating alternative forms of dispute settlement" (Horwitz 1977:154).

30. The form of "relations with others" in capitalist society is "hierarchical structures of power." In a passage that reveals much about the theoretical and political concerns of critical theorists Kennedy observes that "the kicker is that the abolition of these illegitimate structures, the fashioning of an unalienated collective experience, appears to imply such a massive increase of collective

343

control over our lives that it would defeat its purpose" (1979:212). This presentation of the dilemma of orthodox socialism is what leads him to favor the transformation politics of Roberto Unger, in which "revolutionary reformism" offers the prospect of a cumulative transcendence of egoism and domination in a quest for the creation of the conditions for "community."

31. Kennedy's analysis of the broad trends of doctrinal development suggested the predominance of altruism in the postbellum period followed by the classical period with the dominance of individualism. His periodization of the twentieth century can be read as either a more rapid oscillation between the competing principles or as a period of increased tension between the two organizing principles (Kennedy 1976).

32. Dworkin, "Hard Cases" and "Can Rights be Controversial?" (1978). The unitary character of Dworkin's principles is given not by some assumption of moral consensus but rather from the institutional or constitutional unity of the nation state.

33. Habermas identifies the central concern of critical theory with "society as a system of action by human beings, who communicate through speech and thus must realise social intercourse within the context of conscious communication" (Habermas 1976:255).

34. Robert Gordon argues that "what we experience as social reality is something that we are constantly constructing" (1982:287). In a more ambiguous formulation Karl Klare insists that "we are the ensemble of our social relations and shared meanings, and that our individuality is in many ways defined in relationship to our shared meanings and symbols" (Klare 1982d:419).

35. Unger is explicit about the limited theoretical development of both of the two strands of critical scholarship he identifies; both "have yet to take a clear position on the method, the content, and even the possibility of prescriptive and programmatic thought" (Unger 1982:563).

36. A subsidiary problem that stems from the theoretical eclecticism of CLS is that it tends toward a rather superficial appropriation of concepts and insights from different theoretical traditions, which all too often take the form of a simple listing of influential texts; this approach to theory construction ignores all the most important problems of theory construction that revolve around the compatibility of different conceptual apparatuses.

37. Reference is to "Invasion of the Body Snatchers" (1956) in which a small American town comes perilously close to being taken over by aliens who have sent "pods" to earth that, when they are in proximity to sleeping humans, take over or "snatch" the body as a repository for the alien beings.

38. Peter Gabel very explicitly commits himself to the "relative autonomy" position, which he links directly to his emphasis on the legitimation function of law (Gabel 1980:49). Karl Klare also is explicit in his adoption of this concept (Klare 1979).

39. The intellectual origins of the concept of relative autonomy are to be found in the rejection by both Marx and Engels of economic determinist interpretations of their general theory. Its most coherent articulation is to be found in the letters of Engels written between 1890 and 1895 (Marx and Engels 1975).

40. Without engaging in too much self-reflection I should comment that *The Sociological Movement in Law* (1978) was very dependent on the idea, if

not the explicit concept, of the relative autonomy of law; later in collaboration with Maureen Cain, *Marx and Engels on Law* (1979) began to pose relative autonomy as a problem.

41. The most important attempt to theoretically identify the limits of relative autonomy is that provided by Althusser and Balibar with their discussion of "determination in the last instance" (1970:216–224).

42. Other critical scholars also make passing reference to structuralism; for example, Mark Tushnet refers to legal doctrine as "structures of thought with internal coherence" (Tushnet 1979a:1350), whereas Peter Gabel, although he makes some use of structuralist ideas, finds structuralism incompatible with the radical phenomenology that provides his primary theoretical orientation (Gabel 1977a:606).

43. The most important modern defense and development of Marxism as a philosophy of internal relations are provided in Bertell Ollman (1971). It is interesting to note that this text, which is arguably the most important piece of Marxist scholarship to have been produced in the United States, is never (to the best of my knowledge) discussed by the critical legal scholars despite its compatibility with many of their own ideas.

44. This criticism has real force, but it should be disassociated from the rather "Leftist" association with a concern for the association of doctrinal analysis with elite law schools; such a criticism is an unnecessary ad hominem, which weakens the force of their more important criticism of "the failure to develop any theory of the relationship between law, as legal doctrine, and the socio-political context of law" (Munger and Seron 1984:257).

45. In this chapter I have been anxious to examine the critical legal studies movement as a whole. I have not found it necessary to focus on the internal differences, whether theoretical, methodological, or political, except where specific differences have been relevant to some specific topic under consideration. Since many recent discussions concentrate on these differences it is necessary to make a brief comment. That there exist differences of substance is not in dispute, but whether there is a clear line of differentiation, as argued most forcibly by Hutchinson and Monahan (1984), is more debatable; they question whether the movement can continue to embrace the divergencies within it. My objection, which leads me to focus on continuity rather than divergence within CLS, is that the differences do not follow the neat dichotomies proposed. There is no consistent division between "revisionists" and "nonrevisionists" (Hutchinson and Monahan 1984), or between "reformist" and "irrationalist" (Dalton 1983). The eclecticism of the intellectual inspiration of the movement makes possible a variety of classifications, but there is little consistency to the patterns.

46. I take it for present purposes that his concept of "motive" has the same role as Unger's concept of "principles."

47. "A complete rationalization of the criminal law would remove those very elements of discretion, such as the pardon, which contributed so much to the maintenance of order and deference" (Hay 1977:57–58).

48. The label "constitutive theory of law" appears explicitly in Karl Klare's essay on "Law-Making as Praxis" (1979:28–33). He continues to employ it elsewhere (1982d:57). It is also invoked by Mark Tushnet (1983a:285–287).

49. It should be stressed that Thompson does not employ the concept of constitutive theory.

50. Thompson's language is not entirely satisfactory in expressing his wider theoretical intent. The idea of "imbrication" conjures up the image of an "overlapping" relation between the legal and economic dimensions of relations. More adequate in conveying the attempt to break with the idea of two separate spheres in the other term he uses "interpenetration." But it should be noted that this still fails to provide a new discourse that is not founded on the separation of two entities "law" and "economy." What we confront is a fundamental problem of the language available to us that, with apparent inescapability, endows social reality with the solidity of Newtonian physical "objects."

51. For a beginning of such an examination see Hugh Collins (1982:81–85).

52. The sense of lack of certainty as to the precise claim being made that is imported by the phrase "at least in part" is not, I think, accidental; there is a similar hesitancy when Mark Tushnet observes that this trend of analysis within CCLS "treats law as *in some way* constitutive of society" (Tushnet 1979b:32; emphasis added).

53. In defense of the ugly neologism "effectivity" it is intended to make clear that the concern is not with the "effects" of law conceived as one independent variable acting on another social element. "Effectivity" is intended to demarcate the consequences for the development of some complex social elements of its legal dimension or manifestation.

54. In the same article he employs the formulation that identifies the role of the legal process as "one of the primary forms, if not the primary form, of social practice through which the actual relationships embodying class power were created and articulated" (Klare 1979:130).

55. Marx employed the concept "conditions of existence" in a distinctive manner. "Like all its predecessors, the capitalist process of production proceeds under definite material conditions, which are, however, simultaneously the bearers of definite social relations entered into by individuals in the process of reproducing their life. These conditions, like those relations, are on the one hand prerequisites, on the other hand results and creations of the capitalist process of production; they are produced and reproduced by it" (Marx 1959:798). The distinctive feature of Marx's formulation is that while certain "conditions" are a *prerequisite* of capitalism, their existence is the *creation* of the capitalist process of production. In other words capitalism provides its own prerequisites.

56. Brenner, it should be stressed, does not make use of the conceptual apparatus through which I represent his thesis. I take Brenner's analysis to illustrate the methodology being proposed because I hope to supplement the way in which Robert Gordon invokes Brenner in illustrating constitutive theory.

57. For an interesting discussion of how this conceptualization can be applied within sociological study of law see Fitzpatrick (1983:45–49).

58. Of particular interest are Gordon (1984) and Trubek (1984).

Notes to Chapter 8

1. It should be noted that this formulation goes beyond the mere adoption of a hermeneutic approach that insists that social relations cannot be under-

stood outside the associated meanings of participants; such a position is agnostic as to whether such meanings are part of the conception of the relationship itself.

2. I take it that Cohen employs the notion of "matching" concepts to indicate that the two concepts are functionally equivalent in that both formulations, whether in terms of rights and powers, say the same and no more about the relations of production thus identified.

3. In discussing the exchange between Lukes and Cohen, I will adopt the context that Lukes imposes, namely, of posing the issues in terms of the relationship between "norms" and relations of production; I simply assume that for present purposes law is but a particular instance of norms.

4. It is significant that Cohen's discussion of slavery is generally posed in terms very close to the gun-man situation, i.e., as if it could satisfactorily be analyzed in terms of face-to-face coercion.

5. Nothing in this account denies the validity of proposing a form of analysis that abstracts from the concrete determination of specific social relations in order to produce a conception, for example, of a social relation of production in order to fulfill some heuristic purpose. In any such restricted concept the social relation remains constituted by those elements or forms of social relations that are retained within the conception employed. Thus Cohen quite properly commences his comparison of the production relations of slavery and of capitalism by employing an "ideal-typical" slave and a proletarian owning his or her own labor.

6. My point here has much in common with Cohen's own account of his divergence with what he calls Marx's "philosophical anthropology." He criticizes Marx for going "too far" in the materialist direction with the result that he neglected "the subject's relation to itself, and that aspects of the subject's relations to others which is a mediated (that is indirect) form of relation to itself" (Cohen 1983a:233).

7. He admits that this involves a simplification and discusses as a special case negative rights (e.g., a right that another not enter one's land, which involves "not doing") (Cohen 1978:237). His discussion of this issue is not relevant to my present concerns.

8. On performatives see Austin (1962) and for its extension to problems of legal theory Hart (1961).

9. For a fuller critique of a systematic attempt at a fully behaviorial account of legal phenomena, see Hunt (1982a:19).

10. Cohen's conceptualization is very similar to the theory of power that Foucault calls the "economic theory" (Foucault 1980). Foucault reacts against the temptation to think of power as a "thing" to be possessed by some agents and consequentially not possessed by others (i.e., the common-sense "zero-sum" view of power). His response was to insist that power is "omnipresent." "Power is everywhere—not because it encompasses everything, but because it comes from everywhere" (Foucault 1978:93). While providing a valuable corrective against the narrow conceptions of power that he sought to transcend, his strategy, by going to the opposite extreme, tends to reproduce the same weakness by again rendering power as somewhat mysterious and elusive.

11. The concept "social totality" is employed as a partial check against falling into unreflective assumptions about the unity imported by the concept "society." I agree with Michael Mann that if we take cognizance of the

problems associated with the concept "society" we can then allow ourselves to continue to employ it (Mann 1985). Mann's focus on "socio-spatial" and "organizational levels of analysis" goes some way to inscribe the societal conditions within which power exists and hereby avoids the abstraction of the possessory conception of power. He emphasizes the collective dimension of power by focusing on a typology of social networks within which power exists and eschews any attempt to offer a theory of "power as such."

12. I refrain from pursuing this objection because it involves a much more general challenge to the conceptual apparatus of historical materialism. For present purposes I abstain from any such broad assessment of Marxism.

13. Note that I do not insist that every account of production relations must include reference to legal relations; it is possible to provide an adequate account of certain short-term relations between economic agents in terms of purely economic or other powers, but such relations are atypical since they lack the persistence, that is the production and reproduction of the relationship, that I take to be the hallmark of Marx's conception of social relations of production.

14. Somewhat surprisingly Cohen argues that "work relations," which intuitively suggest themselves as preeminently relations of production, are excluded from the important category "social relations of production" and thus do not form part of the base or economic structure. It is not my purpose to challenge this conceptual separation between work relations and social relations of production; but it is necessary to comment that his treatment leaves the identification of social relations of production somewhat hazy; they are left hanging as involving a higher level of abstraction than the immediacy of work relations. One is tempted to feel that his relative neglect of social relations is not unconnected to his subsequent claim that productive forces take casual primary over relations of production. An alternative attempt to solve "the legal problem in Marx" is advanced by William Shaw. He distinguishes between "work relations of production" and "ownership relations of production," the latter being "understood in a non-legal, non-normative sense as the relations of control over the productive forces" (Shaw 1978:43). Precisely the same objection may be raised against his nonlegal relations of ownership as those leveled against Cohen, but his conceptualization of relations of production ("work" and "ownership") avoids the lack of specification of Cohen's "social" relations of production.

15. An illegal squatter's regime may become legitimated by usage or subsequent legal recognition and may thus, in the long run, be able to establish an instance of the prevailing relations of production.

16. Lakoff and Johnson refer to such cases as "spatialization metaphors"; they note that metaphors impose their own criteria of systematization and coherence once a particular metaphor is adopted (Lakoff and Johnson 1980). White argues that metaphorical strategies represent, in developmental terms, a naive or early phase of consciousness (White 1978).

17. For an extended discussion see Hall (1977).

18. Cohen also provides two variant illustrative cases, since my argument is not relevant to the variations introduced I ignore these cases.

19. It is interesting to note that although I follow others in quoting Thompson's phrase, his normally elegant use of the English language rather fails him and he falls back on an architectural metaphor no richer than that of base and

superstructure; to "imbricate" or overlap (as in roof tiling) fails to express the idea that law is so deeply imbedded in and interdependent on economic relations that any attempt to separate out legal and economic relations is doomed to failure and to produce a mechanistic or reductionist account of their interaction.

20. Apart from this brief comment on Cohen's "Marxist functionalism" I do not propose to engage with his account of functionalism (Cohen 1978:Chpts. 9 and 10).

Notes to Chapter 9

1. In the United States some exponents have explicitly celebrated the joys of "trashing" (Kelman 1984).

2. There exists a continuing hesitancy about the relationship between critical legal theory and socialism. In the United States this is part of the deeper consequences of the absence of a strong socialist tradition. In Britain the hesitancy is a manifestation of the wide-ranging debate on the Left about both the characteristics and possibility of a viable socialism.

3. For a very readable presentation of Rorty's view see the set of three articles in *London Review of Books* (1986). On realism see the very spirited defence by Sayers (1985).

4. In contrast, sociology of law has generated interesting accounts of the criminal process by adopting a defendant perspective; a classic illustration is Blumberg (1967). The adoption of a "victim" perspective has been urged by at least one critical legal theorist (Freeman 1982a:96).

5. For an extended discussion of the application of the concept of ideology to legal studies see Chapter 6.

6. Both Althusser and Foucault stress that theoretical closures render alternatives invisible. Althusser makes the important additional qualification that alternatives are rendered invisible to theory (1971:27).

7. The absence of anything beyond a naive theory of the state gives rise to a paradox in Dworkin's theory. On the one hand, the state is nothing other than the organized expression of the community but, on the other, it is against this state that citizens are empowered with rights as trumps against the state. Beyond a common-sense suspicion of the state he offers no account of why the state so conceived might be the enemy of citizen's rights.

8. It must be stressed that the conceptualization of the terrain of legal theory is not completed by the formula "law–state complex." Though important, this is only the most immediate illustration of that process. The remaining questions are more difficult and are (fortunately) outside the scope of my immediate concerns, although some of these issues are taken up again in the final section.

9. I bracket "reality" out of deference to the philosophical problems considered in the third section above. However, I want to insist that even the most committed pragmatist/relativist accepts the self-evidence of our common and shared experience; their reservations are primarily concerned with absolutist claims, which Rorty demarcates with capitalization: "Truth," "Reality," etc. Just as Rorty is correct in contending that there is nobody who defends

full-blooded relativism, so it is true that there are no defenders of "Truth," "Reality," etc. in the form that Rorty objects to them.

10. A powerful pleas for the importance of empirical material within critical legal studies is made in Trubek (1984).

11. A working model of relational theory would, of course, require a more elaborate typology of social relations.

Notes to Chapter 10

1. Maureen Cain's interesting paper on Gramsci and the law is concerned with the general debate about historicism (between Althusser and Gramsci) but does not draw out many implications of Gramsci's interesting, but fleeting, comments about law (Cain 1983); short papers by Greer and Kennedy on Gramsci and the law are insubstantial (Greer 1982; Kennedy 1982b).

2. Gramsci's distinction between "East" and "West" is a distinction between Russia as the exemplification of the east with an underdeveloped civil society that made possible the Bolshevik Revolution being directed toward the seizure of power—symbolically, the storming of the Winter Palace—and the extended development of civil society in the West (and, it should be added, of political society in the form of representative democracy) rules out the possibility of the frontal or insurrectionary seizure of power. It is the articulation of the East/West distinction and the conception of hegemony that marks a degree of rupture between Gramsci and Lenin far beyond Gramsci's own immediate recognition; it was in this sense that Gramsci broke from Leninism while remaining a Leninist.

3. Gramsci's concept "historical bloc" signifies that economic classes rarely, if ever, rule directly, but that political power is always constituted as a bloc of classes and other social forces (for example, national or ethic groups).

4. My term, not Gramsci's.

5. While I have generally stressed Gramsci's break with Lenin it is important to note that although different in content, both Lenin and Gramsci provide major critiques of economism and stress that there is no necessary or developmental connection between trade union consciousness and socialist political consciousness.

6. It should be noted that a major pole of difference that runs through the contemporary debates on Gramsci is with respect to the extent to which he should be understood as effecting a series of breaks with the Leninist tradition. As a counter to the line of argument advanced in this chapter Perry Anderson (1977) seeks to demonstrate the continuity between Gramsci and Lenin (and Trotsky).

7. This idea of "blocked" hegemonic projects is akin to the concept developed by Barrington Moore in his idea of "blocked historical possibilities" (Moore 1978:Chpt. 11). I am indebted to Rianne Mahon for suggesting the applicability of Moore's concept to the theory of hegemony.

8. This location of the law at the intersection of state and civil society is significant because of its implicit rejection of the reduction of law to state within classical Marxism that tended to see law as a dependent "instrument" of the state and hence of a ruling class.

9. Without entering more fully into all the problematic ramifications that

underlie the innocent concept of "accountability," I will make the general observation that what renders the equilibrium achievable by law between state and civil society problematic and unstable is the resistance of the state to a mutuality with civil society. A major source of tension and instability is the incapacity of the state to abide by the ideological doctrine and most centrally associated with modern law, namely, the rule of law. It is this tension between "state" and "rule of law" that makes E. P. Thompson's justly renowned conclusion to *Whigs and Hunters* (1975), that the rule of law is a universal human good, of such continuing importance; it is this "tension" rather than the "celebration" of the rule of law that is the fertile field of discussion that Thompson opens up.

10. Since I have suggested a "link" between Gramsci and Foucault let me suggest some parallels with other social theorists. There is a suggestive parallel between the "educative" function that Norbert Elias attributes to manners that parallels that which Gramsci assigns to law; this is especially pertinent with reference to the self-eduction of the dominant bloc (Elias 1978). A similar linkage can also be glimpsed with Pierre Bourdieu's notion of "habitus," and I think this holds even though he is at pains to distinguish "habitus" from "rules," practices regulated without express regulation or any institutionalized call to order (Bourdieu 1977:17). My suggestion is that Gramsci's sense of law is not a conception of law as orders/commands, but rather of an authoritative form through which social values are articulated and regularized and thus become part of the "common sense" of the age and culture. My final linkage allows me to make the point that what has been overlooked in the tendency to dump on structuralism is that Althusser was more Gramscian than generally recognized and that his discussion of "ideological state apparatuses" seeks to capture a line of thought very similar to that invoked by Gramsci's talk about the educative role of law (Althusser 1971).

11. Joel Handler has sought to take account of the characteristics of social movements in his study of public interest law. His focus has been on size, on ability to attract elite support, and on capacity to provide meaningful incentives to leaders and staff (Handler 1978:5). My reservation is that these characteristics are far too narrowly drawn and thus miss the issue of the hegemonic capacity of the movements being studied.

Notes to Chapter II

1. The reference to structural inequalities stresses that the most important inequalities of class, race, and gender are manifestations of relations that are structural in the sense that they define the general characteristics of a particular form of social life. For example, paid or wage labor and a sexual division of domestic labor are two structural features of modern capitalist societies that go a long way to influence many other features of such societies.

2. Despite the burgeoning literature on Marxist theory of law that has appeared since the late 1970s there has as yet been no attempt to trace its historical development.

3. To talk about "the law" in the singular is strictly unsatisfactory because it implies a degree of unity and centralization that misrepresents the real complexity of the variety of laws, within which "state law" is generally para-

mount and that continually seeks to assert control over the diverse forms of law that make up the richness of legal phenomena (legal pluralism).

4. For a discussion of the connection between law, citizenship, and politics (Hall and Held 1989).

5. The argument that follows can be read as a criticism of Hugh Collins' "solution" to the "legal problem in Marx," which relies on the distinction between "social rules," reflecting the requirements of the dominant ideology, and "legal rules," which remain superstructural (Collins 1982:84–90).

6. That the paradoxical nature of trade union law in Britain is not confined to the topic of strike ballots is indicated by the fact that the imposition of direct elections for trade union office, and of membership ballots before a trade union may establish a political fund, has increased membership participation and caused the unions to improve significantly their communication and contract with their members. These examples are good illustrations of the unintended consequences of law, that is where legislative policy results in outcomes at variance with those intentions.

Notes to Chapter 12

1. The significant and early exception, among the now voluminous literature that Foucault's work has generated, to this neglect of Foucault's treatment of law was Nicos Poulantzas; much of the course of the argument to be developed in this chapter owes much to Poulantzas. I seek to flesh out Poulantzas' seminal thesis that "law is a constitutive element of the politico-social field" (Poulantzas 1978:83).

2. The use of "discipline(s)" catches Foucault's double usage of "discipline" as a distinctly modern form of domination and of the plurality of modern "discipline" rooted in the medical and human sciences.

3. Foucault's relationship with Marxism is complex; for discussion see Sheridan (1980); Mark Poster (1984), and Smart (1983). Politically he made an early breach with the French Communist Party. Theoretically he treated Marxism as a tradition irretrievably marked by economic reductionism. The paradoxical result was that in the 1960s and 1970s when Western Marxism was undergoing its most fertile development and breaking, among other things, with a narrow equation of power, state, and repression, we find Foucault invoking what we might call "Marxism at its worst" as the intellectual spur driving forward his reconceptualization of power.

4. One of Foucault's most elusive concepts is his notion of a "field of force relations"; it is linked to his diagrammatic metaphor of power relations, but he never explicates the connection between "force" and "power"; for discussion see Chris Weedon (1987:110–111).

5. This is not to imply that interesting reflections on law were absent from his earlier work. In *Madness and Civilization* (1965) Foucault identifies the interconnection between the rise of psychiatry and the elaboration of the juridical subject endowed with rights.

6. In an interview in 1983 Foucault identified three sequential axes of his general project, by that time labeled "genealogy," consisting of the axes of "truth," "power," and "ethics" (1983).

7. It is by no means clear whether Foucault's shift of attention to govern-

mental rationality toward the end of the 1970s involves the implication that he dropped or at least downgraded his equation of premodernity with absolutism, law, and sovereignty. Colin Gordon offers this interpretation, but there is little or no textual evidence to support it (Gordon 1987).

8.   The "repressive hypothesis" arises in the context of Foucault's account of the history of sexuality. He repudiates what he takes to be the common sense of the modern age that there was once sexual openness and naturalness that came to be suppressed by a rising wave of repression, captured for us by the label "Victorian," from which the twentieth century has been struggling to liberate itself (Foucault 1978:17–23).

9.   For fuller discussion of Foucault's relationship to Marxism, in addition to the references in note 3 above, see Cousins and Hussain (1984). While both Smart and Poster seek to "recover" a Foucault that is compatible with at least some aspects of the Marxist legacy, most other commentators, including Cousins and Hussain, stress his breach with Marxism.

10.   Foucault's negative view of the significance of state power is exemplified in the following formulation: "The idea that the state must, as the sources or point of confluence of power, be invoked to account for all the apparatuses in which power is organized, does not seem to me very fruitful for history" (Foucault 1980:188). The problem with this rhetoric is that there is, of course, no one who argues that the state accounts for "all" the manifestations of power. Indeed one of the odd features of Foucault's critique of orthodox Marxism is the claim that it exhibited a narrowly state-centered view of power; statism there is in Marx, but that provides no justification for entirely ignoring the much more developed analysis that Marx provided of economic power that is dramatically and revealingly absent from Foucault's own work.

11.   The evidence that Jessop relies on for his interpretation is to be found in the following passages in Foucault's texts: (1978:94; 1980:99–100, 142, 188–189, 202–203). Another invaluable source that informs my discussion is provided by Jeffrey Minson (1980).

12.   The most developed example that Foucault gives of an unintended "strategy" is one of the key themes in *Discipline and Punish,* which contends that the productivity of prisons for capitalism was "discovered" rather than "invented."

13.   Foucault (1978:102). Jeff Minson, while critical of Foucault's conception of strategy along similar lines to those argued here, makes an interesting attempt to retrieve a conception of strategy for the project of socialist politics (1980). Boaventura de Sousa Santos criticizes Foucault along similar lines when he suggest that Foucault simply went too far in stressing the dispersion and fragmentation of power and that this results in a lack of attention to the conjunctural formation of hierarchy among the forms of power (Santos 1985).

14.   This view is both confirmed and denied by Foucault's discussion of the discourses of sexuality: "We must not expect the discourse on sex to tell us, above all, what strategy they derive from: . . . rather we must question them on the two levels of their tactical productivity (what reciprocal effects of power and knowledge they ensure) and their strategical integration (what conjunction and what force relationships make their utilization necessary in a given episode of the various confrontations that occur" (Foucault 1980:102). Unfortunately he tells us nothing about how the ascent from the investigation of "tactical productivity" to "strategical integration" is to be made.

15.   Jessop (1986:78) arrives at a similar conclusion when he argues that Foucault, having insisted on the multiplicity of power relations and rejected their structural determination in favor of the pure immanence of power, reveals the poverty of his account of global strategies that left him with no means to explain "hegemonic effects." This is especially clear in the vagueness of his approach to global strategies and *surpouvoir* and his unreasoned assumption of the inherent neutrality of the techniques of power.

16.   Foucault gives the example of the way in which judges have gradually absorbed the role of "experts" in the criminal process.

17.   It should be noted that there are significant variations in Foucault's own periodization. In the short paper on "Governmentality" (1979:21) he pushes the juridical state back into the feudal period, with the "administrative state" grounded in "regulation" emerging in the fifteenth century, and the "governmental state" in the seventeenth and eighteenth centuries.

18.   The idea of juridification was used by Otto Kirchheimer to indicate the way in which law comes to be used as a means of neutralizing political conflicts by subjecting them to formal legal regulation (Kirchheimer 1969). More recently the idea has come to refer to the process by which the state intervenes in areas of social life in ways that limit the autonomy of individuals or groups to determine their own affairs; see, e.g., Habernas's discussion of "Tendencies of Juridification" in (Habermas 1987b:356–373), and Teubner (1986). These tendencies have led some commentators to worry about a new social disease of hyperlexis or legal overload (Trubek 1984a).

19.   This assessment of Foucault's views on the place of law in modern society is at odds with the interpretation offered by Mark Poster, who contends that Foucault "argues that in 'modern politics', the law is the center of power, a function which variously impedes or promotes the actions of individuals" (Poster 1990:133). Unfortunately, Poster offers no evidence, textual or otherwise, to support this interpretation.

20.   He elsewhere formulates this point in the following terms: "The discourse of discipline has nothing in common with that of law, rule, or sovereign will. . . . The code they come to define is not that of law but that of normalization" (Foucault 1980:106).

21.   As normalization spreads both its targets and its instruments, so does judging become transformed. Judges become the bearers of normalizing power, while at the same time the judicial role is taken on by other agents. "The judges of normality are present everywhere. We are in the society of the teacher-judge, the doctor-judge, the educator-judge, the social worker-judge; it is on them that the universal reign of the normative is based" (Foucault 1977:304).

22.   In a second and very similar formulation Foucault insists that "the powers of modern society are exercised through, on the basis of, and by virtue of, this very heterogeneity between a public right of sovereignty and polymorphous disciplinary mechanism" (1980:106).

23.   A survey of Foucault's varied formulations of the relationship between law and discipline reveals a preponderant strain toward the counterposing of law and discipline; some of these are particularly sharply drawn as is manifest in the following formulation: "the juridical system . . . is utterly incongruous with the new methods of power whose operation is not ensured by right but by technique" (1979:89).

24.   It is perhaps significant that his attempts to formulate an alternative

principle of unification are at best suggestive, and at worst simply hazy. "[U]lti-mately what presides over all the mechanisms is not the unitary functioning of an apparatus or an institution, but the necessity of combat and the rules of strategy" (Foucault 1977:308). The looseness of this formulation is all the more striking since it appears in the penultimate paragraph of this text.

25. Paul Hirst, in characteristically blunt terms, describes Foucault's move from "the disciplines" to "disciplinary society" as an absurdity. "These prac-tices [the disciplines] have no unity of objective, content or effect" (Hirst 1986:49).

26. Foucault's sketch of an expanding disciplinarity shares much in com-mon with the currently popular theme of juridification that contends that we have been witnessing a steady advance of legal intervention into ever deeper spheres of social life. The juridification thesis comes in versions from different political stables (Mandel 1989; Hayek 1973).

27. Foucault's last texts from the uncompleted history of sexuality marked a shift, even though they had a fragmentary and undertheorized character, to a concern with the "techniques of the self" that went a long way to overcome his earlier schematic separation between the premodern and the modern (Foucault 1985, 1986). He formulates this problematic in the following terms: "How did we directly constitute our identity through some ethical techniques of the self that developed through antiquity down to now?" (Foucault 1988b:146).

28. Other sources of the renewed attention to government are to be found in the debate about "state formation" (Corrigan and Sayer 1985; Gerhard Oestreich 1982; Elias 1982).

29. It should be stressed that Foucault does not suggest any simple displace-ment of law by discipline; indeed he is at pains to show how the problematic of law and sovereignty persists. This idea he captures with his insight that modernity has "not yet cut off the King's head" (1980:121). For reasons that he does not explicate he sees law as lacking the capacity "for the codification of a continuous surveillance" (1980:104).

30. A slightly different periodization can be found in "Governmentality" (1979:21); (i) State of Justice or "society of law," (ii) Administrative state or "society of regulation," and (iii) "Governmental State."

31. The notion of cameralist reason draws on the tradition of economic thought of cameralism as a distinctive governmentalization of the mercantilist phase of capitalist development. Foucault emphasizes the "étatism"—taking into state control the detailed regulation and supervision of individual con-duct—of this type of regulation. For a general account of the distinction between cameralism and mercantilism, see Spengler (1960).

32. These lectures have not, as yet, been translated into English but are extensively summarized and discussed in Gordon (1991).

33. "Legal imperialism" comes in a number of different guises; it is most explicitly present in Ronald Dworkin's liberalism (Dworkin 1986), Posner's much more conservative liberalism (Posner 1988), but also in recent German legal sociology with its reliance on systems theory and the model of autopoietic law (Luhmann 1985; Teubner 1988). It is in turn linked to the various forms of juridification thesis.

34. The most significant example is the formation of the modern corpora-tion with limited liability; these are legal creations in the important sense that

it is precisely the ability to confer a legal status that limits the liability of participants that makes the relationship not only distinctive but a viable vehicle for the cooperation of capitals drawn from a range of different sources to some particular economic project.

35. A discursive formation can be viewed as a constellation of discourses that, in order to distinguish it from Foucault's usage, we might call a "discursive bloc."

36. For example, Foucault was correct in his contention that the Victorian discourses on sex never silenced the endless talk of sexuality and that other voices of sexuality coexisted. Yet he was wrong in not admitting that the discursive constellation, which we so readily label Victorianism, did succeed in consolidating itself as the hegemonic discourse capable of marginalizing, expelling, and disallowing other discursive traditions, and still forms a powerful component of significant variants of contemporary radical feminism whose discursive formation draws heavily on the rhetoric of "social purity" (male vice and female virtue) that was central to the Victorian discourse of sexuality (Snitow et al. 1983; Valverde 1990).

37. The exemplary study of the discursive formation of hegemony remains Stuart Hall et al. (1978); it not only situates the very specific discourses around the invention of "mugging" in Britain, but it convincingly demonstrates the reactionary hegemonic potential of the complex articulation of the disparate discourses of race, urban decay, and youth.

38. Jessop seeks to avoid the presupposition of a taken-for-granted unitary conception of "society" by employing the linguistically clumsy but theoretically attractive innovation of speaking of "societalization" processes and effects (1990:4–7).

39. We should perhaps also add Foucault's concept "tactics," but I omit consideration of tactics because I see no problem with his use of this concept.

40. This formulation is pitched at a rather general level; it is the focus of work in hand. The line of thinking being explored here is that the intensification of contemporary structural couplings within which law in imbricated is to be explained by something akin to what Mark Poster calls the mode of information. Poster argues a general case for the expansion of social control in which, for example, electronic data bases give rise to a new Superpanopticon that provides new and expanded means of controlling population in postindustrial societies. My own interest in both the positive and negative sides of structural coupling seems to imply a less Orwellian vision of the present.

41. Foucault also, rather confusingly, refers to this process as "collective sovereignty" (1980:105).

Notes to Chapter 13

1. The complexity of shifts and developments in the history of legal theory is underlined when we note that the contemporary form of an undoubtedly advanced social theoretical trend, epitomized with the autopoietic theories of Niklas Luhmann and Gunther Teubner, has returned to this preoccupation with the self-referentiality of law (Luhmann 1985; Teubner 1988); this approach has the merit in providing a systematic break with a temptation to

lapse back into any version of a "reflection theory" in which law is conceived as merely the resultant of other societal processes.

2. I explore the connection between liberal legal theory and the claims about "legal autonomy" more fully in Hunt (1992a).

3. In an earlier period this argument over the self-referentiality of jurisprudence can be found in the opposition between what was usually referred to as the historical school and analytical jurisprudence. There is an absence of a good treatment of the jurisprudential debates of the late eighteenth and nineteenth centuries in light of the concerns and controversies of the twentieth century; Roscoe Pound's overview of the history of legal theory still remains valuable (Pound 1923).

4. The opposition between "internal" and "external" legal theory is exemplified by Dworkin's increasingly explicit defense of internalism as the distinguishing mark of an adequate legal theory. I have argued that the general deficiency of most criticism of Dworkin's project has been its failure to challenge in any coherent way this internalism and to avoid the adoption, through a simple negation, of an unsustainable externalism (Hunt 1992a).

5. Having suggested above that modern autopoietic theory was akin to self-referentiality, it should now be noted that one of its most significant claims is that its objective is precisely to locate law as a subsystem existing in exchange with its environment. For present purposes I remain neutral as to whether this biological model can achieve the relationalism for which I argue.

6. This sense of "governance" and "government of the self" is captured especially well by Nikolas Rose (1990) and Colin Gordon (1991).

7. For overviews of modern legal pluralism see Henry (1983), Griffiths (1986), and Merry (1988).

8. For an overview of and important contribution to the trajectory of the Marxist theories of the state see Jessop (1990).

9. One of his clearest articulations of this conception of policing is to be found in a short paper on the politics of health in the eighteenth century (Foucault 1980:170). However, the concern with "population" is found in many earlier periods, for example, in Augustan Rome, where economic penalties were imposed on the childless, and in medieval Florence, where the commune provided dowries to help reduce the age of marriage.

10. The positive dimension of constitutive practices can be further underlined by borrowing the distinctive inflection given to the term "individuation" by Abercrombie and his co-authors (Abercrombie et al. 1986); in contrast to the atomizing connotations of "individualization," "individuation" refers to those information practices that identify the specific characteristics of individuals and groups in order to provide appropriate resources and entitlements. For example, the provision of child benefits necessitates the collection of information about the numbers, ages, distribution, and location of children.

11. Michael Mann provides an important resource on the articulation of different forms of power (Mann 1985).

12. I borrow the slogan aptly coined in Evans et al. (1985).

13. The concept moral regulation is developed by Corrigan and Sayer (Corrigan 1981; Corrigan and Sayer 1985) and is closely related to Foucault's concept "normalization."

14. I recall that as a child encountering the last gasps of one such minor regulatory object: there was a school rule that boys were not allowed to keep

their hands in their pockets. As far as I recall no reason was ever given for this rule. Accordingly it became a target for resistance and among my friends it became the height of fashion to spend as much time as possible with hands thrust deep into our pockets. It was only much later that I discovered that this rule was a remnant of an earlier preoccupation with masturbation and juvenile sexuality.

15. Joseph Gusfield's study of the rise and fall of the temperance movement remains the classic study of symbolic political struggles (Gusfield 1963). The moral panic surrounding AIDS is an important current exemplar of the construction of new objects of regulation (Sontag 1989).

16. The contests over the number, powers, and duties of nineteenth-century factory inspectors is a well-documented case of contests around the creation of regulatory agents (Carson 1974).

17. For the purpose of the present argument I am content to accept Santos' neat thesis that workers gained on one front and lost on another. I merely wish to register a caution against too ready acceptance that capital was the exclusive winner in the workplace. The forms of regularization of employment relations that factory legislation introduced laid the conditions for many modern trade union practices; it reduced dependence on the discourse of "custom and practice" and made possible arguments around turnover, profitability, etc.

18. Bourdieu's notion of the legal, or as he prefers, juridical field are partially exempt from this objection. His concept of "field" does not imply some geographically identifiable "place" inhabited by law. His sense of "field" draws instead on analogy with magnetic or electrical fields suggesting a set of forces (or magnetic pull) that is capable of organizing and controlling a certain set of practices. Hence his concept of the "force of law" carries the double sense; a "field" organized by the practices of lawyers and judges, and force in the sense of "violence" in which law exhibits a close interpenetration of actual "violence" in the sense of punishment and coercion, but also the "symbolic violence" through which law normalizes and universalizes social relations (Bourdieu 1987). While I have much sympathy with Bourdieu's intent the term "field" is too strongly "spatial" in the sense of suggesting the bounded field of agriculture.

19. For the recent work on "law in everyday life" from within the traditions of the law and society movement (Merry 1990; Sarat and Kearns 1992).

20. For an extended discussion and development of the critique of legal ideology see the assessments by Trubek and Esser (1989) and Coombe (1989).

21. For an interesting current engagement see Fitzpatrick (1992).

22. It is interesting to note that his one substantive engagement with the field of law, his paper on "The Force of Law" (1987), does not engage with this developmental line of enquiry; it is more narrowly concerned with the mechanisms whereby legal professionals secure control over the "field" of law and of the ideological consequences that result from the induced misapprehension or "miscognition" that flows from the "autonomous field of law" that is the result of the work of legal professionals. One consequence of this line of thought is that it leads him to be very pessimistic about the political utility of "struggle in the law."

BIBLIOGRAPHY *

Abel, Richard. 1982. "The Contradictions of Informal Justice." In R. Abel
(ed.), *The Politics of Informal Justice:* Vol. I, *The American Experience.*
Academic Press, New York.

Abercrombie, Nicholas, Steven Hill, and Bryan Turner. 1986. *Sovereign Individuals of Capitalism.* Allen & Unwin, London.

Abrahamson, B., and A. Brostrom. 1980. *The Rights of Labour.* Sage, Beverly
Hills.

Acton, H. B. 1970. "On Some Criticisms of Historical Materialism." Suppl.
44 *Proc. Aristotelian Soc.* 143–156.

Adlam, Diana et al. (eds.). 1981. *Politics and Power IV: Law, Politics and
Justice.* Routledge & Kegan Paul, London.

Aglietta, Michel. 1979. *A Theory of Capitalist Regulation: The US Experience.*
New Left Books, London.

Albrow, Martin. 1981. ". . . law, ideology, law, ideology, law, ideology, . . .
sociology. . . ?" **32** *Br. J. Sociol.* 127–136.

Althusser, Louis. 1969. *For Marx.* Penguin, Harmondsworth.

Althusser, Louis. 1971. "Ideology and Ideological State Apparatuses." In *Lenin
and Philosophy and Other Essays.* New Left Books, London.

Althusser, Louis, and Étienne Balibar. 1970. *Reading Capital.* New Left Books,
London.

Anderson, Perry. 1976–1977. "The Antimonies of Antonio Gramsci." **100**
New Left Rev. 5.

Arthur, Chris. 1977. "Towards a Materialist Theory of Law." **7** *Critique* 31–
46.

Arthurs, Harry. 1985. *Without the Law: Administrative Justice and Legal
Pluralism in Nineteenth Century England.* University of Toronto Press,
Toronto.

Atiyah, Patrick. 1979. *The Rise and Fall of Freedom of Contract.* Clarendon
Press, Oxford.

Atkinson, Dick. 1971. *Orthodox Consensus and Radical Alternative.* Heinemann, London.

Auden, W. H. 1976. *Collected Poems.* Faber & Faber, London.

* N.B. Where relevant, dates of first publication are given between square
brackets.

Austin, John. 1954. *The Province of Jurisprudence Determined*. [1861] Nicholson, London.

Austin, J. L. 1962. *How To Do Things With Words* (ed. J. O. Urmson). Harvard University Press, Cambridge, MA.

Balbus, Isaac. 1973. *The Dialectics of Legal Repression: Black Rebels Before the American Criminal Courts*. Russell Sage Foundation, New York.

Balbus, Isaac. 1977. "Commodity Form and Legal Form: An Essay on the 'Relative Autonomy' of Law." 11 *Law Soc. Rev.* 571–588.

Baldwin, R., and R. Kinsey. 1980. "Behind the Politics of Police Powers." 7 *Br. J. Law Soc.* 242–265.

Bankowski, Zenon, and Geoff Mungham. 1976. *Images of Law*. Routledge & Kegan Paul, London.

Bartholomew, Amy, and Alan Hunt. 1990. "What's Wrong With Rights?" 9 *J. Law Inequality* 501–558.

Beirne, Piers, and Richard Quinney (eds.). 1982. *Marxism and Law*. John Wiley, New York.

Beirne, Piers, and Robert Sharlet (eds.). 1980. *Pashukanis: Selected Writings on Marxism and Law*. Academic Press, London.

Benn, Tony. 1979. "Democracy and Human Rights." 1979 *Haldane Society Bulletin* 1–15.

Berger, Peter and Thomas Luckmann. 1966. *Social Construction of Reality: A Treatise in the Sociology of Knowledge*. Doubleday, Garden City, NY.

Black, Donald. 1972. "The Boundaries of Legal Sociology." 81 *Yale Law J.* 1086–1100.

Black, Donald. 1976. *The Behavior of Law*. Academic Press, New York.

Blumberg, Abraham. 1967. "The Practice of Law as a Confidence Game." 1 *Law Soc. Rev.* 15.

Bourdieu, Pierre. 1977. *Outline of a Theory of Practice* (trans. Richard Nice). Cambridge University Press, Cambridge.

Bourdieu, Pierre. 1987. "The Force of Law: Toward a Sociology of the Juridical Field." 38 *Hastings Law J.* 805–853.

Bowles, Samuel, and Herbert Gintis. 1986. *Democracy and Capitalism: Property, Community, and the Contradictions of Modern Social Thought*. Basic Books, New York.

Boyer, R. 1990. *The Regulation School: A Critical Introduction*. Columbia University Press, New York.

Boyle, Kevin, Tom Hadden, and Paddy Hillyard. 1975. *Law and State: The Case of Northern Ireland*. Martin Robertson, Oxford.

Brenner, Robert. 1976. "Agrarian Class Structure and Economic Development in Pre-Industrial Europe." 70 *Past Present* 30–75.

Brest, Paul. 1981. "The Fundamental Rights Controversy: The Essential Contradictions of Normative Constitutional Scholarship." 90 *Yale Law J.* 1063.

Brodsky, Gwen, and Shelagh Day. 1989. *Canadian Charter Equality Rights For Women: One Step Forward or Two Steps Back?* Canadian Advisory Council on the Status of Women, Ottawa.

Bumiller, Kristin. 1988. *The Civil Rights Society: The Social Construction of Victims*. Johns Hopkins University Press, Baltimore.

Burchell, Graham, Colin Gordon, and Peter Miller (eds.). 1991. *The Foucault Effect: Studies in Governmentality.* Harvester Wheatsheaf, Hemel Hempstead.

Cain, Maureen. 1983. "Gramsci, the State and the Place of Law." In D. Sugarman (ed.), *Legality, Ideology and the State.* Academic Press, London, pp. 95–117.

Cain, Maureen, and Alan Hunt. 1979. *Marx and Engels on Law.* Academic Press, London.

Callinicos, Alex. 1987. *Making History: Agency, Structure and Change in Social Theory.* Polity Press, Cambridge.

Campbell, Bea. 1987. "Signs of Crisis: Child Sexual Abuse and the Pro-Family State in Britain." 21:4 *Radical America* 7–19.

Campbell, Colin. 1972. "The Expansion of the Sociology of Law," mimeo.

Campbell, Tom. 1983. *The Left and Rights: A Conceptual Analysis of the Idea of Socialist Rights.* Routledge & Kegan Paul, London.

Carson, W. G. 1974. "Symbolic and Instrumental Dimensions of Early Factory Legislation: A Case Study in the Social Origins of Criminal Law." In R. Hood (ed.), *Crime, Criminology and Public Policy.* Heinemann, London.

Carver, Terrell. 1976. *Karl Marx: Texts on Method.* Harper & Row, New York.

Centre for Contemporary Cultural Studies. 1977. "On Ideology." 10 *Working Papers in Cultural Studies.* CCCS, Birmingham.

Center for Research on Criminal Justice. 1975. *The Iron Fist and the Velvet Glove: An Analysis of the U.S. Police.* Center for Research on Criminal Justice, Berkeley.

Cloke, Kenneth. 1971. "The Economic Basis of Law and State." In R. Lefcourt (ed.), *Law Against the People.* Random House, New York.

Cohen, G. A. 1978. *Karl Marx's Theory of History: A Defence.* Oxford University Press, Oxford.

Cohen, G. A. 1983a. "Reconsidering Historical Materialism." In J. R. Pennock and J. W. Chapman (eds.), *Marx and Legal Theory: Nomos XXVI.* NYU Press, New York.

Cohen, G. A. 1983b. "Reply to Four Critics." 5 *Analyse Kritik* 212–221.

Cohen, Jean. 1982. *Class and Civil Society: The Limits of Marxian Critical Theory.* University of Massachusetts Press, Amherst, MA.

Cohen, M. et al. (eds.). 1980. *Marx, Justice and History.* Princeton University Press, Princeton, NJ.

Cohen, Stanley. 1972. *Folk Devils and Moral Panics.* MacGibbon & Kee, London.

Collins, Hugh. 1982. *Marxism and Law.* Oxford University Press, Oxford.

Collins, Hugh. 1987. "The Decline of Privacy in Private Law." In P. Fitzpatrick and A. Hunt (eds.), *Critical Legal Studies.* Basil Blackwell, Oxford.

Coombe, Rosemary. 1989. "Room For Manoeuver: Toward Theory of Practice in Critical Legal Studies." 14 *Law Social Inquiry* 69–121.

Corrigan, Philip. 1975. "Dichotomy is Contradiction." 23 *Sociol. Rev.* 211–243.

Corrigan, Philip. 1980. *Capitalism, State Formation and Marxist Theory.* Quartet, London.

Corrigan, Philip. 1981. "On Moral Regulation." **29** *Sociol. Rev.* 313–327.

Corrigan, Philip, and Derek Sayer. 1985. *The Great Arch: English State Formation as Cultural Revolution.* Basil Blackwell, Oxford.

Cotterrell, Roger. 1980. "Review of Beirne and Sharlet (eds.) *Pashukanis: Selected Writings on Marxism and Law.*" **7** *Br. J. Law Soc.* 317–321.

Cotterrell, Roger. 1981. "Conceptualising Law: Problems and Prospects of Contemporary Legal Theory." **10** *Econ. Soc.* 348–366.

Cotterrell, Roger. 1983. "Legality and Political Legitimacy in the Sociology of Max Weber." In D. Sugarman (ed.), *Legality, Ideology and the State.* Academic Press, London.

Cousins, Mark, and Atthar Hussain. 1984. *Michel Foucault.* St. Martins Press, New York.

Coward, Rosalind, and John Ellis. 1977. *Language and Materialism: Developments in Semiology and the Theory of the Subject.* Routledge & Kegan Paul, London.

Currie, Elliot. 1971. "Sociology of Law: The Unasked Questions." **81** *Yale Law J.* 134–147.

Cutler, Anthony, Barry Hindess, Paul Hirst, and Athar Hussain. 1977 and 1978. *Marx's 'Capital' and Capitalism Today* (2 vols). Routledge & Kegan Paul, London.

Dalton, Clare. 1983. "Review of Kairys *The Politics of Law.*" **6** *Harvard Women's Law J.* 229–248.

Dawe, Alan. 1970. "The Two Sociologies." **21** *Br. J. Sociol.* 207–218.

Demos, John. 1982. *Entertaining Satan: Witchcraft and the Culture of Early New England.* Oxford University Press, New York.

Dews, Peter. 1989. "The Return of the Subject in the Late Foucault." **52** *Radical Philos.* 37–41.

Dicey, A. V. 1967. *Introduction to the Study of the Constitution* [1885]. Macmillan, London.

Durkheim, Emile. 1964. *The Division of Labour in Society* [1893]. Macmillan, New York.

Durkheim, Emile. 1973. "Two Laws of Penal Evolution" [1900]. **2** *Econ. Soc.* 285–308.

Dworkin, Ronald. 1978. *Taking Rights Seriously.* Duckworth, London.

Dworkin, Ronald. 1981. "What Is Equality?" **10** *Philos. Pub. Affairs* 185–335.

Dworkin, Ronald. 1986. *Law's Empire.* Harvard University Press, Cambridge, MA.

Echeverria, Rafael. 1978. "Critique of Marx's 1857 'Introduction.' " **7** *Econ. Soc.* 333–366.

Edelman, M. 1971. *Politics as Symbolic Action: Mass Arousal and Quiescence.* Markham Books, Chicago.

Eder, Klaus. 1977. "Rationalist and Normative Approaches to the Sociological Study of Law." **12** *Law Soc. Rev.* 133–144.

Edwards, Richard. 1979. *Contested Terrain: The Transformation of the Workplace in the Twentieth Century.* Basic Books, New York.

Ehrlich, Eugen. 1962. *Fundamental Principles of the Sociology of Law* [1913] (trans. W. L. Moll and intro. Roscoe Pound). Russell & Russell, New York.

Elias, Norbert. 1978. *The Civilizing Process:* Vol I: *The History of Manners* [1939]. Basil Blackwell, Oxford.

Elias, Norbert. 1982. *The Civilizing Process:* Vol II: *State Formation and Civilization.* Basil Blackwell, Oxford.

Engels, Frederick. 1960. "Letter to C. Schmidt" [27/10/1890] *Marx–Engels Selected Correspondence.* Progress Books, Moscow.

Engels, Frederick. 1970. *The Origin of the Family, Private Property and the State.* Lawrence & Wishart, London.

Evans, Peter, Dietrich Rueschemeyer, and Theda Skocpol. 1985. *Bringing the State Back In.* Cambridge University Press, Cambridge.

Ewald, François. 1990. "Norms, Discipline and the Law." 30 *Representations* 138–161.

Fine, Bob. 1984. *Democracy and the Rule of Law: Liberal Ideals and Marxist Critiques.* Pluto Press, London.

Fine, Bob et al. (eds.). 1979. *Capitalism and the Rule of Law.* Hutchinson, London.

Fitzpatrick, Peter. 1983. "Marxism and Legal Pluralism." 1 *Aust. J. Law Soc.* 45–59.

Fitzpatrick, Peter. (1992). "Terminal Legality? Administration and the Complicity of Law." In Raes, K. (ed.), in press.

Fitzpatrick, Peter, and Alan Hunt (eds.). 1987. *Critical Legal Studies.* Basil Blackwell, Oxford.

Foucault, Michel. 1965. *Madness and Civilization: A History of Insanity in the Age of Reason* [1961]. Pantheon Books, New York.

Foucault, Michel. 1977. *Discipline and Punish: The Birth of the Prison* [1975]. Pantheon Books, New York.

Foucault, Michel. 1978. *The History of Sexuality:* Vol. I. *An Introduction* [1976]. Random House, New York, 1978.

Foucault, Michel. 1979. "Governmentality." 6 *Ideology Consciousness* 5–21 [reprinted in Burchell, Graham, Colin Gordon, and Peter Miller (eds.), *The Foucault Effect: Studies in Governmentality.* Harvester-Wheatsheaf, Hemel Hempstead, 1991].

Foucault, Michel. 1980. *Power/Knowledge: Selected Interviews and Other Writings 1972–1977.* (ed. Colin Gordon). Harvester Press, Brighton.

Foucault, Michel. 1981. "Omnes et Singulatim: Towards a Criticism of 'Political Reason'." In S. McMurrin (ed.), *The Tanner Lectures on Human Values* (Vol. II). Cambridge University Press, Cambridge, pp. 223–54.

Foucault, Michel. 1982a. "The Subject and Power." In Herbert Dreyfus and Paul Rabinow (eds.), *Michel Foucault: Beyond Structuralism and Hermeneutics* (2nd ed.). University of Chicago Press, Chicago, pp. 208–226.

Foucault, Michel. 1982b. "On the Genealogy of Ethics: An Overview of Work in Progress." In Herbert Dreyfus and Paul Rabinow (eds.), *Michel Foucault: Beyond Structuralism and Hermeneutics* (2nd ed.). University of Chicago Press, Chicago, pp. 229–252.

Foucault, Michel. 1983. "Structuralism and Poststructuralism: An Interview." 55 *Telos* 195–211.

Foucault, Michel. 1985. *The Care of the Self:* Vol III. *The History of Sexuality.* Pantheon Books, New York.

Foucault, Michel. 1986. *History of Sexuality:* Vol II. *The Use of Pleasure.* Penguin, Harmondsworth.

Foucault, Michel. 1988a. "Technologies of the Self." In Luther H. Martin et al. (eds.), *Technologies of the Self.* University of Massachusetts Press, Amherst, MA.

Foucault, Michel. 1988b. "On Power." In L. D. Kritzman (ed.), *Politics, Philosophy, Culture: Interviews and Other Writings 1977–1984.* Routledge, New York.

France, Anatole. 1927. *Le Lys Rouge.* W. Stephens, London.

Freeman, Alan. 1981. "Truth and Mystification in Legal Scholarship." 90 *Yale Law J.* 1229.

Freeman, Alan. 1982a. "Antidiscrimination Law: A Critical Review." In D. Kairys (ed.), *The Politics of Law.* Pantheon Books, New York.

Freeman, Alan. 1982b. "Legitimizing Racial Discrimination Through Anti-Discrimination Law." In P. Beirne and R. Quinney (eds.), *Marxism and Law.* John Wiley, New York.

Friedmann, Wolfgang. 1972. *Law in a Changing Society.* Penguin, Harmondsworth.

Frug, Gerald. 1980. "The City as a Legal Concept." 93 *Harvard Law Rev.* 1057.

Fuller, Lon. 1964. *The Morality of Law.* Yale University Press, New Haven.

Gabel, Peter. 1977a. "Intention and Structure in Contractual Conditions: Outline of a Method for Critical Legal Theory." 61 *Minnesota Law Rev.* 601–643.

Gabel, Peter. 1977b. "Review of Dworkin's *Taking Rights Seriously.*" 91 *Harvard Law Rev.* 302.

Gabel, Peter. 1980. "Reification in Legal Reasoning." In S. Spitzer (ed.) *Research in Law and Sociology,* Vol. III, JAI Press, Greenwood, CT, pp. 25–51.

Gabel, Peter. 1984. "The Phenomenology of Rights-Consciousness and the Pact of the Withdrawn Selves." 62 *Texas Law Rev.* 1563–1599.

Gabel, Peter, and Jay Feinman. 1982. "Contract Law as Ideology." In D. Kairys (ed.), *The Politics of Law.* Pantheon, New York.

Gabel, Peter, and Duncan Kennedy. 1984. "Roll Over Beethoven." 36 *Stanford Law Rev.* 1–55.

Galanter, Marc. 1981. "Justice in Many Rooms: Courts, Private Ordering and Indigenous Law." 19 *J. Legal Pluralism* 1–47.

Gallie, W. B. 1955–1956. "Essentially Contested Concepts." 56 *Proc. Aristotelean Soc.* 167–198.

Genovese, Eugene G. 1976. "The Hegemonic Function of the Law." In *Roll, Jordon, Roll.* Random House, New York, pp. 25–49.

Giddens, Anthony. 1972. "Four Myths in the History of Social Thought." 1:4 *Econ. Soc.* 357–385.

Glasbeek, Harry, and Michael Mandel. 1984. "The Legalisation of Politics in Advanced Capitalism: The Canadian Charter of Rights and Freedoms." 2 *Socialist Studies* 84–124.

Godelier, Maurice. 1978. "Infrastructures, Societies and History." 112 *New Left Rev.* 84–96.

Gordon, Colin. 1987. "The Soul of the Citizen: Max Weber and Michel

Foucault on Rationality and Government." In Scott Lasch and Sam Whimster (eds.), *Max Weber, Rationality and Modernity*. Allen & Unwin, London.

Gordon, Colin. 1991. "Governmental Rationality." In Burchell, Graham, Colin Gordon, and Peter Miller (eds.), *The Foucault Effect: Studies in Governmentality*. Harvester-Wheatsheaf, Hemel Hempstead.

Gordon, Robert. 1981. "Historicism in Legal Scholarship." 90 *Yale Law J.* 1017–56.

Gordon, Robert. 1982. "New Developments in Legal Theory." In D. Kairys (ed.), *The Politics of Law*. Pantheon Books, New York.

Gordon, Robert. 1984. "Critical Legal Histories." 36 *Stanford Law Rev.* 57–125.

Gramsci, Antonio. 1971. *Selections From the Prison Notebooks* (ed. and trans. Q. Hoare and G. Nowell-Smith). Lawrence & Wishart, London.

Greer, Edward. 1982. "Antonio Gramsci and Legal Hegemony." In D. Kairys (ed.), *The Politics of Law*. Pantheon Books, New York.

Griffiths, John. 1986. "What is Legal Pluralism?" 24 *J. Legal Pluralism* 1–55.

Gusfield, Joseph. 1963. *Symbolic Crusade: Status Politics and the American Temperance Movement*. University of Illinois Press, Urbana.

Gusfield, Joseph. 1981. "Social Movements and Social Control: Perspectives of Linearity and Fluidity." In *Research in Social Movements, Conflict, and Change* (Vol. IV). JAI Press, Greenwood, CT, pp. 317–339.

Habermas, Jürgen. 1976. *Legitimation Crisis*. Heinemann, London.

Habermas, Jürgen. 1987a. *The Philosophical Discourse of Modernity: Twelve Lectures*. MIT Press, Cambridge, MA.

Habermas, Jürgen. 1987b. *The Theory of Communicative Action* Vol. II: *Lifeworld and System: A Critique of Functionalist Reason*. Beacon Press, Boston.

Hall, Stuart. 1977. "Re-thinking the 'Base-and-Superstructure' Metaphor." In John Bloomfield (ed.), *Class, Hegemony and Party*. Lawrence & Wishart, London, pp. 43–72.

Hall, Stuart. 1988. "The Toad in the Garden: Thatcherism Among the Theorists." In C. Nelson and L. Grossberg (eds.), *Marxism and the Interpretation of Culture*. University of Illinois Press, Urbana, pp. 35–73.

Hall, Stuart, Chas Critcher, Tony Jefferson, John Clarke, and Brian Roberts. 1978. *Policing the Crisis: Mugging, the State, and Law and Order*. Macmillan, London.

Hall, Stuart, and David Held. 1989. "Left and Rights." 33:6 *Marxism Today* 16–23.

Handler, Joel. 1978. *Social Movements and the Legal System: A Theory of Law Reform and Social Change*. Academic Press, New York.

Handler, Joel. 1988. "Dependent People, the State, and the Modern/Postmodern Search for the Dialogic Community." 35 *U.C.L.A. Law Rev.* 999–1113.

Harrington, Christine. 1985. *Shadow Justice: The Ideology and Institutionalization of Alternatives to Courts*. Greenwood Press, Westport, CT.

Harrington, Christine. 1988. "Reforming Regulation: Creating Gaps and Making Markets." 10 *Law Policy* 293–316.

Hart, H. L. A. 1961. *The Concept of Law*. Clarendon Press, Oxford.

Hay, Doug. 1977. "Property, Authority and the Criminal Law." In D. Hay et al., *Albion's Fatal Tree: Crime and Society in Eighteenth Century England*. Penguin, Harmondsworth.

Hay, Doug, Peter Linebaugh, John Rule, Edward Thompson, and Cal Winslow. 1977. *Albion's Fatal Tree: Crime and Society in Eighteenth Century England*. Penguin, Harmondsworth.

Hayek, F. A. 1973–1979. *Law, Legislation and Liberty* (3 vols). Routledge & Kegan Paul, London.

Hazard, J. N., and H. W. Babb (eds.). 1951. *Soviet Legal Philosophy*. Harvard University Press, Cambridge, MA.

Henriques, Julian *et al.* 1984. *Changing the Subject: Psychology, Social Regulation and Subjectivity*. Methuen, London.

Henry, Stuart. 1983. *Private Justice: Towards Integrated Theorizing in Sociology of Law*. Routledge & Kegan Paul, London.

Henry, Stuart. 1987. "Disciplinary Pluralism: Four Models of Private Justice in the Workplace." **35** *Sociol. Rev.* 279–319.

Hirst, Paul. 1979a. "The Law of Property and Marxism." In *On Law and Ideology*. Macmillan, London.

Hirst, Paul. 1979b. *On Law and Ideology*. Macmillan, London.

Hirst, Paul. 1980. "Law, Socialism and Rights." In Pat Carlen and Mike Collison (eds.), *Radical Issues in Criminology*. Martin Robertson, Oxford, pp. 58–105.

Hirst, Paul. 1986. *Law, Socialism and Democracy*. Allen & Unwin, London.

Hirst, Paul, and Phil Jones. 1987. "The Critical Resources of Established Jurisprudence." In P. Fitzpatrick and A. Hunt (eds.), *Critical Legal Studies*. Basil Blackwell, Oxford.

Hobsbawm, Eric, and Ranger Terence. 1983. *The Invention of Tradition*. Cambridge University Press, Cambridge.

Holmes, O. W. 1897. "The Path of Law." **10** *Harvard Law Rev.* 457–478.

Horwitz, Morton. 1975. "The Rise of Legal Formalism." **19** *Am. J. Legal Hist.* 251–264.

Horwitz, Morton. 1977. *Transformation of American Law 1780–1860*. Harvard University Press, Cambridge, Ma.

Horwitz, Morton. 1982a. "The History of the Public/Private Distinction." **130** *Univ. Pennsylvania Law Rev.* 1423–428.

Horwitz, Morton. 1982b. "The Doctrine of Objective Causation." In D. Kairys (ed.), *The Politics of Law*. Pantheon Books, New York, pp. 201–213.

Hunt, Alan. 1976a. "Perspectives in the Sociology of Law." In P. Carlen, *The Sociology of Law*. Sociological Review Monographs, University of Keele, Keele.

Hunt, Alan. 1976b. "Lenin and Sociology." **24:1** *Sociol. Rev.* 5–22.

Hunt, Alan. 1976c. "Law, State and Class Struggle." **20** *Marxism Today* 178–187.

Hunt, Alan. 1978. *The Sociological Movement in Law*. Macmillan, London.

Hunt, Alan. 1979. "The Sociology of Law of Gurvitch and Timasheff: A Critique of Theories of Normative Integration." In S. Spitzer (ed.), *Research in Law and Sociology* (Vol. 2). JAI Press, Greenwood, CT.

Hunt, Alan. 1981a. "The Politics of Law and Justice." In D. Adlam et al. (eds.), *Politics and Power IV: Law, Politics and Justice*. Routledge & Kegan Paul, London.

Hunt, Alan. 1981b. "Dichotomy and Contradiction in the Sociology of Law." 8 *Br. J. Law Soc.* 47–77.

Hunt, Alan. 1983a. "Behavioral Sociology of Law: A Critique of Donald Black." 10:1 *J. Law Soc.* 19–46.

Hunt, Alan. 1983b. "Marxist Legal Theory and Legal Positivism." 46:2 *Modern Law Rev.* 236–243.

Hunt, Alan. 1988. "Living Dangerously on the Deconstructive Edge." 26 *Osgoode Hall Law J.* 867–895.

Hunt, Alan. 1992a. "Law's Empire or Legal Imperialism?" In *Reading Dworkin Critically.* Berg Publishers, New York.

Hunt, Alan (ed.). 1992b. *Reading Dworkin Critically.* Berg Publishers, New York.

Hutchinson, Allan. 1988. *Dwelling on the Threshold.* Carswell, Toronto.

Hutchinson, Allan, and Patrick Monahan. 1984. "Law, Politics and the Critical Legal Scholars: The Unfolding Drama of American Legal Thought." 36 *Stanford Law Rev.* 199–246.

Hyde, Alan. 1983. "The Conception of Legitimacy in the Sociology of Law." 1983 *Wisconsin Law Rev.* 379–426.

Ignatieff, Michael. 1978. *A Just Measure of Pain: Penitentiaries in the Industrial Revolution 1750–1850.* Macmillan, London.

Ireland, Paddy *et al.* 1987. "The Conceptual Foundations of Modern Company Law." In P. Fitzpatrick and A. Hunt (eds.), *Critical Legal Studies.* Basil Blackwell, Oxford.

Jenkins, Iredell. 1980. *Social Order and the Limits of Law: A Theoretical Essay.* Princeton University Press, Princeton, NJ.

Jessop, Bob. 1977. "Recent Theories of the Capitalist State." 1 *Cambridge J. Econ.* 353–373.

Jessop, Bob. 1982. *The Capitalist State: Marxist Theories and Methods.* Martin Robertson, Oxford.

Jessop, Bob. 1986. "Poulantzas and Foucault on Power and Strategy." 3 *Ideas Production* 59–84 [reprinted in Bob Jessop *State Theory: Putting the Capitalist State in its Place.* Polity Press, Cambridge, 1990].

Jessop, Bob. 1990. *State Theory: Putting the Capitalist State in its Place.* Polity Press, Cambridge.

Jones, Kelvin. 1982. *Law and Economy: The Legal Regulation of Corporate Capital.* Academic Press, London.

Kahn-Freund, Otto. 1972. "Introduction." In Karl Renner, *The Institutions of Private Law and their Social Functions* [1949] (ed. Otto Kahn-Freund) Routledge & Kegan Paul, London.

Kairys, David. 1982a. "Freedom of Speech." In *The Politics of Law: A Progressive Critique.* Pantheon Books, New York.

Kairys, David (ed.). 1982b. *The Politics of Law: A Progressive Critique.* Pantheon Books, New York.

Kamenka, Eugene, and Alice Tay. 1975. "Beyond Bourgeois Individualism: The Contemporary Crisis in Law and Legal Ideology." In E. Kamenka and R. S. Neale (eds.), *Feudalism, Capitalism and Beyond.* Edward Arnold, London.

Kamenka, Eugene, and Alice Tay (eds.). 1978. *Law and Society: The Crisis in Legal Ideals.* Edward Arnold, London.

Katz, Al. 1979. "Studies in Boundary Theory: Three Essay in Adjudication and Politics." 28 *Buffalo Law Rev.* 383.

Keane, John. 1984. *Public Life in Late Capitalism: Toward a Socialist Theory of Democracy.* Cambridge University Press, Cambridge.

Kelman, Mark. 1981. "Interpretive Construction in the Substantive Criminal Law." 33 *Stanford Law Rev.* 591–673.

Kelman, Mark. 1984. "Trashing." 36 *Stanford Law Rev.* 293–348.

Kennedy, Duncan. 1973. "Legal Formality." 2 *J. Legal Stds.* 351–398.

Kennedy, Duncan. 1976. "Form and Substance in Private Law Adjudication." 89 *Harvard Law Rev.* 1685–1778.

Kennedy, Duncan. 1979. "The Structure of Blackstone's Commentaries." 28 *Buffalo Law Rev.* 205–382.

Kennedy, Duncan. 1980. "Toward an Historical Understanding of Legal Consciousness: The Case of Classical Legal Thought in America 1850–1940." In S. Spitzer (ed.), *Research in Law and Sociology* (Vol. III). JAI Press, Greenwood, CT, pp. 3–24.

Kennedy, Duncan. 1981a. "Cost-Benefit Analysis of Entitlement Problems: A Critique." 33 *Stanford Law Rev.* 387.

Kennedy, Duncan. 1981b. "Critical Labor Law Theory: A Comment." 4 *Ind. Rel. Law J.* 503.

Kennedy, Duncan. 1982a. "Distributive and Paternalist Motives in Contract and Tort Law, With Special Reference to Compulsory Terms and Unequal Bargaining Power." 41 *Maryland Law Rev.* 563–649.

Kennedy, Duncan. 1982b. "Antonio Gramsci and the Legal System." 6 *Legal Studies Forum* 32–37.

Kennedy, Duncan. 1982c. "Legal Education as Training for Hierarchy." In D. Kairys (ed.), *The Politics of Law: A Progressive Critique.* Pantheon Books, New York.

Kirchheimer, Otto. 1969. *Politics, Law and Social Change: Selected Essays of Otto Kirchheimer* (eds. F. S. Burin and K. L. Shell). Columbia University Press, New York, 1969.

Klare, Karl. 1979. "Law-Making as Praxis." 40 *Telos* 123–135.

Klare, Karl. 1981. "Labor Law as Ideology: Towards a New Historiography of Collective Bargaining Law." 4 *Industrial Rel. Law J.* 450.

Klare, Karl. 1982a. "Judicial Deradicalization of the Wagner Act and the Origins of Modern Legal Consciousness 1937–1941." In P. Beirne and R. Quinney (eds.), *Marxism and Law.* John Wiley, New York.

Klare, Karl. 1982b. "The Quest for Industrial Democracy and the Struggle Against Racism: Perspectives from Labor Law and Civil Rights Law." 61 *Oregon Law Rev.* 157–200.

Klare, Karl. 1982c. "Critical Theory and Labor Relations Law." In D. Kairys (ed.), *The Politics of Law.* Pantheon Books, New York.

Klare, Karl. 1982d. "The Public/Private Distinction in Labor Law." 130 *U. Penn. Law Rev.* 1358.

Kronman, Anthony. 1983. *Max Weber.* Stanford University Press, Stanford, CA.

Laclau, Ernesto. 1977. *Politics and Ideology in Marxist Theory.* New Left Books, London.

Laclau, Ernesto. 1983. "The Impossibility of Society." 7 *Can. J. Political Social Theory* 21–24.
Lakoff, George, and Mark Johnson. 1980. *Metaphors We Live By*. University of Chicago Press, Chicago.
Larrain, Jorge. 1979. *The Concept of Ideology*. Hutchinson, London.
Larrain, Jorge. 1983. *Marxism and Ideology*. Macmillan, London.
Lefcourt, Robert (ed.). 1971. *Law Against the People: Essays to Demystify Law, Order and the Courts*. Random House, New York.
Lenin, V. I. 1960–1970. *Collected Works* (45 vols). Lawrence & Wishart, London.
Lenin, V. I. 1960. "The Development of Capitalism in Russia." *Lenin Collected Works*, Vol. 3. Lawrence & Wishart, London.
Lipietz, Alain. 1985. *The Enchanted World: Inflation, Credit and the World Crisis*. Verso, London.
Livingston, Debra. 1982. " 'Round and 'Round the Bramble Bush: From Legal Realism to Critical Legal Scholarship." 95 *Harvard Law Rev.* 1669–690.
Llewellyn, Karl, and Adamson Hoebel. 1941. *The Cheyenne Way: Conflict and Case Law in Primitive Jurisprudence*. University of Oklahoma Press, Norman.
Lofland, Lyn. 1973. *The World of Strangers: Order and Action in Urban Public Space*. Basic Books, New York.
Luhmann, Niklas. 1985. *A Sociological Theory of Law*. Routledge & Kegan Paul, London.
Lukes, Steven. 1982. "Can the Base Be Distinguished from the Superstructure?" 4 *Analyse Kritik* 211–222.
Macaulay, Stewart. 1963. "Non-Contractual Relations in Business: A Preliminary Study." 28 *Am. Sociol. Rev.* 55–66.
Mandel, Michael. 1989. *The Charter of Rights and the Legalisation of Politics in Canada*. Wall & Thompson, Toronto.
Mann, Michael. 1970. "The Social Cohesion of Liberal Democracy." 35 *Am. Soc. Rev.* 423–439.
Mann, Michael. 1985. *The Sources of Social Power*: Vol. I. *A History of Power From the Beginning to AD 1760*. Cambridge University Press, Cambridge.
Marshall, T. H. 1963. "Citizenship and Social Class." In *Sociology at the Crossroads*. Heinemann, London, pp. 67–127.
Marx, Karl. 1843. "Letter to Ruge" (Sept.).
Marx, Karl. 1958. *Marx–Engels Selected Works* (2 vols). Foreign Languages Publishing House, Moscow.
Marx, Karl. 1959. *Capital: A Critique of Political Economy*, Vol. III. Foreign Languages Publishing House, Moscow.
Marx, Karl. 1961. *Capital: A Critique of Political Economy*, Vol. I. Foreign Languages Publishing House, Moscow.
Marx, Karl. 1969. *Grundrisse: Foundations of the Critique of Political Economy*. Penguin, Harmondsworth.
Marx, Karl. 1971. "Preface to the Contribution to the Critique of Political Economy." In *A Contribution to the Critique of Political Economy* (ed. and intro. Maurice Dobb). Lawrence & Wishart, London.

Marx, Karl. 1973. *Surveys From Exile: Political Writings* (Vol. II) (ed. and intro. David Fernbach). Penguin, Harmondsworth.

Marx, Karl, and Engels, Frederick. 1968. *The German Ideology.* Foreign Languages Publishing House, Moscow.

Marx, Karl, and Engels, Frederick. 1975. *Selected Correspondence* (3rd. rev. ed.). Progress, Moscow.

McCann, Michael. 1986. *Taking Reform Seriously: Perspectives on Public Interest Liberalism.* Cornell University Press, Ithaca.

McLennan, Gregor, Victor Molina, and Roy Peters. 1977. "Althusser's Theory of Ideology." 10 *Working Papers in Cultural Studies* 77–105.

Mensch, Betty. 1982. "The History of Mainstream Legal Thought." In D. Kairys (ed.), *The Politics of Law.* Pantheon Books, New York.

Merry, Sally. 1988. "Legal Pluralism." 22 *Law Soc. Rev.* 869–896.

Merry, Sally. 1990. *Getting Justice and Getting Even: Legal Consciousness Among Working-Class Americans.* University of Chicago Press, Chicago.

Miliband, Ralph. 1969. *The State in Capitalist Society.* Weidenfeld & Nicolson, London.

Mills, C. W. 1959. *The Power Elite.* Oxford University Press, New York.

Minson, Jeff. 1980. "Strategies for Socialists? Foucault's Conception of Power." 9 *Econ. Soc.* 1–43.

Moore, Barrington. 1978. *Injustice: The Social Basis of Obedience and Revolt.* Sharpe, White Plains, NY.

Munger, Frank, and Carroll Seron. 1984. "Critical Legal Studies Versus Critical Legal Theory: A Comment on Method." 6 *Law Policy* 257–297.

Nonet, Philippe, and Philip Selznick. 1978. *Law and Society in Transition: Toward Responsive Law.* Harper & Row, New York.

Oestreich, Gerhard. 1982. *Neostoicism and the Early Modern State.* Cambridge University Press, Cambridge.

Ollman, Bertell. 1971. *Alienation: Marx's Conception of Man in Capitalist Society.* Cambridge University Press, Cambridge.

Olsen, Frances. 1983. "The Family and the Market: A Study of Ideology and Legal Reform." 96 *Harvard Law Rev.* 1497–1578.

O'Malley, Pat. 1990. "Legal Networks and Domestic Security." In Austin Sarat and Susan Sibley (eds.), *Studies in Law, Politics and Society.* JAI Press, Greenwood, CT.

Parsons, Talcott. 1959. *Politics and Social Structure.* Free Press, New York.

Parsons, Talcott. 1966. *Societies: Evolutionary and Comparative Perspectives.* Prentice-Hall, Englewood Cliffs, NJ.

Parsons, Talcott. 1977. "Review of Unger *Law in Modern Society.*" 12 *Law Soc. Rev.* 145–149.

Pashukanis, E. V. 1978. *Law and Marxism: A General Theory* (ed. C. J. Arthur). Ink Links, London.

Pearce, Frank. 1976. *Crimes of the Powerful: Marxism, Crime and Deviance.* Pluto Press, London.

Pearce, Frank. 1989. "Durkheim and the Juridical Relation." In *The Radical Durkheim.* Unwin Hyman, London.

Pearson, G. 1980. "Popular Justice and the Lay Magistracy." In Z. Bankowski and G. Mungham (eds.), *Essays in Law and Society*. Routledge & Kegan Paul, London.

Picciotto, Sol. 1979. "The Theory of the State, Class Struggle and the Role of Law." In B. Fine et al. (eds.), *Capitalism and the Rule of Law*. Hutchinson, London.

Plamenatz, John. 1954. *German Marxism and Russian Communism*. Longmans, London.

Posner, Richard. 1987. "The Decline of Law as an Autonomous Discipline." 100 *Harvard Law Rev.* 761.

Posner, Richard. 1988. "Conventionalism: The Key to Law as an Autonomous Discipline?" 38 *Univ. Toronto Law J.* 333–354.

Poster, Mark. 1984. *Foucault, Marxism and History: Mode of Production versus Mode of Information*. Polity Press, Cambridge.

Poster, Mark. 1990. *The Mode of Information: Poststructuralisms and Contexts*. University of Chicago Press, Chicago.

Poulantzas, Nicos. 1973. *Political Power and Social Classes*. New Left Books, London.

Poulantzas, Nicos. 1978. *State, Power, Socialism*. New Left Books, London.

Pound, Roscoe. 1923. *Interpretations of Legal History*. Macmillan, New York.

Pound, Roscoe. 1942. *Social Control Through Law*. Yale University Press, New Haven.

Pritt, D. N. 1970. *Law, Class and Society*. Lawrence & Wishart, London.

Quinney, Richard. 1972. "The Ideology of Law: Notes for a Radical Alternative to Legal Oppression." 7 *Issues Criminol.* 1–35.

Quinney, Richard. 1973. "Crime Control in Capitalist Society: A Critical Philosophy of Legal Order." 8 *Issues Criminol.* 75–99.

Raeff, Marc. 1983. *The Well-Ordered Police State: Social and Institutional Change Through Law in the Germanies and Russia, 1600–1800*. Yale University Press, New Haven.

Rawls, John. 1971. *A Theory of Justice*. Harvard University Press, Cambridge, MA.

Redhead, Steve. 1978. "The Discrete Charm of Bourgeois Law: A Note on Pashukanis." 9 *Critique* 113–120.

Reich, N. 1984. "The Regulatory Crisis: Does It Exist and Can It Be Solved?" 2 *Govern. Policy* 177–179.

Renner, Karl. 1949. *The Institutions of Private Law and their Social Functions* (ed. Otto Kahn-Freund). Routledge & Kegan Paul, London.

Rifkin, Janet. 1982. "Toward a Theory of Law and Patriarchy." In P. Beirne and R. Quinney (eds.), *Marxism and Law*. John Wiley, New York.

Rorty, Richard. 1979. *Philosophy and the Mirror of Nature*. Princeton University Press, Princeton, NJ.

Rorty, Richard. 1982. *Consequences of Pragmatism*. Harvester Press, Sussex.

Rorty, Richard. 1986. "The Contingency of Language", "The Contingency of Selfhood", and "The Contingency of Community." 8 *London Rev. Books* (April–July).

Rose, Nikolas. 1987. "Beyond the Public/Private Division: Law, Power and the Family." In P. Fitzpatrick and A. Hunt (eds.), *Critical Legal Studies*. Basil Blackwell, Oxford.

Rose, Nikolas. 1990. *Governing the Soul: Technologies of Human Subjectivity.* Routledge, London.

Rostow, Eugene (ed.). 1970. *Is Law Dead?* Simon & Schuster, New York.

Ryan, Michael. 1982. *Marxism and Deconstruction: A Critical Articulation.* Johns Hopkins University Press, Baltimore.

Santos, Boaventura de Sousa. 1979. "Popular Justice, Dual Power and Socialist Strategy." In Bob Fine *et al.* (eds.), *Capitalism and the Rule of Law: From Deviancy Theory to Marxism.* Hutchinson, London.

Santos, Boaventura de Sousa. 1985. "On Modes of Production of Law and Social Power." 13 *Int. J. Sociol. Law* 299–336.

Sarat, A., and T. Kearns (eds.). 1992. *The Law in Everyday Life.* University of Michigan Press, Ann Arbor.

Sayer, Derek. 1979. *Marx's Method: Ideology, Science and Critique in 'Capital.'* Harvester Press, Brighton.

Sayers, Sean. 1985. *Reality and Reason: Dialectic and the Theory of Knowledge.* Basil Blackwell, Oxford.

Scheingold, Stuart. 1974. *The Politics of Rights: Lawyers, Public Policy and Political Change.* Yale University Press, New Haven.

Schwendinger, Herman, and Julia Schwendinger. 1975. "Defenders of Order or Guardians of Human Rights?" In Ian Taylor, Paul Walton and Jock Young (eds.), *Critical Criminology.* Routledge & Kegan Paul, London.

Scull, Andrew. 1977. *Decarceration.* Prentice-Hall, Englewood Cliffs, NJ.

Shaw, William. 1978. *Marx's Theory of History.* Stanford University Press, Stanford.

Sheridan, Alan. 1980. *Michel Foucault: The Will to Truth.* Tavistock, London.

Shklar, Judith. 1964. *Legalism: An Essay on Law, Morals and Politics.* Harvard University Press, Cambridge, MA.

Simon, Jonathan. 1987. "The Emergence of a Risk Society: Insurance, Law, and the State." 95 *Socialist Rev.* 61–89.

Skillen, Anthony. 1977. *Ruling Illusions: Philosophy and the Social Order.* Harvester Press, Hassocks, 1977.

Skolnick, Jerome. 1966. *Justice Without Trial: Law Enforcement in the Democratic Society.* John Wiley, New York.

Smart, Barry. 1983. *Foucault, Marxism and Critique.* Routledge, London.

Smart, Carol. 1990. *Feminism and the Power of Law.* Routledge, London.

Snitow, Ann, Christine Stansell, and Sharon Thompson (eds.). 1983. *Powers of Desire: The Politics of Sexuality.* Monthly Review Press, New York.

Sontag, Susan. 1989. *AIDs and its Metaphors.* Allen Lane, London.

Sparer, Ed. 1984. "Fundamental Human Rights, Legal Entitlements, and the Social Struggle: A Friendly Critique of the Critical Legal Studies Movement." 36 *Stanford Law Rev.* 509–574.

Spengler, Joseph. 1960. "Mercantilist and Physiocratic Growth Theory." In Bert Hoselitz (ed.), *Theories of Economic Growth.* Free Press, New York, pp. 3–64.

Stansell, Christine. 1982. *City of Women: Sex and Class in New York, 1789–1860.* Alfred A. Knopf, New York.

Stone, Julius. 1966. *Law and the Social Sciences in the Second Half Century.* University of Minnesota Press, Minneapolis.

Sugarman, David (ed.). 1983. *Legality, Ideology and the State.* Academic Press, London.

Sumner, Colin. 1979. *Reading Ideologies: An Investigation into the Marxist Theory of Ideology and Law.* Academic Press, London.

Taub, Nadine, and Elizabeth Schneider. 1982. "Perspectives on Women's Subordination and the Role of Law." In D. Kairys (ed.), *The Politics of Law.* Pantheon Books, New York.

Taylor, Ian, Paul Walton, and Jock Young. 1972. *The New Criminology.* Routledge & Kegan Paul, London.

Teubner, Gunther. 1984. "After Legal Instrumentalism? Strategic Models of Post-Regulatory Law." 12 *Int. J. Soc. Law* 375–400.

Teubner, Gunther (ed.). 1986. *Dilemmas of Law in the Welfare State.* Walter de Gruyter, New York.

Teubner, Gunther. 1987. "Juridification: Concepts, Aspects, Limits, Solutions." In Gunther Teubner (ed.), *Juridification of Social Spheres: A Comparative Analysis in the Areas of Labor, Corporate, Antitrust and Social Welfare Law.* Walter de Gruyter, New York.

Teubner, Gunther. 1988. *Autopoietic Law: A New Approach to Law and Society.* Walter de Gruyter, New York.

Timasheff, N. S. 1939. *An Introduction to the Sociology of Law.* Harvard University Press, Cambridge, MA.

Therborn, Göran. 1980. *The Ideology of Power and the Power of Ideology.* New Left Books, London.

Thompson, E. P. 1965. "The Peculiarities of the English." In R. Miliband and R. Saville (eds.), *1965 Socialist Register.* Merlin Press, London.

Thompson, E. P. 1975. *Whigs and Hunters: The Origin of the Black Act.* Allen Lane, London.

Thompson, E. P. 1978. *The Poverty of Theory and Other Essays.* Merlin Press, London.

Thompson, E. P. 1979a. "Introduction." In J. Friedman (ed.), *Review of Security and the State.* CSE Books, London.

Thompson, E. P. 1979b. "The Rule of Law in English History." 10 *Bull. Haldane Soc.* 7–10.

Thompson, E. P. 1980. *Writing by Candlelight.* Merlin Press, London.

Thompson, John. 1984. *Studies in the Theory of Ideology.* Polity Press, Cambridge.

Tomlins, Christopher. 1985. *The State and the Unions: Labor Relations, the Law, and the Organized Labour Movement in America 1880–1960.* Cambridge University Press, Cambridge.

Tribe, Keith. 1978. *Land, Labour and Economic Discourse.* Routledge & Kegan Paul, London.

Trubek, David. 1972a. "Toward a Social Theory of Law: An Essay on the Study of Law and Development." 82 *Yale Law J.* 1–50.

Trubek, David. 1972b. "Max Weber on Law and the Rise of Capitalism." 1972 *Wisconsin Law Rev.* 720–753.

Trubek, David. 1977. "Complexity and Contradiction in the Legal Order: Balbus and the Challenge of Critical Social Thought About Law." 11 *Law Soc. Rev.* 529–69.

Trubek, David. 1984a. "Turning Away From Law." 82 *Michigan Law Rev.* 824–835.

Trubek, David. 1984b. "Where the Action Is: Critical Legal Studies and Empiricism." 36 *Stanford Law Rev.* 576–622.

Trubek, David. 1986. "Max Weber's Tragic Modernism and the Study of Law in Society." 20 *Law Soc. Rev.* 573–598.

Trubek, David. 1990. "Back to the Future: The Short, Happy Life of the Law and Society Movement." 18:1 *Florida State Univ. Law Rev.* 4–55.

Trubek, David, and John Esser. 1989. " 'Critical Empiricism' in American Legal Studies: Paradox, Program or Pandora's Box." 14 *Law Social Inquiry* 3–52.

Tushnet, Mark. 1977. "Perspectives on the Development of American Law: A Critical Review of Friedman's *A History of American Law*." 1977 *Wisconsin Law Rev.* 81.

Tushnet, Mark. 1978. "A Marxist Analysis of American Law." 1 *Marxist Perspectives* 96.

Tushnet, Mark. 1979a. "Truth, Justice and the American Way: Constitutional Law Scholarship in the '70s." 57 *Texas Law Rev.* 1307–59.

Tushnet, Mark. 1979b. "Post-Realist Legal Scholarship." 15 *J. Soc. Public Teachers Law* 20–32.

Tushnet, Mark. 1981a. "Legal Scholarship: Its Causes and Cure." 90 *Yale Law J.* 1205–228.

Tushnet, Mark. 1981b. "The Dilemmas of Liberal Constitutionalism." 42 *Ohio State Law J.* 411–426.

Tushnet, Mark. 1982. "Corporations and Free Speech." In D. Kairys (ed.), *The Politics of Law*. Pantheon Books, New York.

Tushnet, Mark. 1983a. "Marxism as Metaphor: Review of Collins *Marxism and Law*." 68 *Cornell Law Rev.* 282.

Tushnet, Mark. 1983b. "Following the Rules Laid Down: A Critique of Interpretivism and Neutral Principle." 96 *Harvard Law Rev.* 781–827.

Tushnet, Mark. 1984. "An Essay on Rights." 62 *Texas Law Rev.* 1363–1403.

Unger, Roberto. 1975. *Knowledge and Politics.* Free Press, New York.

Unger, Roberto. 1976. *Law in Modern Society: Toward a Criticism of Social Theory.* Free Press, New York.

Unger, Roberto. 1982. "The Critical Legal Studies Movement." 96 *Harvard Law Rev.* 561–675.

Valverde, Mariana. 1990. *The Age of Light, Soap and Water: Social Purity and Philanthropy in Canada, 1885–1925.* McClelland & Stewart, Toronto.

von Hirsch, A. 1976. *Doing Justice: The Choice of Punishments.* Hill & Wang, New York.

Walkowitz, Judith. 1980. *Prostitution and the Victorian Society: Women Class and the State.* Cambridge University Press, Cambridge.

Warrington, Ronnie. 1981. "Pashukanis and the Commodity Form Theory." 9 *Int. J. Sociol. of Law* 1–22.

Weber, Max. 1966. *Law in Economy and Society* (ed. Max Rheinstein). Harvard University Press, Cambridge, MA.

Wedderburn, K. W. 1965. *The Worker and the Law.* Penguin, Harmondsworth.

Weedon, Chris. 1987. *Feminist Practice and Poststructuralist Theory.* Basil Blackwell, Oxford.

White, Hayden. 1978. *Tropics of Discourse: Essays in Cultural Criticism.* Johns Hopkins University Press, Baltimore.

Williams, Raymond. 1977. *Marxism and Literature.* Oxford University Press, Oxford.

Winkler, J. 1975. "Corporatism." 2 *Br. J. Law Soc.* 103.

Wolff, Robert (ed.). 1971. *The Rule of Law.* Simon & Schuster, New York.

Woodiwiss, Anthony. 1990a. *Rights v. Conspiracy: A Sociological Essay on the Development of Labour Law in the United States.* Berg, Oxford.

Woodiwiss, Anthony. 1990b. *Social Theory After Postmodernism: Rethinking Production, Law and Class.* Pluto Press, London.

Wright, Erik. 1978. *Class, Crisis and the State.* New Left Books, London.

Young, Jock. 1979. "Left Idealism, Reformism and Beyond." In B. Fine et al. (eds.), *Capitalism and the Rule of Law.* Hutchinson, London.

INDEX